D1743884

SIXTH EDITION

Study Guide to accompany
MANAGERIAL ECONOMICS
Principles and Worldwide Applications

DOMINICK
SALVATORE

Not for Sale in USA or
Canada

This adapted version has
been specially created for
Europe, the Middle East,
Asia, and Australasia by
the author.

ROBERT F.
BROOKER

Gannon University

New York   Oxford
OXFORD UNIVERSITY PRESS
2008

Oxford University Press, Inc., publishes works that further
Oxford University's objective of excellence in research, scholarship,
and education.

Oxford New York
Auckland Cape Town Dar es Salaam Hong Kong Karachi
Kuala Lumpur Madrid Melbourne Mexico City Nairobi
New Delhi Shanghai Taipei Toronto

With offices in
Argentina Austria Brazil Chile Czech Republic France Greece
Guatemala Hungary Italy Japan Poland Portugal Singapore
South Korea Switzerland Thailand Turkey Ukraine Vietnam

Copyright © 2008 by Oxford University Press, Inc.

Published by Oxford University Press, Inc.
198 Madison Avenue, New York, New York 10016
http://www.oup.com

Oxford is a registered trademark of Oxford University Press

All rights reserved. No part of this publication may be reproduced,
stored in a retrieval system, or transmitted, in any form or by any means,
electronic, mechanical, photocopying, recording, or otherwise,
without the prior permission of Oxford University Press.

ISBN: 978-0-19-532698-7

Printing number: 9 8 7 6 5 4 3 2 1

Printed in the United States of America
on acid-free paper

CONTENTS

PREFACE

This Study Guide consists of fourteen chapters that correspond to those in the text. The chapters in this Study Guide include the sections that are listed below:

Learning Objectives: A concise summary of the outcomes you should anticipate from a study of the chapter.

Summary of Notation and Formulas: A summary list of the important formulas and equations presented in the chapter and definitions of the notation used in each.

True-False Questions

Multiple Choice Questions

Problems

True-False Answers

Multiple Choice Answers

Solutions to Problems

The purpose of this Study Guide is to help you to make the time that you spend studying the material in this course more productive. By providing you with summaries and with ways to test your understanding of the material as you go along, it can help you to focus your efforts in a more effective way.

To get the best use out of this Study Guide, begin with the textbook. After you have read a chapter in the text, use the Learning Objectives section to gauge your familiarity with the chapter's major topics. If you draw a blank on any of them, return to the text to refresh your memory. Use the Summary of Notation and Formulas in a similar way. These sections will help you to assess your broad understanding of the topics. Next, go through the true-false and multiple choice questions to test your understanding of the details. Don't check your answers until you have completed all of the questions. When you do, concentrate on determining **why** your answer differs from the one provided here. Finally, work the problems and then refer to the detailed solutions.

Robert F. Brooker
February 26, 2007

CHAPTER 1

THE NATURE AND SCOPE OF MANAGERIAL ECONOMICS

Learning Objectives

After a careful reading of this chapter, you should be able to list and define the functional skills and areas of knowledge that comprise managerial economics and to describe the five steps involved in the decision-making process. You should understand the objectives and constraints that influence the behavior of firms, the function of profit in motivating a firm's behavior and in allocating society's resources, the role of business ethics in defining appropriate conduct by a firm and its employees, and the influence of globalization on the nature of the modern business environment.

The Appendix to Chapter 1 is a review of supply, demand, and market equilibrium that should refresh your understanding of these topics. Finally, you should have developed an appreciation for the contribution that a knowledge of managerial economics can make to the quality of managerial decisions and, consequently, to the efficiency with which firms operate.

Summary of Notation and Formulas

(1-1) $Q = f(P, Y, P_C, P_S)$

Equation 1-1 is a mathematical expression that represents a demand function, where Q is the quantity demanded of a commodity per time period, P is the price of the commodity, Y is consumer income, P_C is the price of a complementary commodity, and P_S is the price of a substitute commodity. The equation is presented as an example of a general mathematical model that is used to represent an economic theory.

(1-2) $PV = \dfrac{\pi_1}{(1+r)^1} + \dfrac{\pi_2}{(1+r)^2} + \cdots + \dfrac{\pi_n}{(1+r)^n}$

(1-2a) $PV = \sum\limits_{t=1}^{n} \dfrac{\pi_t}{(1+r)^t}$

(1-3) Value of Firm $= \sum\limits_{t=1}^{n} \dfrac{TR_t - TC_t}{(1+r)^t}$

Equations 1-2, 1-2a, and 1-3 are equivalent. They define the value of a firm as the total dixcounted value of future profits, where PV is present value, n is the number of time periods, π_t is the profit in time period t, which is equal to total revenue in time t (TR_t) minus total cost in time t (TC_t), and r is the interest rate used to discount future cash flows to present value.

True-False Questions

T F 1.   The single most important element in managerial economics is the microeconomic theory of the firm.

T F 2.   A theoretical model attempts to identify every possible determinant of an event.

T F 3.   Managerial economics involves the application of economic theory and decision science.

T F 4.   Management decision problems are not encountered by government agencies or non-profit organizations.

T F 5.   Management decision problems typically involve objectives and constraints.

T F 6.   The economic theory of the firm assumes that businesses attempt to maximize their contribution to social welfare.

T F 7.   The ultimate test of the value of an economic theory is whether it is based on reasonable assumptions.

T F 8.   Mathematical economics involves the application of statistical tools to estimate economic models.

T F 9.   The functional areas of business administration are largely irrelevant to the study of managerial economics.

T F 10. Most of the goods and services in the United States are produced by government and the rest are produced by firms and not-for-profit organizations.

T F 11. Firms exist because they facilitate the efficient organization of factors of production.

T F 12. The function of a firm is to purchase resources and then to transform them into goods and services and offer them for sale.

T F 13. The value of a firm is equal to the sum of all future profits that will be generated by the firm.

T F 14. If there was no inflation, the value of a dollar received now would be greater than the value of a dollar received a year from now.

T F 15. The concept of the circular flow of economic activity illustrates the point that all economic activities are interdependent.

T F 16. The theory of the firm holds that the primary goal of a firm is to maximize the discounted present value of the positive difference between the firm's total revenue and the firm's total cost or to minimize the present value of the negative difference between the firm's total revenue and total cost.

T F 17. The value of a firm will increase if there is a reduction in the uncertainty associated with the firm's cash flows.

T F 18. An increase in the uncertainty associated with a firm's cash flows will cause a decrease in the discount rate that is applied to the valuation of the firm.

T F 19. Profit is a constraint on the operation of a firm.

T F 20. The value of a firm under constrained optimization is generally below what it would be under unconstrained optimization.

T F 21. The firm, as an organizational structure, exists in order to reduce transactions costs.

T F 22. Transaction cost refers to the price paid for a good or service.

T F 23. The costs of negotiating and enforcing contracts are transaction costs.

T F 24. Firms purchase goods and services from other firms, instead of producing the goods and services internally, because it will reduce transaction costs.

T F 25. The principal-agent problem can occur when the person who manages a firm is not the owner of the firm.

T F 26. Satisficing refers to the fact that profit maximization by corporate managers is a way of satisfying stockholders.

T F 27. Alternative theories of the firm have proven to be more satisfactory than the theory of profit maximization.

T F 28. Business profit is generally greater than economic profit.

T F 29. The wages paid to workers employed by a firm are an example of an explicit cost.

T F 30. Sales taxes paid to the state by a retail firm are an example of an implicit cost.

T F 31. Business profit is equal to total revenue minus all implicit costs.

T F 32. A building owned by a firm has an explicit cost of zero, but its implicit cost is not zero.

T F 33. Businesses are taxed on the basis of their economic profit.

T F 34. Implicit costs refer to the value of inputs owned and used by a firm.

T F 35. Economic profit is equal to total revenue minus all implicit costs.

T F 36. Business profit minus economic profit is equal to the total of all implicit costs.

T F 37. Economic cost is equal to the sum of explicit and implicit costs.

T F 38. Firms that operate in industries with relatively high levels of risk tend to have lower levels of profit.

T F 39. In the long run, competitive firms tend to earn risk-adjusted levels of economic profit equal to zero.

T F 40. The frictional theory of profits holds that firms in a competitive industry can have economic profits that differ from zero for long periods of time.

T F 41. The monopoly theory of profits argues that restricted entry into an industry tends to keep profits low.

T F 42. The idea that profits are a form of reward for the successful introduction of a new product or process is the frictional theory of profit.

T F 43. The managerial efficiency theory of profit holds that firms that enjoy higher levels of profit do so because they are more efficient than their competitors.

T F 44. Economic profit is an important mechanism for the efficient reallocation of resources in a free-enterprise economy.

T F 45. Managerial economics is largely independent of the internationalization of economic activity.

T F 46. Business ethics refers to enforceable laws of business conduct.

T F 47. Business ethics provides quidelines as to what is acceptable behavior in business transactions.

T F 48. Many firms have responded to the need for ethical behavior by establishing codes of ethical behavior.

T F 49. Firms typically provide employees with a list of all possible forms of unethical behavior.

T F 50. The Internet has had very little impact on the way that business is conducted.

Multiple Choice Questions

1. Which of the following is the best definition of managerial economics? Managerial economics is

   A. a distinct field of economic theory.
   B. a field that applies economic theory and the tools of decision science.
   C. a field that combines economic theory and mathematics.
   D. none of the above.

2. The value of an economic theory in practice is determined by

   A. how accurate the assumptions are.
   B. how well the theory can be represented by a graph.
   C. how well the theory can predict or explain.
   D. how parsimonious the model is.

3. Management decision problems are comprised of three elements. Which of the following is not one of them?

   A. Profitability
   B. Alternatives
   C. Constraints
   D. Objectives

4. Which of the following areas of economic theory is the single most important element of managerial economics?

   A. Mathematical economics
   B. Econometrics
   C. Macroeconomics
   D. Microeconomics

5.   Which of the following is defined as the study of the aggregate economy studied as a whole?

   A. Mathematical economics
   B. Econometrics
   C. Macroeconomics
   D. Microeconomics

6.   Which of the following is the discipline that studies the use of statistical tools to estimate economic models?

   A. Mathematical economics
   B. Econometrics
   C. Macroeconomics
   D. Microeconomics

7.   Firms do not continue to grow without limit because of

   A. managerial limitations.
   B. government regulation.
   C. income taxes.
   D. antitrust laws.

8.   The modern theory of the firm holds that firms behave in a way that is designed to maximize

   A. profit.
   B. the value of the firm.
   C. monopoly power.
   D. total revenue.

9.   Which of the following functional areas of business has primary responsibility for a firm's total revenue?

   A. Accounting
   B. Finance
   C. Marketing
   D. Personnel

10.   Which of the following is an example of a resource constraint?

   A. Pollution control laws
   B. Inadequate demand
   C. Excessive production costs
   D. Inadequate financial capital

11.   The last stage in the five-step decision process described in the text is to

   A. determine the objective.
   B. select the best possible solution.
   C. implement the decision.
   D. explain the decision to managers.

12. The first stage in the five-step decision process described in the text is to

    A. define the problem.
    B. select the best possible solution.
    C. determine the objective.
    D. identify possible solutions.

13. The economic term for the costs associated with negotiating and enforcing a contract is

    A. opportunity costs.
    B. real costs.
    C. functional costs.
    D. transaction costs.

14. The tendency for managers to operate a firm in a way that maximizes their personal utility rather than the firm's profits is referred to as the

    A. consumer utility incentive.
    B. principal-agent problem.
    C. hidden agenda scenario.
    D. Modigliani hypothesis.

15. By tying a manager's compensation to the performance of the firm relative to that of its competitors, corporate stockholders and directors create incentives that tend to resolve the

    A. possibility of bankruptcy.
    B. hidden agenda scenario.
    C. principal-agent problem.
    D. firm's opportunity costs.

16. The globalization of business is reflected in all of the following except

    A. the international convergence of consumer tastes.
    B. the increase in barriers to international trade.
    C. the emphasis on global marketing-management training.
    D. increasing domestic competition from foreign producers.

17. Which of the following is not a result of the spread of information technology?

    A. More rapid deliveries of products to consumers
    B. Reduced inventories
    C. Reduced productivity of workers
    D. Reduced need for middle management

18. Which of the alternatives to the modern theory of the firm holds that managers attempt to meet some goal that is defined in terms of a specified level of sales, profits, growth, or market share?

    A. Sales maximization model
    B. Management utility maximization model
    C. Satisficing model
    D. Profit maximization model

19. Business profit is equal to total revenue minus

   A. economic costs.
   B. explicit costs.
   C. implicit costs.
   D. managerial costs.

20. Which of the following is an example of an implicit cost?

   A. Dividends paid out to stockholders
   B. The uncompensated services of the spouse of a firm's owner
   C. Payments made to workers who are unproductive
   D. All of the above are implicit costs.

21. Implicit cost is equal to

   A. business profit minus economic profit.
   B. business profit plus economic profit.
   C. economic profit minus business profit.
   D. economic profit minus explicit cost.

22. Which theory of profit holds that profit will be higher in industries characterized by a high degree of variability in their revenues or their costs?

   A. Risk-bearing theory
   B. Frictional theory
   C. Monopoly theory
   D. Innovation theory

23. Which theory of profit holds that profit will be higher in industries where firms in the industry are able to prevent other firms from entering the industry?

   A. Risk-bearing theory
   B. Frictional theory
   C. Monopoly theory
   D. Managerial efficiency theory

24. Which theory of profit holds that a firm's profits can differ from zero only in the short run?

   A. Risk-bearing theory
   B. Frictional theory
   C. Monopoly theory
   D. Managerial efficiency theory

25. Which theory of profit views profit as a reward for introducing a new product or technique?

   A. Risk-bearing theory
   B. Frictional theory
   C. Monopoly theory
   D. Innovation theory

26. Which theory of profit views profit as a firm's reward for keeping costs below or revenues above the levels experienced by other firms in the industry?

   A. Risk-bearing theory
   B. Frictional theory
   C. Innovation theory
   D. Managerial efficiency theory

27. What social function is served by profits in a free-enterprise system?

   A. Taxes on profits support government programs
   B. They provide an incentive for the reallocation of resources
   C. Profits allow individuals to accumulate wealth and engage in capital investment
   D. Profits result in higher levels of employment

28. Business ethics refers to any behavior by businesses that may

   A. be illegal.
   B. violate social or moral standards.
   C. result in the maximization of profits.
   D. All of the above.

29. Businesses have responded to incentives for ethical behavior by doing all of the following except

   A. lobbying for the abolition of laws that require ethical behavior.
   B. appointing "ethics officers" with responsibility for ensuring that employees behave in an ethical manner.
   C. providing training sessions in ethical behavior for employees.
   D. establishing codes of ethical behavior for employees.

30. Which of the following is a question that is uniquely relevant to the subject of business ethics?

   A. Should a firm make false and slanderous statements about its competitior's products?
   B. Should a firm attempt to conceal evidence of the harmful effects of its products on the health of consumers?
   C. Should a firm engage in illegal practices?
   D. Should a firm use a production method in foreign countries that is banned in its home country?

Multiple Choice Questions (Appendix)

31. The market demand curve shows

   A. the effect on market supply of a change in the demand for a good or service.
   B. the quantity of a good that consumers would like to purchase at different prices.
   C. the marginal cost of producing and selling different quantities of a good.
   D. the effect of advertising expenditures on the market price of a good.

32. At a price of $4.95, a pulp fiction novel is expected to sell 9,000 copies. If the novel is offered for sale at a price of $3.95, then the publisher can expect to sell

A. less than 9,000 copies.
B. 9,000 copies.
C. more than 9,000 copies.
D. It is impossible to predict the effect of a lower price on sales.

33. During a recession, economies experience increased unemployment and a reduced level of activity. How would a recession be likely to affect the market demand for new cars?

A. Demand will shift to the right.
B. Demand will shift to the left.
C. Demand will not shift, but the quantity of cars sold per month will decrease.
D. Demand will not shift, but the quantity of cars sold per month will increase.

34. The market supply curve shows

A. the effect on market demand of a change in the supply of a good or service.
B. the quantity of a good that firms would offer for sale at different prices.
C. the quantity of a good that consumers would be willing to buy at different prices.
D. All of the above are correct.

35. At a price of $299.95, the manufacturer of a portable gas-powered generator is willing to produce 19,000 units per quarter. At a price of $349.95, it is likely that the manufacturer will be willing to produce

A. more than 19,000 units per quarter.
B. 19,000 units per quarter.
C. less than 19,000 units per quarter.
D. It is impossible to predict the effect of a higher price on the number of units of a product that a firm will be willing to produce.

36. Unionized workers may be able to negotiate with management for higher wages during periods of economic prosperity. Suppose that workers at automobile assembly plants successfully negotiate a significant increase in their wage package. How would the new wage contract be likely to affect the market supply of new cars?

A. Supply will shift to the right.
B. Supply will shift to the left.
C. Supply will not shift, but the quantity of cars produced per month will decrease.
D. Supply will not shift, but the quantity of cars produced per month will increase.

37. If automobile manufacturers are producing cars faster than people want to buy them,

A. there is an excess supply and price can be expected to decrease.
B. there is an excess supply and price can be expected to increase.
C. there is an excess demand and price can be expected to decrease.
D. there is an excess demand and price can be expected to increase.

38. If a computer software company introduces a new program and finds that orders from wholesalers far exceed the number of units that are being produced,

   A. there is an excess supply and price can be expected to decrease.
   B. there is an excess supply and price can be expected to increase.
   C. there is an excess demand and price can be expected to decrease.
   D. there is an excess demand and price can be expected to increase.

39. Market equilibrium refers to a situation in which market price

   A. is high enough to allow firms to earn a fair profit.
   B. is low enough for consumers to buy all that they want.
   C. is at a level where there is neither a shortage nor a surplus.
   D. is just above the intersection of the market supply and demand curves.

40. If the price of a good increases while the quantity of the good exchanged on markets increases, then the most likely explanation is that there has been

   A. an increase in demand.
   B. a decrease in demand.
   C. an increase in supply.
   D. a decrease in supply.

41. If the price of a good decreases while the quantity of the good exchanged on markets increases, then the most likely explanation is that there has been

   A. an increase in demand.
   B. a decrease in demand.
   C. an increase in supply.
   D. a decrease in supply.

42. If the price of a good increases while the quantity of the good exchanged on markets decreases, then the most likely explanation is that there has been

   A. an increase in demand.
   B. a decrease in demand.
   C. an increase in supply.
   D. a decrease in supply.

43. If the price of a good decreases while the quantity of the good exchanged on markets decreases, then the most likely explanation is that there has been

   A. an increase in demand.
   B. a decrease in demand.
   C. an increase in supply.
   D. a decrease in supply.

44. An increase in the demand for a good will cause

   A. an increase in equilibrium price and quantity.
   B. a decrease in equilibrium price and quantity.
   C. an increase in equilibrium price and a decrease in equilibrium quantity.
   D. a decrease in equilibrium price and an increase in equilibrium quantity.

45.   An increase in the supply of a good will cause

    A. an increase in equilibrium price and quantity.
    B. a decrease in equilibrium price and quantity.
    C. an increase in equilibrium price and a decrease in equilibrium quantity.
    D. a decrease in equilibrium price and an increase in equilibrium quantity.

Problems

1.   Use the graph that follows to plot the relationship between the present value of $1 and the number of years in the future that it will be received when the interest rate is 10%. What is the general relationship between present value and time?

Chapter 1: Problem 1

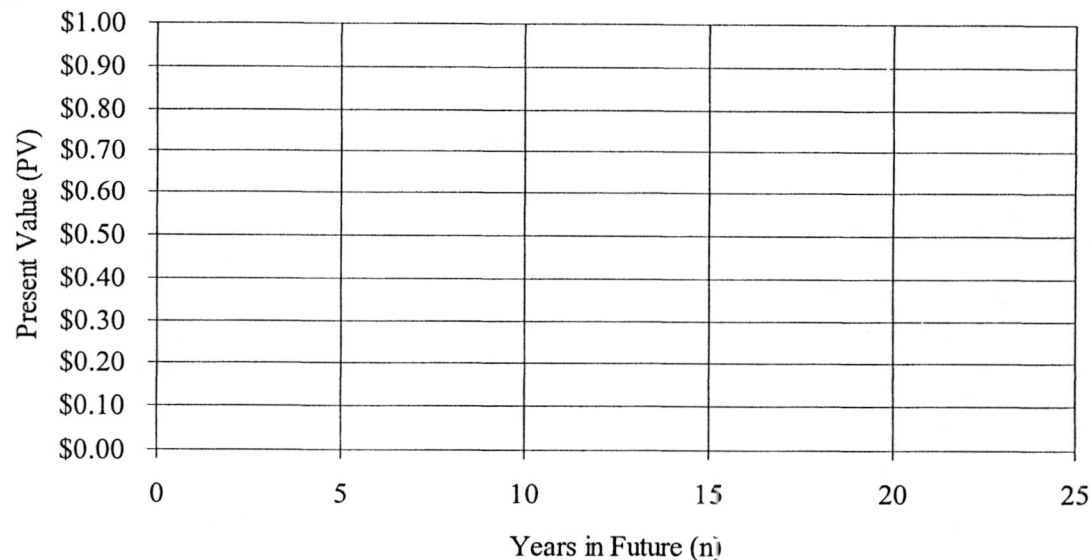

2.   Use the graph that follows to plot the relationship between the present value of $1 received five years from now and the interest rate. What is the general relationship between present value and the interest rate?

Chapter 1: Problem 2

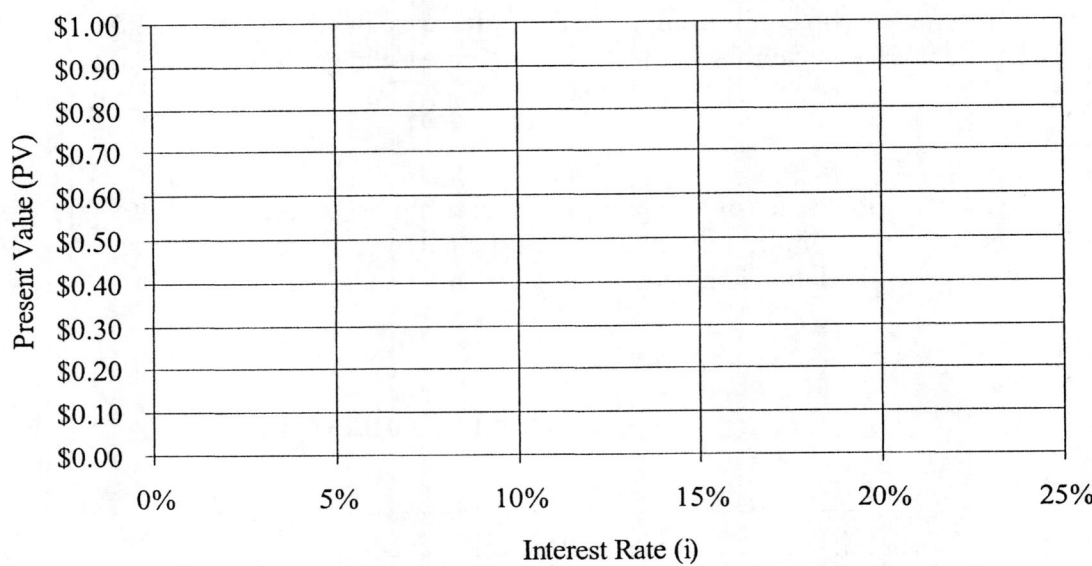

3.   Firms frequently find themselves in situations where they must choose between pursuing short-term projects that will increase profits immediately (for example, an advertising campaign) and long-term projects that will not increase profits until several years have passed (for example, research designed to develop a new technology.) Based on your analysis of the effects of time and the interest rate on present value in Problems 1 and 2, how do you think changes in the interest rate will influence a firm's choice between a short term and a long-term project?

4. Abe is thinking of buying a piece of commercial property as an investment. The property will cost $100,000. Abe believes that he can lease the property for $6,000 per year, payable at the beginning of every year, just as soon as he buys it. He also believes that he can sell the property at the end of five years for $120,000. Calculate the present value (PV) of profits for Abe's business at each of the following discount rates: 8%, 9%, 10%, and 12%. Enter each of your calculated values in the table that follows and indicate whether or not Abe should buy the property at each of the discount rates. Finally, plot the PV for each of the discount rate on the graph and connect the plotted points with straight lines. At approximately what interest rate will Abe be indifferent between buying the property and not buying the property?

Discount Rate (i)	8%	9%	10%	12%
Present Value				
Should Abe buy?				

Chapter 1: Problem 4

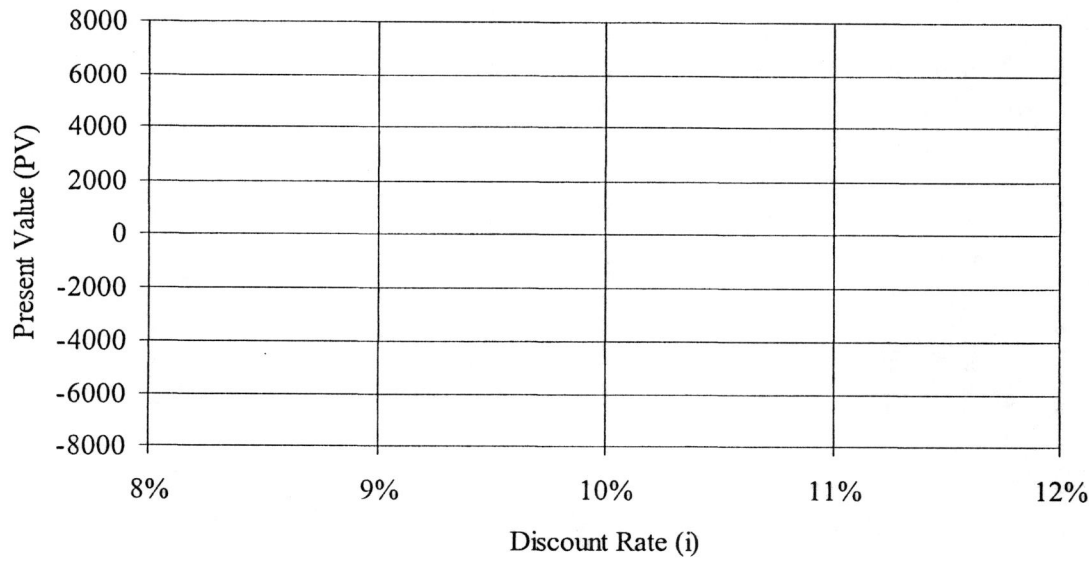

5. Brenda is a college professor who earns $40,000 a year. She decides to open an automobile body shop. She anticipates annual revenues of $150,000. Her expenses will be as follows:

Employee salaries	$ 65,000
Insurance	4,000
Utilities	3,000
Lease	6,000
Supplies	12,000
Interest payments	10,000

Calculate Brenda's anticipated explicit costs, implicit costs, business profits, and economic profits. What is the minimum revenue that is required for Brenda to earn a normal profit (i.e., an economic profit of zero)?

Explicit Costs	Implicit Costs	Business Profits	Economic Profits

6. Charlie is considering the purchase of a laundry business, but does not know how much it is worth. The business generates $18,000 in profit per year and will not require any of Charlie's time to operate. Charlie plans to buy the business, keep it for 10 years, and then sell it for the same price he pays for. If the appropriate discount rate is 18%, what is the most Charlie should pay for the business?

7. Refer to the information in Problem 6. If the discount rate falls to 9% at the end of 10 years, what will happen to the price at which Charlie can sell the business?

8. Dr. Doug is considering two business opportunities. Both require an initial investment of $200,000. The first will return $50,000 at the end of each of the next six years, while the second will return $35,000 at the end of each of the next 10 years. Calculate the present value of the profit from these two businesses at each of the following discount rates: 7%, 8%, 9%, 10%, and 12%. Use the graph that follows to plot the relationship between the present value (PV) of profit from each of the two businesses and the interest rate. At approximately what interest rate would Dr. Doug be indifferent between the two businesses? Over what range of interest rates would Business 1 be preferred? Over what range would Business 2 be preferred?

Discount Rate (i)	7%	8%	9%	10%	12%
Business 1					
Business 2					

Chapter 1: Problem 8

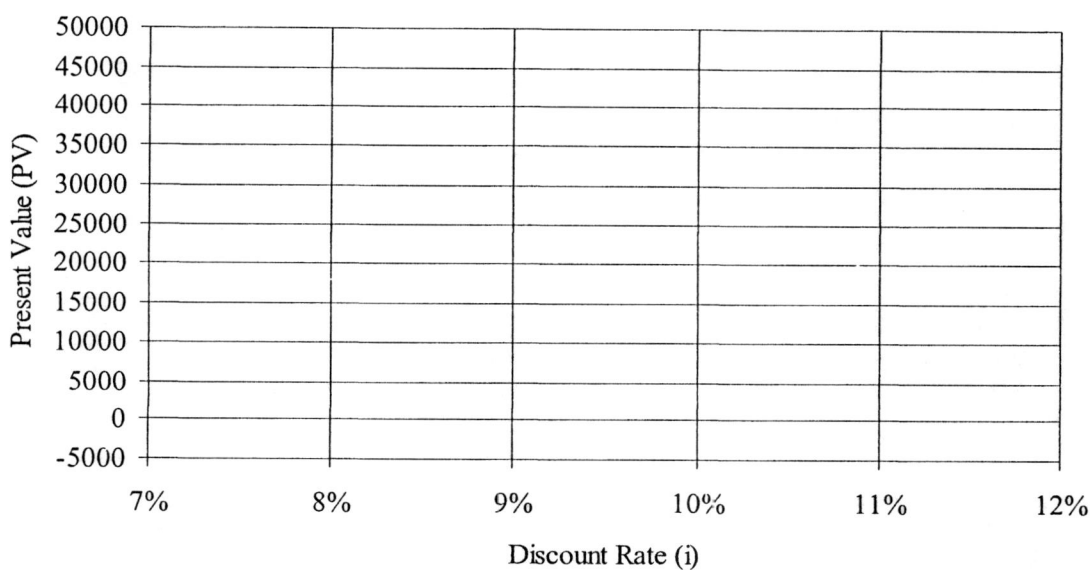

9.   Elaine had always wanted to operate a restaurant, so one day she took a leave of absence from her job, which pays $25,000 per year, and bought a restaurant for $100,000 in cash. At the end of the year, she had to decide whether to go back to her old job or to continue operating the restaurant, so she examined her revenues and expenses for the year. She found that her revenues were $185,000 and that her operating expenses were $68,000 for labor, $80,000 for food and supplies, and $12,000 for utilities, repairs and insurance. She also found that she can sell the restaurant back to the old owner for exactly what she paid for it. If she came to you, what advice would you give her? Should she keep the restaurant or go back to her old job? Why?

10.   Fred has $10,000 to invest. If he invests in Business A, he will receive $18,000 at the end of five years. If he invests in Business B, he will receive $2,000 at the end of each of the next 10 years. If Fred does not invest in a business, he can earn a rate of return equal to the discount rate from a certificate of deposit. If the appropriate discount rate is 10%, should Fred invest in A, B, or neither?

11.   Refer to the information in Problem 10 and determine what Fred should do if the appropriate discount rate is 20%.

12.   Refer to the information in Problem 10. If Fred decides to invest in a certificate of deposit that pays an amount equal to the discount rate, how much will he have at the end of five years if the discount rate is 10%?

13.   Refer to the information in Problem 10. If Fred decides to invest in a certificate of deposit that pays an amount equal to the discount rate, how much will he have at the end of five years if the discount rate is 20%?

14. Refer to the information in Problem 10. If Fred decides to invest in an annuity that repays his investment in 10 equal payments made at the end of each of the next 10 years, what will the annual payments be if the discount rate is 10%?

15. Refer to the information in Problem 10. If Fred decides to invest in an annuity that repays his investment in 10 equal payments made at the end of each of the next 10 years, what will the annual payments be if the discount rate is 20%?

16. Problems involving the time value of money, or discounting, can always be solved in more than one way. This is illustrated by the answers to Problems 10 through 15. Compare the results of your calculations for Problem 10 with those for Problems 12 and 14. Now compare the results of your calculations or Problem 11 with those for Problems 13 and 15. Devise a general rule based on these comparisons.

17. Use the graph that follows to plot a demand curve and a supply curve. Label them D_0 and S_0. Identify the equilibrium price and quantity and label them P_0 and Q_0. Now plot a second demand curve that is parallel to the first and that represents an **increase in demand** and label it D_1. Identify the new equilibrium price and quantity and label them P_1 and Q_1. What has happened to price and quantity as a result of the change in demand? Finally, draw two new supply curves, parallel to the first supply curve. Draw the first one so that the equilibrium price defined by the new supply curve and demand curve D_1 is equal to P_0. Label the first new supply curve S_P. Draw the second supply curve so that the equilibrium quantity defined by the new supply curve and demand curve D_1 is equal to Q_0. Label the second new supply curve S_Q. Explain the general implications of this exercise by answering the following question: what happens to equilibrium price and quantity if a demand increase is accompanied by a change in supply?

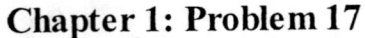

Chapter 1: Problem 17

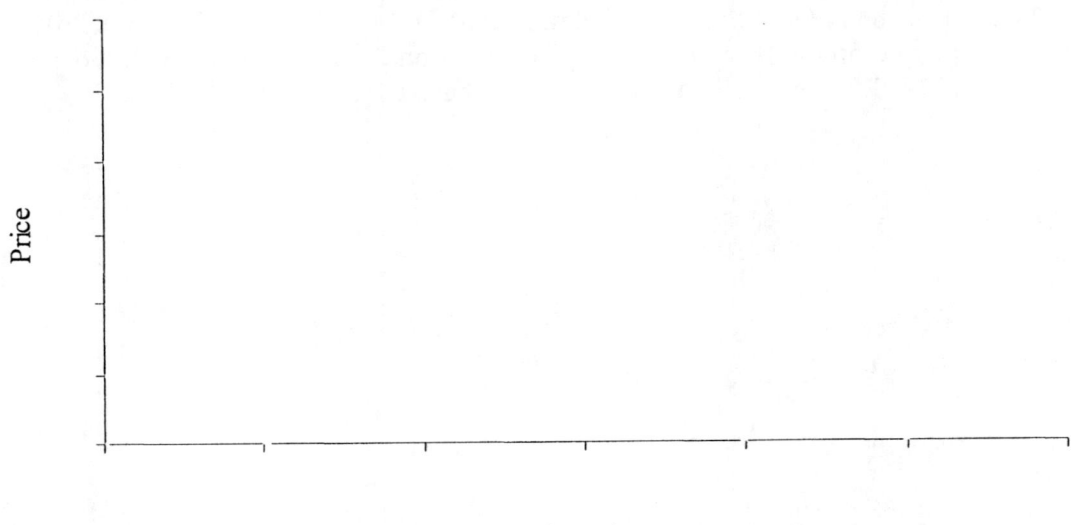

Quantity

18. Use the graph that follows to plot a demand curve and a supply curve. Label them D_0 and S_0. Identify the equilibrium price and quantity and label them P_0 and Q_0. Now plot a second demand curve that is parallel to the first and that represents a **decrease in demand** and label it D_1. Identify the new equilibrium price and quantity and label them P_1 and Q_1. What has happened to price and quantity as a result of the change in demand? Finally, draw two new supply curves, parallel to the first supply curve. Draw the first one so that the equilibrium price defined by the new supply curve and demand curve D_1 is equal to P_0. Label the first new supply curve S_P. Draw the second supply curve so that the equilibrium quantity defined by the new supply curve and demand curve D_1 is equal to Q_0. Label the second new supply curve S_Q. Explain the general implications of this exercise by answering the following question: what happens to equilibrium price and quantity if a demand decrease is accompanied by a change in supply?

Chapter 1: Problem 18

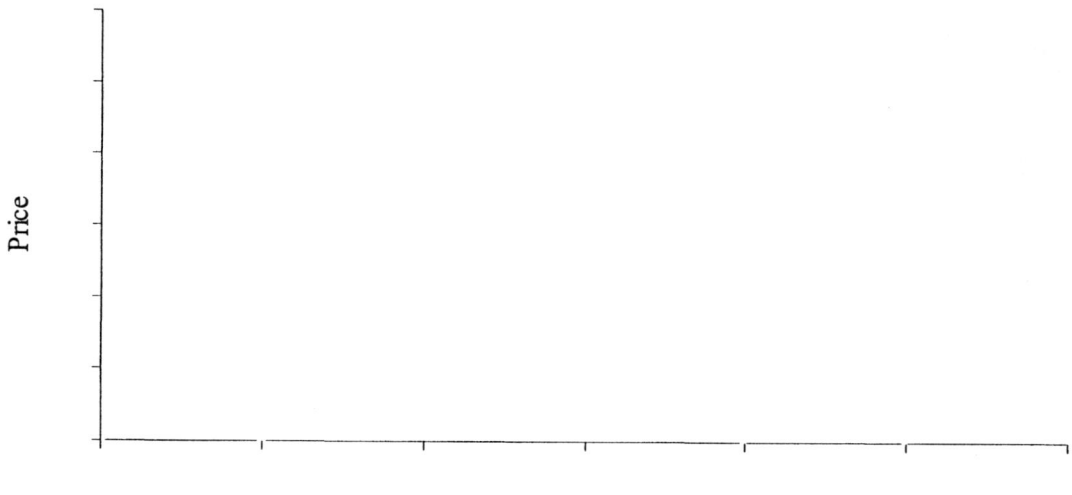

Quantity

---

19.   Use the graph that follows to plot a demand curve and a supply curve. Label them D_0 and S_0. Identify the equilibrium price and quantity and label them P_0 and Q_0. Now plot a second supply curve that is parallel to the first and that represents an **increase in supply** and label it S_1. Identify the new equilibrium price and quantity and label them P_1 and Q_1. What has happened to price and quantity as a result of the change in supply? Finally, draw two new demand curves, parallel to the first demand curve. Draw the first one so that the equilibrium price defined by the new demand curve and supply curve S_1 is equal to P_0. Label the first new demand curve D_P. Draw the second demand curve so that the equilibrium quantity defined by the new demand curve and supply curve S_1 is equal to Q_0. Label the second new demand curve D_Q. Explain the general implications of this exercise by answering the following question: what happens to equilibrium price and quantity if a supply increase is accompanied by a change in demand?

Chapter 1: Problem 19

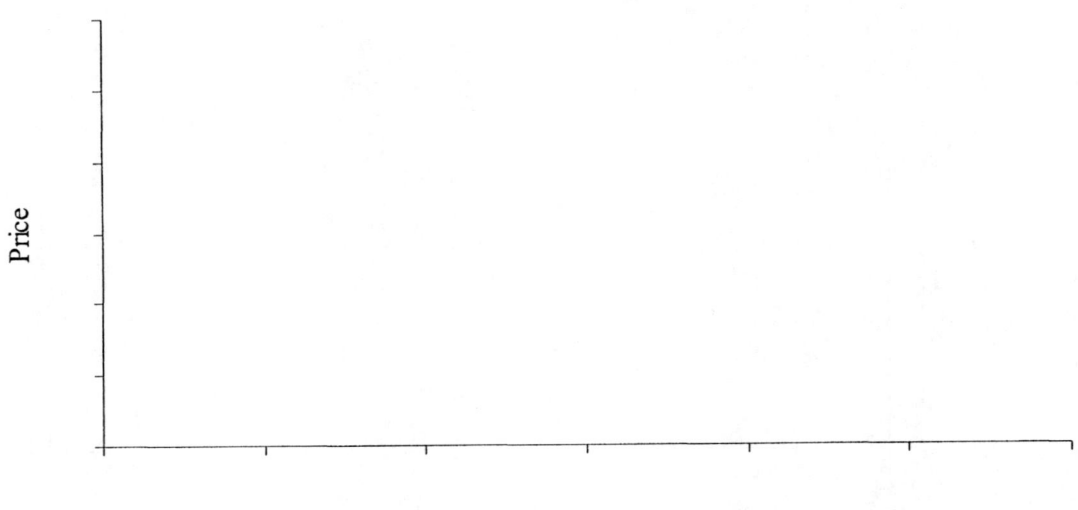

20.   Use the graph that follows to plot a demand curve and a supply curve. Label them D_0 and S_0. Identify the equilibrium price and quantity and label them P_0 and Q_0. Now plot a second supply curve that is parallel to the first and that represents a **decrease in supply** and label it S_1. Identify the new equilibrium price and quantity and label them P_1 and Q_1. What has happened to price and quantity as a result of the change in supply? Finally, draw two new demand curves, parallel to the first demand curve. Draw the first one so that the equilibrium price defined by the new demand curve and supply curve S_1 is equal to P_0. Label the first new demand curve D_P. Draw the second demand curve so that the equilibrium quantity defined by the new demand curve and supply curve S_1 is equal to Q_0. Label the second new demand for D_Q. Explain the general implications of this exercise by answering the following question: what happens to equilibrium price and quantity if a supply decrease is accompanied by a change in demand.

Chapter 1: Problem 20

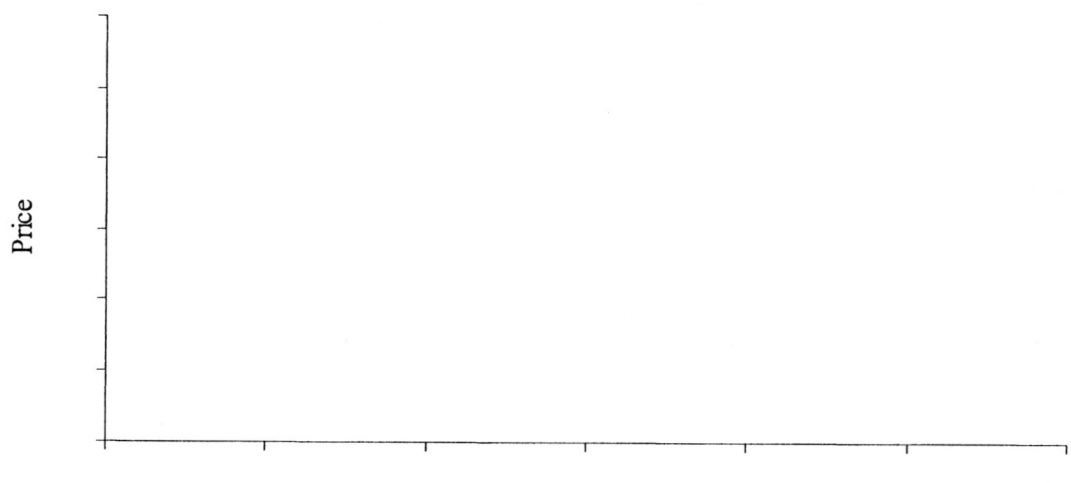

Quantity

True-False Answers

1	T	11	T	21	T	31	F	41	F
2	F	12	T	22	F	32	T	42	F
3	T	13	F	23	T	33	F	43	T
4	F	14	T	24	F	34	T	44	T
5	T	15	T	25	T	35	F	45	F
6	F	16	T	26	F	36	T	46	F
7	F	17	T	27	F	37	T	47	T
8	F	18	F	28	T	38	F	48	T
9	F	19	F	29	T	39	T	49	F
10	F	20	T	30	F	40	F	50	F

Multiple Choice Answers

1	B	10	D	19	B	28	B	37	A
2	C	11	C	20	B	29	A	38	D
3	A	12	A	21	A	30	D	39	C
4	D	13	D	22	A	31	B	40	A
5	C	14	B	23	C	32	C	41	C
6	B	15	C	24	B	33	B	42	D
7	A	16	B	25	D	34	B	43	B
8	B	17	C	26	D	35	A	44	A
9	C	18	C	27	B	36	B	45	D

Solutions to Problems

1. Conclusion: The present value of a dollar that will be received in the future will be lower if it is received further in the future. In other words, the longer you have to wait to get a dollar, the less the dollar is worth to you.

   General formula for the present value (PV) of an amount received t periods in the future when the discount rate is equal to i:

   PV = Future Amount c $1/(1 + i)^t$ = Future Amount x $PVIF_{i,n}$

   Present value of $1 received now:

   PV = $1 \times 1/(1 + 0.10)^0$ = $1 \times PVIF_{0.10,0}$ = $1

   Present value of $1 received in five years:

   PV = $1 \times 1/(1 + 0.10)^5$ = $1 \times PVIF_{0.10,5}$ = $0.62

   Present value of $1 received in ten years:

   PV = $1 \times 1/(1 + 0.10)^{10}$ = $1 \times PVIF_{0.10,10}$ = $0.39

Present value of $1 received in fifteen years:

$$PV = \$1 \times 1/(1 + 0.10)^{15} = \$1 \times PVIF_{0.10,15} = \$0.24$$

Present value of $1 received in twenty years:

$$PV = \$1 \times 1/(1 + 0.10)^{20} = \$1 \times PVIF_{0.10,20} = \$0.15$$

Present value of $1 received in twenty-five years:

$$PV = \$1 \times 1/(1 + 0.10)^{25} = \$1 \times PVIF_{0.10,25} = \$0.09$$

The relationship between the present value of money and the period of into the future that it will be received can be clearly seen in the graph that follows.

Chapter 1: Problem 1

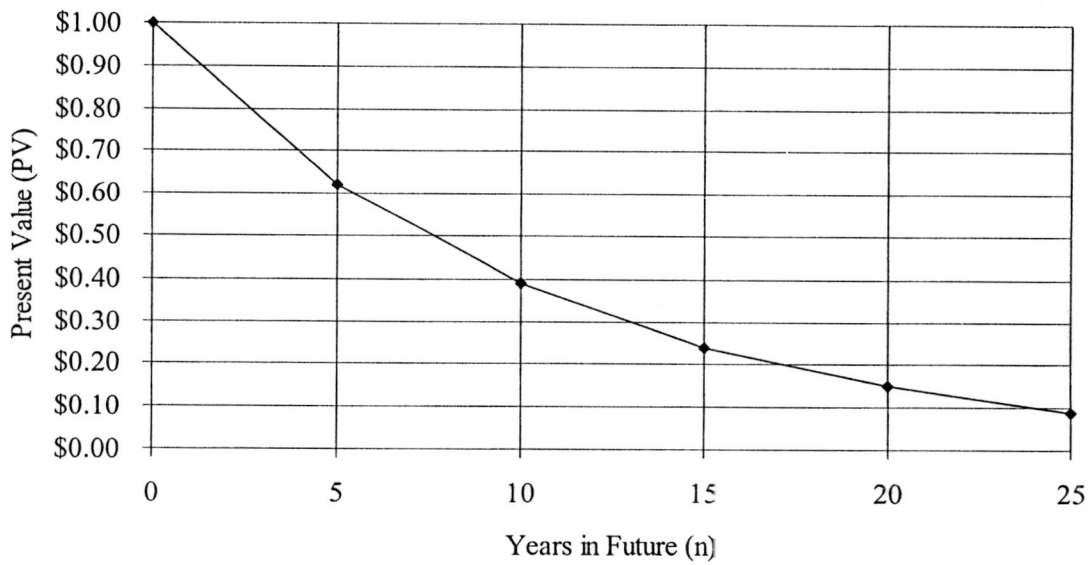

2. Conclusion: The present value of a dollar that will be received in the future will be lower if the discount rate is higher.

Present value of $1 received in five years if i = 0:

$$PV = \$1 \times 1/(1 + 0.00)^{5} = \$1 \times PVIF_{0.00,5} = \$1.00$$

Present value of $1 received in five years if i = 0.05:

$$PV = \$1 \times 1/(1 + 0.05)^{5} = \$1 \times PVIF_{0.05,5} = \$0.78$$

Present value of $1 received in five years if i = 0010:

$$PV = \$1 \times 1/(1 + 0.10)^{5} = \$1 \times PVIF_{0.10,5} = \$0.62$$

Present value of $1 received in five years if $i = 0015$:

$$PV = \$1 \times 1/(1 + 0.15)^5 = \$1 \times PVIF_{0.15,5} = \$0.50$$

Present value of $1 received in five years if $i = 0.20$:

$$PV = \$1 \times 1/(1 + 0.20)^5 = \$1 \times PVIF_{0.20,5} = \$0.40$$

Present value of $1 received in five years if $i = 0.25$:

$$PV = \$1 \times 1/(1 + 0.25)^5 = \$1 \times PVIF_{0.25,5} = \$0.33$$

The relationship between the present value of money and the interest rate at which it is discounted can be seen clearly in the graph that follows.

Chapter 1: Problem 2

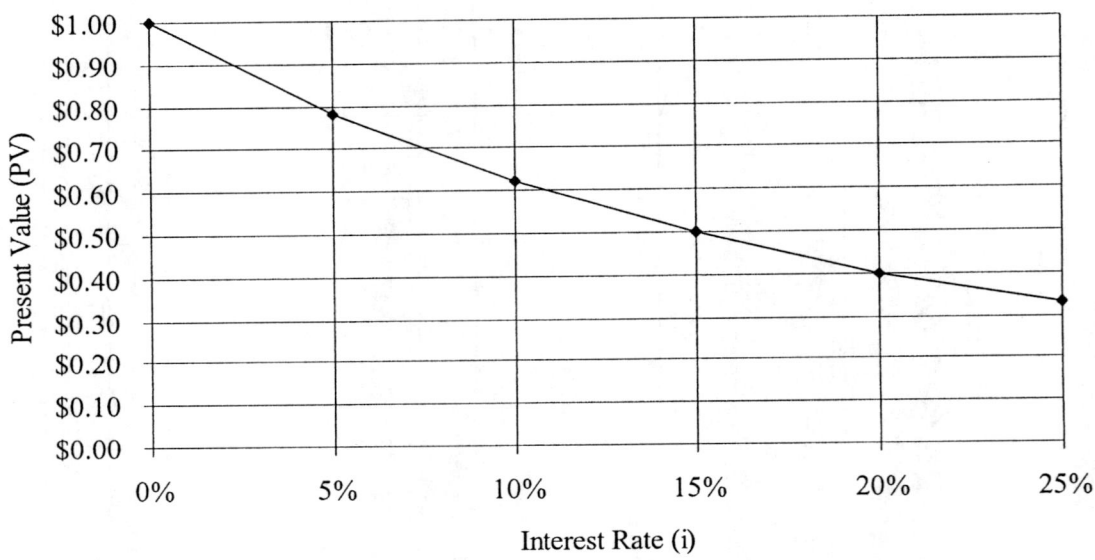

3.   If the interest rate used for discounting is higher, then a short term project is more likely to be selected because profits in the near future are not as heavily discounted by higher interest rates as are profits in the distant future. Conversely, if the interest rate used for discounting is lower, then a long-term project is more likely to be selected because profits in the distant future will not be as heavily discounted as they would be if rates were higher.

The cash flows associated with Abe's investment are listed below (note that all cash flows are listed at the end of the relevant period, which is the beginning of the following period):

Time Period	Cash Flows ($1,000s)
0	-100 + 6 = -94
1	6
2	6
9	6
4	6
5	120

The following are general formulas for the present value of a series of n equal periodic payments (that is, of an annuity of n periods) that begin one time period from the present:

$$PV = Payment \times [1/(1 + i)^1 + 1/(1 + i)^2 + \cdots + 1/(1 + i)^n]$$

$$PV = Payment \times [PVIF_{i,1} + PVIF_{i,2} + \cdots + PVIF_{i,n}]$$

A more effective way to calculate the present value of this type of cash flow sequence is by using a factor that is based on the general formulas given above, the present value interest factor for an annuity (PVIFA), in the following way:

$$PV = Payment \times PVIFA_{i,n}$$

Present Value of the cash flow in $1,000s if i = 0.08:

$$PV = -94 + (6 \times PVIFA_{0.08,4}) + (120 \times PVIF_{0.08,5}) = 7.5446$$

$$PV = -94 + (6 \times 3.3121) + (120 \times 0.6806) = 7.5446$$

Present Value of the cash flow in $1,000s if i = 0.09:

$$PV = -94 + (6 \times PVIFA_{0.09,4}) + (120 \times PVIF_{0.09,5}) = 3.4262$$

$$PV = -94 + (6 \times 3.2397) + (120 \times 0.6499) = 3.4262$$

Present Value of the cash flow in $1,000s if i = 0.10:

$$PV = -94 + (6 \times PVIFA_{0.10,4}) + (120 \times PVIF_{0.10,5}) = -0.4726$$

$$PV = -94 + (6 \times 3.1699) + (120 \times 0.6209) = -0.4726$$

Present Value of the cash flow in $1,000s if i = 0.12:

$$PV = -94 + (6 \times PVIFA_{0.12,4}) + (120 \times PVIF_{0.12,5}) = -7.6882$$

$$PV = -94 + (6 \times 3.0373) + (120 \times 0.5674) = -7.6882$$

The relationship between the present value of the cash flows and the discount rate is evident in the graph that follows, as is the location of the breakeven interest rate.

Chapter 1: Problem 4

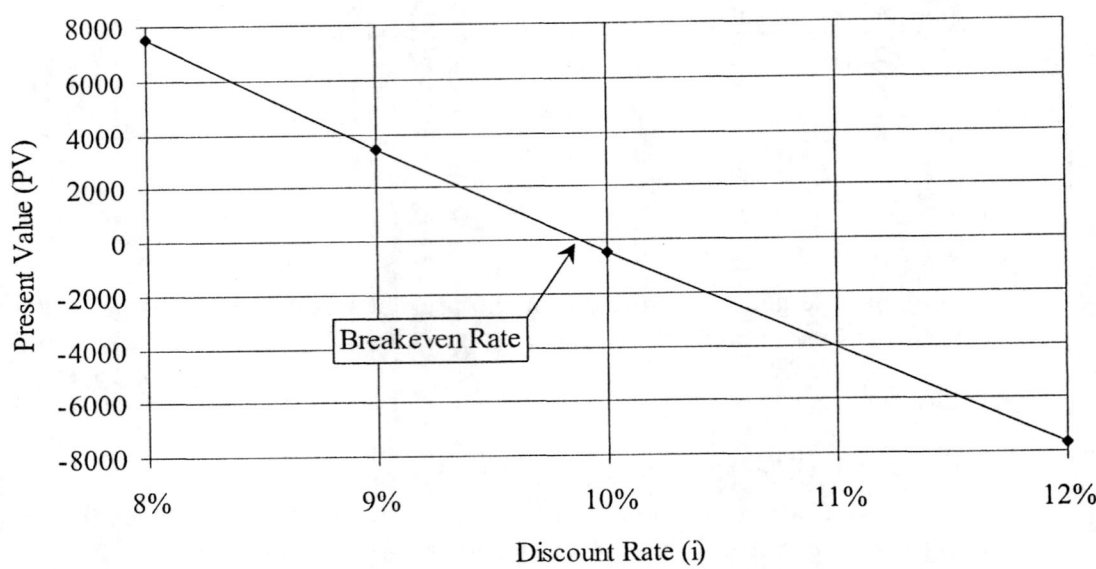

4. Abe should invest in the property if the discount rate is below the breakeven rate and should not invest in the property if the discount rate is above the breakeven rate. If you refer to the graph, you can see that the PV is equal to zero when the discount rate is just below 10%. Below this rate, the PV is positive and the investment is desirable. Above the breakeven rate, the PV is negative and the investment is not desirable.

5. Explicit costs include all of the listed expenses. They total to $100,000. The only implicit cost is Brenda's foregone salary of $40,000. Business profit is equal to total revenue minus explicit costs, $150,000 - $100,000 or $50,000. Economic profit is equal to total revenue minus explicit and implicit costs, $150,000 - $140,000 or $10,000. The minimum revenue required for Brenda to earn a normal profit (that is, an economic profit equal to zero) is $140,000.

6. The most Charlie should pay for the laundry business is an amount that has an implicit annual cost that results in an economic profit of zero; i.e., an implicit cost equal to the annual profit of $18,000. The implicit cost of the purchase price is equal tot the purchase price multiplied by the discount rate. This yields the following relationship:

Profit = Cost = Price × Rate

Substituting in the know values and solving yields:

$18,000 = Price × 0.18 so Price = $18,000/0.18 = $100,000

The most Charlie should pay is $100,000.

7.	If the discount rate falls to 9%, then the price of the business will double to $200,000. Note that, if Charlie anticipated this decrease in the discount rate at the time he purchased the business, he would have been willing to pay a higher price for the business.

8.	The general formulas for the present values of the two businesses (in $1,000s) are:

$$PV_1 = -200 + 50 \times PVIFA_{i,6} \text{ and } PV_2 = -200 + 35 \times PVIFA_{i,10}$$

When the discount rate is 7%, the solutions are:

$$PV_1 = -200 + 50 \times 4.7665 = 38.325$$

$$PV_2 = -200 + 35 \times 7.0236 = 45.826$$

When the discount rate is 8%, the solutions are:

$$PV_1 = -200 + 50 \times 4.6229 = 31.145$$

$$PV_2 = -200 + 35 \times 6.7101 = 34.8535$$

When the discount rate is 9%, the solutions are:

$$PV_1 = -200 + 50 \times 4.4859 = 24.295$$

$$PV_2 = -200 + 35 \times 6.4177 = 24.6195$$

When the discount rate is 10%, the solutions are:

$$PV_1 = -200 + 50 \times 4.3553 = 14.765$$

$$PV_2 = -200 + 35 \times 6.1446 = 15.061$$

When the discount rate is 12%, the solutions are:

$$PV_1 = -200 + 50 \times 4.1114 = 5.57$$

$$PV_2 = -200 + 35 \times 5.6502 = -2.243$$

The two businesses are equivalent at the discount rate where the present value of each is the same. From the graph that follows, you can see that this point of indifference is located at an interest rate of about 9.1%. If the discount rate is below this rate than Business 2 is preferred. If it is above this rate, then Business 1 is preferred.

Chapter 1: Problem 8

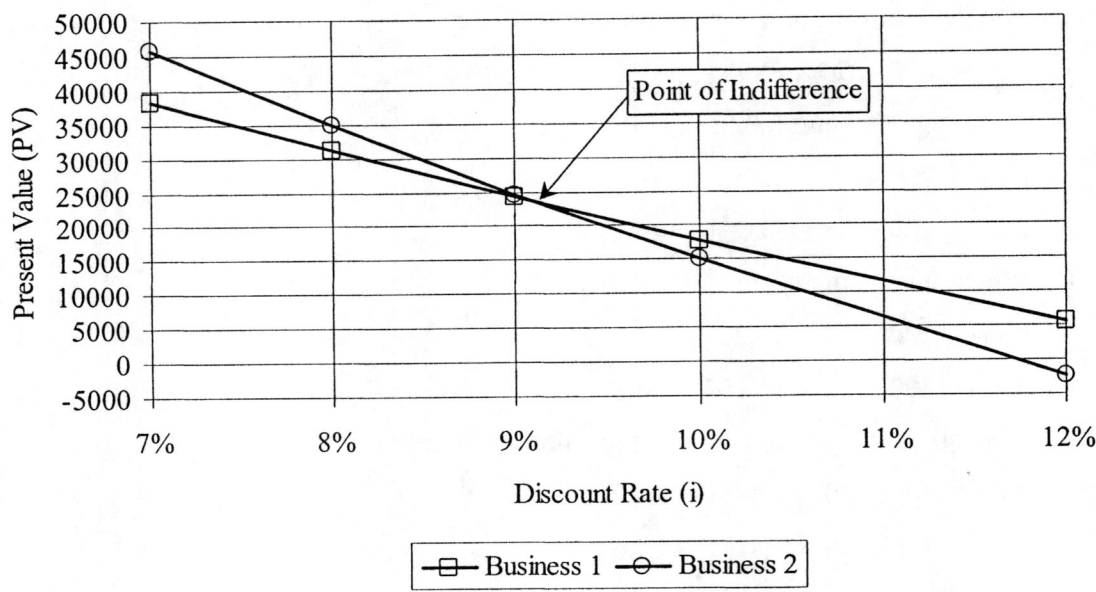

9. She should go back to her old job. Her explicit costs total $68 + 80 + 12 = 160$ and the implicit cost of her time is 25. The sum of her explicit costs and the cost of her time is 185, which is equal to her total revenue. However, the implicit cost of the $100,000 investment in the restaurant is equal to the appropriate discount rate multiplied by $100,000. Thus, her economic profit is negative and she will be better off if she takes her old job back.

10. The present value formulas for the two businesses (in $1,000s) are:

$PV_A = -10 + 18 \times PVIF_{0.10,5}$ and $PV_B = -10 + 2 \times PVIF_{0.10,10}$

$PV_A = -10 + 18 \times 0.6209 = 1.1762$

$PV_B = -10 + 2 \times 6.1446 = 2.2892$

Fred should select Business B because it has a higher positive present value than does Business A.

11. The present value formulas for the two alternatives (in $1,000s) are:

$PV_A = -10 + 18 \times PVIF_{0.20,5}$ and $PV_B = -10 + 2 \times PVIF_{0.20,10}$

$PV_A = -10 + 18 \times 0.4019 = -2.7658$

$PV_B = -10 + 2 \times 4.1925 = -1.615$

Fred should invest in the CD because neither of the two business opportunities have a positive present value. The implication of this result is that neither business yields a rate of return as high as 20%, but the CD does, so it is the preferred alternative.

12. The formula for the future value (FV) of the CD (in $1,000s) is:

$$FV = 10 \times 1/(1 + 0.10)5 = 16.105$$

This can also be written using factor notation as:

$$FV = 10 \times FVIF_{0.20,5} = 10 \times 1.6105 = 16.105$$

13. If the interest rate on the CD is 20%, then the future value of the CD is calculated as follows:

$$FV = 10 \times FVIF_{0.20,5} = 10 \times 2.4883 = 24.883$$

14. The formula for the annual payment amount (R) is derived from the definition of the PVIFA as follows:

$$PV = R \times PVIFA_{i,n} \text{ so } R = PV \times 1/PVIFA_{i,n}$$

The formula for the annual payment amount (in $1,000s) is:

$$R = 10 \times 1/PVIFA_{0.10,10} = 10 \times 1/6.1446 = 1.6274$$

15. $$R = 10 \times 1/PVIFA_{0.20,10} = 10 \times 1/4.1925 = 2.3852$$

16. There are always at least three ways to solve problems that involve the comparison of projects using the time value of money. The first method, present value, was used in Problems 10 and 11 above. When the interest rate was 10%, the present value of Business A ($1,176) was smaller than the present value of Business B ($2,289) and both were positive, so Business B was preferred to Business A and both were preferred to the CD. When the interest rate was 20%, the present values of Business A (-$2,766) and of Business B (-$1,615) were both negative, so neither was preferred to the CD.

The second method, future value, involves comparing the future value of alternatives. Notice that, when the interest rate is 10%, the future value of the CD ($16,105) is less than the future value of Business A ($18,000), which indicates that Business A is preferred to the CD. If the interest rate is 20%, the future value of the CD ($24,883) will be greater than the future value of Business A, so the CD is preferred.

The third method, annual payment, involves comparing the equivalent annual payments of alternatives. Again, note that, when the interest rate is 10%, the annual payment that is equivalent to the CD ($1,627) is less than the annual payment that would be derived from Business B ($2,000) so the business is preferred. If the interest rate is 20%, then the annual payment that is equivalent to the CD ($2,385) is greater than the annual payment from Business B. The result is the same as that noted previously, namely, that Business B is preferred to the CD at 10%, but the CD is preferred at 20%.

The general rule that can be derived from this example is that the alternative with the highest equivalent present value, future value, and annual payment value is preferred to other alternatives. Note, also, that all three of these methods of computing time value equivalence will yield the same ranking of alternatives.

17. An increase in demand will cause both the equilibrium price and equilibrium quantity to increase.

If an increase in demand is accompanied by an increase in supply, then equilibrium quantity will increase while equilibrium price may increase, decrease, or remain the same, depending upon whether the rightward shift in the supply curve is less than, greater than, or equal to the rightward shift in the demand curve, respectively.

If an increase in demand is accompanied by a decrease in supply, then equilibrium price will increase while equilibrium quantity may increase, decrease, or remain the same depending upon whether the upward shift in the supply curve is less than, greater than, or equal to the upward shift in the demand curve, respectively.

Chapter 1: Problem 17

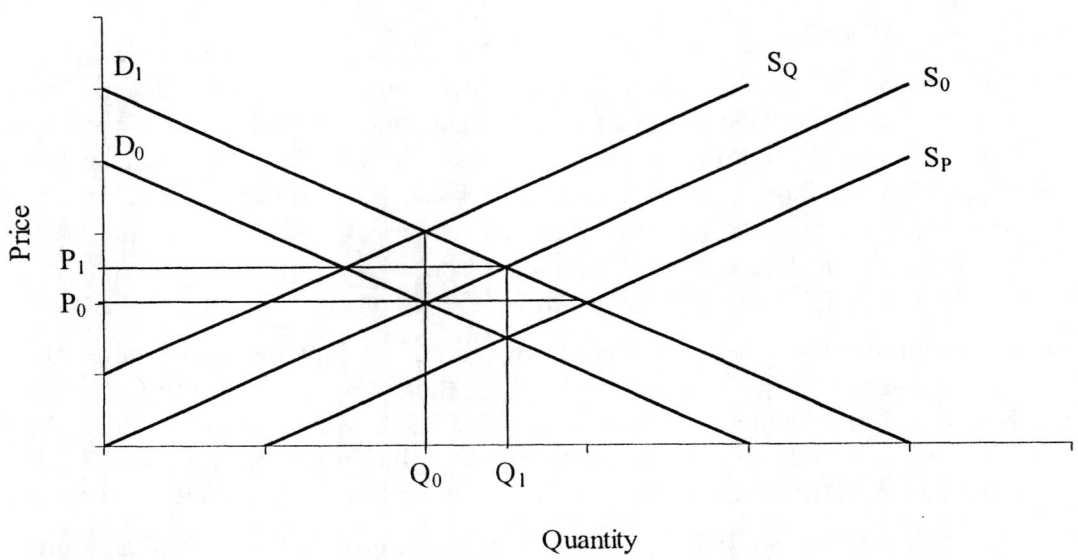

18. A decrease in demand will cause both equilibrium price and equilibrium quantity to decrease.

If a decrease in demand is accompanied by an increase in supply, then equilibrium price will decrease while equilibrium quantity may increase, decrease, or remain the same, depending upon whether the downward shift in the supply curve is greater than, less than, or equal to the downward shift in the demand curve, respectively.

If a decrease in demand is accompanied by a decrease in supply, then equilibrium quantity will decrease while equilibrium price may increase, decrease, or remain the same depending upon whether the leftward shift in the supply curve is greater than, less than, or equal to the leftward shift in the demand curve, respectively.

Chapter 1: Problem 18

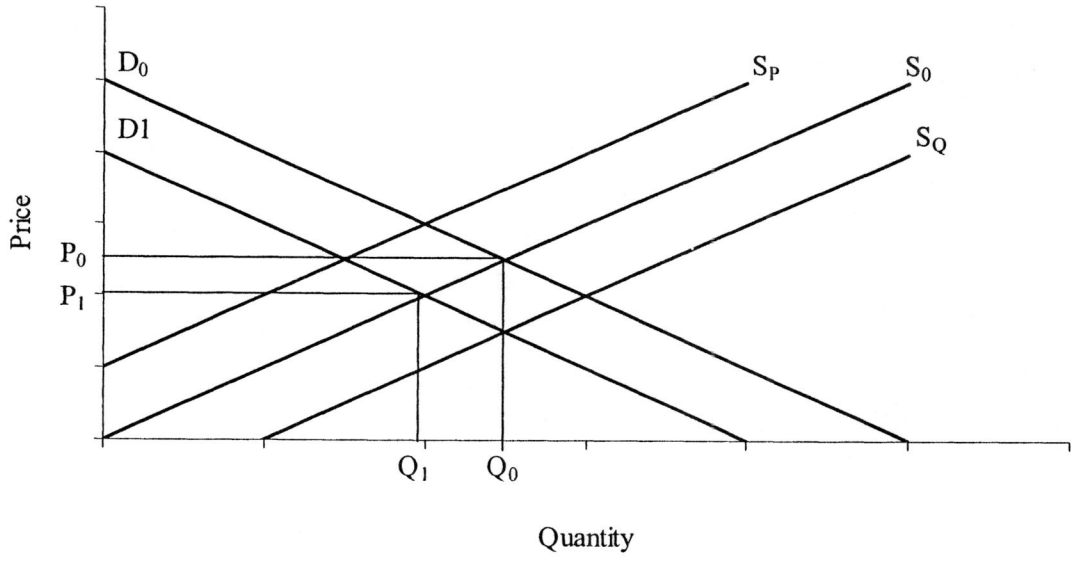

19.   An increase in supply will cause equilibrium price to decrease and equilibrium quantity to increase.

If an increase in supply is accompanied by an increase in demand, then equilibrium quantity will increase while equilibrium price may increase, decrease, or remain the same, depending upon whether the rightward shift in the demand curve is greater than, less than, or equal to the rightward shift in the supply curve, respectively.

If an increase in supply is accompanied by a decrease in demand, then equilibrium price will increase while equilibrium quantity may increase, decrease, or remain the same, depending upon whether the downward shift in the demand curve is less than, greater than, or equal to the downward shift in the supply curve, respectively.

Chapter 1: Problem 19

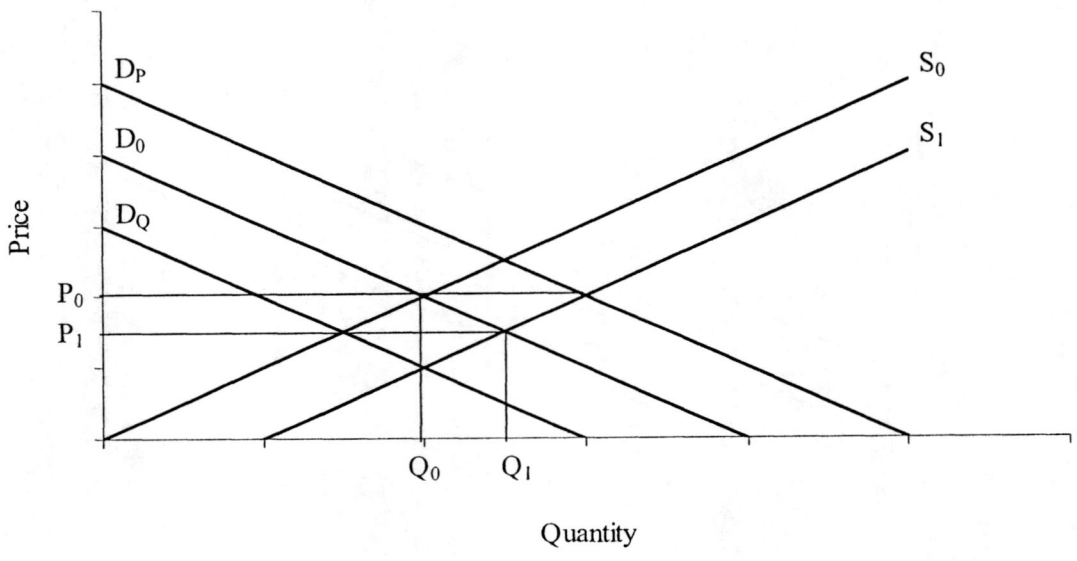

20. A decrease in supply will cause equilibrium price to increase and equilibrium quantity to decrease.

If a decrease in supply is accompanied by an increase in demand, then equilibrium price will increase while equilibrium quantity may increase, decrease, or remain the same, depending upon whether the upward shift in the demand curve is greater than, less than, or equal to the upward shift in the supply curve, respectively.

If an increase in supply is accompanied by a decrease in demand, then equilibrium quantity will decrease while equilibrium price may increase, decrease, or remain the same, depending upon whether the leftward shift in the demand curve is less than, greater than, or equal to the leftward shift in the supply curve, respectively.

Chapter 1: Problem 20

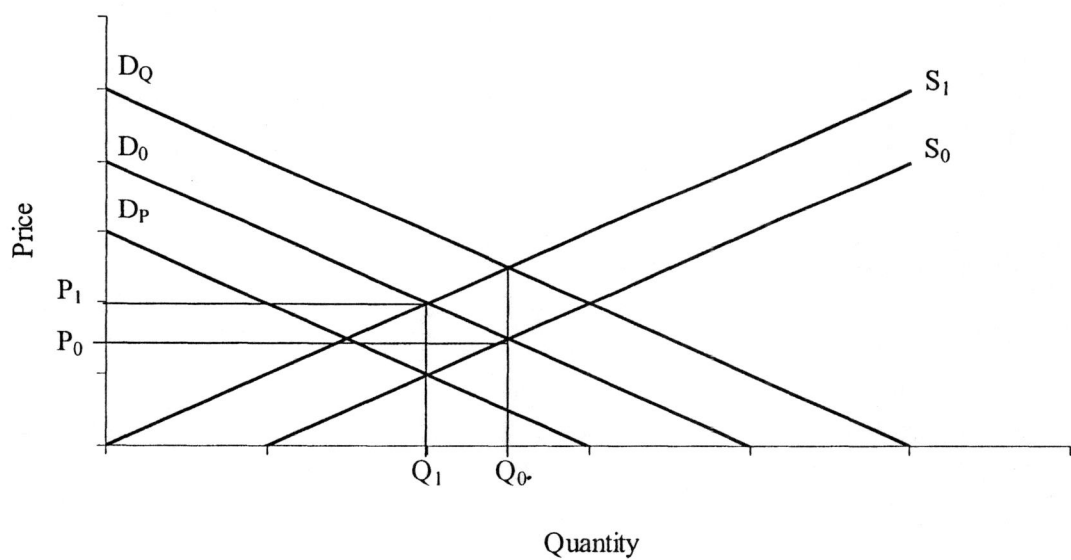

CHAPTER 2

OPTIMIZATION TECHNIQUES AND NEW MANAGEMENT TOOLS

Learning Objectives

This chapter explains some of the fundamental tools of managerial economics. After reading this chapter, you should understand the relationship between total, average, and marginal measures. Further, you should have a thorough understanding of the general concept of an optimum and of how marginal analysis can be used to identify an optimum. Finally, you should be familiar with the many new management tools for optimization that are described in the chapter.

Summary of Notation and Formulas

(2-1) $TR = 100Q - 10Q^2$

Equation 2-1 represents a firm's total revenue per time period (TR) as a function of quantity sold per time period (Q). This type of total revenue function is implied by a linear demand function. In the text, the function is plotted on a graph in Figure 2-1 and is presented in the form of a schedule in Table 2-1.

True-False Questions

T F 1.   Economic relationships can be expressed as equations, graphs, and schedules.

T F 2.   If an economic relationship is complex, it must generally be expressed as an equation.

T F 3.   Differential calculus can be applied directly to the graph of an economic relationship.

T F 4.   The optimal solution to a problem refers to the best solution.

T F 5.   For any given total function, the total is always larger than the average and the average is always larger than the marginal.

T F 6.   The form of the relationship between total, average, and marginal functions is the same whether it is applied to total revenue, product, cost, or profit.

T F 7.   Total cost is equal to average cost times marginal cost.

T F 8.   Average revenue is equal to marginal revenue between zero units of output and one unit of output.

T F 9.   If total cost is increasing, marginal cost is positive.

T F 10. If total revenue is decreasing, average revenue is negative.

T F 11. If total profit is at a maximum, marginal profit is zero.

T F 12. The concept that corresponds most closely to the derivative is the concept of an average value.

T F 13. Marginal cost is plotted (as an approximation) halfway between successive units of output.

T F 14. If an average value is equal to its corresponding marginal value, the average value must be at either a maximum or a minimum.

T F 15. Average revenue reaches a maximum at the same level of sales that total revenue reaches a maximum.

T F 16. Marginal revenue reaches a maximum at the same level of output that total revenue reaches a maximum.

T F 17. If a straight line that is tangent to total cost passes through the origin of a graph, then the slope of the line is equal to average cost at the point of tangency.

T F 18. If a straight line that is tangent to total cost passes through the origin of a graph, then the slope of the line is equal to marginal cost at the point of tangency.

T F 19. If a straight line that intersects a total cost line passes through the origin of a graph, then the slope of the straight line is equal to marginal cost at the point of intersection.

T F 20. If a firm's marginal revenue is negative, then total revenue will decrease if the firm sells more output.

T F 21. The slope of a tangent to a total curve is equal to the marginal value at the point of tangency.

T F 22. The inflection point refers to the point where a marginal curve has a slope of zero.

T F 23. The point where a total value changes from increasing at an increasing rate to increasing at a decreasing rate is called the inflection point.

T F 24. The point where a total value changes from increasing at a decreasing rate to increasing at an increasing rate is called the inflection point.

T F 25. If a marginal value is greater than its corresponding average value, the average value must be decreasing.

T F 26. If an average value is greater than its corresponding marginal value, the average value must be decreasing.

T F 27. If a marginal value is greater than its corresponding average value, the marginal value must be decreasing.

T F 28. If a firm is producing a level of output where marginal profit is equal to zero, then the level of output is optimal.

T F 29. If a firm's total cost curve is a straight line, then its marginal cost curve will be defined by a horizontal straight line.

T F 30. If a firm's total cost curve is a straight line, then its average total cost curve will also be a straight line.

T F 31. If a firm's total cost curve is an upward-sloping straight line, then its average total cost curve will slope upward.

T F 32. A firm's total profit is generally at a maximum when total revenue is at a maximum.

T F 33. A firm's total profit is generally at a maximum when total cost is at a minimum.

T F 34. A firm's total profit is generally at a maximum when the firm's average revenue curve is above its average cost curve and the vertical distance that separates the two curves is at a maximum.

T F 35. A firm's total profit is generally at a maximum when the firm's total revenue curve is above its total cost curve and the vertical distance that separates the two curves is at a maximum.

T F 36. A firm should continue to increase an activity so long as the marginal revenue from the activity exceeds the marginal cost of the activity.

T F 37. A firm should continue to increase an activity so long as the total revenue from the activity exceeds the total cost of the activity.

T F 38. If marginal revenue is equal to marginal cost, profit must be at a maximum.

T F 39. If total cost is equal to total revenue, then profit is equal to zero.

T F 40. The optimal amount of pollution is found where the marginal benefit of pollution is equal to the marginal cost of pollution.

Multiple Choice Questions

1. Relationships between economic variables can be expressed in the form of

    A. a graph.
    B. an equation.
    C. a table.
    D. any of the above.

2. The optimal solution to a problem is best defined as the solution that

    A. is superior to any other possible solution.
    B. costs less than any other possible solution.
    C. generates more revenue than any other possible solution.
    D. corresponds to the inflection point on a total product or total cost curve.

3. Differential calculus can be used to solve problems in cases where economic relationships are expressed in the form of

    A. a graph.
    B. a table.
    C. an equation.
    D. any of the above.

4. Average cost is defined as

   A. total cost divided by marginal cost.
   B. total cost divided by total output.
   C. total output times cost per unit.
   D. total output times marginal cost.

5. The marginal cost when output = 10 is equal to

   A. the slope of a line drawn tangent to the total cost curve where output = 10.
   B. the total cost of 10 units of output divided by 10.
   C. the average cost of 10 units of output.
   D. the slope of a ray drawn from the origin to the point on the total cost curve where output = 10.

6. If a firm's total revenue function is a straight line that begins at the origin, then

   A. marginal revenue is zero.
   B. average revenue is zero.
   C. marginal revenue is equal to average revenue.
   D. all of the above are true.

7. If marginal revenue is equal to zero, then

   A. total revenue is zero.
   B. average revenue is zero.
   C. total revenue is at a maximum or a minimum.
   D. average revenue is at a maximum or a minimum.

8. If average cost is at a minimum, then

   A. it is equal to marginal cost.
   B. total cost is also at a minimum.
   C. profit is at a maximum.
   D. all of the above are true.

9. The level of output where a straight line drawn from the origin is tangent to the total cost curve is where

   A. total cost is at a minimum.
   B. average cost is equal to marginal cost.
   C. profit is at a maximum.
   D. all of the above are correct.

10. The economic concept that corresponds most closely to a "derivative" in calculus is the concept of

    A. an average value.
    B. a total value.
    C. a marginal value.
    D. economic profit.

11. The marginal principle asserts that, in general, when net benefit is maximized

   A. total benefit will be equal to total cost.
   B. average benefit will be equal to average cost.
   C. marginal benefit will be equal to marginal cost.
   D. average cost will be above total cost but below average benefit.

12. When total revenue is at a maximum

   A. average revenue is at a maximum.
   B. marginal revenue is at a maximum.
   C. average revenue is equal to zero.
   D. none of the above is correct.

13. If both average cost (AC) and marginal cost (MC) are U shaped, then

   A. AC will reach a minimum at a level of output that is less than that at which MC reaches a minimum.
   B. the total cost curve will be a straight line.
   C. AC will reach a minimum at a level of output that is greater than that at which MC reaches a minimum.
   D. both AC and MC will reach a minimum at the same level of output.

14. If a firm's marginal revenue is greater than its marginal cost, then the firm should

   A. increase output to increase profit.
   B. decrease output to increase profit.
   C. keep output the same.
   D. collect additional information before taking any action.

15. If a firm's average cost is equal to its average revenue, then

   A. profit is at a maximum.
   B. profit is at a minimum.
   C. profit is equal to zero.
   D. the firm is in equilibrium.

16. The inflection point refers to the point on a total cost curve where

   A. average cost is at a minimum.
   B. average cost is at a maximum.
   C. marginal cost is at a minimum.
   D. marginal cost is at a maximum.

17. If an average curve has a negative slope, then the corresponding

   A. marginal curve is below the average curve.
   B. total curve has a negative slope.
   C. marginal curve is above the average curve.
   D. total curve has a positive slope.

18.   If a firm's total cost curve is defined by a straight line that has a positive intercept that is equal to fixed costs, then

    A. average cost is equal to marginal cost for all levels of output.
    B. average cost is negatively sloped and marginal cost is horizontal.
    C. both average cost and marginal cost are negatively sloped, but they are not equal to each other.
    D. both average cost and marginal cost are horizontal, and average cost is below marginal cost at all levels of output.

19.   If a firm is producing a level of output where marginal cost is equal to marginal revenue, then

    A. profit is at a maximum if marginal cost has a negative slope and marginal revenue is horizontal.
    B. profit is at a minimum if marginal cost has a negative slope and marginal revenue is horizontal.
    C. profit is at a maximum if average revenue is greater than average cost.
    D. profit is at a minimum if average revenue is greater than average cost.

20.   The optimal amount of pollution to society is where

    A. the total cost of pollution is equal to zero.
    B. the total benefit of pollution is equal to zero.
    C. the marginal benefit of pollution equals the marginal cost of pollution.
    D. there is no pollution at all.

Problems

1.   Fill in the blanks in the table below, which lists output quantity and total cost, and then plot the values on the graphs that follow.

Quantity	0	1	2	3	4	5	6	7	8
Total	4	6	8	10	12	14	16	18	20
Average									
Marginal									

Chapter 2: Problem 1

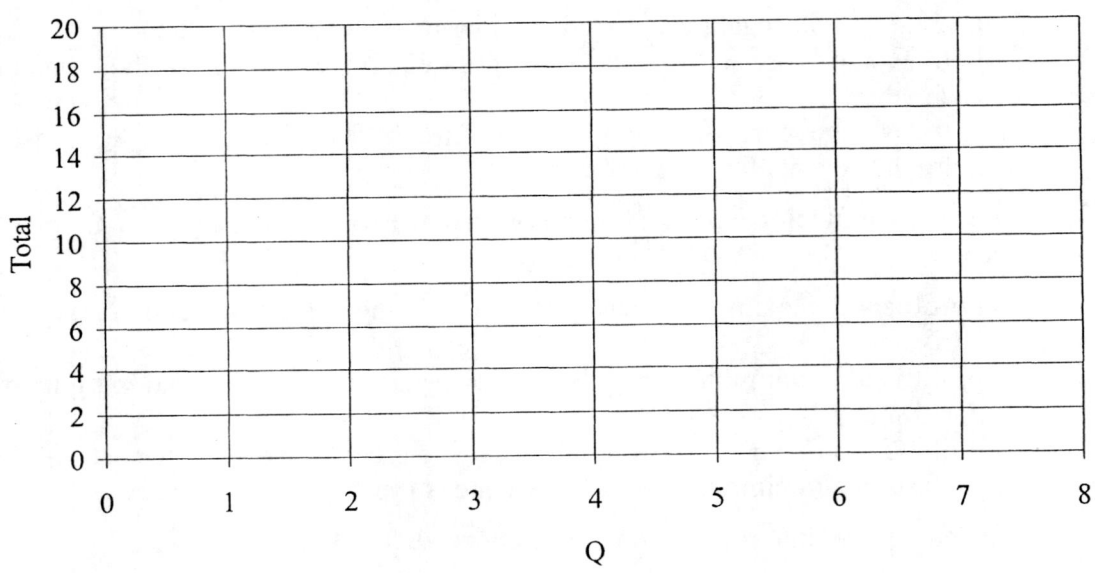

Chapter 2: Problem 1

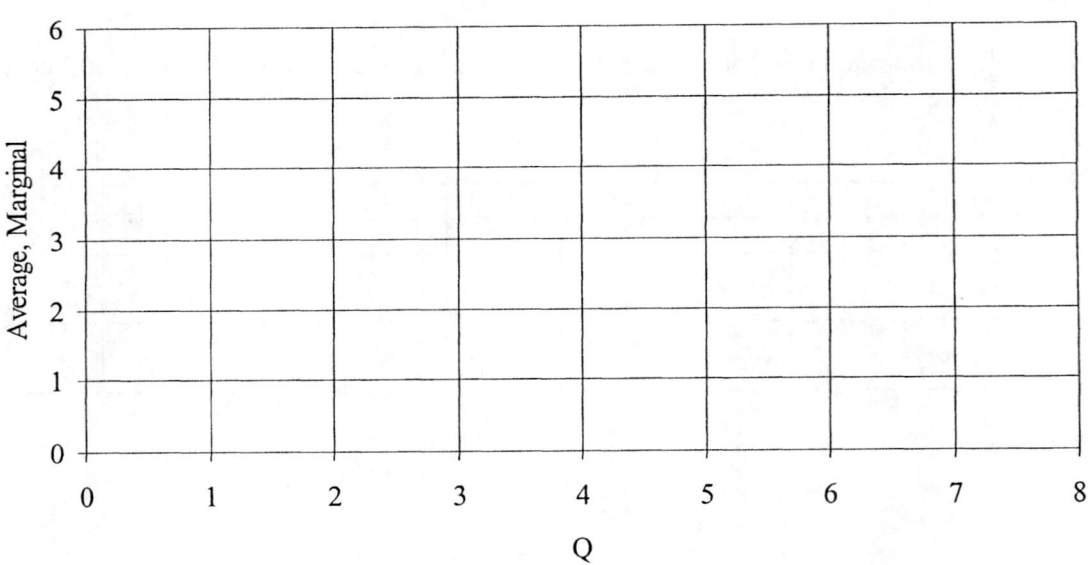

2. Fill in the blanks in the table below, which shows quantity sold and total revenue, and then plot the values on the graphs that follow.

Quantity	0	1	2	3	4	5	6	7
Total	0	6	10	12	12	10	6	0
Average								
Marginal								

Chapter 2: Problem 2

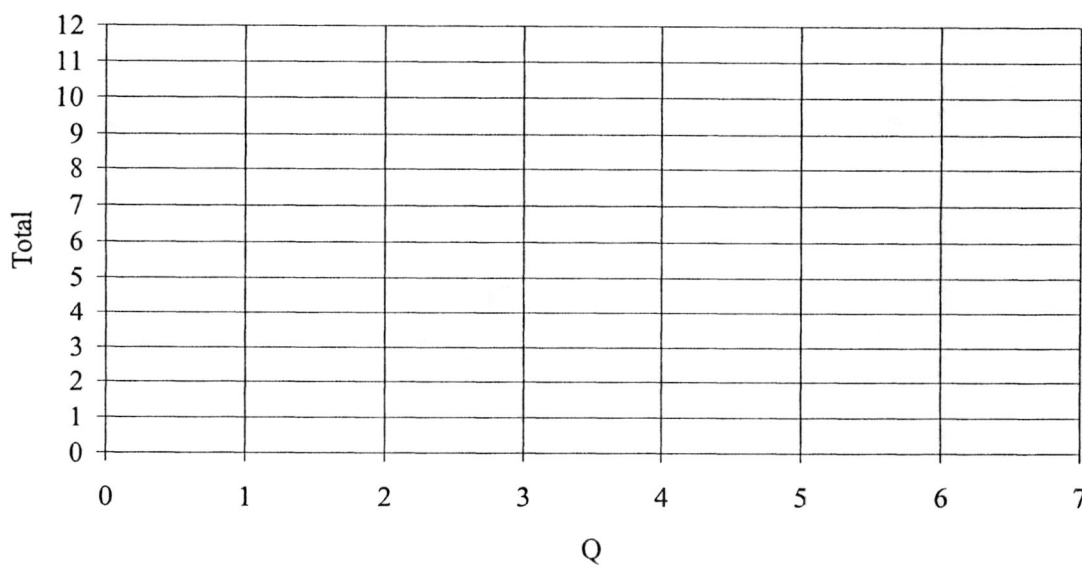

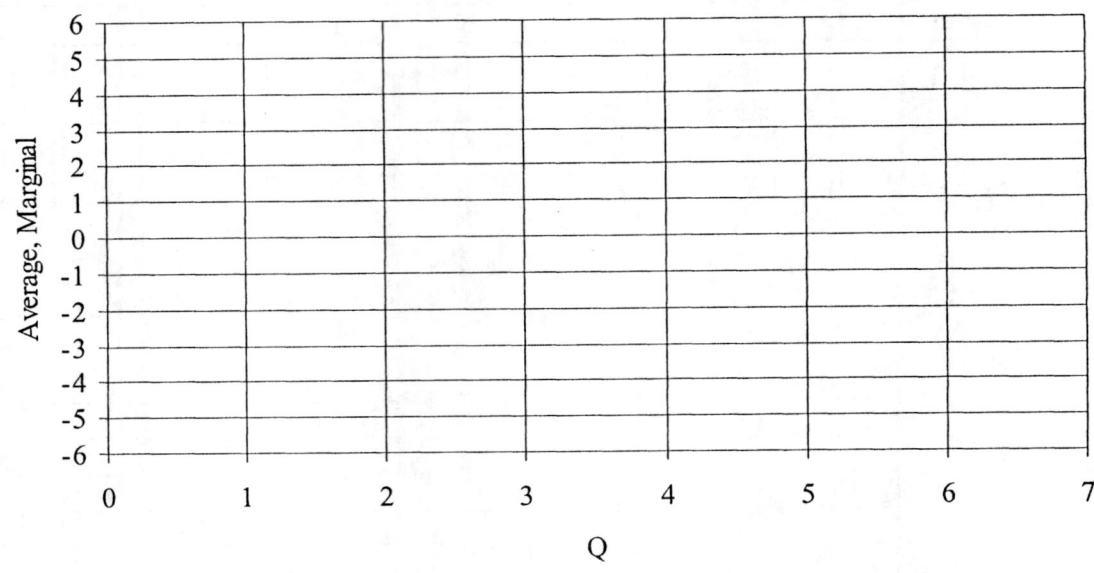

3. Fill in the blanks in the table below, which shows the relationship between quantity of labor employed and total product, and then plot the values on the graphs provided.

Labor	0	1	2	3	4	5	6	7	8
Quantity	4	5	8	12	15	17	18	18	17
Average									
Marginal									

Chapter 2: Problem 3

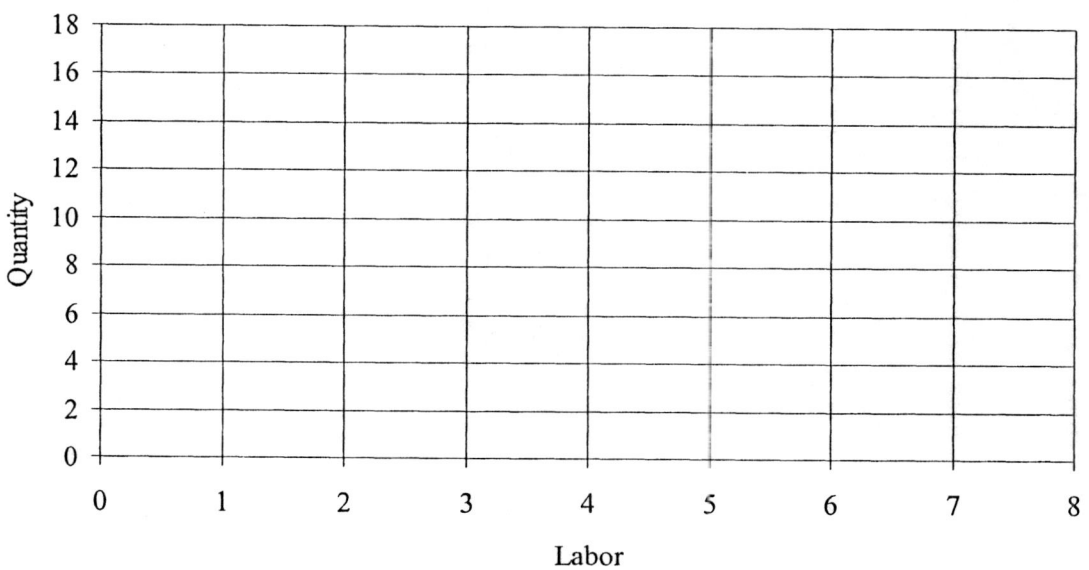

Chapter 2: Problem 3

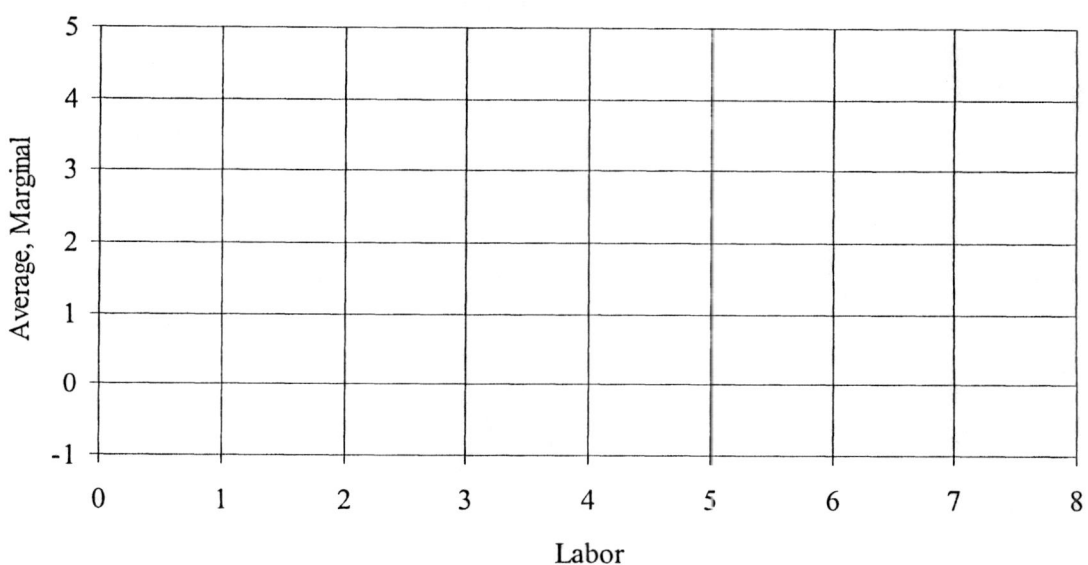

4. Fill in the blanks in the table below, which shows the relationship between quantity produced and total cost, and then plot the values on the graphs that follow.

Quantity	0	1	2	3	4	5	6	7	8
Total	4	8	11	13	14	16	19	23	29
Average									
Marginal									

Chapter 2: Problem 4

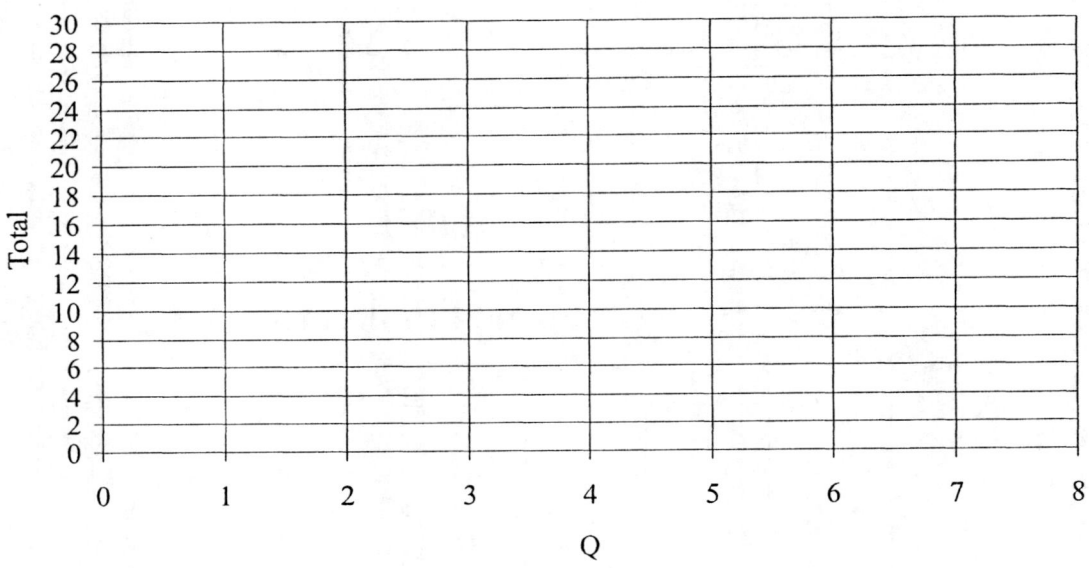

Chapter 2: Problem 4

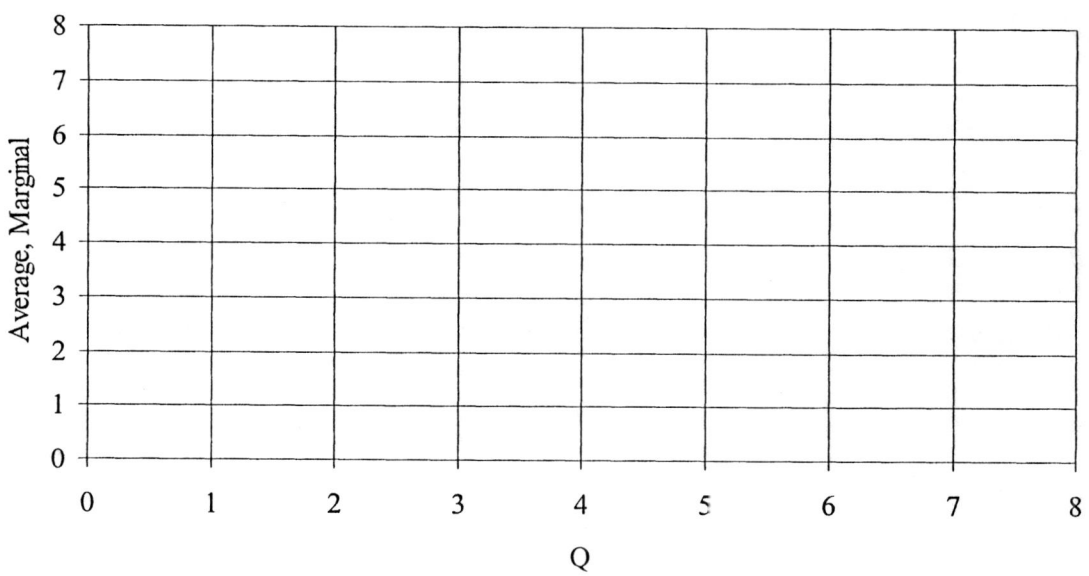

5. A firm has the total cost and total revenue functions defined below. Use these functions to fill in the table and then plot total revenue and total cost on the first graph and marginal revenue and marginal cost on the second graph.

$$TC = 6 + Q - 0.03\,Q^2 + 0.001\,Q^3$$

$$TR = 6\,Q - 0.1\,Q^2$$

Quantity	TR	MR	TC	MC	Profit
0					
10					
20					
30					
40					
50					

Chapter 2: Problem 5

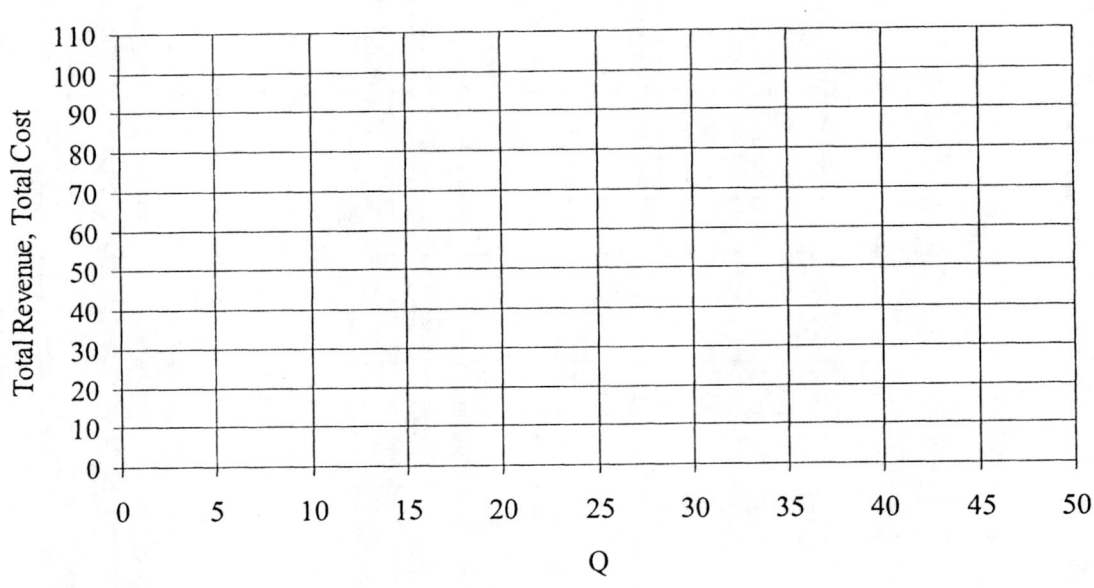

Chapter 2: Problem 5

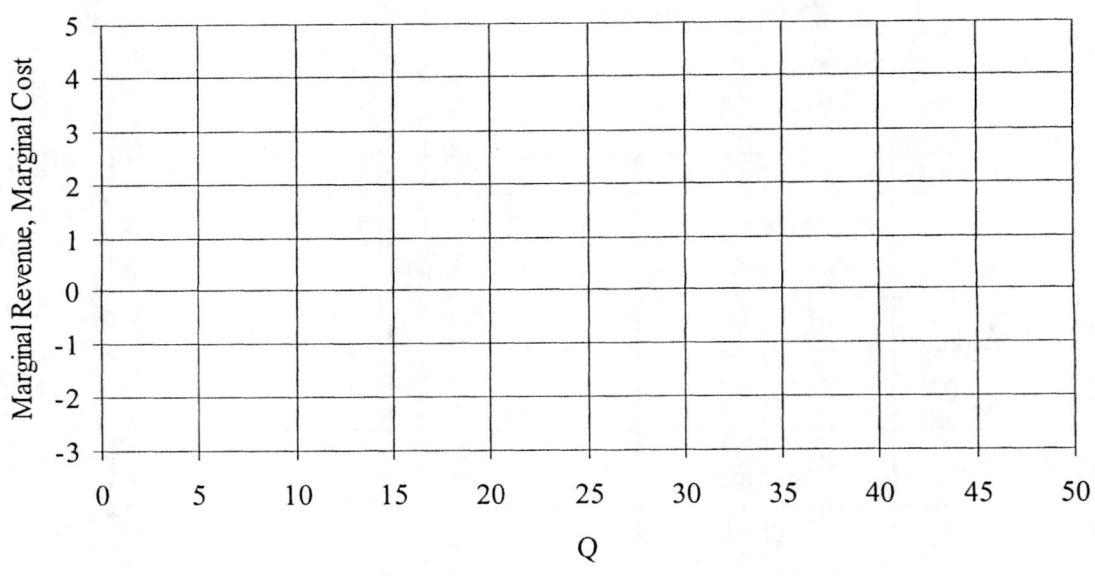

True-False Answers

1	T	9	T	17	T	25	F	33	F
2	T	10	F	18	T	26	T	34	F
3	F	11	T	19	F	27	F	35	T
4	T	12	F	20	T	28	T	36	T
5	F	13	T	21	T	29	T	37	F
6	T	14	T	22	T	30	F	38	F
7	F	15	F	23	T	31	F	39	T
8	T	16	F	24	T	32	F	40	T

Multiple Choice Answers

1	D	5	A	9	B	13	C	17	A
2	A	6	C	10	C	14	A	18	B
3	C	7	C	11	C	15	C	19	B
4	B	8	A	12	D	16	C	20	C

Solutions to Problems

1. This schedule shows the relationship between total, marginal, and average values when the total function is linear. The marginal value is constant, yielding a horizontal marginal curve, and the average is described by a curve that descends continuously and asymptotically to the marginal curve. Note that marginal and average values are plotted above the midpoint of each interval.

Quantity	0	1	2	3	4	5	6	7	8
Total	4	6	8	10	12	14	16	18	20
Average	-	6.0	4.0	3.3	3.0	2.8	2.7	2.6	2.5
Marginal	-	2.0	2.0	2.0	2.0	2.0	2.0	2.0	2.0

Chapter 2: Problem 1

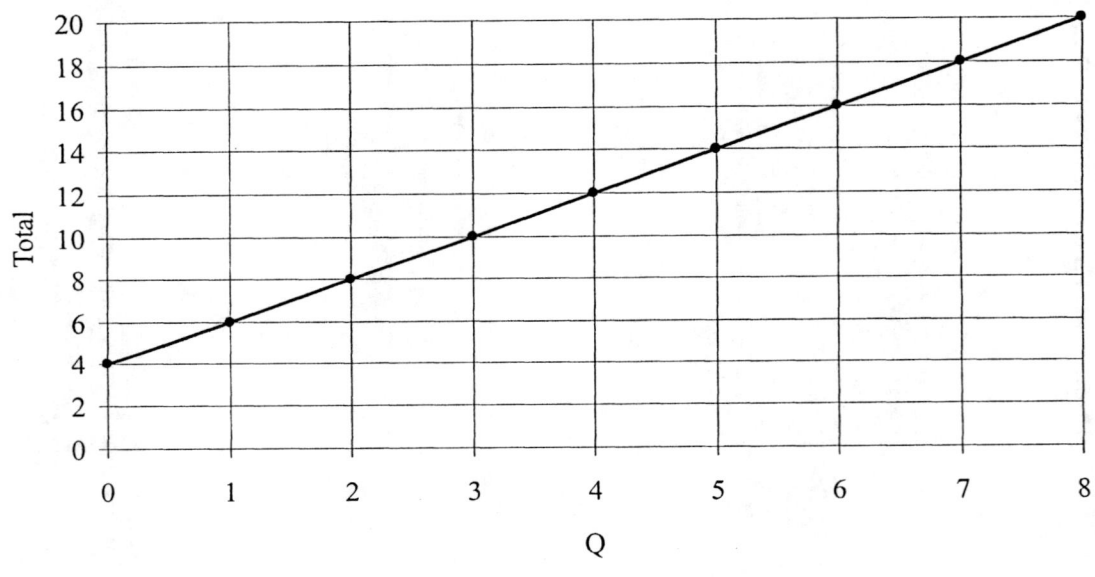

Chapter 2: Problem 1

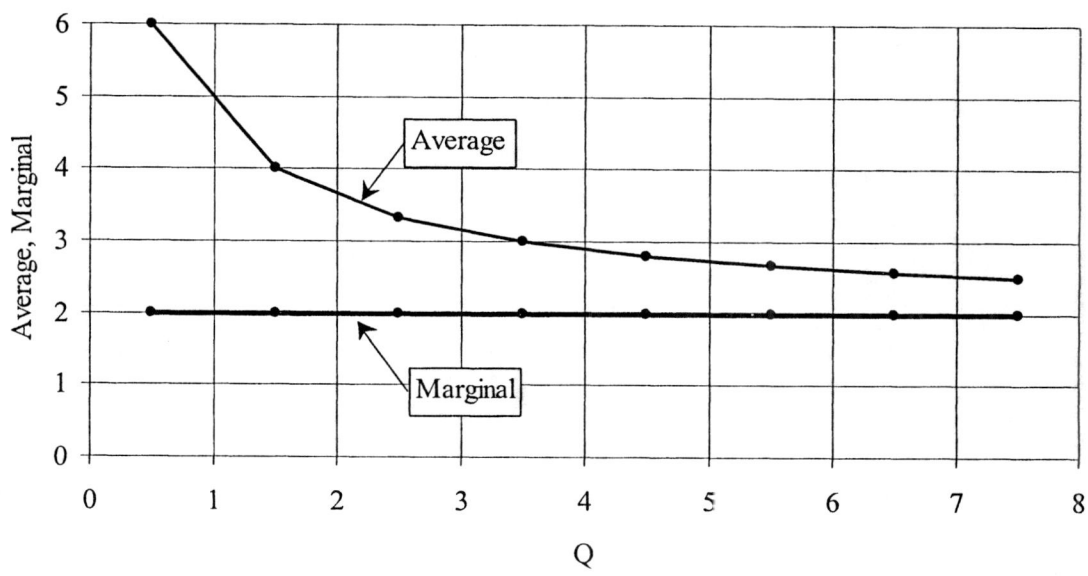

2. This schedule shows the relationship between total, marginal, and average values when the total function rises smoothly to a maximum and then descends. The marginal values and the average values are described by downward-sloping linear functions.

Quantity	0	1	2	3	4	5	6	7
Total	0	6	10	12	12	10	6	0
Average	-	6.0	5.0	4.0	3.0	2.0	1.0	0.0
Marginal	-	6.0	4.0	2.0	0.0	-2.0	-4.0	-6.0

Chapter 2: Problem 2

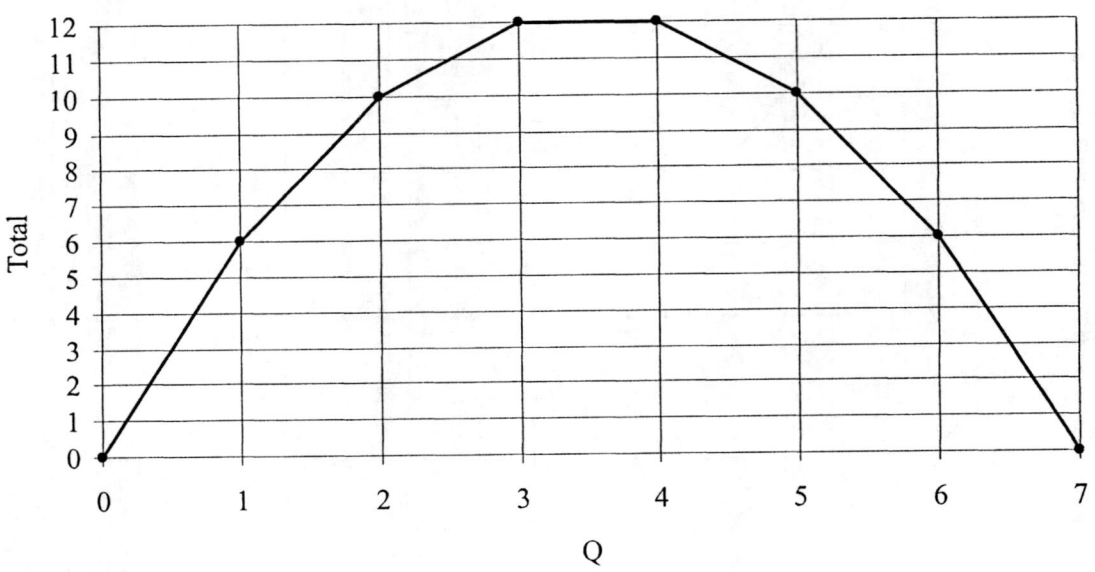

Chapter 2: Problem 2

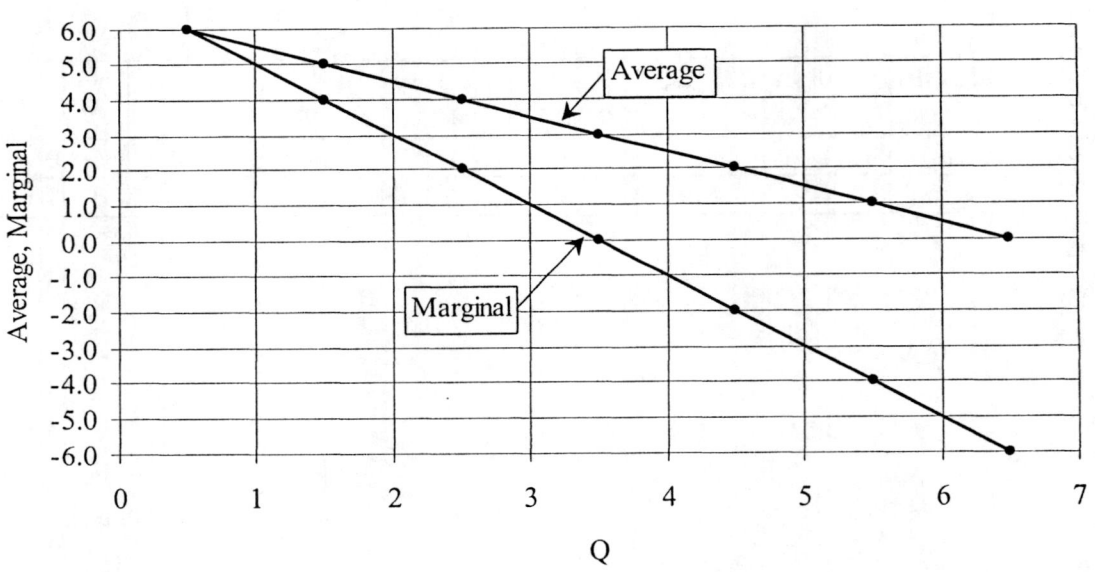

3. This schedule shows the relationship between total, marginal, and average values when the total function rises at a rate that first accelerates and then decelerates, reaches a maximum and then begins to descend. The marginal values rise to a maximum as the total function rises at an accelerating rate and then declines as the rate of increase in the total function slows. Finally, the marginal function reaches zero when the total function is at a maximum. The average value declines continuously.

Labor	0	1	2	3	4	5	6	7	8
Quantity	4	5	8	12	15	17	18	18	17
Average		5.0	4.0	4.0	3.8	3.4	3.0	2.6	2.1
Marginal		1.0	3.0	4.0	3.0	2.0	1.0	0.0	-1.0

Chapter 2: Problem 3

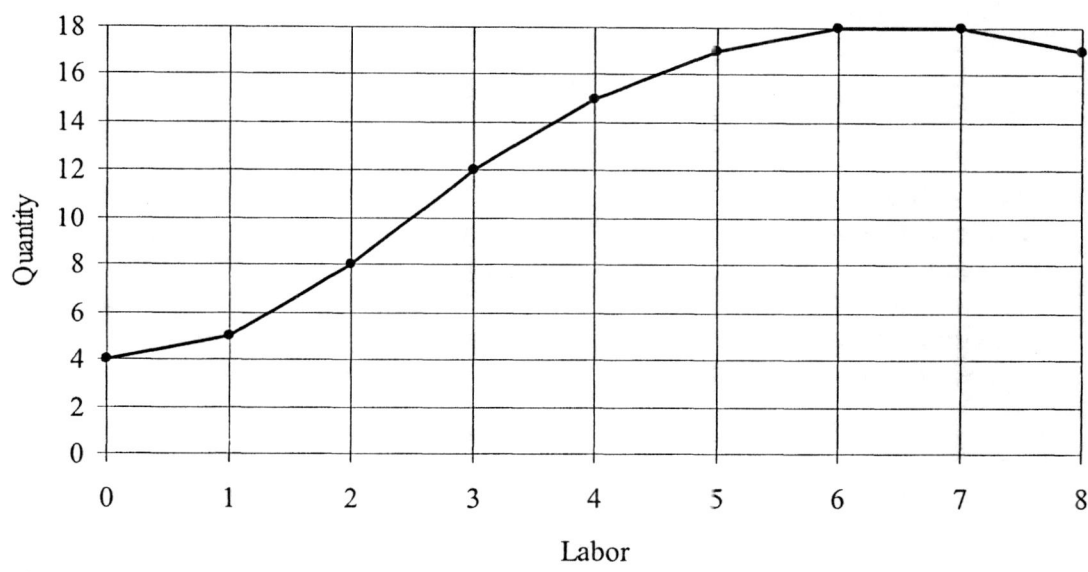

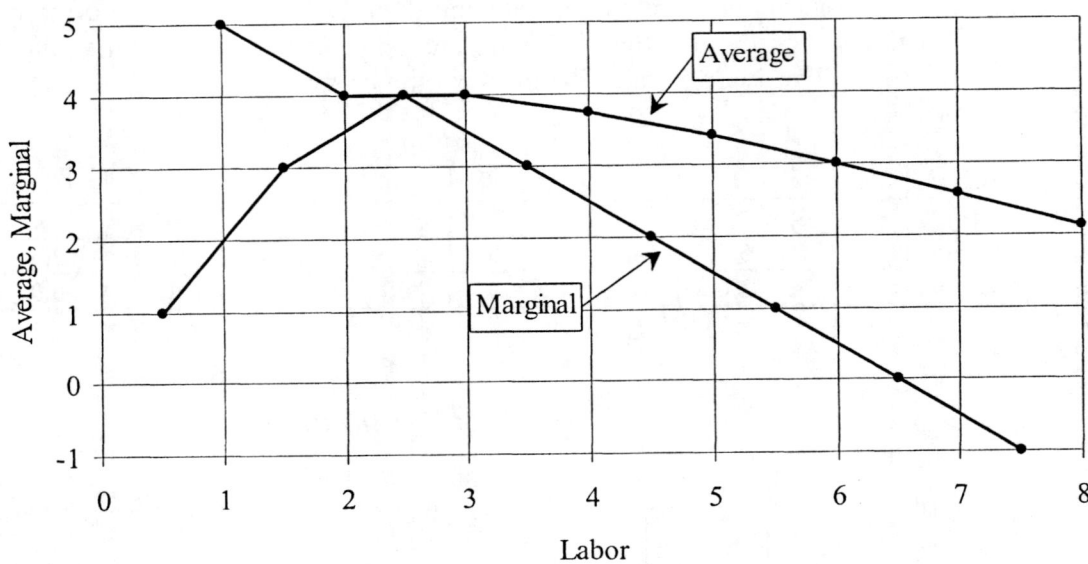

4.   This schedule shows the relationship between total, marginal, and average values when the total function rises at a rate that first decelerates and then accelerates. The marginal values fall to a minimum as the total function rises at a decelerating rate and then rise as the rate of increase in the total function accelerates. At the same time, the average function declines to a minimum that corresponds to its intersection with the marginal curve and then increases after the marginal curve rises above it.

Quantity	0	1	2	3	4	5	6	7	8
Total	4	8	11	13	14	16	19	23	29
Average	-	8.0	5.5	4.3	3.5	3.2	3.2	3.3	3.6
Marginal	-	4.0	3.0	2.0	1.0	2.0	3.0	4.0	6.0

Chapter 2: Problem 4

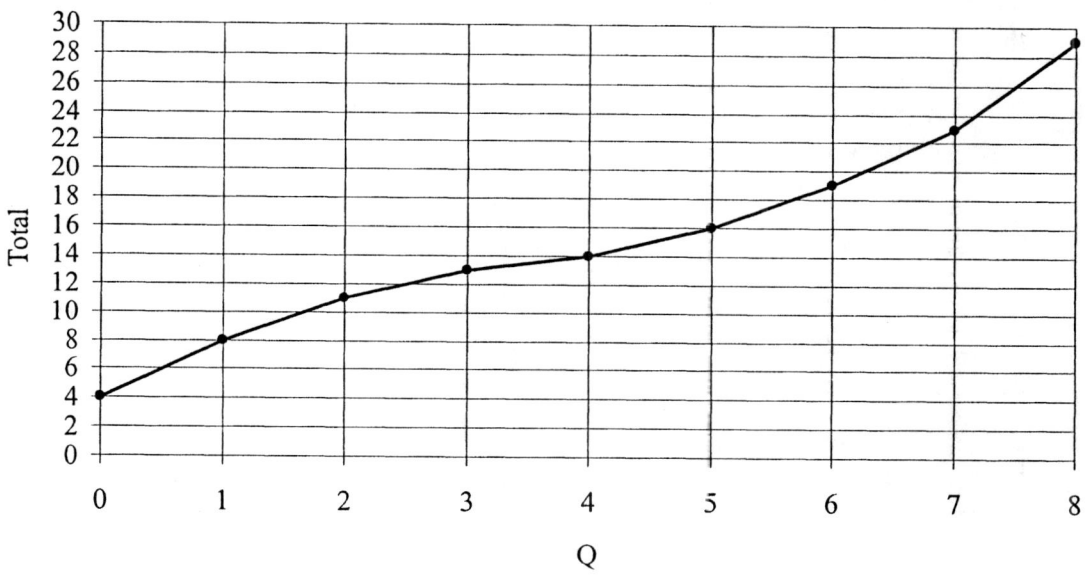

Chapter 2: Problem 4

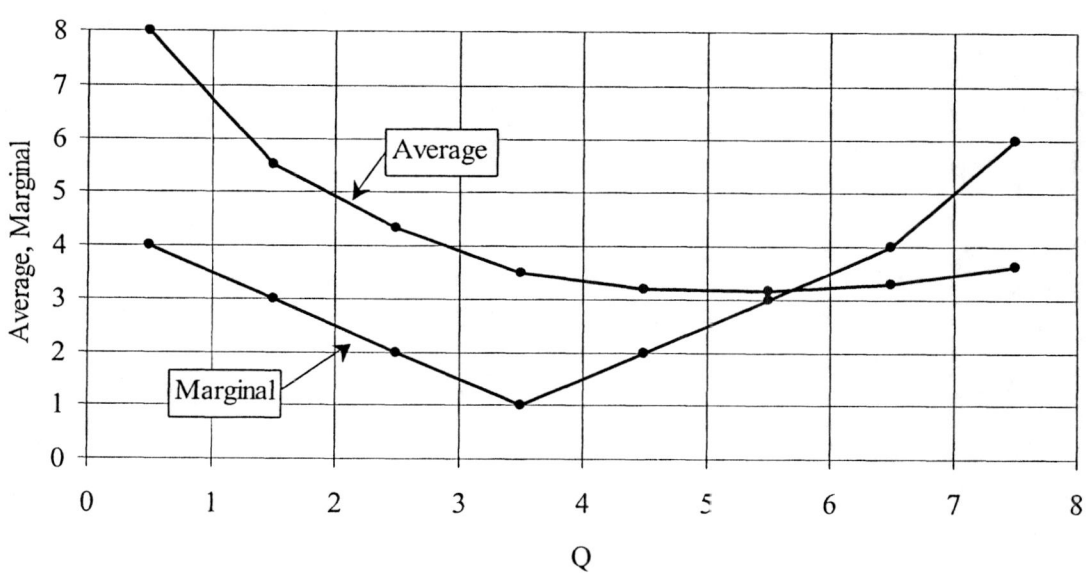

5. This schedule shows the relationship between total cost and total revenue, the determinants of profit, and the corresponding values of marginal and average revenue and cost. Total revenue rises to a maximum and then falls while the average and marginal revenue curves are linear and decline continuously. Total cost rises continuously while the average and marginal cost curves have a U shape. The minimum value of average cost corresponds to the point where the average and marginal cost curves intersect. The point of maximum profit corresponds to the quantity where marginal cost and marginal revenue are equal.

Quantity	TR	MR	TC	MC	Profit
0	0	-	6	-	-6
10	50	5	14	0.8	36
20	80	3	22	0.8	58
30	90	1	36	1.4	54
40	80	-1	62	2.6	18
50	50	-3	106	4.4	-56

Chapter 2: Problem 5

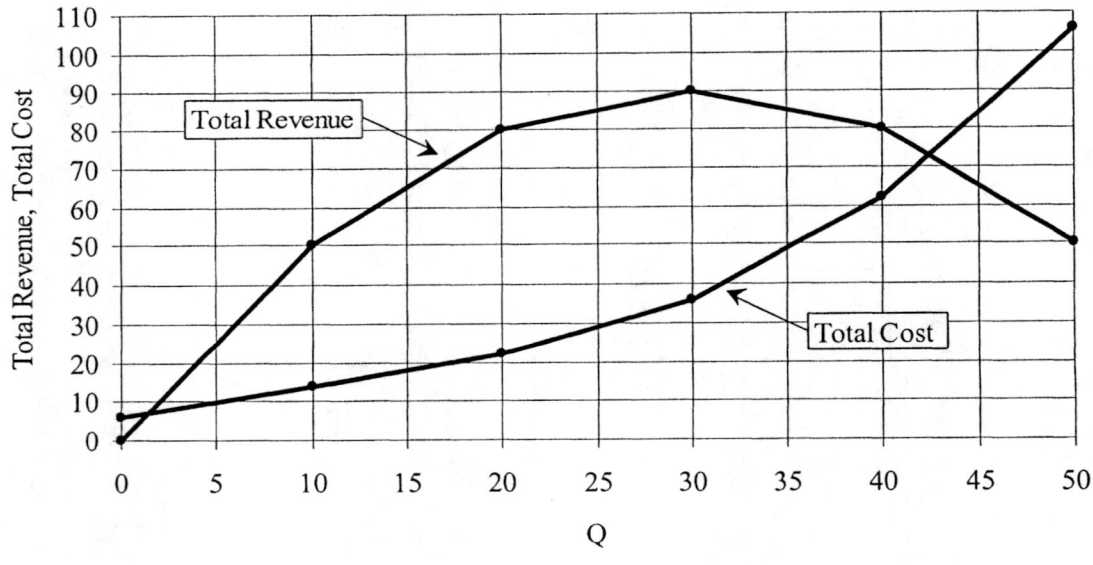

Chapter 2: Problem 5

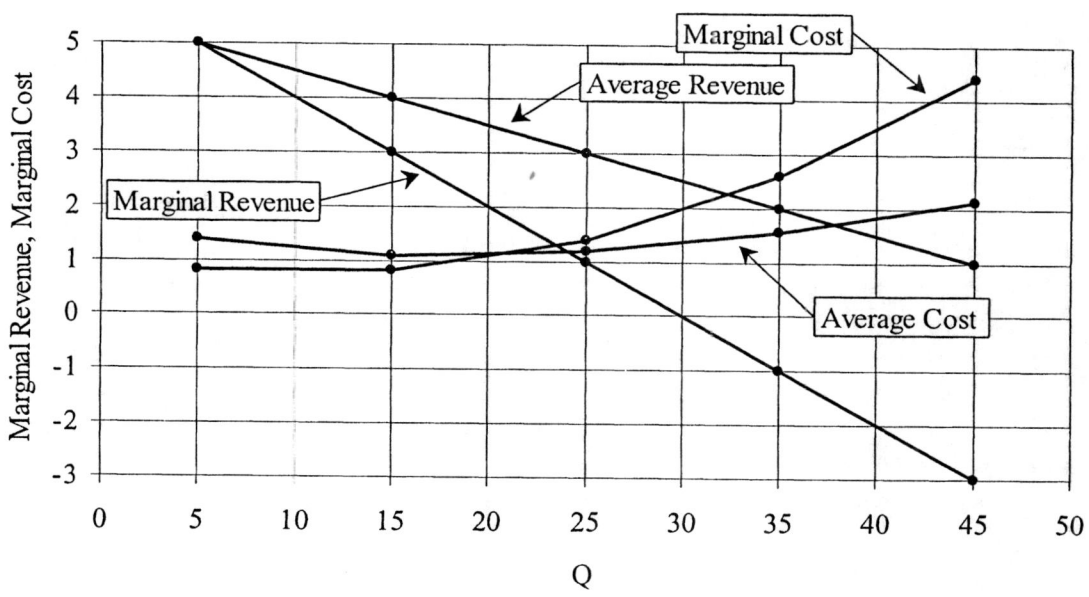

CHAPTER 3

DEMAND THEORY

Learning Objectives

When you finish reading this chapter, you should understand the determinants of consumers' demand for commodities and of firms' derived demand for inputs. Further, you should understand how elasticities are defined and calculated and how they are used to measure the responsiveness of the quantity demanded of a commodity per time period to changes in the determinants of demand. You should also appreciate the vital contribution that a knowledge of demand can make to the successful operation of a firm. Most firms have some control over the price charged for their output and over other factors, such as advertising expenditures, that influence market demand. Without knowledge of the demand for its products, a firm cannot make optimal decisions regarding product price or the allocation of resources among activities designed to increase sales. In the extreme case, if the demand for a firm's output is inadequate, then the firm will earn negative economic profits in the short run and will go out of business in the long run.

Summary of Notation and Formulas

(3-1) $Qd_X = f(P_X, I, P_Y, T)$

(3-2) $QD_X = F(P_X, N, I, P_Y, T)$

Equation 3-1 and 3-2 represent the demand for a commodity by an individual consumer and by all consumers (the entire market), respectively. The quantity demanded of a commodity per time period by an individual consumer (Qd_X) is a function of the price of the commodity (P_X), consumer income (I), the prices of related commodities (P_Y), and consumer tastes (T). The quantity demanded of a commodity per time period by the entire market (QDX) is a function of all of the same variables as the individual consumer's demand function plus one additional variable, the number of consumers in the market (N).

(3-3) $Q_X = a_0 + a_1 P_X + a_2 N + a_3 I + a_4 P_Y + a_5 T + \cdots$

Equation 3-3 is the market demand function for a firm's output represented in linear form. The quantity demanded of the firm's output (Q_X) is a function of the variables defined above. The parameters of the equation (a_0, a_1, a_2, a_3, a_4, a_5, etc.) represent the change in Q_X due to a one unit change in the associated independent variable while all other independent variables are held constant.

(3-4) $E_P = \dfrac{\Delta Q/Q}{\Delta P/P} = \dfrac{\Delta Q}{\Delta P} \dfrac{P}{Q}$

(3-5) $E_P = a_1 \dfrac{P}{Q}$

$$(3-6) \quad E_P = \frac{\Delta Q}{\Delta P} \frac{(P_2 + P_1)/2}{(Q_2 + Q_1)/2} = \frac{Q_2 - Q_1}{P_2 - P_1} \frac{P_2 + P_1}{Q_2 + Q_1}$$

Equations 3-4, 3-5, and 3-6 define the price elasticity of demand (E_P). The first is the point formula, which defines the price elasticity as the slope of the demand curve ($\Delta Q/\Delta P$) multiplied times the ratio of price (P) divided by quantity demanded per time period (Q). The second is a specific version of the point formula that is defined in terms of the price slope coefficient ($a_1 = \Delta Q/\Delta P$) of the linear demand equation (Equation 3-3) that was defined previously. The third is the arc formula, which is used to calculate the price elasticity of demand between two points on a demand curve.

$$(3-7) \quad TR = PQ$$

$$(3-8) \quad MR = \frac{\Delta TR}{\Delta Q}$$

$$(3-9) \quad MR = P(1 + \frac{1}{E_P})$$

Equations 3-7, 3-8, and 3-9 define total revenue (TR) and marginal revenue (MR). The third of these defines MR in terms of the price elasticity of demand (E_P) and product price (P).

$$(3-10) \quad E_I = \frac{\Delta Q/Q}{\Delta I/I} = \frac{\Delta Q}{\Delta I} \frac{I}{Q}$$

$$(3-11) \quad E_I = a_3 \frac{I}{Q}$$

$$(3-12) \quad E_I = \frac{\Delta Q}{\Delta I} \frac{(I_2 + I_1)/2}{(Q_2 + Q_1)/2} = \frac{Q_2 - Q_1}{I_2 - I_1} \frac{I_2 + I_1}{Q_2 + Q_1}$$

Equations 3-10, 3-11, and 3-12 define the income elasticity of demand (E_I). The first is the point formula, which defines the income elasticity as the slope of the demand function with respect to income ($\Delta Q/\Delta I$) multiplied times the ratio of income (I) divided by quantity demanded per time period (Q). The second is a specific version of the point formula that is defined in terms of the income slope coefficient ($a_3 = \Delta Q/\Delta I$) of the linear demand equation (Equation 3-3) that was defined previously. The third is the arc formula, which is used to calculate the income elasticity of demand between two levels of income.

$$(3-13) \quad E_{XY} = \frac{\Delta Q_X/Q_X}{\Delta P_Y/P_Y} = \frac{\Delta Q_X}{\Delta P_Y} \frac{P_Y}{Q_X}$$

$$(3-14) \quad E_{XY} = a_4 \frac{P_Y}{Q_X}$$

$$(3-15) \quad E_{XY} = \frac{\Delta Q_X}{\Delta P_Y} \frac{(P_{Y_2} + P_{Y_1})/2}{(Q_{X_2} + Q_{X_1})2} = \frac{Q_{X_2} - Q_{X_1}}{P_{Y_2} - P_{Y_1}}$$

Equations 3-13, 3-14, and 3-15 define the cross-price elasticity of demand (E_{XY}) for good X with respect to the price of good Y. The first is the point formula, which defines the cross-price elasticity as the slope of the demand function with respect to the price of a related good ($\Delta Q_X / \Delta P_Y$) multiplied times the ratio of the price of the related good (P_Y) divided by quantity demanded per time period (Q_X). The second is a specific version of the point formula that is defined in terms of the price of the related commodity slope coefficient ($a_4 = \Delta Q_X / \Delta P_Y$) of the linear demand equation (Equation 3-3) that was defined previously. The third is the arc formula, which is used to calculate the cross-price elasticity between two levels of the price of the related commodity.

(3-16) $\quad Q_X = 1.5 - 3.0 P_X + 0.8I + 2.0 P_Y - 0.6 P_S + 1.2A$

Equation 3-16 is an example of an estimated linear market demand function. In this case, the demand function defines the quantity demanded of a firm's output (Tasty Company brand X). The quantity demanded of the commodity per time period (Q_X) is a function of the price of the commodity (P_X), income (I), the prices of two related commodities (another brand of coffee $= P_Y$ and sugar $= P_S$, which are substitute and complementary goods, respectively), and a variable that represents the effect of advertising on consumer tastes (expenditures $= A$). The parameters of the equation are $a_0 = 1.5$, $a_1 = -3.0$, etc.

True-False Questions

T F 1. The cost of production is a major determinant of consumer demand.

T F 2. Managerial economics is primarily concerned with the market demand for an individual firm's output.

T F 3. The quantity of a commodity demanded by a consumer is influenced by the price of the commodity.

T F 4. The demand for an individual firm's output depends on the demand for the industry's output, the number of firms in the industry, and the structure of the industry.

T F 5. The quantity of a commodity demanded by a consumer is influenced by the number of consumers in the market.

T F 6. The quantity of a commodity demanded by a consumer is influenced by the prices of related commodities.

T F 7. The law of demand refers to the relationship between consumer income and the quantity of a commodity demanded per time period.

T F 8. An increase in price of a commodity will generally lead to a decrease in the quantity of the commodity demanded per time period.

T F 9. A commodity is referred to as normal if an increase in its price leads to an increase in the quantity of the commodity demanded per time period.

T F 10. Most goods are normal.

T F 11. Inferior goods are generally purchased at low levels of income but not at high levels of income.

T F 12. If an increase in the price of one commodity leads to an increase in demand for a second commodity, then the two commodities are complements.

T F 13. An individual's demand curve is formulated under the assumption that price is held constant and all other determinants of demand are allowed to vary.

T F 14. The substitution effect holds that an increase in the price of a commodity will cause an individual to search for substitutes.

T F 15. The income effect holds that a decrease in the price of a commodity is, in some respects, the same as an increase in income.

T F 16. A change in the price of a commodity will cause the demand curve for that commodity to shift.

T F 17. If a decrease in income causes an individual's demand curve for a good to shift to the left, then the good is inferior.

T F 18. If a good is normal, then both the substitution effect and the income effect cause quantity demanded to change in the same direction.

T F 19. There is an inverse relationship between the quantity demanded of a commodity and its price.

T F 20. Butter and bread are substitutes.

T F 21. A shift in demand is referred to as a change in quantity demanded.

T F 22. If the independent individual consumer demand curves for a commodity are horizontally summed, the result is the market demand curve for the commodity.

T F 23. If the consumption decisions of individual consumers are not independent, then the horizontal sum of individual consumer demand curves is the market demand curve for the commodity.

T F 24. The bandwagon effect refers to the importance of musical backgrounds in TV advertising.

T F 25. The bandwagon effect tends to make the market demand curve flatter than the horizontal summation of individual demand curves.

T F 26. The snob effect tends to make the market demand curve flatter than the horizontal summation of individual demand curves.

T F 27. Monopoly refers to a situation in which there is only one producer of a commodity for which there are many close substitutes.

T F 28. If the demand for a firm's output is horizontal, then the firm is a perfect competitor.

T F 29. Oligopoly refers to a type of market organization that is characterized by large number of firms selling a differentiated commodity.

T F 30. Monopolistic competition is a form of market organization that combines elements of perfect competition and monopoly.

T F 31. Under every form of market organization except monopolistic competition, the firm faces a downward-sloping demand curve.

T F 32. If consumers expect the price of a commodity to increase in the future, then demand for the commodity will decrease.

T F 33. Consumers find it easier to postpone the purchase of a durable good than to postpone the purchase of a nondurable good, so the demand for durable goods is more unstable than the demand for nondurable goods.

T F 34. Derived demand refers to the mathematical derivation of a market demand curve from individual consumers' demand curves.

T F 35. Derived demand by a firm will generally increase if the demand for the firm's output increases.

T F 36. According to the estimated linear demand function presented in Case 3-1, sweet potatoes are normal goods.

T F 37. Elasticity is a measure that does not depend on the units used to measure prices and quantities.

T F 38. The price elasticity of demand is the same as the slope of a demand curve.

T F 39. The arc price elasticity of demand measures the price elasticity at a point on the demand curve.

T F 40. The price elasticity of demand for a firm's output is generally more elastic than the price elasticity of demand for the industry's output of the commodity.

T F 41. If price elasticity of demand for a firm's output becomes more elastic, then the firm's marginal revenue will increase.

T F 42. If a firm increases the price of its product and total revenue increases, then the price elasticity of demand must be less than minus one.

T F 43. If the price elasticity of demand for a firm's output is inelastic, then a decrease in price will reduce the firm's total revenue.

T F 44. If the price elasticity of demand for a firm's output is unit elastic, then marginal revenue is equal to zero and total revenue is at a maximum.

T F 45. If a firm is a perfect competitor, then its marginal revenue is equal to the price of its commodity.

T F 46. If a firm is not a perfect competitor, then its marginal revenue is greater than the price of its commodity.

T F 47. An increase in the number of available substitutes for a commodity will decrease the price elasticity of demand for the commodity.

T F 48. The long-run price elasticity of demand for a commodity is generally greater then the short-run price elasticity of demand for the commodity.

T F 49. The income elasticity of demand for an inferior good is negative.

T F 50. For most goods, the income elasticity of demand is negative.

T F 51. The cross-price elasticity of demand for two goods is negative if the goods are substitutes.

T F 52. The cross-price elasticity of demand measures the percentage change in the demand for one good that results from a one percent change in the quantity demanded of a second good.

T F 53. If two goods are very close complements, then the cross-price elasticity of demand between the two goods will be large and negative.

T F 54. It is likely that the cross-price elasticity of demand between two goods produced by different firms in the same industry will be positive and large.

T F 55. Estimates of demand elasticities are used by firms to determine optimal operational policies.

T F 56. If the price elasticity of demand for a firm's output is inelastic, then the firm could increase its revenue by reducing price.

T F 57. Decreased barriers to international trade have increased the differences in consumer preferences between countries.

T F 58. The international convergence in tastes has progressed to the point where there are virtually no international differences in consumer preferences.

T F 59. Improved telecommunication technology has contributed to the globalization of markets.

T F 60. Middle-class life styles are fundamentally different in different countries.

T F 61. Electronic commerce currently accounts for no more than 10% of total U.S. retail sales.

T F 62. About 90% of the total world revenue accounted for by electronic commerce in 1999 involved business-to-business transactions.

T F 63. The growth of electronic commerce has been limited by the fact that it increases the costs to retailers of executing sales.

T F 64. Retail firms that have developed electronic commerce distribution channels typically have not maintained their traditional retail outlets.

T F 65. The ability of consumers to do comparison shopping on the Internet is likely to put pressure on profit margins at the retail level.

Multiple Choice Questions

1. Which of the following is not a determinant of a consumer's demand for a commodity?

    A. Income
    B. Population
    C. Prices of related goods
    D. Tastes

2. The law of demand refers to the

    A. inverse relationship between the price of a commodity and the quantity demanded of the commodity per time period.
    B. direct relationship between the desire a consumer has for a commodity and the amount of the commodity that the consumer demands.
    C. inverse relationship between a consumer's income and the amount of a commodity that the consumer demands.
    D. direct relationship between population and the market demand for a commodity.

3. If the price of a good increases, then

    A. the demand for complementary goods will increase.
    B. the demand for the good will increase.
    C. the demand for substitute goods will increase.
    D. the demand for the good will decrease.

4.   If consumer income declines, then the demand for

    A. normal goods will increase.
    B. inferior goods will increase.
    C. substitute goods will increase.
    D. complementary goods will increase.

5.   Which of the following will cause a decrease in quantity demanded while leaving demand unchanged?

    A. An increase in the price of a complementary good.
    B. An increase in income when the good is inferior.
    C. A decrease in the price of a substitute good.
    D. An increase in the price of the good.

6.   Which of the following will not decrease the demand for a commodity?

    A. The price of a substitute decreases
    B. Income falls and the good is normal
    C. The price of a complement increases
    D. The commodity's price increases

7.   Demand curves have a negative slope because

    A. firms tend to produce less of a good that is more costly to produce.
    B. the substitution effect always leads consumers to substitute higher quality goods for lower quality goods.
    C. the substitution effect always causes consumers try to substitute away from the consumption of a commodity when the commodity's price rises.
    D. an increase in price reduces real income and the income effect always causes consumers to reduce consumption of a commodity when income falls.

8.   If a good is normal, then a decrease in price will cause a substitution effect that is

    A. positive and an income effect that is positive.
    B. positive and an income effect that is negative.
    C. negative and an income effect that is positive.
    D. negative and an income effect that is negative.

9.   If the consumption decisions of individual consumers are independent, then

    A. the market demand curve will be flatter because of the bandwagon effect.
    B. the market demand curve will be steeper because of the snob effect.
    C. the market demand curve will not be equal to the horizontal summation of the demand curves of individual consumers.
    D. none of the above is correct.

10.   If the demand curve for a firm's output is perfectly elastic, then the firm is

    A. a monopolist.
    B. perfectly competitive.
    C. an oligopolist.
    D. monopolistically competitive.

11. Firms in an industry that produces a differentiated product

   A. are either monopolists or oligopolists.
   B. are either monopolistically competitive or perfectly competitive.
   C. are either monopolistically competitive or oligopolists.
   D. are either perfectly competitive or oligopolists.

12. The type of industry organization that is characterized by recognized interdependence and non-price competition among firms is called

   A. monopoly.
   B. perfect competition.
   C. oligopoly.
   D. monopolistic competition.

13. The demand by a firm for inputs used in the production of a commodity that the firm offers for sale

   A. is called a derived demand.
   B. is directly related to the demand for the commodity.
   C. is negatively sloped.
   D. is all of the above.

14. If the price elasticity of demand for a firm's output is elastic, then the firm's marginal revenue is

   A. positive, and an increase in price will cause total revenue to increase.
   B. positive, and an increase in price will cause total revenue to decrease.
   C. negative, and an increase in price will cause total revenue to increase.
   D. negative, and an increase in price will cause total revenue to decrease.

15. If a firm that produces carrots operates in a perfectly competitive industry, then

   A. the demand for the firm's carrots must be horizontal.
   B. the demand by individual consumers for carrots must be horizontal.
   C. the market demand for carrots must be horizontal.
   D. all of the above must be true.

16. If a firm raises its price by 10% and total revenue remains constant, then

   A. the price elasticity of demand for its output is unitary.
   B. marginal revenue is equal to zero.
   C. quantity demanded has decreased by 10%.
   D. all of the above are correct.

17. The price elasticity of demand for a good will tend to be more elastic if

   A. the good is broadly defined (e.g., the demand for food as opposed to the demand for carrots).
   B. the good has relatively few substitutes.
   C. a long period of time is required to fully adjust to a price change in the good.
   D. none of the above are true.

18. If a good is inferior, then

   A. the income elasticity of demand will be negative.
   B. the income elasticity of demand will be zero.
   C. the income elasticity of demand will be positive.
   D. a decrease in income will cause demand to decrease.

19. If two goods are complements, then

   A. the cross-price elasticity of demand will be negative.
   B. the cross-price elasticity of demand will be zero.
   C. the cross-price elasticity of demand will be positive.
   D. an increase in the price of one good will increase demand for the other.

20. The cross-price elasticity of demand between two differentiated goods produced by firms in the same industry will be

   A. negative and large.
   B. negative and small.
   C. positive and large.
   D. positive and small.

21. Which of the following is <u>not</u> viewed by firms as an advantage of electronic commerce over traditional commerce?

   A. Consumers have the ability to easily compare product prices.
   B. The cost of executing a transaction is much lower.
   C. Firms have the ability to gather useful information about buyers.
   D. Firms can reduce their reaction times to changing market conditions and increase their sales reach.

22. Electronic commerce is a significant market channel for the sale of

   A. travel services.
   B. books.
   C. computer products.
   D. All of the above.

Problems

Gary operates an automobile detailing business in a mid-sized town in Pennsylvania. An automobile detailer restores a car to the level of cleanliness and perfection that it had when it was new. His fastidious nature, attention to detail, and ability to effectively manage employees have helped to make his business profitable, but he believes that more information about the market would allow him to operate more efficiently. He uses regression analysis to estimate the demand function for his business and gets the following result:

$$Q_X = 235 - 3P_X + 40A - 20U + 8P_W$$

The number of detailing jobs he gets per month (Q_X) depends on the price he charges per job (P_X), his monthly advertising expenditures (A) measured in $1,000s, the regional percentage unemployment rate (U), and the average price charged by local car wash businesses (P_W) for a standard wash and wax.

Use the estimated demand function given above to solve Problems 1 through 8.

1.   Is automobile detailing a normal good or an inferior good? How can you tell?

2.   Is a wash and wax at the local car wash a complement or a substitute for automobile detailing? How can you tell?

3.   Gary is currently charging $65 per detailing job and spending $3,500 per month on advertising. The regional unemployment rate is 7.5% and the average price of a wash and wax at a local car wash is $15. How many detailing jobs per month can Gary expect under these conditions?

4.   Derive the demand curve for detailing jobs under current conditions. Calculate the values needed to fill in the demand schedule below and then plot the schedule on the graph provided.

P_X	105	95	85	75	65	55	45	35	25	15
Q_X										

Chapter 3: Problem 4

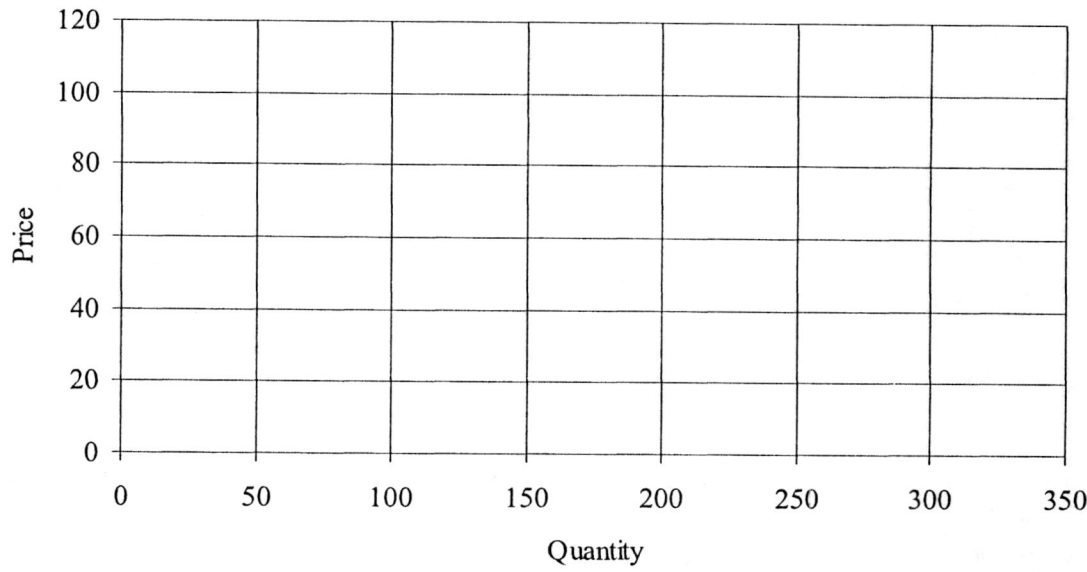

5. Calculate the point price elasticity of demand under current conditions. Is it elastic or inelastic? Also calculate marginal revenue. If the marginal cost of a detailing job is equal to $12, should Gary increase price, lower price, or hold price constant?

6. Calculate the point advertising elasticity of demand ($\%\Delta QX/\%\Delta A$) under current conditions. Is it elastic or inelastic? How many additional detailing jobs would result if Gary spent an additional $1,000 on advertising? How much additional revenue will be generated, under current conditions, if an additional $1,000 is spent on advertising?

7.   Assume that Gary increases his advertising expenditures to $4,500 while all other conditions remain unchanged. Derive the new demand curve for detailing jobs. Calculate the values needed to fill in the demand schedule that follows and then plot this schedule on the same axes you used for Problem 4. How does an increase in advertising expenditures influence the demand curve? How would an increase in the price charged for a detailing job influence the demand curve?

P_X	105	95	85	75	65	55	45	35	25	15
Q_X										

8.   Assume that Gary increases his advertising expenditures to $4,500 and raises his price to $70 and that all other conditions remain unchanged. Calculate the point price elasticity of demand and use it to calculate marginal revenue. If the marginal cost of a detailing job is equal to $12, should Gary increase price, lower price, or hold price constant?

Henry Dan is a researcher for Hugo University, a small private school in Wego, Ohio. Using regression analysis, he estimated the following demand equation for enrollment at Hugo.

$$Q_X = 94 - 50P_X + 8P_E + 6P_S + 5I + 15R + 3N + 20G$$

Dr. Dan determined that the number of new freshman entering Hugo in the fall (Q_X) depends on the annual tuition and housing costs at Hugo measured in $1,000s ($P_X$), the annual tuition and housing costs at Eyego College (P_E) and Wego State University (P_S), Hugo's chief competitors for local students, measured in $1,000s, regional per capita annual income measured in $1,000s (I), the financial aid rebate at Hugo measured as a percentage of tuition revenue (R), the number of students who graduated from local high schools in the previous spring measured in 1,000s (N), and the number of games won in the previous season by Hugo's football team (G).

Use the estimated demand function given above to solve Problems 9 through 13.

9. Hugo, Eyego, and Wego are currently charging $11,000, $15,000, and $6,000, respectively, for tuition and housing. Per capita income in the region is $11,000 and 90,000 students are expected to graduate from local high schools this spring. Hugo's financial aid rebate is 25% and the football team won 5 games last season. How many new freshmen should Hugo expect in the fall?

10. Calculate the point price elasticity of demand and marginal revenue under the current conditions. If Hugo wants to maximize revenue, should the annual cost of tuition and housing be increased, decreased, or kept the same?

11. Calculate the point income elasticity of demand. Is attendance at Hugo normal or inferior? Is it a luxury, a necessity, or neither?

12. Calculate the point cross-price elasticity of demand with Eyego's cost of tuition and housing. Are Eyego and Hugo substitutes or complements?

13. Calculate the remaining elasticities associated with Hugo's demand function and write out the function in terms of percentage changes.

14. Fill in the blanks in the table below. Use the arc elasticity formula to calculate the price elasticity of demand (E_P). Plot the demand schedule and marginal revenue on the graph provided. What is the relationship between the demand curve and the marginal revenue curve? Between demand, marginal revenue, and total revenue? Between demand, marginal revenue, total revenue, and the price elasticity of demand?

Q	P	TR	Q	MR	EP
2	10				
4	9		3		
6	8		5		
8	7		7		
10	6		9		
12	5		11		
14	4		13		
16	3		15		
18	2		17		
20	1		19		

Chapter 3: Problem 14

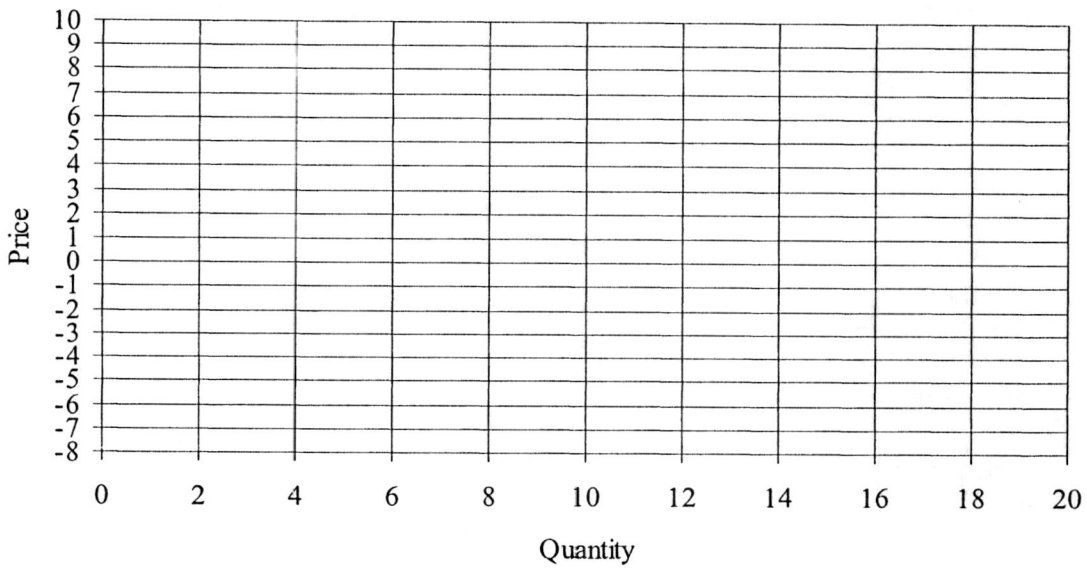

Price

Quantity

15. Fill in the blanks in the table below. Use the arc elasticity formula to calculate the price elasticity of demand (E_P). Plot the demand schedule on the graph that follows.

Q	P	TR	Q	MR	EP
1	24				
2	12		1.5		
3	8		2.5		
4	6		3.5		
5	4.8		4.5		
6	4		5.5		
8	3		7		
10	2.4		9		
12	2		11		
15	1.6		13.5		
16	1.5		15.5		
20	1.2		18		

Chapter 3: Problem 15

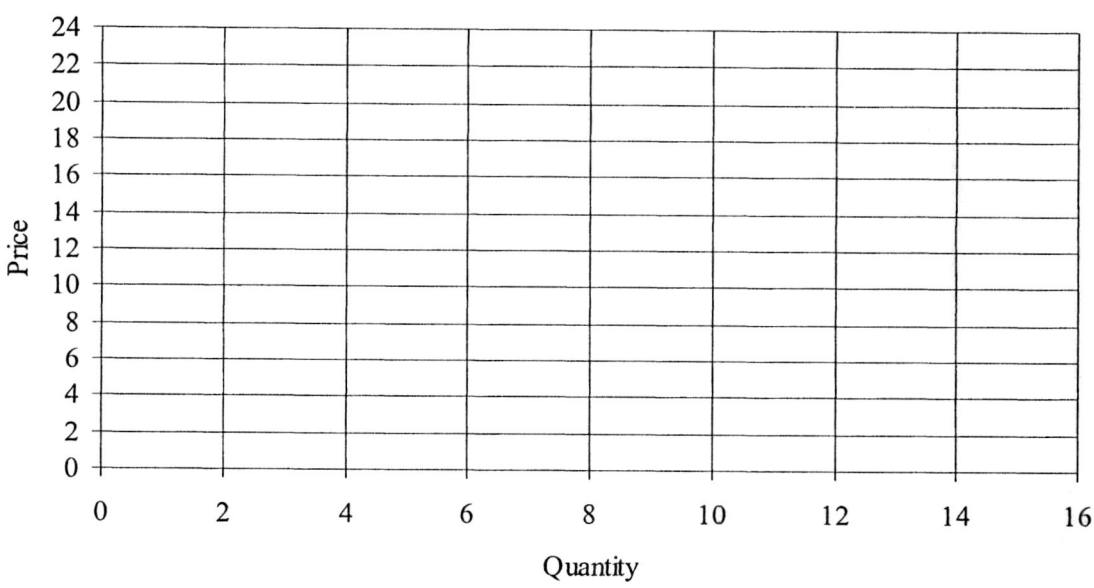

16. Suppose that three consumers comprise the total demand for a good and that their demand functions are defined by the following three demand functions:

   (1)   Q = 16 - 4P

   (2)   Q = 10 - 2P

   (3)   Q = 6 - P

   Given these three individual demand functions, calculate the market demand schedule and enter the values in the table below and then plot the market demand curve on the graph that follows.

P	6	5	4	3	2	1	0
Q							

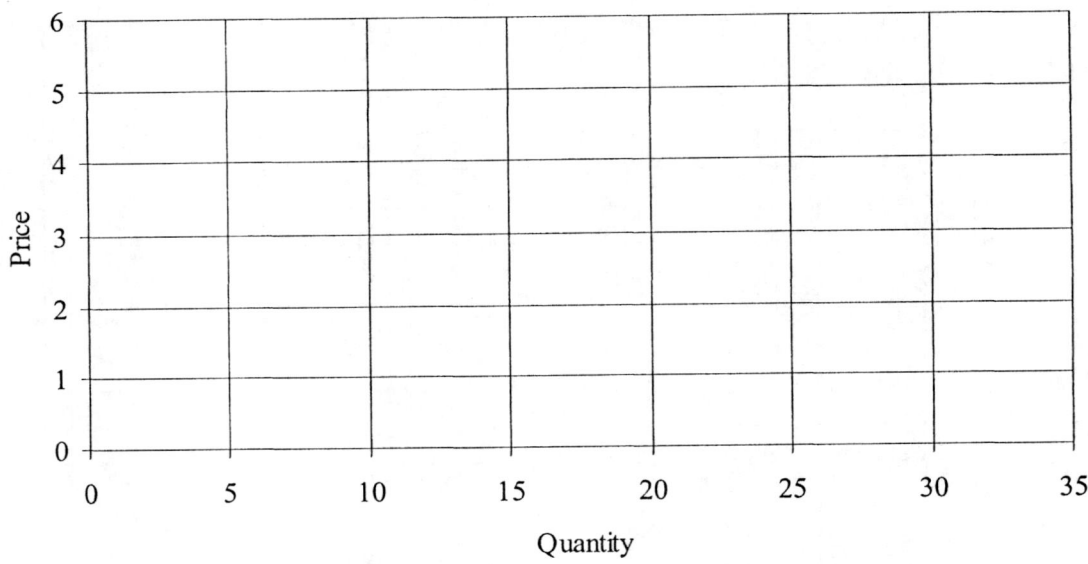

17.   Chelsea Izkowski owns a fast food restaurant named Mickey Doodle's Burgers. She recently took a course in managerial economics and is eager to apply her knowledge to the management of her business. She decides to estimate the price elasticity (E_P) and income elasticity (E_I) of demand for DoodleBurgers and the cross-price elasticity (E_{DF}) of demand for DoodleBurgers with respect to the price of FiddleBurgers, her chief competitor. In order to estimate these elasticities, she collects the information that is listed in the table below, where Q is the quantity of DoodleBurgers sold in a week, P_D is the price of a DoodleBurger during the week, I is per capita annual income, and P_F is the price of a FiddleBurger during the week. Use this information to calculate the arc price, income, and cross-price elasticities of demand for DoodleBurgers.

Q	1,000	1,100	983	831
P_D	$1.20	$1.20	$1.20	$1.40
I	$10,000	$10,000	$11,000	$10,000
P_F	$1.00	$1.10	$1.00	$1.00

18. Injecto Plant Foods, Inc. estimated the demand elasticities for the Squirtomatic, a product that they distribute nationally. They found that the price elasticity of demand (E_P) is -4, the income elasticity (E_I) of demand is 2, the cross-price elasticity of demand (E_{SK}) with respect to the price of the King Autospritzer is 1.5, the cross-price elasticity with respect to the price of PrimoPlants MIX-O-SQUIRT (E_{SM}) is -2, and the demand elasticity with respect to advertising expenditures (E_A) is 5.

The current price of a Squirtomatic is $29.95, per capita income is $11,000, the price of an Autospritzer is $39.99, the cost of a quart of MIX-O-SQUIRT is $8.45, and advertising expenditures are $84,000 per month.

If Injecto Plastics increases the price of the Squirtomatic by 10%, per capita income rises by 5%, the price of an Autospritzer increases by 4%, and the cost of a quart of MIX-O-SQUIRT falls by 2%, by how much will advertising expenditures have to change in order to keep sales of Squirtomatics from changing?

True-False Answers

1	F	14	T	27	F	40	T	53	T
2	T	15	T	28	T	41	T	54	T
3	T	16	F	29	F	42	F	55	T
4	T	17	F	30	T	43	T	56	F
5	F	18	T	31	F	44	T	57	F
6	T	19	T	32	F	45	T	58	F
7	F	20	F	33	T	46	F	59	T
8	T	21	F	34	F	47	F	60	F
9	F	22	T	35	T	48	T	61	F
10	T	23	F	36	T	49	T	62	T
11	T	24	F	37	T	50	F	63	F
12	F	25	T	38	F	51	F	64	F
13	F	26	F	39	F	52	F	65	T

Multiple Choice Answers

1	B	6	D	11	C	16	D	21	A
2	A	7	C	12	C	17	D	22	D
3	C	8	A	13	D	18	A		
4	B	9	D	14	B	19	A		
5	D	10	B	15	A	20	C		

Solutions to Problems

1. Automobile detailing is a normal good. The slope coefficient associated with the variable U (the regional unemployment rate measured as a percentage) is an indirect, or proxy, measure of income. If the unemployment rate increases, then per capita income will generally decrease. Thus, since the slope coefficient is negative, an increase in unemployment (and decrease in income) will cause demand to decrease, which means that the good is normal.

2. A wash and wax at the local car wash is a substitute for detailing. If the demand for one good increases when the price of a second good increases then the two goods are substitutes. In this case, the slope coefficient associated with the variable P_W (the price of a wash and wax at the local car wash) is positive, which means that the goods are substitutes.

3. $Q_X = 235 - (3)(65) + (40)(3.5) - (20)(7.5) + (8)(15) = 150$

4. $Q_X = 235 - 3P_X + (40)(3.5) - (20)(7.5) + (8)(15) = 345 - 3P_X$

P_X	105	95	85	75	65	55	45	35	25	15
Q_X	30	60	90	120	150	180	210	240	270	300

Chapter 3: Problems 4 and 7

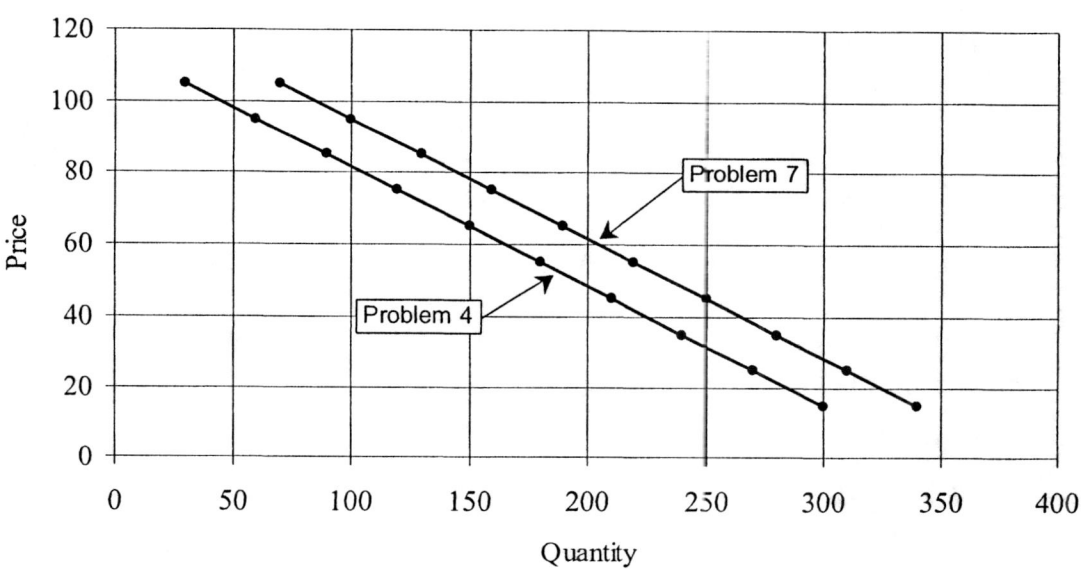

5. $E_P = -3(65/150) = -1.3$ and $MR = 65(1 - (1/1.3)) = 15$

If MC = 12, then MR > MC. This means that an increase in quantity sold will increase total revenue by more than it will increase total cost, so an increase in quantity sold is desirable. Because the demand curve has a negative slope, an increase in quantity sold requires a decrease in price. Consequently, when MR > MC, a firm with a negatively sloped demand curve should lower price.

6. $E_A = 40(3.5/150) = 0.93$

The advertising elasticity is between zero and one, so demand is inelastic with respect to advertising expenditures. If advertising expenditures are increased by $1,000, 40 more detailing jobs per month will result. At $65 per job, the increase in revenue will be:

$(40)(65) = \$2,600$

7. $Q_X = 235 - 3P_X + (40)(4.5) - (20)(7.5) + (8)(15) = 385 - 3P_X$

P_X	105	95	85	75	65	55	45	35	25	15
Q_X	70	100	130	160	190	220	250	280	310	340

An increase in advertising expenditures shifts the demand curve to the right. The horizontal intercept increases by the change in advertising expenditures multiplied by the slope of the demand function with respect to advertising expenditures. A change in P_X will have no influence on the demand curve at all. It will just cause a change in quantity demanded; i.e., a movement along the demand curve.

8. $Q_X = 235 - (3)(70) + (40)(4.5) - (20)(7.5) + (8)(15) = 175$

$E_P = -3(70/175) = -1.2$ and $MR = 70(1-(1/1.2)) = 11.67$

If MC = 12, then MR < MC. This means that an increase in quantity sold will increase total revenue by less than it will increase total cost, so an increase in quantity sold is undesirable and quantity sold should be reduced. Because the demand curve has a negative slope, quantity sold will decrease only if price is increased. Consequently, when MR < MC, a firm with a negatively sloped demand curve should increase price.

9. $Q_X = 94 - (50)(11) + (8)(15) + (6)(6) + (5)(11) + (15)(25) + (3)(90) + (20)(5) = 500$

10. $E_P = -50(11/500) = -1.1$ and $MR = 11(1-(1/1.1)) = 1$

Revenue is at a maximum when marginal revenue is equal to zero. An increase in quantity sold (in this case, an increase in enrollment) when MR > 0 will cause total revenue to increase. Because the demand curve has a negative slope, quantity sold can be increased by reducing price.

11. $E_I = 5(11/500) = 0.11$

The income elasticity of demand is positive, so attendance at Hugo is a normal good. Further, since the elasticity is between zero and one, attendance can be classified as a necessity. Typically, higher education is a luxury; i.e., it has an income elasticity of demand that is greater than one.

12. $E_{XY} = 8(15/500) = 0.24$

The cross-price elasticity of demand is positive, so Hugo and Eyego are substitutes.

13. $\%\Delta Q_X = -1.1(\%\Delta P_X) + 0.24(\%\Delta P_E) + 0.07(\%\Delta P_S) + 0.11(\%\Delta I) +$

$0.75(\%\Delta R) + 0.54(\%\Delta N) + 0.20(\%\Delta G)$

$\%\Delta Q_X/\%\Delta P_S = 6(6/500) = 0.07$

$\%\Delta Q_X/\%\Delta R = 15(25/500) = 0.75$

$\%\Delta Q_X/\%\Delta N = 3(90/500) = 0.54$

$\%\Delta Q_X/\%\Delta G = 20(5/500) = 0.20$

14. The marginal revenue curve is linear. It has the same vertical intercept as the demand curve and it has a horizontal intercept that is halfway between the origin and the horizontal intercept of the demand curve. Marginal revenue is below the demand curve, and thus below price, at every quantity.

The equation for the demand curve is $Q = 22 - 2P$. The equation for the marginal revenue curve is $Q = 11 - MR$.

Total revenue is equal to zero at quantities that correspond to both the horizontal and the vertical intercept of the demand curve. Total revenue is at a maximum at the quantity that corresponds to the midpoint of the demand curve and to the horizontal intercept of the marginal revenue curve, where marginal revenue is equal to zero. To the left of the maximum, marginal revenue is positive and total revenue has a positive slope. To the right of the maximum, marginal revenue is negative and total revenue has a negative slope.

The price elasticity of demand is elastic (less than -1) along the upper portion of the demand curve, where marginal revenue is positive and total revenue is increasing. It is unit elastic (equal to -1) at the midpoint of the demand curve, where marginal revenue is equal to zero and total revenue is at a maximum. It is inelastic (greater than -1) along the lower portion of the demand curve, where marginal revenue is negative and total revenue is decreasing.

Q	P	TR	Q	MR	EP
2	10	20	-	-	-
4	9	36	3	8	-6.33
6	8	48	5	6	-3.40
8	7	56	7	4	-2.14
10	6	60	9	2	-1.44
12	5	60	11	0	-1.00
14	4	56	13	-2	-0.69
16	3	48	15	-4	-0.47
18	2	36	17	-6	-0.29
20	1	20	19	-8	-0.16

TR = PQ so, for example, $(2)(10) = 20$

$MR = \Delta TR/\Delta Q = (TR_2 - TR_1)/(Q_2 - Q_1)$ at $Q = (Q_2 + Q_1)/2$ so, for example,

$MR = (36-20)/(4-2) = 8$ at $Q = (2 + 4)/2 = 3$.

$E_P = [((Q_2 - Q_1)/(P_2 - P_1)][(P_2 + P_1)/(Q_2 + Q_1)]$ at $Q = (Q_2 + Q_1)/2$ so, for example,

at $Q = (2 + 4)/2 = 3$, $E_P = [(4 - 2)/(9 - 10)][(9 + 10)/(4 + 2)] = -6.33$

15. This demand function has the following equation: $Q = 24P^{-1}$. It is referred to as a constant elasticity function.

Q	P	TR	Q	MR	EP
1	24	24	-	-	-
2	12	24	1.5	0	-1.00
3	8	24	2.5	0	-1.00
4	6	24	3.5	0	-1.00
5	4.8	24	4.5	0	-1.00
6	4	24	5.5	0	-1.00
8	3	24	7	0	-1.00
10	2.4	24	9	0	-1.00
12	2	24	11	0	-1.00
15	1.6	24	13.5	0	-1.00
16	1.5	24	15.5	0	-1.00
20	1.2	24	18	0	-1.00

Chapter 3: Problem 15

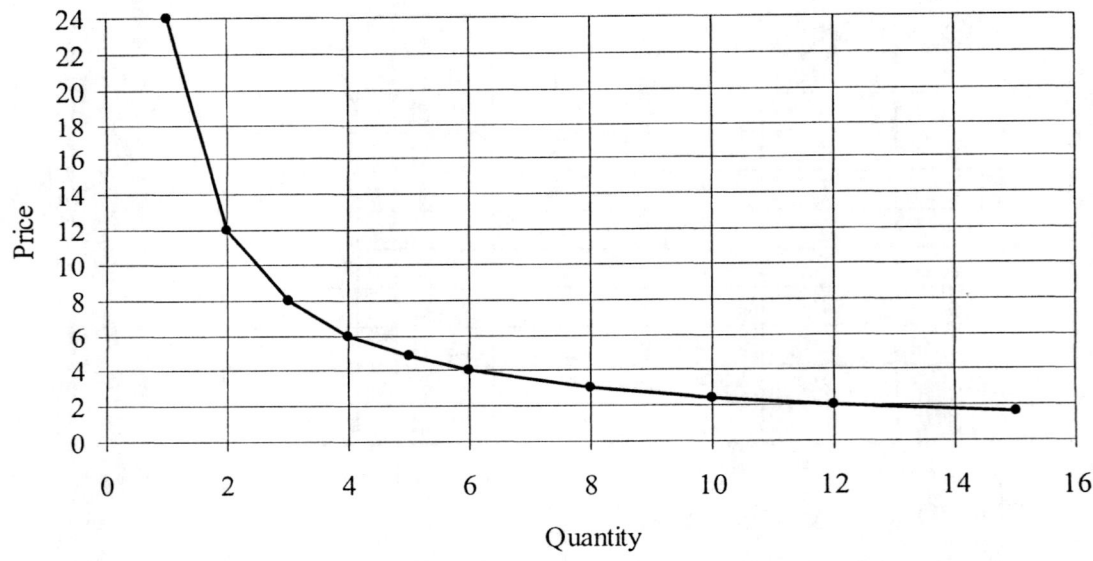

TR = PQ so, for example, (10)(2) = 20

MR = ΔTR/ΔQ = (TR$_2$ - TR$_1$)/(Q$_2$ - Q$_1$) at Q = (Q$_2$ + Q$_1$)/2 so, for example,

MR = (24 - 24)/(2 - 1) = 0 at Q = (1 + 2)/2 = 1.5.

$E_P = [((Q_2 - Q_1)/(P_2 - P_1))][(P_2 + P_1)/(Q_2 + Q_1)]$ at $Q = (Q_2 + Q_1)/2$ so, for example,

at $Q = (1+2)/2 = 1.5$, $E_P = [(2 - 1)/(12 - 24)][(12 + 24)/(2 + 1)] = -1$

16. The three demand functions are horizontally summed to yield the market demand schedule (QD) by adding together the three quantities at each price. For example, where $P = 3$:

$Q = 16 - (4)(3) = 4$

$Q = 10 - (2)(3) = 4$

$Q = 6 - (1)(3) = 3$

$QD = 4 + 4 + 3 = 11$

Consider this second example, where $P = 5$:

$Q = 16 - (4)(5) = -4$ (so $Q = 0$ because it cannot be negative)

$Q = 10 - (2)(5) = 0$

$Q = 6 - (1)(5) = 1$

$QD = 0 + 0 + 1 = 1$

P	6	5	4	3	2	1	0
Q	0	1	4	11	18	25	32

Chapter 3: Problem 16

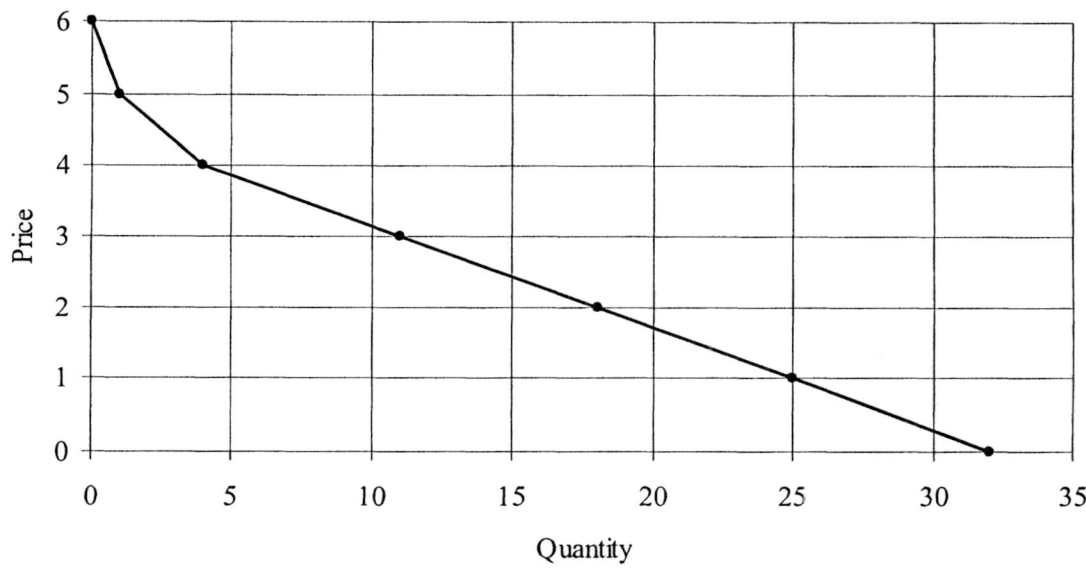

17. Elasticities, like slopes, are defined as the response of a dependent variable to a change in an independent variable when all other independent variables are held constant. This problem requires you to use the table to find values that will allow you to calculate the requested elasticities.

$E_P = [((Q_2 - Q_1)/(P_2 - P_1)][(P_2 + P_1)/(Q_2 + Q_1)]$

$E_P = [(1,000 - 831)/(1.2 - 1.4)][(1.2 + 1.4)/(1,000 + 831)]$

$E_P = -1.20$

$E_I = [((Q_2 - Q_1)/(I_2 - I_1)][(I_2 + I_1)/(Q_2 + Q_1)]$

$E_I = [(1,000 - 983)/(10 - 11)][(10 + 11)/(1,000 + 983)]$

$E_I = -0.18$

$E_{XY} = [((Q_{X2} - Q_{X1})/(P_{Y2} - P_{Y1})][(P_{Y2} + P_{Y1})/(Q_{X2} + Q_{X1})]$

$E_{XY} = [(1,000 - 1,100)/(1.0 - 1.1)][(1.0 + 1.1)/(1,000 + 1,100)]$

$E_{XY} = 1.00$

18. The demand equation can be written in terms of percentage changes as

$\%\Delta Q_S = -4(\%\Delta P_S) + 2(\%\Delta I) + 1.5(\%\Delta P_K) - 2(\Delta P_M) + 5(\%\Delta A)$

Notice that the Autospritzer is a substitute and MIX-O-SQUIRT is a complement to the Squirtomatic.

The problem is solved by substituting in the known values and then solving for the one unknown value, the percentage change in advertising expenditures. None of the price information is required to solve this problem.

$\%\Delta Q_S = (-4)(0.10) + (2)(0.05) + (1.5)(0.04) - (2)(-0.02) + 5\%\Delta A = 0$

$\%\Delta A = (-0.20)/(-5) = 0.04$

Thus, in order to maintain sales at a constant level, advertising expenditures must increase by 4%.

CHAPTER 4

DEMAND ESTIMATION

Learning Objectives

After working through this chapter, you should be conversant with the methods that can be applied to the estimation of demand. Primary among these is regression analysis, a statistical technique that is used to estimate the parameters of mathematical functions from empirical data. Regression analysis is an essential tool of managerial economics, not only for the estimation of demand, but for other applications as well. Consequently, it is crucial that you approach this chapter with the goal of developing a thorough knowledge of regression procedures.

Summary of Notation and Formulas

(4-1) $\quad Y = a + bX$

(4-1') $\quad Y_t = a + bX_t + e_t$

(4-2') $\quad e_t = Y_t - \hat{Y}_t$

Equation 4-1 is a linear function. It defines a straight line relationship between a dependent variable (Y) and an independent variable (X) in terms of the Y intercept (a) and the slope (b) of the line. This equation can be written in statistical form as Equation 4-1' by adding a subscript index (t) to identify specific observations and by adding a third variable (e_t) that represents the influence of random factors on the dependent variable. This third variable accounts for the fact that the dependent variable will not generally be exactly equal to the value that results from the calculation of a + bX for specific values of a, b, and X. As a consequence, it is referred to as the random error in the equation. Equation 4-2' defines the error term as the difference between the observed value of the dependent variable (Y_t) and the value of the dependent variable that is predicted by the estimated linear equation ($\hat{Y}_t$)

(4-3) $\quad \hat{Y}_t = \hat{a} + \hat{b}X_t$

(4-4) $\quad e_t = Y_t - \hat{Y}_t = Y_t - \hat{a} - \hat{b}X_t$

(4-5) $\quad \displaystyle\sum_{t=1}^{n} e_t^2 = \sum_{t=1}^{n} (Y_t - \hat{Y}_t)^2 = \sum_{t=1}^{n} (Y_t - \hat{a} - \hat{b}X_t)^2$

Equations 4-3 to 4-5 define the components of the ordinary least squares model for simple linear regression. Equation 4-3 is the ordinary least squares estimate of Equation 4-1'. It states that the estimated value of the dependent variable for a given value of t ($\hat{Y}$) is equal to the estimated intercept ($\hat{a}$) plus the estimated slope ($\hat{b}$) times the value of the independent variable for a given value of t (X_t). Notice that the random error term (e_t) is absent from this equation.

Since it is random, its value for a given value of t cannot be predicted. However, it can be calculated if the value of Y_t is known.

Equation 4-4 defines the random error's value for a given t as the difference between the observed value of Y and the estimated value of Y for a given t. Equation 4-5 employs the definition in Equation 4-4 to develop the definition of the sum of the squared random error terms. This sum is important because it is the basis for regression analysis by ordinary least squares (OLS), which identifies the intercept and slope (or slopes in the case of multiple regression) that together minimize the sum of the squared errors for a given set of data.

$$(4\text{-}6) \quad \hat{b} = \frac{\sum_{t=1}^{n}(X_t - \bar{X})(Y_t - \bar{Y})}{\sum_{t=1}^{n}(X_t - \bar{X})^2}$$

$$(4\text{-}6') \quad \hat{b} = \frac{\sum_{t=1}^{n} X_t Y_t - (\frac{1}{n})(\sum_{t=1}^{n} X_t)(\sum_{t=1}^{n} Y_t)}{\sum_{t=1}^{n} X_t^2 - (\frac{1}{n})(\sum_{t=1}^{n} X_t)^2}$$

$$(4\text{-}7) \quad \hat{a} = \bar{Y} - \hat{b}\bar{X}$$

Equations 4-6, 4-6', and 4-7 are formulas that can be used to calculate the OLS estimates of the slope and intercept. Equation 4-6' is an alternative version of 4-6 that is more convenient for carrying out hand calculations. Notice that the mean values of Y and X are used in Equation 4-7 to calculate the intercept estimate. One consequence of this is that the estimated slope and intercept always define a line that passes through a point corresponding to these two mean values.

$$(4\text{-}9) \quad s_{\hat{b}} = \sqrt{\frac{\sum(Y_t - \hat{Y})^2}{(n-k)\sum(X_t - \bar{X})^2}} = \sqrt{\frac{\sum e_t^2}{(n-k)\sum(X_t - \bar{X})^2}}$$

$$(4\text{-}9') \quad s_{\hat{b}} = SE \frac{1}{\sqrt{\sum(X_t - \bar{X})^2}}$$

Equations 4-9 and 4-9' are two alternative definitions of the standard error of the slope estimate ($s_{\hat{b}}$), which is a measure of the variability of $\hat{b}$ relative to b. Notice that the variability in $\hat{b}$ is directly related to the sum of the squared errors and inversely related to both the sum of the squared deviations of X around its mean and the difference between the number of observations used in estimation (n) and the number of estimated coefficients (k), which is two (k = 2) in the case of simple linear regression. The second of these two equations defines $s_{\hat{b}}$ in terms of the standard error of the regression (SE) and the sum of the squared deviations of X around its mean. The standard error of the regression, which is generally a part of the output presented by computer programs that carry out regression calculations, is equal to the square root of the sum of the squared errors divided by n - k.

(4-10) $\quad t = \dfrac{\hat{b}}{s_{\hat{b}}}$

(4-10') $\quad \hat{b} \pm t s_{\hat{b}}$

Equation 4-10 defines the t test statistic or "t-ratio" that is used to test whether or not the estimated slope coefficient is significantly different from zero. The t-ratio is compared to a value of the t distribution with degrees of freedom equal to n - k in order to determine significance. If the t-ratio is larger in absolute value than the value taken from the t distribution, then the slope is significantly different from zero. Equation 4-10' defines a confidence interval on the slope estimate. The value of t in this equation is taken from the table of the t distribution with n - k degrees of freedom and the interval that results is an interval estimate of b, which is the true value of the slope coefficient.

(4-11) $\quad Total\ variation\ in\ Y = \displaystyle\sum_{t=1}^{n}(Y_t - \bar{Y})^2$

(4-12) $\quad Explained\ variation\ in\ Y = \displaystyle\sum_{t=1}^{n}(\hat{Y}_t - \bar{Y})^2$

(4-13) $\quad Unexplained\ variation\ in\ Y = \displaystyle\sum_{t=1}^{n}(Y_t - \hat{Y}_t)^2$

(4-14) $\quad \displaystyle\sum(Y_t - \bar{Y})^2 = \sum(\hat{Y}_t - \bar{Y})^2 + \sum(Y_t - \hat{Y}_t)^2$

Equations 4-11 through 4-14 define the decomposition of the sum of squares from a regression analysis. Equation 4-11 defines the total variation in Y as the sum of the squared deviations of Y around its mean value ($\bar{Y}$). Note that division of this sum by n - 1 would yield the sample variance of the Y variable. Equation 4-12 defines the explained variation in Y as the sum of the squared deviations of the estimated value of Y ($\hat{Y}_t$) from the mean value of Y. Note that, defined graphically, these deviations correspond to vertical distances between the estimated regression line and a horizontal line that corresponds to the mean value of Y for each value of X. Equation 4-13 defines the unexplained variation in Y as the sum of the squared deviations of the actual value of Y from the estimated value of Y. Note that this sum is identical to the sum of squared random errors which was used as the basis for defining OLS estimates of the intercept and slope coefficients. Finally, Equation 4-14 defines the relationship between the total, explained, and unexplained variation in Y. This is also referred to as the decomposition of the total sum of squares because it shows that the total sum of squares is composed of an explained and an unexplained component. This relationship is used in developing some of the measures that are defined below.

(4-15) $\quad R^2 = \dfrac{\sum(\hat{Y}_t - \bar{Y})^2}{\sum(Y_t - \bar{Y})^2}$

(4-15') $\quad R^2 = 1 - \dfrac{\sum(Y_t - \hat{Y}_t)^2}{\sum(Y_t - \bar{Y})^2}$

Equations 4-15 and 4-15' are alternative definitions of the coefficient of determination (R^2), which is more commonly referred to as R-square. The second of the two equations is the more convenient way to calculate R^2. Notice that the value of R^2 can be calculated in either of two ways. First, it is equal to the proportion of the total variation in Y that is "explained" by the regression equation. Second, it is equal to one minus the proportion of the total variation in Y that is "unexplained" by the regression equation. Thus, the smaller the sum of squared errors is relative to the sum of squared deviations in Y, the larger R^2 will be. Recall that OLS determines the intercept and slope estimates that minimize the sum of squared errors. This means that these estimates also maximize R^2.

$$(4\text{-}16) \quad r = \sqrt{R^2}$$

$$(4\text{-}16') \quad t = \frac{r}{\sqrt{\dfrac{1-r^2}{n-2}}}$$

Equation 4-16 defines the estimated correlation coefficient (r) as the square root of the coefficient of determination (R^2) with the sign of the slope estimate ($\hat{b}$). Note that this relationship only holds for simple linear regression, not for an R^2 calculated from a multiple regression analysis. The correlation coefficient is a general measure of the strength and direction of the linear relationship between the X and the Y variable. It can take values ranging from negative one, which implies a perfect inverse relationship, to zero, which implies that there is no linear relationship, to positive one, which implies a perfect direct relationship. Unlike the coefficient of determination, the correlation coefficient can be tested for significance. Equation 4-16' defines the test statistic that is used for this purpose. Like the t-ratio used to test the significance of a slope coefficient, this value is compared to a value from the t distribution with n - 2 degrees of freedom. If the absolute value of the test statistic is greater than the value taken from the t distribution, then the correlation coefficient is significantly different from zero and there is evidence of significant correlation between Y and X. Otherwise, there is not. The test on the correlation coefficient yields results identical to those obtained from the t-ratio test on the slope for simple linear regression.

$$(4\text{-}18) \quad Y = a + b_1 X_1 + b_2 X_2 + \cdots + b_{k'} X_{k'}$$

$$(4\text{-}18') \quad Y_t = a + b_1 X_{1t} + b_2 X_{2t} + \cdots + b_{k'} X_{k't} + e_t$$

Equation 4-18 is a function that defines a linear relationship between a dependent variable (Y) and multiple independent variables (X_1, X_2, ... , $X_{k'}$) in terms of an intercept (a) and multiple slope coefficients (b_1, b_2, ... , $b_{k'}$). Note that k' denotes the number of independent variables in the equation. Equation 4-18' is the statistical form of Equation 4-18. Compare these two equations with Equations 4-1 and 4-1' above. Equation 4-18' is converted to statistical form by adding a subscript index (t) to identify specific observations and by adding an additional variable (e_t) that represents the influence of random factors on the dependent variable.

$$(4\text{-}20) \quad \bar{R}^2 = 1 - (1 - R^2)(\frac{n-1}{n-k})$$

$$(4\text{-}20') \quad k = k' + 1$$

Equations 4-20 and 4-20' define the adjusted value of the coefficient of determination or adjusted R^2 (R-bar^2) and the relationship between k and k', respectively. Notice that the higher k is for a given value of n and R^2, the smaller the adjusted R^2 will be. This is a way of adjusting for the fact that the addition of an X variable (which will increase k) will generally increase the value of R^2 even if there is little reason to include the variable in the equation. The adjusted R^2 will decrease if the addition of a variable is not justified.

$$(4\text{-}21) \quad F = \frac{\text{explained variation} / (k-1)}{\text{unexplained variation} / (n-k)}$$

$$(4\text{-}22) \quad F = \frac{R^2 / (k-1)}{(1-R^2) / (n-k)}$$

Equations 4-21 and 4-22 define the F test statistic. This statistic is used to test the overall significance of a regression model. The value of the F test statistic is compared to a value from the F probability distribution with numerator degrees of freedom equal to k - 1 (or k') and denominator degrees of freedom equal to n - k (or n - k' - 1). If the test statistic is greater than the value from the probability distribution, then the model is significant; i.e., at least one slope coefficient is significantly different from zero. The F test yields results identical to the t-ratio test on the slope if it is applied to simple linear regression.

$$(4\text{-}24') \quad \hat{Y} \pm 2(SE)$$

Equation 4-24' defines an approximate interval estimate on the value of the dependent variable given the value of the X variable (for simple linear regression) or the values of the X variables (for multiple regression). The point estimate of the dependent variable ($\hat{Y}$) is calculated from the estimated regression equation. The estimate is based on the empirical rule, which states that approximately 95% of the values of a random variable will be found within two standard deviations of the mean of the variable. Here, that is taken to mean that a confidence level of 95% can be applied to interval estimates that range from two standard errors (SE) below the point estimate to two standard errors above the point estimate.

$$(4\text{-}25) \quad d = \frac{\sum_{t=2}^{n} (e_t - e_{t-1})^2}{\sum_{t-1}^{n} (e_t)^2}$$

One of the problems commonly encountered in the analysis of time-series data is first-order autocorrelation. The most common test for this condition uses the Durbin-Watson statistic (d) that is defined in Equation 4-25. The calculated value of d is compared to values from the Durbin-Watson table that are based on the number of X variables (k') and the number of observations (n). If the value of d is below the lower value from the table (d_L) then there is significant evidence of first-order autocorrelation. If the value of d is above the upper value from the table (d_U) then there is no evidence of first-order autocorrelation. If the value of d is between the lower value and the upper value (between d_L and d_U) then the result is inconclusive and no conclusion can be drawn.

$$(4\text{-}28') \quad Y_t = a X_{1t}^{b_1} X_{2t}^{b_2} \cdots X_{k't}^{b_{k'}} \exp(e_t)$$

(4-29') $Y_t = \ln a + b_1 \ln X_{1t} + b_2 \ln X_{2t} + \cdots + b_{k'} \ln X_{k't} + e_t$

Equation 4-28' is the statistical form of a formula that is referred to as the Cobb-Douglas, log-linear, or constant-elasticity function, where exp() is the exponential function. It can be estimated using OLS after it is transformed into the form given in Equation 4-29'. The transformation is accomplished by converting all values of the Y and X variable(s) into their natural logarithms. For example, $\ln Y_t$ denotes the natural logarithm of Y_t. After the transformation, the slope coefficients from OLS are equal to the exponents in the original function. This form is particularly useful in demand analysis because the coefficients are equal to the elasticities of the dependent variable with respect to the corresponding independent variable. One minor limitation results from the fact that the natural logarithm of a negative number does not exist, so the observed values of all variables must be positive or this functional form can't be used.

True-False Questions

T F 1. Cross-sectional data are made up of observations that are collected across a period of time.

T F 2. The demand curve for a commodity can generally be approximated by drawing a graph with price on the horizontal axis and quantity on the vertical axis, plotting a series of points that represent observed combinations of price and quantity, and then drawing lines that connect the points.

T F 3. If the price of a commodity rises and the quantity sold increases, it does not prove that the demand curve for the commodity slopes upward.

T F 4. If the supply curve for a commodity shifts while the demand curve does not shift, then the demand identification problem will not be encountered.

T F 5. The identification problem is dealt with in practice by including all of the determinants of demand in the estimated demand function.

T F 6. Observational research involves questioning a sample of consumers about their responses to actual and potential market conditions.

T F 7. One advantage of consumer clinics over market experiments is the ability to control the environment and screen out the effects of external events.

T F 8. A market experiment is carried out by providing consumers with a sum of money that must be spent in a simulated store.

T F 9. The use of electronic devices designed to gather information about which television stations people are watching is an example of observational research.

T F 10. A scatter diagram is a graph of a linear function.

T F 11. In the linear function Y = a + bX, Y is the intercept and X is the slope of the function.

T F 12. The slope of a linear function is equal to the change in the dependent variable divided by the corresponding change in the independent variable.

T F 13. The Y intercept of a linear function is equal to the value of X when Y is equal to zero.

T F 14. If a one unit increase in the value of X results in a two unit decrease in the value of Y, then b = -2.

T F 15. If a linear function that is plotted on a graph passes through the origin of a graph, then b = 0.

T F 16. If a regression line that was calculated by ordinary least squares is plotted on a scatter diagram, all of the points in the data set will be on the line.

T F 17. A regression line that is calculated by ordinary least squares will have an intercept and slope that minimize the sum of the squared differences between the observed value of the Y variable and the regression line.

T F 18. Unexplained variation in the Y variable is denoted e_t.

T F 19. If OLS is used to estimate a linear function, then the sum of the e_t will always be equal to zero.

T F 20. One of the crucial assumptions of regression analysis is that the error term has a normal probability distribution.

T F 21. A significance test on the slope coefficient using the t ratio tests the hypothesis that the slope is equal to zero.

T F 22. If the absolute value of the t ratio is larger than the t value taken from the table, then the conclusion is that the slope does not differ from zero.

T F 23. A t test on the slope takes, as its alternative hypothesis, the position that there is no relationship between the dependent variable and the relevant independent variable.

T F 24. For a given sample size, the more independent variables are incorporated in a regression model, the more degrees of freedom the relevant t distribution has.

T F 25. The significance level of a t test on the slope of a simple linear regression equation measures the probability of drawing an incorrect conclusion when the test indicates that X and Y have a significant relationship.

T F 26. The coefficient of determination is equal to the explained variation in the Y variable divided by the unexplained variation in the Y variable.

T F 27. Ordinary least squares minimizes the total variation in the dependent variable.

T F 28. Ordinary least squares maximizes the coefficient of determination.

T F 29. If R^2 is equal to one, then the coefficient of correlation must also be equal to one.

T F 30. The adjusted coefficient of determination is generally larger than the unadjusted coefficient of determination.

T F 31. Omission of an important independent variable from a multiple regression model tends to bias estimates.

T F 32. The more explanatory power a regression model has, the smaller the F test statistic is.

T F 33. The F test has, as its null hypothesis, the proposition that none of the estimated slope coefficients is different from zero.

T F 34. If the F test statistic is greater than the appropriate critical value, it means that at least one of the estimated slope coefficients is significantly different from zero.

T F 35. The standard error of the regression line is an estimate of the standard deviation of the dependent variable relative to the regression line.

T F 36. Multicollinearity refers to a situation in which two or more of the independent variables in a regression model are highly correlated.

T F 37. Heteroskedasticity refers to violation of the assumption that the mean of the error terms is zero.

T F 38. Autocorrelation refers to a situation that is often encountered in time-series data.

T F 39. The Durbin-Watson statistic is used to test the significance of the standard error of the regression.

T F 40. If the observed values of the dependent and independent variables are transformed into their natural logarithms, then each estimated slope coefficient is equal to the elasticity of the dependent variable with respect to the corresponding independent variable.

Multiple Choice Questions

1.   The identification problem refers to the difficulties that a researcher encounters when trying to

   A. determine which independent variables influence quantity demanded.
   B. find accurate data on the price of a commodity and on the quantity demanded of a commodity.
   C. estimate a demand function from data on commodity price and quantity demanded.
   D. measure the impact of extraneous variables on experimental market data.

2.   The estimation of consumer demand by questioning a sample of consumers is referred to as the

   A. consumer survey approach.
   B. observational research approach.
   C. consumer clinic approach.
   D. market experiment approach.

3.   The estimation of consumer demand by setting up simulated stores, providing a sample of consumers with money, and then allowing them to purchase and keep the commodities they select in the stores is called the

   A. consumer survey approach.
   B. observational research approach.
   C. consumer clinic approach.
   D. market experiment approach.

4. The estimation of consumer demand by monitoring actual purchasing and consumption behavior by a sample of consumers is called the

    A. consumer survey approach.
    B. observational research approach.
    C. consumer clinic approach.
    D. market experiment approach.

5. If the t ratio for the slope of a simple linear regression equation is -2.48 and the critical values of the t distribution at the 1% and 5% levels, respectively, are 3.499 and 2.365, then the slope is

    A. not significantly different from zero.
    B. significantly different from zero at both the 1% and the 5% levels.
    C. significantly different from zero at the 1% level but not at the 5% level.
    D. significantly different from zero at the 5% level but not at the 1% level.

6. Ordinary least squares is used to estimate a linear relationship between a firm's quantity sold per month and its total promotional expenditures and the slope of the linear function is found to be positive and significantly different from zero. Assuming that all other variables, including product price, were constant during the period covered by the data set, this result implies that

    A. the firm should spend more on promotional expenditures.
    B. the firm should spend less on promotional expenditures.
    C. promotional expenditures influence demand.
    D. promotional expenditures have no influence on demand.

7. Ordinary least squares is used to estimate a linear relationship between a firm's total revenue per week (in $1,000s) and the average percentage discount from list price allowed to customers by salespersons. A 95% confidence interval on the slope is calculated from the regression output. The interval ranges from 1.05 to 2.38. Based on this result, the researcher

    A. can conclude that the slope is significantly different from zero at the 5% level of significance.
    B. can be 95% confident that the effect of a 1% increase in the average price discount will increase weekly total revenue by between $1,050 and $2,380.
    C. has one chance in twenty of incorrectly concluding that the slope is within the estimated confidence interval.
    D. All of the above are correct.

8. The coefficient of determination

    A. is maximized by ordinary least squares.
    B. has a value between zero and one.
    C. will generally increase if additional independent variables are added to a regression analysis.
    D. All of the above are correct.

9.   The coefficient of correlation is

   A. a measure of the strength and direction of the linear relationship between two variables.
   B. equal to the size of the change in the Y variable that is caused by a change in the X variable.
   C. is equal to the proportion of the variation in the Y variable that is due to variations in the X variable.
   D. All of the above are correct.

10.   Multiple regression analysis is used when

   A. there is not enough data to carry out simple linear regression analysis.
   B. the dependent variable depends on more than one independent variable.
   C. one or more of the assumptions of simple linear regression are not correct.
   D. the relationship between the dependent variable and the independent variables cannot be described by a linear function.

11.   The adjusted value of the coefficient of determination

   A. will always increase if additional independent variables are added to the regression model.
   B. is equal to the proportion of the sum of the squared deviations of the dependent variable from its mean that is explained by the regression model.
   C. is always greater than the proportion of the sum of the squared deviations of the dependent variable from its mean that is explained by the regression model.
   D. is always less than the proportion of the sum of the squared deviations of the dependent variable from its mean that is explained by the regression model.

12.   If the F test statistic for a regression is greater than the critical value from the F distribution, it implies that

   A. none of the independent variables in the regression model have a significant effect on the dependent variable.
   B. all of the independent variables in the regression model have significant effects on the dependent variable.
   C. one or more of the independent variables in the regression model have a significant effect on the dependent variable.
   D. None of the above is correct.

13.   The standard error of the regression measures the

   A. variability of the independent variable(s) relative to its (their) mean.
   B. variability of the dependent variable relative to its mean.
   C. variability of the dependent variable relative to the regression line.
   D. average error that will result if the regression line is used to predict.

14. Multicollinearity refers to a situation in which

   A. successive error terms derived from the application of regression analysis to time series data are correlated.
   B. there is a high degree of correlation between the independent variables included in a multiple regression model.
   C. the dependent variable is highly correlated with the independent variable(s) in a regression analysis.
   D. the application of a multiple regression model yields estimates that are nonlinear in form.

15. Autocorrelation refers to a situation in which

   A. successive error terms derived from the application of regression analysis to time series data are correlated.
   B. there is a high degree of correlation between two or more of the independent variables included in a multiple regression model.
   C. the dependent variable is highly correlated with the independent variable(s) in a regression analysis.
   D. the application of a multiple regression model yields estimates that are nonlinear in form.

16. Heteroskedasticity refers to a situation in which the error terms from a regression analysis

   A. do not have equal variance.
   B. are not normally distributed.
   C. do not have a mean of zero.
   D. All of the above are correct.

17. The Durbin-Watson statistic is used to test for

   A. multicollinearity.
   B. autocorrelation.
   C. heteroskedasticity.
   D. All of the above are correct.

18. Autocorrelation may be the result of

   A. the omission of an important explanatory variable.
   B. the presence of a trend in the independent variable.
   C. nonlinearities in the relationship between the dependent and independent variables.
   D. All of the above are correct.

19. One advantage of estimating a function in which all variables have been transformed into their natural logarithms is that

   A. problems with multicollinearity will be eliminated.
   B. problems with heteroskedasticity will be eliminated.
   C. the estimated slope coefficients are all elasticities.
   D. None of the above is correct.

20. One difference between foreign and domestic demand for a commodity exported by the U.S. is that

   A. foreign demand is unrelated to the dollar price of the commodity.
   B. foreign demand depends on the exchange rate between domestic and foreign currencies.
   C. the domestic price elasticity of demand depends on the availability of substitute commodities.
   D. foreign-made commodities are not good substitutes for U.S. made commodities.

Problems

June Bugg Electronics, Inc., manufactures and distributes the BuggOff, a solar powered insect repellent device. June Bugg was founded in 1978, and since that time it has enjoyed fairly consistent increases in sales revenue. The firm's sales manager, Cathy Kollogee, feels that more spending on advertising campaigns that emphasize the non-polluting nature of the BuggOff would cause revenues to grow much more rapidly. The firm's owner, June Bugg, is skeptical. She thinks that a better understanding of the relationship between advertising expenditures and sales revenue is necessary before the advertising budget is increased, so she comes to you for help.

The table below lists annual observations (OBS) over the period from 1981 to 1991 on BuggOff sales (Y) in millions of dollars per year and average advertising expenditures (X) in thousands of dollars per month. Use this information to solve Problems 1 through 3.

OBS	1	2	3	4	5	6	7	8	9	10	11
X	2	3	5	5	10	7	7	7	8	9	9
Y	4	3	3	5	3	4	6	7	5	6	8

1. Plot the points that correspond to these observations on the graph that follows. Next, use a ruler to draw an approximate line of best fit on the graph. That is, draw a line that appears (to your eye) to fit the points well enough to be an adequate description of the relationship between the two variables. Label this line VISUAL.

Chapter 4: Problem 1

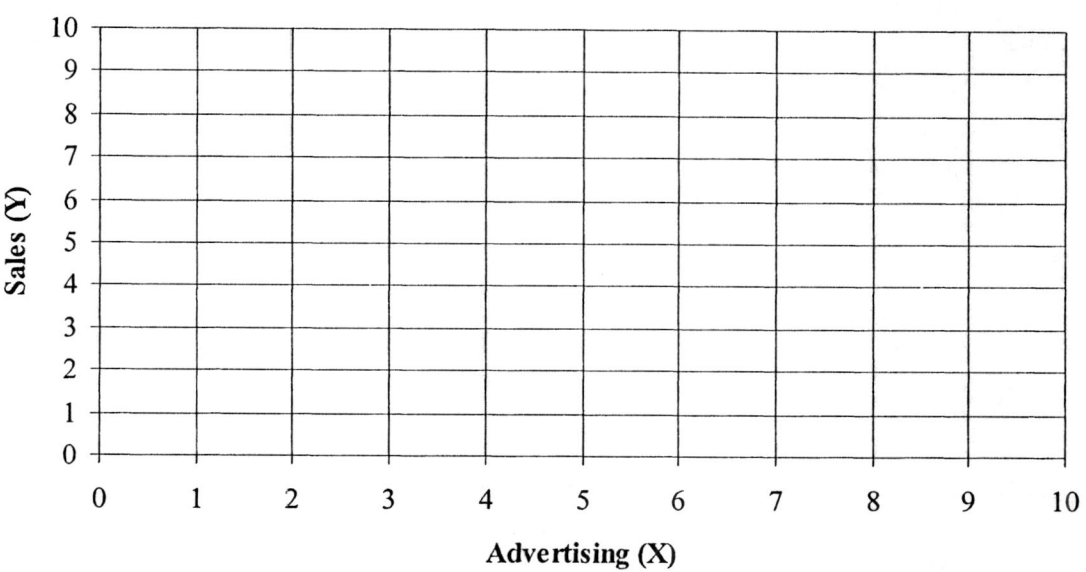

Choose two points on your "visual" line of best fit and use the points to calculate the intercept and slope of the line.

2.   Use OLS to calculate the intercept, the slope, the coefficient of determination, and the standard error of the slope.

Plot the OLS regression line on the graph from Problem 1 and label it OLS1. How does this line differ from your visual line of best fit? Evaluate the fit of this line using the calculated values.

After noticing that observation 5 differs substantially from the other observations, you question the sales manager about events that are related to this observation. She explains that late in 1984 a competing firm, the Lingering Death Insecticide Company, used advertisements in which the BuggOff was represented as a danger to children and pets. June Bugg sales revenues fell substantially in 1985, but the firm responded with a major advertising campaign that was effective in returning things to normal by the end of the year.

3.   Apply OLS to the 10 observations that remain when observation 5 is omitted from the data set. Plot this second OLS regression line on the graph with OLS1 and VISUAL and label it OLS2. Evaluate the fit of this line and compare it with that of OLS1.

Tom Acadvipski operates the Mucho Macho Hair Restoration Clinic in Cranium, Arizona. His son, Ollie, recently completed a course in managerial economics and is eager to apply his skills to the family business. Mucho Macho is one of many clinics around the country that are franchised by Hairball International, so Ollie contacts the regional Hairball representative and asks for cross-sectional data on the demand for hair restoration services. After some persuasion, the representative finally coughs up the Hairball data. Ollie collects some additional data for each of the 32 clinic areas and then uses a computer to calculate regression results from the 32 observations.

The variables employed in the analysis are listed below with their average values in parenthesis:

Q = Number of clients per week (269)

I = Average annual income in $1,000s (23)

M = Single men over 35 in 1,000s (292)

P = Price per restoration treatment (584)

W = Single women over 21 in 1,000s (387)

B = Number of singles bars (33)

A = Advertising expenditures in $1,000s per month (4)

D = Divorce rate in percent (45)

The regression results, with t-ratios in parenthesis, are listed below:

SE of regression   37.62

R^2 0.91

$Q = 187.27 + 2.46I + 0.62M - 0.27P - 0.14W + 1.02B - 3.27A + 0.74D$

$\qquad\qquad$ (1.22) (10.33) (-6.89) (-3.60) (1.52) (-0.77) (0.84)

Use these results to solve Problems 4 through 7.

4. Calculate the adjusted coefficient of determination and explain its meaning.

5. Test the overall explanatory power of the regression equation at a 5% level of significance. Explain, in words, what your test result implies.

6. Test each of the slope parameters at a 5% level of significance. Explain, in words, what the results of each of your tests imply. Should any of the independent variables be eliminated from the equation? Which ones?

7. Use the mean values of the variables and the regression results to calculate the income elasticity of demand and the price elasticity of demand. Comment on these elasticities.

After examining the regression results shown above, Ollie decides to re-estimate the equation using only the significant independent variables. The results, with t-ratios in parentheses, are listed below. Use these results to solve Problems 8 through 12.

SE of regression   40.02

R^2 0.88

$Q = 294.79 + 0.62M - 0.28P - 0.11W$

            (10.72) (-7.84) (-3.27)

8.   Calculate the adjusted coefficient of determination and compare it to the value obtained in Problem 4.

9.   Test the regression equation at a 5% level of significance. Explain, in words, what your test result implies.

10.   Test each of the slope parameters at a 5% level of significance. Explain, in words, what the results of each of your tests imply.

11.   Use the mean values of the variables and the regression results to calculate the price elasticity of demand. Comment on this elasticity. What general advice would you give to Hairball International regarding the prices charged for services at their franchised clinics? Assuming that Hairball International receives a fixed percentage of the total revenue earned by their franchised clinics, what average price per treatment should they recommend?

12. The Cranium area has a population that includes about 110,000 single men over 35 and 170,000 single women over 21. Calculate the demand function for hair restoration in Cranium. Also calculate the corresponding marginal revenue function. Assume that the marginal cost per client per week for Mucho Macho is $250 and calculate marginal cost. Determine what price Mucho Macho should charge in order to maximize profit, how many treatments per week will be sold at that price, and what total revenue per week will be. Also calculate 95% confidence intervals on the number of clients per week and on total revenue per week.

Ulysses Travel Consulting Services is a firm that specializes in organizing every aspect of unique cruise vacations for discriminating travelers who are seeking adventurous odysseys. The owner and general manager, Helena Troy, has operated Ulysses Travel for over twenty years. In that time, as she likes to say, she has launched a thousand ships. She charges a flat fee per person to organize every part of a vacation. Her fee does not include any of the direct costs of travel. The personal qualities that she brings to her job have inspired a remarkable degree of client loyalty. Many of her patrons come to her every year for travel advice and new clients are generally the result of their recommendations.

Her pricing decisions have always been based on an intuitive understanding of the travel market, but recently Helena has started to wonder if a more quantitative understanding of the demand for her services might help her to end up with a better bottom line. As a consequence, she goes through her records and pulls out the consulting price (P_C) in $100s and the number of clients (Q_C) for each of the past twenty years and uses these data to estimate a demand function. The results of her regression calculations, with the t-ratios in parenthesis, follow below. Use them to solve Problems 13 through 15.

SE of regression   206.00

R^2 0.03

Durbin Watson   0.41

$Q_C = 475.65 - 8.47PC$

          (-0.80)

13.   Comment on the regression results obtained by Helena Troy. Identify any problems you see and suggest possible solutions.

Helena Troy is perplexed by the results of her calculations. "I'm sure that the price I charge has some effect on the number of clients I get" she says. When she is asked whether anything else could influence the demand for her services, she suggests that the average income of her clients might have some effect. Consequently, she goes back into her records and, based on her knowledge of her clients, she estimates the average annual income (I) in $1,000s of her clients during each of the past twenty years. She then runs the regression again with both variables in the equation. Her results are shown below.

SE of regression   68.82

R^2 0.90

Durbin Watson   1.92

$QC = 231.30 - 19.08P_C + 4.04I$

          (-5.23)   (12.01)

14.	Compare these regression results with those obtained previously and comment on any differences between the two.

15.	The average values of Q_C, P_C and I are 382.5, 11, and 89.4, respectively. Calculate the price elasticity and income elasticity of demand for Helena Troy's services based on these twenty-year averages. Comment on these elasticities. During the past year, P_C and I were equal to 11 and 174, respectively. Calculate the price elasticity of demand under the current conditions and comment on the price that Helena is currently charging. If the marginal cost per client is about $300, what price should Helena charge?

True-False Answers

1	F	9	T	17	T	25	T	33	T
2	F	10	F	18	T	26	F	34	T
3	T	11	F	19	T	27	F	35	T
4	T	12	T	20	T	28	T	36	T
5	T	13	F	21	T	29	F	37	F
6	F	14	T	22	F	30	F	38	T
7	T	15	F	23	F	31	T	39	F
8	F	16	F	24	F	32	F	40	T

Multiple Choice Answers

1	C	5	D	9	A	13	C	17	B
2	A	6	C	10	B	14	B	18	D
3	C	7	D	11	D	15	A	19	C
4	B	8	D	12	C	16	A	20	B

Solutions to Problems

1. Your VISUAL line will probably not be identical to the one plotted on the graph that follows. However, the method used to find the equation of a straight line from two points on the line is the same regardless of what line you are working with.

    Notice that two of the points on the line that is labeled VISUAL are marked. The first is $(Y_1 = 4, X_1 = 5)$ and the second is $(Y_2 = 7, X_2 = 10)$.

    The equation for the straight line that passes through the two points on the graph is calculated in two steps. First, the slope (b) is calculated by dividing the change in Y by the change in X as follows:

    $b = \Delta Y/\Delta X = (Y_2 - Y_1)/(X_2 - X_1) = (7 - 4)/(10 - 5) = 0.60$

    Next, one of the two points $(X = 5, Y = 4)$ is used to calculate the intercept (a) as follows:

    $a = Y_1 - bX_1 = 4 - (0.60)(5) = Y_2 - bX_2 = 7 - (0.60)(10) = 1$

    The result is an estimated linear function $(Y = 1 + 0.60X)$ based on the visual line of best fit.

Chapter 4: Problem 1

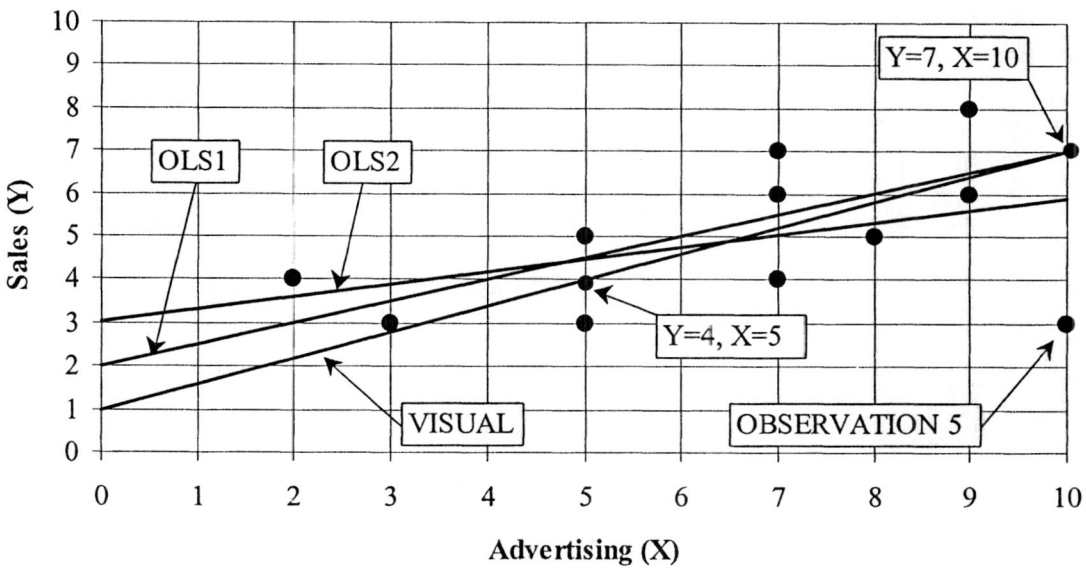

2. The calculations that are used to obtain the OLS estimates from Equations 4-6', 4-9', and 4-15', and a table that shows the required preliminary calculations are shown below.

    As noted previously, your VISUAL line will probably differ from the one plotted on the graph above. It may differ from OLS1 in either of two ways. First, it might be flatter so that it is above OLS1 for small values of X and below OLS1 for large values of X. If this is the case, then you placed a greater emphasis on Observation 5 than ordinary least squares did and so ended up with a larger intercept and a smaller slope. Second, your VISUAL line might be steeper than OLS1, as is the line plotted on the graph above. If this is the case, you placed less emphasis on Observation 5 than ordinary least squares did. The impact of Observation 5 is explored in more detail in Problem 4.

OBS	X	Y	XY	X^2	Y^2	$\hat{Y}$	e_t	e_t^2
1	2	4	8	4	16	3.61	0.39	0.15
2	3	3	9	9	9	3.89	-0.89	0.79
3	5	3	15	25	9	4.47	-1.47	2.16
4	5	5	25	25	25	4.47	0.53	0.28
5	10	3	30	100	9	5.9	-2.9	8.41
6	7	4	28	49	16	5.04	-1.04	1.08
7	7	6	42	49	36	5.04	0.96	0.92
8	7	7	49	49	49	5.04	1.96	3.84
9	8	5	40	64	25	5.33	-0.33	0.11
10	9	6	54	81	36	5.61	0.39	0.15
11	9	8	72	81	64	5.61	2.39	5.71
SUM	72	54	372	536	294	54.01	-0.01	23.6

$$\hat{b} = \frac{n\sum XY - \sum X \sum Y}{n\sum X^2 - (\sum X)^2} = \frac{(11)(372)-(72)(54)}{(11)(536)-(72)^2} = 0.2865$$

$$\hat{a} = \frac{\sum Y}{n} - \hat{b}\frac{\sum X}{n} = \frac{54}{11} - (0.2865)\frac{72}{11} = 3.03$$

$$s_{\hat{b}} = \sqrt{\frac{\sum e_t^2}{(n-k)\left(\sum X^2 - \frac{(\sum X)^2}{n}\right)}} = \sqrt{\frac{23.60}{(11-2)\left(536 - \frac{72^2}{11}\right)}} = 0.20$$

$$R^2 = 1 - \frac{\sum e_t^2}{\sum Y^2 - \frac{(\sum Y)^2}{n}} = 1 - \frac{23.60}{294 - \frac{54^2}{11}} = 0.18$$

The fit of OLS1 to the data, as measured by the coefficient of determination and by a significance test on the slope, is poor. The coefficient of determination is only 0.18, which means that 82% of the variation in the dependent variable is left "unexplained" by the regression line. The t-ratio for the slope is 0.29/0.20 = 1.45. The critical value of the t distribution for n - k = 11 - 2 = 9 degrees of freedom is 2.262 at a 5% level of significance. Since the t-ratio is less than the critical value, the conclusion is that the slope is not significantly different from zero.

3. The calculations used to obtain the OLS estimates from Equations 4-6', 4-9', and 4-15' follow below. Note that the difference between OLS1 and OLS2 is entirely due to Observation 5. Also, note that the omission of this observation increased the coefficient of determination from 0.18 to 0.52 and reduced the standard error of the slope from 0.20 to 0.17 while increasing the slope from 0.29 to 0.50. As a result, the t-ratio increased from 1.45 to 2.94. The critical value of the t distribution for n - k = 10 - 2 = 8 degrees of freedom is 2.306 at a 5% level of significance. Since the t-ratio exceeds the critical value, the conclusion is that the slope is significantly different from zero and that the equation has significant explanatory power.

OBS	X	Y	XY	X^2	Y^2	$\hat{Y}$	e_t	e_t^2
1	2	4	8	4	16	3.0	1.0	1.00
2	3	3	9	9	9	3.5	-0.5	0.25
3	5	3	15	25	9	4.5	-1.5	2.25
4	5	5	25	25	25	4.5	0.5	0.25
6	7	4	28	49	16	5.5	-1.5	2.25
7	7	6	42	49	36	5.5	0.5	0.25
8	7	7	49	49	49	5.5	1.5	2.25
9	8	5	70	64	25	6.0	-1.0	1.00
10	9	6	54	81	36	6.5	-0.5	0.25
11	9	8	72	81	64	6.5	1.5	2.25
SUM	62	51	342	436	285	51.0	0.0	12.00

$$\hat{b} = \frac{n\sum XY - \sum X \sum Y}{n\sum X^2 - (\sum X)^2} = \frac{(10)(342) - (62)(51)}{(10)(436) - (62)^2} = 0.50$$

$$\hat{a} = \frac{\sum Y}{n} - \hat{b}\frac{\sum X}{n} = \frac{51}{10} - (0.50)\frac{62}{10} = 2.00$$

$$s_{\hat{b}} = \sqrt{\frac{\sum e_t^2}{(n-k)\left(\sum X^2 - \frac{(\sum X)^2}{n}\right)}} = \sqrt{\frac{12}{(10-2)\left(436 - \frac{62^2}{10}\right)}} = 0.17$$

$$R^2 = 1 - \frac{\sum e_t^2}{\sum Y^2 - \frac{(\sum Y)^2}{n}} = 1 - \frac{12}{285 - \frac{51^2}{10}} = 0.52$$

An observation like the one eliminated from the data set in this problem is referred to as an **outlier**. An outlier can generally be identified on the basis of its unusually large error (e_t) value. Note that e_5 is 8.41 (see the table in the solution to Problem 2), which is far larger than any of the other error values. If you find an outlier in a data set, it is important to determine whether there is a good reason to omit the observation. This determination is often difficult, because it requires substantial familiarity with the data and its sources. In this problem, the unusual circumstances that surround Observation 5 justify its omission.

4.   The adjusted coefficient of determination measures the proportion of the variation in the dependent variable that is explained by the regression equation after adjusting for the degrees of freedom lost due to the number of independent variables in the equation. An increase in k reduces the adjusted coefficient. In this case, $R^2 = 0.91$, k = 8, and n = 32. The adjusted coefficient is 0.88.

5.   The F test is used to test the significance of a regression equation. In this case, the numerator degrees of freedom is k - 1 = 8 - 1 = 7 and the denominator degrees of freedom is n - k = 32 - 8 = 24 so the critical value of the F distribution at the 5% level of

significance is 2.42. The F test statistic is 34.7, which implies that at least one of the equation's seven slope coefficients is significantly different from zero at the 5% level.

$$\bar{R}^2 = 1 - (1 - R^2)(\frac{n-1}{n-k}) = 1 - (1 - 0.91)\frac{(32-1)}{(32-8)} = 0.88$$

$$F = \frac{R^2/(k-1)}{(1-R^2)/(n-k)} = \frac{0.91/(8-1)}{(1-0.91)/(32-8)} = 34.7$$

6. The critical value of the t distribution with n - k = 32 - 8 = 24 degrees of freedom at the 5% level of significance is 2.064. Therefore, the slope coefficients for I, B, A, and D are not significantly different from zero. These variables can be eliminated from the equation without significantly reducing the explanatory power of the regression model. The slope coefficients for M, P, and W are significantly different from zero, so elimination of any of them from the equation would significantly reduce the model's explanatory power.

7. If the mean values of all of the independent variables are substituted into the estimated regression equation, then the dependent variable will also be equal to its mean value. The income elasticity of demand (E_I) is 0.21, which implies that hair restoration is a necessity. The price elasticity of demand (E_P) is -0.59, which is in the inelastic range, implying that total revenue and total profits could be increased by raising price. Notice that marginal revenue is negative when the price elasticity is in the inelastic range.

$$E_I = \frac{\Delta Q}{\Delta I}\frac{I}{Q} = 2.46\frac{23}{269} = 0.21$$

$$E_P = \frac{\Delta Q}{\Delta P}\frac{P}{Q} = -0.27\frac{584}{269} = -0.59$$

8. For this model, $R^2 = 0.88$, k = 4, and n = 32. The adjusted coefficient of determination is 0.87, which is only slightly lower than the adjusted coefficient of 0.88 that was obtained with the previous model. This result implies that the explanatory power of the four variables that were eliminated from the model was negligible.

$$\bar{R}^2 = 1 - (1 - R^2)(\frac{n-1}{n-k}) = 1 - (1 - 0.88)\frac{(32-1)}{(32-4)} = 0.87$$

9. For this model, the numerator degrees of freedom is k - 1 = 4 - 1 = 3 and the denominator degrees of freedom is n - k = 32 - 4 = 28 so the critical value of the F distribution at the 5% level of significance is 2.95. The F test statistic is 68.4, which implies that at least one of the equation's three slope coefficients is significantly different from zero at the 5% level.

$$F = \frac{R^2/(k-1)}{(1-R^2)/(n-k)} = \frac{0.88/(4-1)}{(1-0.88)/(32-4)} = 68.4$$

10. The critical value of the t distribution with n - k = 32 - 4 = 28 degrees of freedom at the 5% level of significance is 2.048. The slope coefficients for M, P, and W are significantly different from zero.

---

11. If the mean values of all of the independent variables are substituted into the estimated regression equation, then the dependent variable will also be equal to its mean value. The price elasticity of demand (E_P) is -0.61; i.e., demand is price inelastic and marginal revenue is negative. Hairball should recommend that their clinics act to increase the average price charged for hair restoration. When demand is price inelastic, an increase in price will increase total revenue while reducing total quantity sold and, therefore, the variable cost of production. If Hairball receives a fixed percentage of the total revenue of their clinics, they should encourage the clinics to operate where the price elasticity of demand is unitary because the point of unit elasticity corresponds to a marginal revenue of zero and the maximum possible total revenue. The price that yields this result is 774 and the quantity that will be sold at that price is 217. The calculations that yield this result are shown below.

$$E_P = \frac{\Delta Q}{\Delta P}\frac{P}{Q} = -0.28\frac{584}{269} = -0.61$$

$$Q = 294.79 + (0.62)(292) - 0.28P - (0.11)(387) = 433.26 - 0.28P$$

$$E_P = -1 = \frac{\Delta Q}{\Delta P}\frac{P}{Q} = -0.28\frac{P}{433.26 - 0.28P}$$

$$P = 433.26/0.56 = 774 \text{ and } Q = 433.26 - (0.28)(774) = 217$$

12. Solution of this problem involves several steps. First, the demand curve for Mucho Macho must be determined.

$$Q = 294.79 + (0.62)(110) - 0.28P - (0.11)(170)$$

$$Q = a - bP = 344.29 - 0.28P$$

Next, the demand curve must be used to derive the total revenue function. To accomplish this, the curve is solved for P and then both sides are multiplied by Q.

$$P = (a/b) - (1/b)Q = (344.29/0.28) - (1/0.28)Q$$

$$TR = PQ = (a/b)Q - (1/b)Q^2 = 1229.61Q - 3.57Q^2$$

The marginal revenue curve (MR) is equal to the derivative of the total revenue curve. If you are not familiar with derivatives, just use the formula given below.

$$MR = (a/b) - (2/b)Q = 1229.61 - 7.14Q$$

Next, to plot the MR curve on the same graph as the demand curve, it is useful to solve the MR equation for Q. Note that the horizontal (Q) intercept of the MR curve is equal to the intercept of the demand curve divided by two, that the slope of the MR curve is equal to the slope of the demand curve divided by two, and that the demand curve and the MR curve have the same vertical (P) intercept.

$$Q = (a/2) - (b/2)MR = 172.15 - 0.14MR$$

Now, the profit-maximizing quantity can be determined by setting marginal revenue equal to marginal cost (MC) and solving for Q as follows.

$$MC = 250 = MR = 1229.61 - 7.14Q$$

$Q = (1229.61 - 250)/7.14 = 137.2$

This value of Q is then used to determine price from the demand equation.

$P = 1229.61 - (3.57)(137.2) = 739.8$

So, in order to maximize profit, Mucho Macho should charge $740 per treatment and expect to have 137 clients per week with a weekly total revenue of $(740)(137) = \$101,380$.

The confidence intervals are calculated by adding and subtracting twice the standard error (SE) to the quantity estimate as follows.

$Q \pm (2)(SE) = 137 \pm (2)(40.02) = 57$ to 217

$TR \pm (2)(SE)(P) = 101,380 \pm (2)(40)(740) = 42,180$ to $160,580$

Notice that the relatively large standard error yields confidence intervals that are rather wide. This suggests that the results of this analysis should be employed with some caution.

13. The coefficient of determination of 0.03 is quite small and the t ratio of -0.80 is not significantly different from zero. These results indicate that the regression equation has little explanatory power. The Durbin-Watson critical values for k' = 1 and n = 20 at the 5% level of significance are 1.20 and 1.41. The Durbin-Watson test statistic is below the lower critical value, which implies that there is significant autocorrelation. Autocorrelation can be the result of an incorrect functional form, the presence of a time trend in the data, or the omission of an important explanatory variable from the model.

14. Compared to the previous model, this one is substantially better. The coefficient of determination is 0.90, which indicates that 90% of the variation in Qc is explained by the regression model. The critical value of the F distribution for k - 1 = 3 - 1 = 2 numerator degrees of freedom and n - k = 20 - 3 = 17 denominator degrees of freedom at the 5% level of significance is 3.59 and the F test statistic is 76.5, which implies that the model has significant explanatory power. The critical value of the t distribution for n - k = 20 - 3 = 17 degrees of freedom at the 5% level of significance is 2.11. The t ratios for both slope coefficients are larger than this value, which implies that both slope coefficients are significantly different from zero. Finally, the Durbin-Watson critical values for k' = 2 and n = 20 at the 5% level of significance are 1.10 and 1.54. The Durbin-Watson test statistic is above the upper critical value, which implies that there is no evidence of significant autocorrelation. The source of the autocorrelation that was present in the previous model appears to have been the failure to include income as an explanatory variable.

15. The income elasticity of demand (E_I) is 0.94, which implies that expenditures on travel consulting services tend to be a fairly constant share of total expenditures. The price elasticity of demand (E_P) is -0.55, which is in the inelastic range, implying that total revenue and total profits could be increased by raising price. Notice that marginal revenue is negative when the price elasticity is in the inelastic range. Under the current conditions, $Q_C = 231.30 - (19.08)(11) + (4.04)(174)$ so $Q_C = 724.4$ and $E_P = -0.29$, which means that marginal revenue is negative and price is lower than the optimum.

$$E_I = \frac{\Delta Q}{\Delta I} \frac{I}{Q} = 4.04 \frac{89.4}{382.5} = 0.94$$

$$E_P = \frac{\Delta Q}{\Delta P} \frac{P}{Q} = -19.08 \frac{11}{382.5} = -0.55$$

$$E_P = \frac{\Delta Q}{\Delta P} \frac{P}{Q} = -19.08 \frac{11}{724.4} = -0.29$$

The optimum price is determined by the same procedure that was used to solve Problem 12. The demand curve and marginal revenue curves are shown below.

$Q_C = a - bP = 934.26 - 19.08P$

$P = (a/b) - (1/b)Q = 48.97 - 0.0524Q_C$

$Q_C = (a/2) - (b/2)MR = 467.13 - 9.54MR$

Substituting MC = 3 for MR, Helena should charge about \$2,600 per client and expect to have about 439 clients per year at that price.

$Q_C = 467.13 - (9.54)(3) = 438.51$

$P = 48.97 - (0.0524)(438.51) = 25.99$

CHAPTER 5

DEMAND FORECASTING

Learning Objectives

After working through this chapter, you should understand what forecasting is, why every organization must engage in forecasting, and how the fundamental techniques of forecasting are applied in practice. You should be able to distinguish between qualitative and quantitative forecasting methods and identify the circumstances in which each is appropriate. You should know how to generate quantitative forecasts using time series analysis, moving averages, and exponential smoothing and how to measure the accuracy of forecasts using the root mean square error. You should also understand the role of leading economic indicators, econometric models, and input-output models in forecasting.

Summary of Notation and Formulas

(5-1) $\quad S_t = S_0 + bt$

Equation 5-1 is a linear trend forecasting equation that defines the value of a variable (S_t) at time = t as a function of a starting value (S_0), a constant amount of change (b) per time period, and t.

(5-3) $\quad S_t = S_0(1+g)^t$

(5-4) $\quad \ln S_t = \ln S_0 + t\ln(1+g)$

Equation 5-3 and 5-4 are different ways of expressing a constant growth rate trend forecasting equation. The first states that the value of a variable (S_t) at time = t is equal to a starting value (S_0) multiplied by one plus a constant rate of growth (g) raised to the power t. Notice that this is identical to the formula used for compound interest calculations. The second equation is obtained by transforming the first using natural logarithms. It is linear, and so can be readily estimated by ordinary least squares. The intercept is ln S_0, the slope is ln(1 + g), the dependent variable is S_t, and the independent variable is t.

(5-9) $\quad RMSE = \sqrt{\dfrac{\sum (A_t - F_t)^2}{n}}$

Equation 5-9 defines the root-mean-square-error (RMSE) as the square root of the mean of the squared forecasting errors, where A_t is the actual observed value of the variable at time = t, F_t is the forecast at time = t, and n is the number of observations in the data set used to create the forecasts. The RMSE is used to compare alternative ways to forecast the same variable. The best method yields the smallest RMSE.

(5-12) $\quad F_{t+1} = wA_t + (1-w)F_t$

Equation 5-12 is the exponential smoothing forecasting equation. It defines the forecast for time $= t + 1$ (F_{t+1}) as a weighted average of the actual observed value of a variable at time $= t$ (A_t) and the forecast value of the variable at time $= t$ (F_t), where w is a value between zero and one that defines the amount of weight placed on the actual observed value at time $= t$ and $(1 - w)$ defines the weight placed on all past observed values.

(5-18) $Q = a_o + a_1 P + a_2 Y + a_3 N + a_4 P_S + a_5 P_C + + a_6 A + e$

Equation 5-18 is a single equation econometric model of the demand for breakfast cereals. It states that the quantity demanded of cereals per time period (Q) is a linear function of the price of cereals (P), consumer income (Y), population (N), the price of a substitute (muffins, P_s), the price of a complement (milk, P_c), the level of advertising (A), and a random error term (e), where a_0 is the intercept of the demand equation and a_1, a_2, ... , a_6, are the slope coefficients.

(5-21) $C = a_1 + b_1 GNP_t + u_{1t}$

(5-22) $I_t = a_2 + b_2 \pi_{t-1} + u_{2t}$

(5-23) $GNP_t \equiv C_t + I_t + G_t$

Equations 5-21, 5-22, and 5-23 comprise a three equation econometric model of a national economy and Equation 5-27 is the solution, or reduced form equation, for this model. If you have taken a macroeconomics course, then you have encountered this model before. In this model, C_t is consumption expenditures in year t, GNP_t is gross national product in year t, I_t is investment expenditures in year t, t - 1 is profit in year t - 1, G_t is government spending in year t, u_{1t} and u_{2t} are random error terms, a_1 and a_2 are intercepts, and b_1 and b_2 are slopes. The reduced form equation is obtained by solving the model so that the endogenous (or dependent) variable that you want to forecast is on the left (in this case that is GNP) and the intercepts, slopes, and exogenous (or independent) variables are on the right. In this case, the exogenous variables are profit and government spending. Forecasts are generated by estimating the intercept and slope coefficients and then determining appropriate values of the independent variables.

True-False Questions

T F 1.   Forecasts of commodity demand may be based on macroeconomic forecasts.

T F 2.   Barometric forecasting methods are most useful for long-term forecasts.

T F 3.   The choice of a forecasting method should be based on an assessment of the costs and benefits of each method in a specific application.

T F 4.   Surveys and opinion polls are qualitative techniques.

T F 5.   Qualitative forecasts based on surveys tend to perform particularly well during periods of unexpected international political upheaval.

T F 6.   The Delphi method generates forecasts by surveying consumers to determine their opinions.

T F 7.   One advantage of the Delphi method is that it avoids a "bandwagon effect" that could lead to incorrect or biased conclusions.

T F 8. Councils of distinguished foreign dignitaries and business people are used to obtain qualitative forecasts with a foreign perspective.

T F 9. Time-series analysis generates forecasts by identifying cause and effect relationships between variables.

T F 10. Time-series data are observations on a variable at different points in time.

T F 11. The fundamental assumption of time-series analysis is that past patterns in time-series data will continue unchanged in the future.

T F 12. Time-series forecasting tends to be more accurate than "naive" forecasting.

T F 13. The long-run increase or decrease in time-series data is referred to as a cyclical fluctuation.

T F 14. A time series that displays regular seasonal variation is said to exhibit cyclical fluctuation.

T F 15. Irregular or random influences on time-series data give rise to the secular trend.

T F 16. Expansions and contractions in the general economy result in seasonal variation.

T F 17. Cyclical fluctuations in time-series data are generally forecast using qualitative techniques.

T F 18. The use of a linear trend equation to forecast future values of a variable is based on the assumption of a constant amount of change per time period.

T F 19. The linear trend equation can be estimated by ordinary least squares regression analysis.

T F 20. The constant percentage growth rate model cannot be estimated by ordinary least squares regression analysis.

T F 21. Seasonal variation can be estimated by the use of dummy variables in linear regression analysis.

T F 22. The ratio-to-trend method is used to estimate a linear trend equation.

T F 23. A fundamental assumption of time-series analysis is that past trend and seasonal patterns will not persist in the future.

T F 24. Time-series analysis is particularly useful for forecasting turning points in time-series data.

T F 25. Naive forecasting methods include time-series analysis and smoothing methods.

T F 26. Smoothing techniques are most useful for time-series data that is primarily influenced by irregular variation.

T F 27. A moving average forecast is based on the most recent observed values of time-series data.

T F 28. The greater the number of periods used to calculate a moving average, the more sensitive the forecast is to the most recent observation.

T F 29. In general, the greater the degree of irregular or random variation present in a time series, the more periods should be used to calculate a moving average forecast.

T F 30. If two forecasting methods are applied to the same data set, the method that yields the larger root-mean-square error (RMSE) is better.

T F 31. A forecast calculated using the exponential smoothing method is a weighted average of past observations in which the most recent observation has the greatest weight.

T F 32. The weight (w) that is used to calculate an exponential smoothing forecast defines the contribution of the most recent observation to the forecast.

T F 33. Barometric methods are often used to forecast the cyclical component of a time series.

T F 34. The use of leading indicators to forecast time-series data is an example of econometric forecasting.

T F 35. The diffusion index is a coincident indicator.

T F 36. The use of an estimated demand equation to forecast demand is an example of econometric forecasting.

T F 37. Forecasts based on leading indicators are qualitative.

T F 38. Macroeconomic forecasts are generally based on multiple-equation econometric models.

T F 39. Reduced form equations are derived algebraically from the structural and definitional equations in a multi-equation econometric model.

T F 40. Definitional equations must be estimated using regression analysis.

Multiple Choice Questions

1. A qualitative forecast

    A. predicts the quality of a new product.
    B. predicts the direction, but not the magnitude, of change in a variable.
    C. is a forecast that is classified on a numerical scale from 1 (poor quality) to 10 (perfect quality).
    D. is a forecast that is based on econometric methods.

2. Which of the following is not a qualitative forecasting technique?

    A. Surveys of consumer expenditure plans
    B. Perspectives of foreign advisory councils
    C. Consumer intention polling
    D. Time-series analysis

3.   The first step in time-series analysis is to

A. perform preliminary regression calculations.
B. calculate a moving average.
C. plot the data on a graph.
D. identify relevant correlated variables.

4.   Forecasts are referred to as naive if they

A. are based only on past values of the variable.
B. are short-term forecasts.
C. are long-term forecasts.
D. generally result in incorrect forecasts.

5.   Time-series analysis is based on the assumption that

A. random error terms are normally distributed.
B. there are dependable correlations between the variable to be forecast and other independent variables.
C. past patterns in the variable to be forecast will continue unchanged into the future.
D. the data do not exhibit a trend.

6.   Which of the following is not one of the four types of variation that is estimated in time-series analysis?

A. Predictable
B. Trend
C. Cyclical
D. Irregular

7.   The cyclical component of time-series data is usually estimated using

A. linear regression analysis.
B. moving averages.
C. exponential smoothing.
D. qualitative methods.

8.   In time-series analysis, which source of variation can be estimated by the ratio-to-trend method?

A. Cyclical
B. Trend
C. Seasonal
D. Irregular

9.   If regression analysis is used to estimate the linear relationship between the natural logarithm of the variable to be forecast and time, then the slope estimate is equal to

A. the linear trend.
B. the natural logarithm of the rate of growth.
C. the natural logarithm of one plus the rate of growth.
D. the natural logarithm of the square root of the rate of growth.

10. The use of a smoothing technique is appropriate when

    A. random behavior is the primary source of variation.
    B. seasonality is present.
    C. data exhibit a strong trend.
    D. all of the above are correct.

11. The greatest smoothing effect is obtained by using

    A. a moving average based on a small number of periods.
    B. exponential smoothing with a small weight value.
    C. the root-mean-square error.
    D. the barometric method.

12. The root-mean-square error is a measure of

    A. sample size.
    B. moving average periods.
    C. exponential smoothing.
    D. forecast accuracy.

13. Barometric methods are used to forecast

    A. seasonal variation.
    B. secular trend.
    C. cyclical variation.
    D. irregular variation.

14. A leading indicator is a measure that usually

    A. changes at the same time and in the same direction as the general economy.
    B. responds to a change in the general economy after a time lag.
    C. changes in the same direction as the general economy before the general economy changes.
    D. has all of the properties listed above.

15. If 3 of the leading indicators move up, 2 move down, and the remaining 6 are constant, then the diffusion index is

    A. $3/6 = 50\%$
    B. $3/11 = 27\%$
    C. $5/11 = 45\%$
    D. $6/11 = 55\%$

16. A single-equation econometric model of the demand for a product is a _____ equation in which the quantity demanded of the product is an _____ variable.

    A. structural, exogenous
    B. structural, endogenous
    C. definitional, exogenous
    D. definitional, endogenous

17. A reduced form equation expresses

    A. an exogenous variable as a function of endogenous variables.
    B. an endogenous variable as a function of exogenous variables.
    C. an exogenous variable as a function of both endogenous and exogenous variables.
    D. an endogenous variable as a function of both exogenous and endogenous variables.

18. Trend projection is an example of which kind of forecasting?

    A. Qualitative
    B. Time-series
    C. Barometric
    D. Econometric

19. Turning points in the level of economic activity can be forecast by using

    A. Time-series analysis
    B. Exponential smoothing
    C. Barometric methods
    D. Moving average

20. Econometric forecasts require

    A. accurate estimates of the coefficients of structural equations.
    B. forecasts of future values of exogenous variables.
    C. appropriate theoretical models.
    D. all of the above.

Problems

In 1974, Vanguard World Xpress was founded by Yanos Zarkov, a second generation immigrant from Eastern Europe. The company produces custom crates, boxes, and other packaging materials that are used by exporters of delicate scientific devices. The success of the company is the result of a commitment to quality and service to the customer. Recently, it has become more difficult for Yanos to provide dependable service while, at the same time, containing costs.

One of the tradeoffs faced by VWX is between inventory costs and production backlogs. Inventory costs result from the storage of raw and finished packaging materials. Production backlogs occur if there is not sufficient inventory to fill an order, and they result in unsatisfied customers. Yanos feels that accurate demand forecasts would allow the company to contain inventory costs and eliminate production backlogs.

The local university recently instituted an intern program, so Yanos contacted the director of the program and agreed to hire a student. It turns out to be you. He asks his accountant to obtain accurate quarterly sales data for the past three years, in millions of dollars, and hands it to you. The data are listed below. With the guidance of your crusty old economics adviser you begin to develop a forecasting model for VWX. Your adviser's recommendations are given as Problems 1 through 6 below.

Period	1990.1	1990.2	1990.3	1990.4	1991.1	1991.2
Sales	6.2	8.6	8.8	9	5.2	10
Period	1991.3	1991.4	1992.1	1992.2	1992.3	1992.4
Sales	12.8	12.4	9.4	14.9	13.8	13.9

1. Plot the data on the graph below. Do you see evidence of a secular trend? Seasonal variation? Cyclical variation? Comment on each of these time-series components and on the methods that can be used to estimate them.

Chapter 5: Problem 1

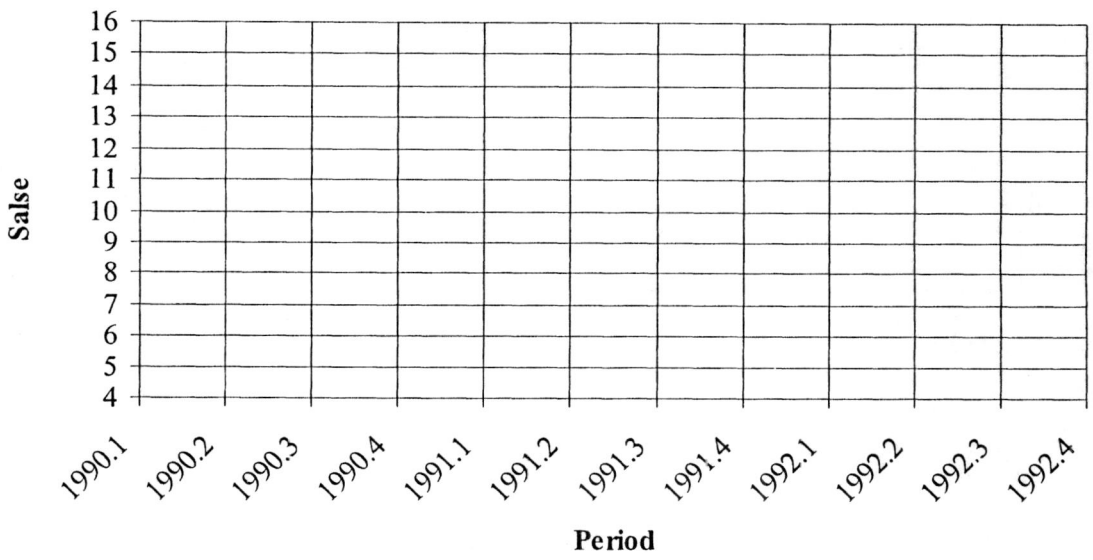

2. Estimate the linear trend using regression analysis. Use the estimated trend equation to fill in the blanks in the table that follows. Note that A is the actual value and F is the forecast value of sales. Plot a line based on the forecast values of sales on the graph for Problem 1. Plot the forecast errors (A-F) on the graph below. What time-series components give rise to these forecast errors? Calculate the RMSE and comment on the accuracy of the forecasts that are derived using this method. Can the RMSE be calculated directly from the regression output?

Period	Trend	Sales (A)	Sales (F)	(A-F)	$(A-F)^2$
1990.1	1	6.2			
1990.2	2	8.6			
1990.3	3	8.8			
1990.4	4	9			
1991.1	5	5.2			
1991.2	6	10			
1991.3	7	12.8			
1991.4	8	12.4			
1992.1	9	9.4			
1992.2	10	14.9			
1992.3	11	13.8			
1992.4	12	13.9			

Chapter 5: Problem 2

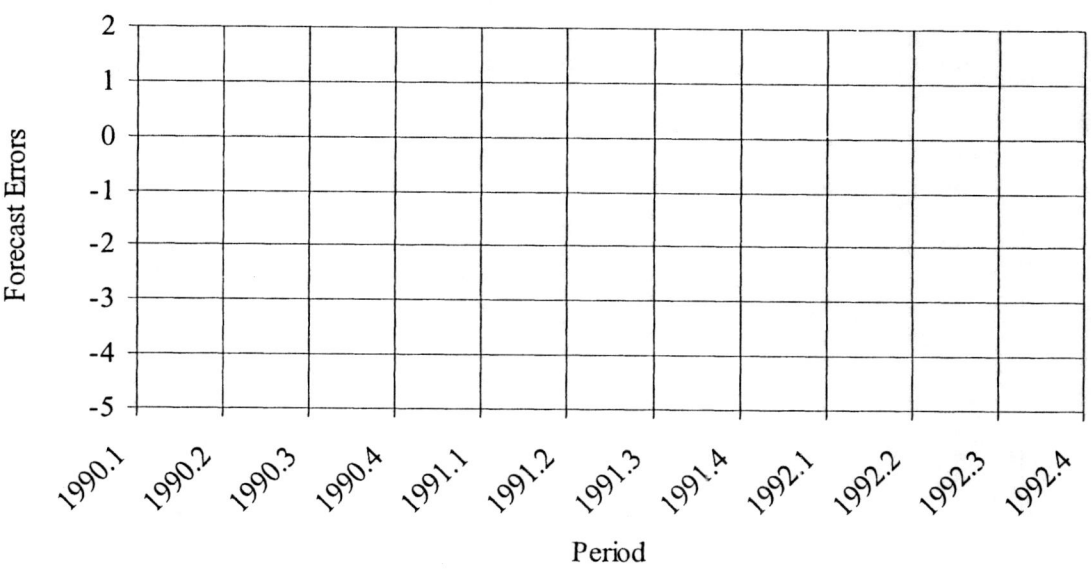

3. Estimate the log-linear trend using regression analysis. Calculate the growth rate that is implied by the estimated slope coefficient. Use the log-linear trend equation to fill in the blanks in the table that follows. Note that lnF is the forecast natural logarithm of sales and the F is the antilog of this value. Calculate the RMSE and comment on the accuracy of the forecasts yielded by this method. Can the RMSE be calculated directly from the regression output? Compare these forecasts with the ones you calculated for Problem 2.

Period	Sales (A)	Sales (lnF)	Sales (F)	(A-F)	$(A-F)^2$
1990.1	6.2				
1990.2	8.6				
1990.3	8.8				
1990.4	9				
1991.1	5.2				
1991.2	10				
1991.3	12.8				
1991.4	12.4				
1992.1	9.4				
1992.2	14.9				
1992.3	13.8				
1992.4	13.9				

4.   Estimate a seasonally adjusted linear trend equation using regression analysis with dummy variables. Use the equation to fill in the blanks in the table below. Plot the forecast errors on the graph that follows. Compare this graph with that from Problem 2. Calculate the RMSE and comment on the accuracy of the forecasts yielded by this method. Compare these forecasts with those you calculated previously.

Period	Trend	Sales (A)	Sales (F)	(A-F)	$(A-F)^2$
1990.1	1	6.2			
1990.2	2	8.6			
1990.3	3	8.8			
1990.4	4	9			
1991.1	5	5.2			
1991.2	6	10			
1991.3	7	12.8			
1991.4	8	12.4			
1992.1	9	9.4			
1992.2	10	14.9			
1992.3	11	13.8			
1992.4	12	13.9			

Chapter 5: Problem 4

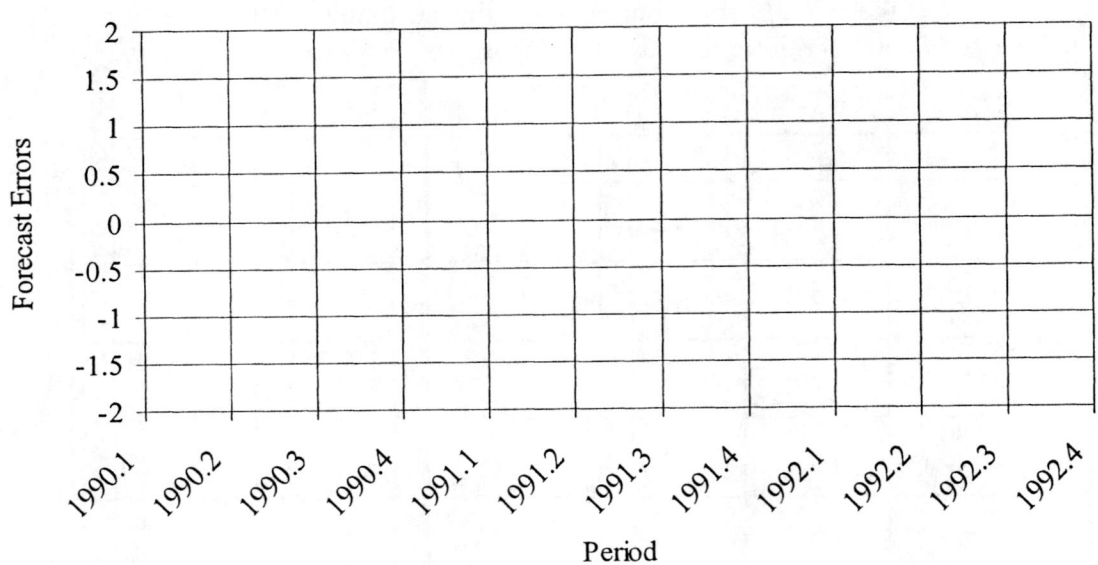

5.   Use the trend equation that was estimated in Problem 2 to calculate ratio-to-trend seasonal adjustment factors. Fill in the blanks in the table below. Note that (A/F) is actual sales divided by the trend forecast and SF is the seasonally adjusted trend forecast. Calculate the RMSE. Comment on the accuracy of the forecasts yielded by this method and compare them with the forecasts you calculated previously.

Period	Sales (A)	Sales (F)	(A/F)	(SF)	$(A-SF)^2$
1990.1	6.2				
1990.2	8.6				
1990.3	8.8				
1990.4	9				
1991.1	5.2				
1991.2	10				
1991.3	12.8				
1991.4	12.4				
1992.1	9.4				
1992.2	14.9				
1992.3	13.8				
1992.4	13.9				

6.   Enter the RMSE and the forecasts for the next four quarters into the table below for each of the four forecasting models estimated in this problem. Use the information in the table to compare the models. Which would you recommend to Yanos Zarkov?

Model	Linear Trend	Constant Growth Rate	Seasonal Dummy Variables	Ratio-To-Trend
RMSE				
1993.1				
1993.2				
1993.3				
1993.4				

Arizona Crystal is a distributor of feldspar, amethyst and other mystically powerful types of crystals. The owner of Arizona Crystal, Geri Moonbeam, is proud to be a part of the movement that is contributing to the higher spirituality of the world. Geri buys crystals from local collectors and then ships them out to wholesalers throughout the country. Geri pays cash for the crystals, but she extends credit to the wholesalers.

As the business has grown, problems have arisen. When Geri buys more crystals than she can sell, inventory increases and cash flow problems arise. When Geri doesn't buy enough crystals, then she can't fill orders and that creates problems with her customers. She needs to base her buying decisions on accurate forecasts of the demand for crystals so she can avoid these problems.

After consulting her tarot cards, Geri visits a friend from El Paso, Texas, who channels for a Wall Street tycoon who didn't survive the crash of 1929. He recommends that, since she only has twelve months of data, she should try using a moving average or exponential smoothing forecasting model. So Geri contacts you. She provides you with data on the number of crystals (in thousands) ordered during each of the past twelve months and asks you to help her develop a forecasting model. To do so, solve Problems 7 through 11 below.

7. Use a three period moving average model to forecast the demand in January of 1993. Also calculate the RMSE for this model. Use the table below.

Month	Demand (A)	Demand (F)	$(A-F)^2$
Jan-92	25.6		
Feb-92	24.7		
Mar-92	21.3		
Apr-92	13.9		
May-92	12.6		
Jun-92	18.0		
Jul-92	21.5		
Aug-92	22.3		
Sep-92	30.7		
Oct-92	15.0		
Nov-92	13.8		
Dec-92	22.6		

8. Use a five period moving average model to forecast the demand in January of 1993. Also calculate the RMSE for this model. Use the table below to carry out your calculations. How does this model compare with the three period model?

Month	Demand (A)	Demand (F)	$(A-F)^2$
Jan-92	25.6		
Feb-92	24.7		
Mar-92	21.3		
Apr-92	13.9		
May-92	12.6		
Jun-92	18.0		
Jul-92	21.5		
Aug-92	22.3		
Sep-92	30.7		
Oct-92	15.0		
Nov-92	13.8		
Dec-92	22.6		

9.   Use an exponential smoothing model with a weight of 0.6 to forecast demand in January of 1993. Also calculate the RMSE for this model. Use the mean value of 20.2 as your initial estimate. Use the table below to carry out your calculations. How does this model compare with the moving average models?

Month	Demand (A)	Demand (F)	$(A-F)^2$
Jan-92	25.6		
Feb-92	24.7		
Mar-92	21.3		
Apr-92	13.9		
May-92	12.6		
Jun-92	18.0		
Jul-92	21.5		
Aug-92	22.3		
Sep-92	30.7		
Oct-92	15.0		
Nov-92	13.8		
Dec-92	22.6		

10. Use an exponential smoothing model with a weight of 0.1 to forecast the demand in January of 1993. Also calculate the RMSE for this model. Use the mean value of 20.2 as your initial estimate. Use the table below to carry out your calculations. How does this model compare with the moving average models and with the previously estimated moving average model?

Month	Demand (A)	Demand (F)	$(A-F)^2$
Jan-92	25.6		
Feb-92	24.7		
Mar-92	21.3		
Apr-92	13.9		
May-92	12.6		
Jun-92	18.0		
Jul-92	21.5		
Aug-92	22.3		
Sep-92	30.7		
Oct-92	15.0		
Nov-92	13.8		
Dec-92	22.6		

11. Recall that the degree of smoothing associated with a moving average model is a function of the number of periods used to calculate the average. Recall also that the degree of smoothing associated with an exponential smoothing model is a function of the weight used to calculate the estimate. What is the moving average forecast of demand for January of 1993 when the maximum possible smoothing is applied? What is the exponential smoothing forecast for January of 1993 when the maximum possible smoothing is applied? What is the weight used to obtain the maximum possible smoothing? Use this weight to fill in the table below and calculate the RMSE. What is your conclusion regarding the best forecasting model?

Month	Demand (A)	Demand (F)	$(A-F)^2$
Jan-92	25.6		
Feb-92	24.7		
Mar-92	21.3		
Apr-92	13.9		
May-92	12.6		
Jun-92	18.0		
Jul-92	21.5		
Aug-92	22.3		
Sep-92	30.7		
Oct-92	15.0		
Nov-92	13.8		
Dec-92	22.6		

12. Continuing in the same vein as Problem 11, what is the moving average forecast of demand for January of 1993 when the minimum possible smoothing is applied? What is the exponential smoothing forecast for January of 1993 when the minimum possible smoothing is applied? What is the weight used to obtain the minimum possible smoothing? Use this weight to fill in the table below and calculate the RMSE. Now what is your conclusion regarding the best forecasting model?

Month	Demand (A)	Demand (F)	$(A-F)^2$
Jan-92	25.6		
Feb-92	24.7		
Mar-92	21.3		
Apr-92	13.9		
May-92	12.6		
Jun-92	18.0		
Jul-92	21.5		
Aug-92	22.3		
Sep-92	30.7		
Oct-92	15.0		
Nov-92	13.8		
Dec-92	22.6		

The Ice Cream Council is an industry group that is funded by contributions by ice cream manufacturers. It engages in advertising and public relations on behalf of the ice cream industry. The Council wants to determine the effect of its advertising expenditures on the market for ice cream. It devises the following three-equation econometric model of the market for ice cream.

(1) $QS_t = S_0 + S_1 P_t$

(2) $QD_t = D_0 - D_1 P_t + D_2 A_t$

(3) $QS_t = QD_t$

QS_t and QD_t are the quantities supplied and demanded of ice cream in month t, P_t is the price per gallon of ice cream in month t, A_t is advertising expenditure in millions of dollars by the Council in month t, and S_0, S_1, D_0, D_1, and D_2 are parameters to be estimated. Equations 1 and 2 are structural equations that define the supply and demand for ice cream, respectively, and Equation 3 defines the condition for market equilibrium.

Regression analysis is used to estimate the two behavioral equations. The results are given below.

(1') $QS_t = 5 + 15 P_t$

(2') $QD_t = 45 - 5 P_t + A_t$

13.   Derive the reduced form equation for Q_t (which is equal to the equilibrium values of both QS and QD at time t) and for P_t, the two endogenous variables in the model. Use Equations 1, 2, and 3. Note that A_t is an exogenous variable that is determined by the actions of the Ice Cream Council.

14.   Use the information in Equations 1' and 2' to forecast price, quantity sold, and total industry revenue before and after an increase in advertising expenditures from $4 to $10 million. Is this increase in advertising expenditures appropriate?

15. The table that follows presents data on four leading indicators for a four month period. Construct a composite index with each indicator assigned equal weight. Next, construct a composite index with the first indicator assigned a weight of 0.40 and the remaining indicators assigned a weights of 0.20. Finally, construct the diffusion index. Compare the implications of the three indexes over the four month period.

Month	Indicator 1	Indicator 2	Indicator 3	Indicator 4
Jan-92	100	40	15	97
Feb-92	120	50	13	65
Mar-92	150	40	17	69
Apr-92	130	40	15	65

True-False Answers

1	T	9	F	17	T	25	T	33	T
2	F	10	T	18	T	26	T	34	F
3	T	11	T	19	T	27	T	35	F
4	T	12	F	20	F	28	F	36	T
5	F	13	F	21	T	29	T	37	T
6	F	14	F	22	F	30	F	38	T
7	T	15	F	23	F	31	T	39	T
8	T	16	F	24	F	32	T	40	F

Multiple Choice Answers

1	B	5	C	9	C	13	C	17	B
2	D	6	A	10	A	14	C	18	B
3	C	7	D	11	B	15	B	19	C
4	A	8	C	12	D	16	B	20	D

Solutions to Problems

1. There is clear evidence of both trend and seasonal variation in the data. The level of sales appears to have increased more or less consistently over time, which indicates the presence of a positive trend. The trend can be estimated by regression analysis. The results of the analysis can be used to determine whether a linear or a constant percentage growth rate model fits the data better.

    The presence of seasonal variation is suggested by the pattern of change in the four quarterly observations for each year. Notice that sales increase between the first and second quarter of every year and decline between the third and fourth quarter of the second year. It is generally somewhat risky to base estimates of seasonal variation on only three years of data; however, it does not seem unreasonable to suppose that sales of packaging materials will be subject to seasonal influences. Seasonality can be estimated by the dummy variable method or by the ratio-to-trend method.

Chapter 5: Problem 1

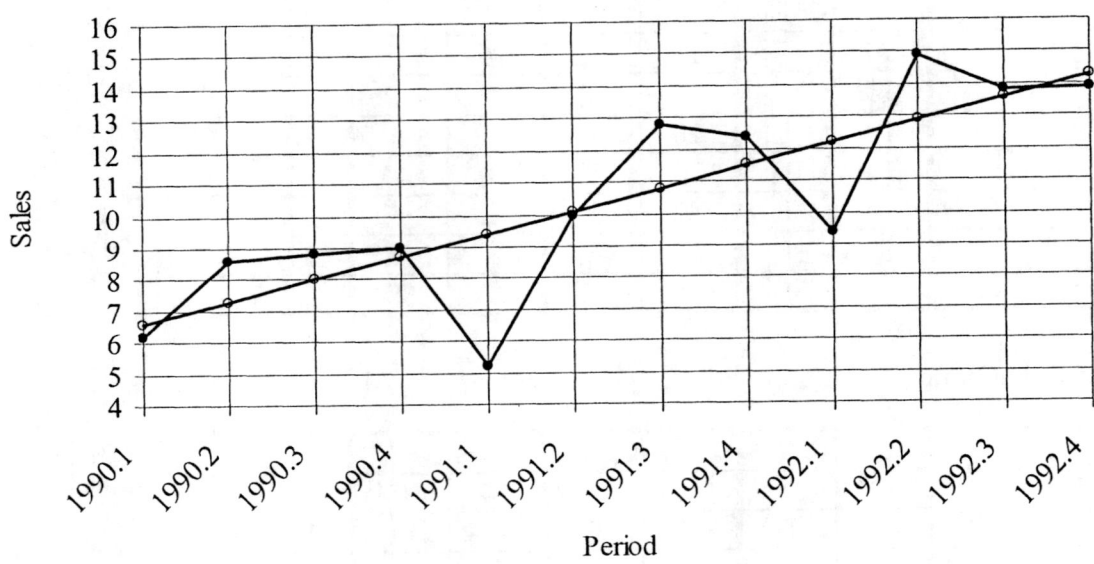

Cyclical variation is typically associated with the economic business cycle, which means that cycles tend to be long (five years or more) and irregular. In data sets that cover relatively short periods of time, it is generally impossible to distinguish cyclical variation from the secular trend. Thus, although a cyclical component may be present in the sales data for VWX, it cannot be identified. The importance of this problem depends largely on the type of forecast that is desired. Cyclical variation is crucial to the accuracy of long-term forecasts. It may be irrelevant when forecasting sales in the short-term. Forecasts that incorporate a cyclical component generally do so by the application of subjectively determined adjustments to forecasts derived by quantitative methods. The magnitudes of the adjustments are usually based on qualitative data derived from market research or barometric methods.

2.   The linear trend estimate is shown below. The standard error of the regression analysis is 1.93 and the coefficient of determination is 0.65. The t-ratio is highly significant.

Sales = 5.9 + 0.7 t

(4.36)

The forecast errors represent the combined effect of random and seasonal variation. Cyclical variation, if present in the time series, may also be a component of the forecast errors. It is not possible to identify cyclical variation without additional information.

The RMSE is equal to the square root of the average of the sum of the squared forecast variations:

$$RMSE = \sqrt{\frac{\sum(A_t - F_t)^2}{n}} = \sqrt{\frac{37.08}{12}} = \sqrt{3.09} = 1.76$$

The RMSE can be calculated directly from the standard error of the regression (SE) by multiplying the standard error by the square root of the ratio of the number of degrees of freedom over the number of observations:

$$RMSE = SE\sqrt{\frac{d.f.}{n}} = 1.93\sqrt{\frac{10}{12}} = 1.76$$

Note that this method only works if the variable to be forecast has <u>not</u> been transformed. See the solution to Problem 3.

The coefficient of determination indicates that this trend equation predicts 65% of the variation in sales. Examination of the forecast errors indicates that some of the remaining unexplained variation is attributable to seasonal variation.

Period	Trend	Sales (A)	Sales (F)	(A - F)	$(A - F)^2$
1990.1	1	6.2	6.6	-0.4	0.16
1990.2	2	8.6	7.3	1.3	1.69
1990.3	3	8.8	8.0	0.8	0.64
1990.4	4	9.0	8.7	0.3	0.09
1991.1	5	5.2	9.4	-4.2	17.64
1991.2	6	10.0	10.1	-0.1	0.01
1991.3	7	12.8	10.8	2.0	4.00
1991.4	8	12.4	11.5	0.9	0.81
1992.1	9	9.4	12.2	-2.8	7.84
1992.2	10	14.9	12.9	2.0	4.00
1992.3	11	13.8	13.6	0.2	0.04
1992.4	12	13.9	14.3	-0.4	0.16

Chapter 5: Problem 2

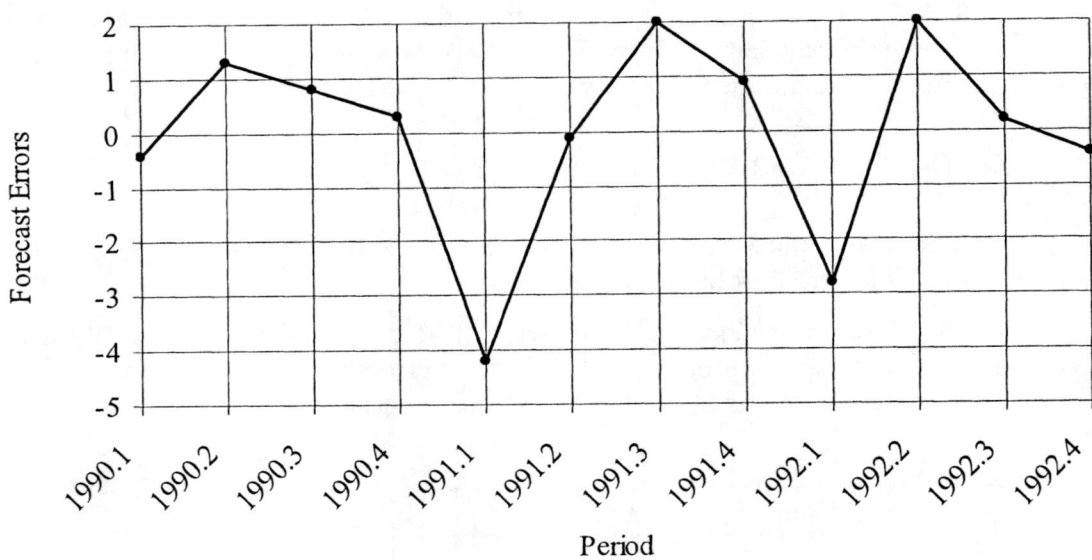

3.   The results obtained by application of linear regression to the transformed values of SALES (ln SALES) are shown below. The standard error of the regression analysis is 0.22 and the coefficient of determination is 0.58. The t-ratio is highly significant.

ln Sales = 1.84 + 0.07 t

(3.74)

The growth rate is calculated as follows:

$\ln(1+g) = 0.07$ so $1 + g = e^{0.07} = 1.0725$ and $g = 0.0725$ or 7.25%

The RMSE is 1.756. It is calculated from the sum of the squared errors in the table by the formula that was used in Problem 2. Note that the standard error of the regression (SE) cannot be used to calculate the RMSE in this case. When the dependent variable has been transformed, then the SE is calculated from the forecast errors associated with the transformed values, which are not the same as the actual forecast errors.

The coefficient of determination (R^2) indicates that 58% of the variation in sales is explained by the constant growth rate model. This is less than the value for the linear trend model. The RMSE is also slightly lower for the linear trend model. As in that model, some of the unexplained variation appears to have a seasonal pattern.

Period	Sales (A)	Sales (lnF)	Sales (F)	(A - F)	$(A - F)^2$
1990.1	6.2	1.91	6.8	-0.6	0.36
1990.2	8.6	1.98	7.2	1.4	1.96
1990.3	8.8	2.05	7.8	1.0	1.00
1990.4	9.0	2.12	8.3	0.7	0.49
1991.1	5.2	2.19	8.9	-3.7	13.69
1991.2	10.0	2.26	9.6	0.4	0.16
1991.3	12.8	2.33	10.3	2.5	6.25
1991.4	12.4	2.40	11.0	1.4	1.96
1992.1	9.4	2.47	11.8	-2.4	5.76
1992.2	14.9	2.54	12.7	2.2	4.85
1992.3	13.8	2.61	13.6	0.2	0.04
1992.4	13.9	2.68	14.6	-0.7	0.49

4.   The seasonally adjusted linear trend estimate is shown below. The standard error of the regression analysis is 1.26 and the coefficient of determination is 0.90. The t-ratio for the trend is highly significant. The t-ratio for the first dummy variable is significant at the 5% level. The t-ratios for the second and third dummy variables are not significant.

$$Sales = 6.9 + 0.6\ t - 3.0\ D_1 + 0.6\ D_2 + 0.6\ D_3$$

$$(5.45)\quad (-2.79)\quad (0.58)\quad (0.62)$$

The dummy variables are defined as follows:

$D_1 = 1$ in quarter 1 and 0 in other quarters

$D_2 = 1$ in quarter 2 and 0 in other quarters

$D_3 = 1$ in quarter 3 and 0 in other quarters

The RMSE is 0.96, a value that is substantially lower than those found for the linear trend model and the constant growth model. It is calculated from the sum of the squared errors (11.14) in the table using the formula that was defined in Problem 2. Note that the RMSE can be calculated directly from the standard error of the regression (SE) in this case because no transformations were applied.

The coefficient of determination indicates that this seasonally adjusted trend equation predicts 90% of the variation in sales. This is a substantial improvement over the value obtained from the linear trend estimated in Problem 2 and the constant growth model estimated in Problem 3. Examination of the forecast errors indicates that the seasonal pattern that was present in the errors in Problem 2 has been eliminated.

Period	Trend	Sales (A)	Sales (F)	(A - F)	$(A - F)^2$
1990.1	1	6.2	4.5	1.7	2.89
1990.2	2	8.6	8.7	-0.1	0.01
1990.3	3	8.8	9.3	-0.5	0.25
1990.4	4	9	9.3	-0.3	0.09
1991.1	5	5.2	6.9	-1.7	2.89
1991.2	6	10	11.1	-1.1	1.21
1991.3	7	12.8	11.7	1.1	1.21
1991.4	8	12.4	11.7	0.7	0.49
1992.1	9	9.4	9.3	0.1	0.01
1992.2	10	14.9	13.5	1.4	1.96
1992.3	11	13.8	14.1	-0.3	0.09
1992.4	12	13.9	14.1	-0.2	0.04

Chapter 5: Problem 4

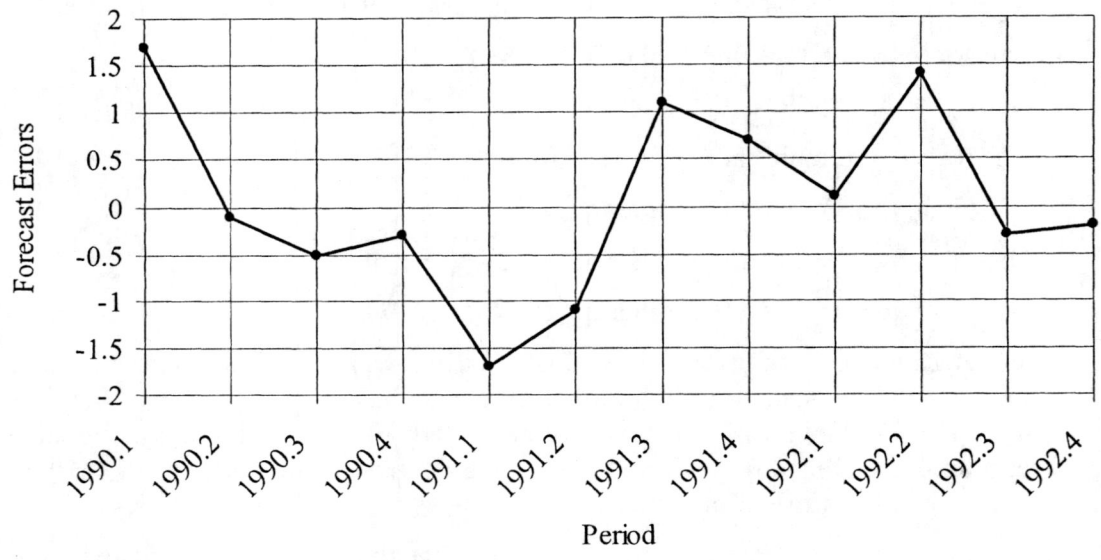

5. The seasonal adjustment factors from the ratio-to-trend method are listed below:

Seasonal 1 (S_1): $(0.94 + 0.55 + 0.77)/3 = 0.75$

Seasonal 2 (S_2): $(1.18 + 0.99 + 1.16)/3 = 1.11$

Seasonal 3 (S_3): $(1.10 + 1.19 + 1.01)/3 = 1.10$

Seasonal 4 (S_4): $(1.03 + 1.08 + 0.97)/3 = 1.03$

The seasonally adjusted forecasts are calculated by multiplying the trend forecasts by the appropriate seasonal adjustment factor; e.g., $SF = (F)(S_1)$ for quarter 1. For example, for 1990 quarter 1 $F = 6.6$ and $S_1 = 0.75$, so the seasonally adjusted value is $SF = (6.6)(0.75) = 5.0$.

The RMSE is 0.93, a value that is substantially lower than those found for the linear trend model and the constant growth model and is slightly lower than that obtained from the seasonally adjusted dummy variable linear trend model. It is calculated from the sum of the squared errors (10.39) in the table using the formula defined in Problem 2.

So far it appears that the linear trend model seasonally adjusted by the ratio-to-trend method is the best sales forecasting model for VWX.

Period	Sales (A)	Sales (F)	(A/F)	(SF)	$(A - SF)^2$
1990.1	6.2	6.6	0.94	5.0	1.44
1990.2	8.6	7.3	1.18	8.1	0.25
1990.3	8.8	8.0	1.10	8.8	0.00
1990.4	9.0	8.7	1.03	9.0	0.00
1991.1	5.2	9.4	0.55	7.1	3.61
1991.2	10.0	10.1	0.99	11.2	1.44
1991.3	12.8	10.8	1.19	11.9	0.81
1991.4	12.4	11.5	1.08	11.8	0.36
1992.1	9.4	12.2	0.77	9.2	0.04
1992.2	14.9	12.9	1.16	14.3	0.36
1992.3	13.8	13.6	1.01	15.0	1.44
1992.4	13.9	14.3	0.97	14.7	0.64

6. The completed table is given below. The forecasts obtained using the ratio-to-trend seasonal adjustment to the linear trend have the lowest RMSE and are, therefore, the logical choice. It turns out that this model does the best job of forecasting the actual observed values for the four quarters of 1993, which are 12.2, 17.1, 19.1, and 17.4.

Model	Linear Trend	Constant Growth Rate	Seasonal Dummy Variables	Ratio-To Trend
RMSE	1.76	1.75	0.96	0.93
1993.1	15.0	15.6	11.7	11.3
1993.2	15.7	16.8	15.9	17.4
1993.3	16.4	18.0	16.5	18.0
1993.4	17.1	19.3	16.5	17.6

7. The three-period moving average forecast of the demand for crystals in January of 1993 is $(15.0 + 13.8 + 22.6)/3 = 17.1$. The RMSE for this model is 7.55; i.e., the square root of $513.1/9 = 57.0$.

Month	Demand (A)	Demand (F)	$(A - F)^2$
Jan-92	25.6		
Feb-92	24.7		
Mar-92	21.3		
Apr-92	13.9	23.9	100.0
May-92	12.6	20.0	54.8
Jun-92	18.0	15.9	4.4
Jul-92	21.5	14.8	44.9
Aug-92	22.3	17.4	24.0
Sep-92	30.7	20.6	102.0
Oct-92	15.0	24.8	96.0
Nov-92	13.8	22.7	79.2
Dec-92	22.6	19.8	7.8

8.	The five-period moving average forecast of the demand for crystals in January of 1993 is (22.3 + 30.7 + 15.0 + 13.8 + 22.6)/5 = 20.9. The RMSE for this model is 6.60; i.e., the square root of 305.1/7 = 43.6. The RMSE for this model is lower than that for the three period model, which indicates that this model fits the data better.

Month	Demand (A)	Demand (F)	$(A - F)^2$
Jan-92	25.6		
Feb-92	24.7		
Mar-92	21.3		
Apr-92	13.9		
May-92	12.6		
Jun-92	18.0	19.6	2.6
Jul-92	21.5	18.1	11.6
Aug-92	22.3	17.5	23.0
Sep-92	30.7	17.7	169.0
Oct-92	15.0	21.0	36.0
Nov-92	13.8	21.5	59.3
Dec-92	22.6	20.7	3.6

9.	The exponential smoothing forecast of the demand for crystals in January of 1993 is (0.6)(22.6) + (1 - 0.6)(16.2) = 20.0. The RMSE for this model is 6.38; i.e., the square root of 488.4/12 = 40.7. The RMSE for this model is lower than that for the three period moving average model and the five period moving average model.

Month	Demand (A)	Demand (F)	$(A-F)^2$
Jan-92	25.6	20.2	29.2
Feb-92	24.7	23.4	1.7
Mar-92	21.3	24.2	8.4
Apr-92	13.9	22.5	74.0
May-92	12.6	17.3	22.1
Jun-92	18.0	14.5	12.3
Jul-92	21.5	16.6	24.0
Aug-92	22.3	19.5	7.8
Sep-92	30.7	21.2	90.3
Oct-92	15.0	26.9	141.6
Nov-92	13.8	19.8	36.0
Dec-92	22.6	16.2	41.0

10. The exponential smoothing forecast of the demand for crystals in January of 1993 is $(0.1)(22.6) + (1 - 0.1)(19.7) = 20.0$. The RMSE for this model is 5.60, i.e., the square root of $376.7/12 = 31.4$. The RMSE for this model is lower than those for the other three models, which indicates that the exponential smoothing model with a weight of 0.1 fits the data better than the other models.

Month	Demand (A)	Demand (F)	$(A - F)^2$
Jan-92	25.6	20.2	29.2
Feb-92	24.7	20.7	16.0
Mar-92	21.3	21.1	0.0
Apr-92	13.9	21.1	51.8
May-92	12.6	20.4	60.8
Jun-92	18.0	19.6	2.6
Jul-92	21.5	19.4	4.4
Aug-92	22.3	19.6	7.3
Sep-92	30.7	19.9	116.6
Oct-92	15.0	21.0	36.0
Nov-92	13.8	20.4	43.6
Dec-92	22.6	19.7	8.4

11. With regard to a moving average model, the degree of smoothing is greatest when every period in the data set is used to calculate the forecast; i.e., when the number of periods is as large as possible. Thus, the moving average forecast of demand for January of 1993 when the maximum possible smoothing is applied is 20.2, the mean of the data set. With regard to an exponential smoothing model, the degree of smoothing is greatest when the weight used to calculate the estimate is zero; i.e., when the forecast is equal to the initial estimate, which is the average of the entire data set. This means that the exponential smoothing forecast is the same as the moving average forecast when smoothing is at a maximum. The RMSE for this model is 5.35, i.e., the square root of $343.2/12 = 28.6$. The RMSE for this model is lower than those for the previous four models, which indicates that the exponential smoothing model with a weight of zero fits the data better than the other models. In other words, the mean of the data set fits the data better than any of the previous models, which implies that demand varies randomly around its mean.

Month	Demand (A)	Demand (F)	$(A - F)^2$
Jan-92	25.6	20.2	29.2
Feb-92	24.7	20.2	20.3
Mar-92	21.3	20.2	1.2
Apr-92	13.9	20.2	39.7
May-92	12.6	20.2	57.8
Jun-92	18.0	20.2	4.8
Jul-92	21.5	20.2	1.7
Aug-92	22.3	20.2	4.4
Sep-92	30.7	20.2	110.3
Oct-92	15.0	20.2	24.0
Nov-92	13.8	20.2	41.0
Dec-92	22.6	20.2	5.8

12.   With regard to a moving average model, the degree of smoothing is least when only one period in the data set is used to calculate the forecast; i.e., when the number of periods in the average is one. Thus, the moving average forecast of demand for January of 1993 when the maximum possible smoothing is applied is 22.6, the last value observed in the data set. With regard to an exponential smoothing model, the degree of smoothing is least when the weight used to calculate the estimate is one; i.e., when the forecast is equal to the most recent observation. This means that the exponential smoothing forecast is the same as the moving average forecast when smoothing is at a minimum. The RMSE for this model is 6.69, i.e., the square root of 536.1/12 = 44.7. The RMSE for this model is higher than those for all but the three period moving average model.

The overall conclusion of this exercise is that this data set exhibits a pattern of variation which is estimated best by a model with the maximum possible degree of smoothing. Arizona Crystal should, accordingly, anticipate a monthly demand equal to the average of all previous month's orders.

Month	Demand (A)	Demand (F)	$(A - F)^2$
Jan-92	25.6	20.2	29.2
Feb-92	24.7	25.6	0.8
Mar-92	21.3	24.7	11.6
Apr-92	13.9	21.3	24.8
May-92	12.6	13.9	1.7
Jun-92	18.0	12.6	29.2
Jul-92	21.5	18.0	12.3
Aug-92	22.3	21.5	0.6
Sep-92	30.7	22.3	70.6
Oct-92	15.0	31.7	246.5
Nov-92	13.8	15.0	1.4
Dec-92	22.6	13.8	77.4

13.   Reduced form equations are derived by a process of substitution. The first step, in this case, is to substitute Equations (1) and (2) into (3). This yields

$S_0 + S_1 P_t = D_0 - D_1 P_t + D_2 A_t$

This equation can be solved to yield the following reduced form equation for price.

$P_t = (D_0 - S_0)/(D_1 + S_1) + A_t D_2/(D_1 + S_1)$

The reduced form equation for quantity is found by substituting the reduced form equation for price into either the supply or the demand equation. In this case, it is more convenient to use the supply equation, which yields the following reduced form equation.

$Q_t = S_0 + S_1 \{(D_0 - S_0)/(D_1 + S_1) + A_t D_2/(D_1 + S_1)\}$

The above equation can be written in the following more convenient form.

$Q_t = S_0 + S_1 (D_0 - S_0)/(D_1 + S_1) + A_t (S_1 D_2)/(D_1 + S_1)$

14. With the insertion of the estimated parameter values, the two reduced form equations become:

$P_t = (45 - 5)/(5 + 15) + A_t /(5 + 15) = 2 + 0.05 A_t$

$Q_t = 5 + 15 (2 + 0.05 A_t) = 35 + 0.75 A_t$

When $A_t = 4$, $P_t = 2.2$, $Q_t = 38$, and $TR_t = 83.6$. When $A_t = 10$, $P_t = 2.5$, $Q_t = 42.5$, and $TR_t = 106.25$. The $6 million increase in expenditures on advertising and promotion yields an increase in industry revenue of $22.65 million, so the expenditure is quite appropriate.

15. The composite index with each indicator assigned equal weight is just the average of the four indicators. The calculations follow:

Jan-92 $(100 + 40 + 15 + 97)/4 = 63$

Feb-92 $(120 + 50 + 13 + 65)/4 = 62$

Mar-92 $(150 + 40 + 17 + 69)/4 = 69$

Apr-92 $(130 + 40 + 15 + 65)/4 = 62.5$

The composite index with the first indicator assigned a weight of 0.40 and the rest assigned a weight of 0.20 is calculated below.

Jan-92 $(0.40)(100) + (0.20)(40) + (0.20)(15) + (0.20)(97) = 70.4$

Feb-92 $(0.40)(120) + (0.20)(50) + (0.20)(13) + (0.20)(65) = 73.6$

Mar-92 $(0.40)(150) + (0.20)(40) + (0.20)(17) + (0.20)(69) = 85.2$

Apr-92 $(0.40)(130) + (0.20)(40) + (0.20)(15) + (0.20)(65) = 76.0$

The diffusion index is equal to the number of indicators that have increased divided by the total number of indicators. The index for each of the three months for which it is possible to calculate it is given below.

Feb-92 $2/4 = 50\%$

Mar-92 $3/4 = 75\%$

Apr-92 $0/4 = 0\%$

The equal weight composite index declines in February and April and increases in March. The unequal weight composite index increases in February and March and declines in April. The diffusion index is most positive in March, but indicates a decline in April. The values of the three indexes are ambiguous in February, they forecast growth in March, and they forecast a cyclical downturn in April.

CHAPTER 6

PRODUCTION THEORY AND ESTIMATION

Learning Objectives

This chapter is a review of the microeconomic theory of production. When you have completed the material in this chapter you should understand how the production function can be used to describe a firm's technology in terms of the relationship between input utilization and output production, how to determine the optimal level and combination of inputs, and how to determine the optimal level of production. Further, you should understand the difference between short and long-run production decisions, the concept of returns to scale, and the importance of technological innovation and its relationship with international competitiveness. Finally, you should understand how the Cobb-Douglas production function is used to empirically estimate output elasticities and how these estimated elasticities are interpreted and used in managerial decisions.

Summary of Notation and Formulas

(6-1) $Q = f(L, K)$

Equation 6-1 is a mathematical expression that represents a production function, where Q is the number of units of output produced per time period (also referred to as total product or TP), L is the quantity of labor employed per time period, and K is the quantity of capital employed per time period.

(6-2) $MP_L = \dfrac{\Delta TP}{\Delta L} = \dfrac{\Delta Q}{\Delta L}$

(6-3) $AP_L = \dfrac{TP}{L} = \dfrac{Q}{L}$

Equations 6-2 and 6-3 define the marginal product (MP) of labor and the average product (AP) of labor in terms of total product (TP or Q) and the quantity of labor (L).

(6-4) $E_L = \dfrac{\%\Delta Q}{\%\Delta L}$

(6-5) $E_L = \dfrac{\Delta Q / Q}{\Delta L / L} = \dfrac{\Delta Q / \Delta L}{Q / L} = \dfrac{MP_L}{AP_L}$

Equations 6-4 and 6-5 define the output elasticity of labor (E_L). Equation 6-4 defines it as the percentage change in output (%ΔQ) divided by the corresponding percentage change in the quantity of labor employed (%ΔL) marginal revenue product. Equation 6-5 defines it in terms of the marginal product of labor (MP_L) and the average product of labor (AP_L).

(6-6) $MRP_L = (MP_L)(MR)$

(6-7) $\quad MRC_L = \dfrac{\Delta TC}{\Delta L}$

Equations 6-6 and 6-7 define the marginal revenue product of labor (MRP$_L$) and the marginal resource cost (MRC$_L$) of labor in terms of the marginal product of labor (MP$_L$), the marginal revenue (MR) of output, the total cost (TC) of output, and the quantity of labor (L).

(6-9) $\quad \dfrac{MP_L}{MP_K} = \dfrac{-\Delta K}{\Delta L} = MRTS$

Equation 6-9 defines the marginal rate of technical substitution (MRTS) in two equivalent ways. First, as the negative of the slope of an isoquant and, second, as the ratio of the marginal products of labor and capital.

(6-10) $\quad C = wL + rK$

(6-11) $\quad K = \dfrac{C}{r} - \dfrac{w}{r}L$

Equations 6-10 and 6-11 define the total cost (C) and the isocost line, respectively, in terms of the quantity of labor (L), the quantity of capital (K), the wage rate (w), and the rental price of capital (r).

(6-12) $\quad MRTS = \dfrac{w}{r}$

(6-13) $\quad \dfrac{MP_L}{MP_K} = \dfrac{w}{r}$

(6-14) $\quad \dfrac{MP_L}{w} = \dfrac{MP_K}{r}$

Equations 6-12, 6-13, and 6-14 are alternative ways of expressing the necessary condition for the optimal combination of inputs. The first states that the optimum combination is found where the absolute value of the slope of an isoquant (MRTS) is equal to the absolute value of the slope of the isocost line. The second notes that the marginal rate of technical substitution is equal to the ratio of the marginal products of labor and capital and is therefore equal to the absolute value of the slope of the isocost line at the optimum. The last rewrites the second to show that it implies that the optimum combination of inputs is found where the marginal product of an input divided its cost per unit is the same for all inputs.

(6-15) $\quad MRP_L = w$

(6-16) $\quad MRP_K = r$

(6-17) $\quad (MP_L)(MR) = w$

(6-18) $\quad (MP_K)(MR) = r$

(6-19) $\quad \dfrac{MP_L}{MP_K} = \dfrac{w}{r}$

Equations 6-15 and 6-16 define the quantities of inputs that a firm should hire in order to maximize profits in terms of the wage (w), the marginal revenue product of labor (MRP_L), the rental price of capital (r), and the marginal revenue product of capital (MRP_K). They also define the firm's input demand functions. Equations 6-17 and 6-18 are obtained by noting that the marginal revenue product of an input is equal to the marginal product (MP) of the input times the marginal revenue of the output. Finally, Equation 6-19 is obtained by taking the ratio of the previous two equations. It is the same as Equation 6-13, which shows that a firm that hires the profit maximizing quantities of inputs and so produces the profit maximizing quantity of output is behaving in a way that will ensure that the optimal, cost minimizing combination of inputs is employed.

(6-20) $\lambda Q = F(hL, hK)$

Equation 6-20 is used to define returns to scale in terms of a production function. If the quantity of labor (L) and the quantity of capital (K) employed by a firm are both increased by the same proportion (h), then the proportional increase (λ) in output (Q) will be greater than, equal to, or less than h depending upon whether the production function exhibits increasing, constant, or decreasing returns to scale, respectively.

(6-21) $Q = AK^a L^b$

(6-22) $\ln Q = \ln A + a \ln K + b \ln L$

Equations 6-21 and 6-22 define the Cobb-Douglas functional form in its general and linearized forms. The second is derived from the first by taking the natural logarithm (ln) of both sides of the function. It is used with linear regression analysis to estimate the output elasticities (a and b) of capital and labor (K and L), respectively.

True-False Questions

T F 1. The production function is an equation, table, or graph that shows the maximum output that can be produced from different combinations of inputs.

T F 2. Production refers to all activities involved in the production of goods and services.

T F 3. Fixed inputs are those that can never be changed.

T F 4. All inputs are variable in the long run.

T F 5. All inputs are fixed in the short run.

T F 6. Scale is a short-run concept.

T F 7. The firm plans in the short run and operates in the long run.

T F 8. The slope of the short-run production function is equal to the average product of the variable input.

T F 9. Output elasticity is equal to the marginal product of an input divided by the average product of the input.

T F 10. The law of diminishing returns is a long-run concept.

T F 11. The marginal product of the variable input is at a maximum at the level of output that corresponds to the inflection point on the short-run production function.

T F 12. The average product and the marginal product of the variable input are equal at the level of output that corresponds to the inflection point on the short-run production function.

T F 13. When an input's average product exceeds its marginal product, average product is increasing.

T F 14. The law of diminishing returns holds that the marginal product of a variable input will eventually decline if output is increased while at least one input is fixed.

T F 15. Stage II of production begins at a level of output where the average product of the variable input is at a maximum and ends where the marginal product of the variable input is equal to zero.

T F 16. Stage I of production begins where the average product of the variable input is equal to the marginal product of the variable input.

T F 17. In general, a firm should continue to hire additional units of an input so long as the marginal revenue product of the input is greater than the marginal resource cost of the input.

T F 18. The marginal revenue product of an input is equal to the change in the firm's total revenue that results from employing an additional unit of a variable input.

T F 19. The marginal resource cost of an input is equal to the change in total cost that results from hiring an additional unit of a variable input.

T F 20. The marginal resource cost of an input is identical to the firm's demand curve for that input.

T F 21. An isoquant shows all combinations of two inputs that will result in the same level of output.

T F 22. Ridge lines drawn on an isoquant map separate Stage II from Stages I and III of production.

T F 23. Firms will only operate at points on an isoquant map that are between the ridge lines.

T F 24. The absolute value of the slope of an isoquant is equal to the ratio of the marginal products of the inputs.

T F 25. The marginal rate of technical substitution measures the number of units of one input that can be dispensed with while holding output constant when one additional unit of the other input is added.

T F 26. The closer an isoquant is to a straight line, the closer the inputs are to being perfect complements.

T F 27. If the marginal rate of technical substitution is the same at all points on an isoquant, then the two inputs are perfect substitutes.

T F 28. The isocost line represents all combinations of inputs that have the same total cost.

T F 29. The absolute value of the slope of the isocost line is equal to the ratio of input prices.

T F 30. If two isocost lines are parallel, then both have the same input price ratio but the one further from the origin represents a higher level of total cost.

T F 31. If a firm is minimizing the total cost of producing a given level of output, then it must also be maximizing the level of output produced at a given level of total cost.

T F 32. The point of tangency between a convex isoquant and an isocost line represents an optimal combination of inputs.

T F 33. Every point on an expansion path represents a combination of inputs that minimizes the cost of producing a given level of output.

T F 34. All expansion paths are straight lines through the origin.

T F 35. If a firm is maximizing profit, then it must be employing a combination of inputs that is on its expansion path.

T F 36. If a firm is employing a combination of inputs that is on its expansion path, then it must be maximizing profits.

T F 37. If the price of an input increases, then the firm will use more of it.

T F 38. If a firm is experiencing increasing returns to scale, then a doubling of output will require more than a doubling of all inputs.

T F 39. Decreasing returns to scale arise because of increased specialization and division of labor at higher levels of output.

T F 40. Most firms operate at a level of output that results in nearly constant returns to scale.

T F 41. One advantage of the use of the Cobb-Douglas production function for empirical estimation is that it can be expressed as a linear function.

T F 42. If the sum of the output elasticities for a production function is greater than one, then the production function exhibits decreasing returns to scale.

T F 43. The law of comparative advantage postulates that even if a nation is less efficient or has an absolute disadvantage with respect to another in the production of all commodities, there is still a basis for mutually beneficial trade.

T F 44. A country that has an absolute advantage in the production of a particular good must also have a comparative advantage in the production of that good.

T F 45. A country that has a comparative advantage in the production of a particular good must also have an absolute advantage in the production of that good.

T F 46. Product differentiation exists when an industry produces goods that are not identical.

T F 47. Intra-industry trade allows each country to specialize in some variation of a product.

T F 48. A country will import goods in which it has a comparative advantage and export goods in which it has a comparative disadvantage.

T F 49. A country that has a relative abundance of cheap labor will tend to have a comparative advantage in the production of goods that are produced using a lot of labor.

T F 50. Most innovations involve revolutionary departures from previous practices and products.

T F 51. Product innovation is shown on an isoquant map by a shift in all isoquants toward the origin.

T F 52. The product cycle model asserts that innovating firms tend to achieve long-term domination of markets.

T F 53. Innovation tends to be stimulated by an environment where firms are protected from competitive forces.

T F 54. American firms generally stress product innovation while Japanese firms stress process innovation.

T F 55. One disadvantage of modern computerized production methods is that they tend to reduce the optimal lot size, thus reducing total profits.

T F 56. Most innovations are based on new technologies and ideas.

T F 57. The use of robots on automobile assembly lines is an example of product innovation.

T F 58. CAD is an acronym that stands for capital-assisted development.

T F 59. CAM is an acronym that stands for computer-aided manufacturing.

T F 60. CAD-CAM allows firms to develop products more rapidly and at a lower cost.

Multiple Choice Questions

1. Which of the following is an example of a capital input?

    A. Money.
    B. Shares of stock.
    C. Long-term bonds.
    D. A hammer.

2. Which of the following is an example of an intermediate product?

    A. A personal computer.
    B. A barrel of crude oil.
    C. A sports car.
    D. A house.

3. Which of the following is not an assumption associated with the definition of a production function?

    A. Technology remains constant.
    B. Both inputs and outputs are measured in monetary units.
    C. The function shows the maximum level of output possible with a given combination of inputs.
    D. All units of the inputs are homogeneous.

4.   The marginal product of labor is equal to

   A. the additional labor required to produce one more unit of output.
   B. average product when average product is at a minimum.
   C. the additional output produced by hiring one more unit of labor.
   D. the slope of a ray drawn from the origin to a point on the total product curve.

5.   The average product of labor is equal to

   A. the additional labor required to produce one more unit of output.
   B. marginal product when average product is at a minimum.
   C. the additional output produced by hiring one more unit of labor.
   D. the slope of a ray drawn from the origin to a point on the total product curve.

6.   The output elasticity of labor is

   A. equal to one at the level of output where average product is at a maximum.
   B. the percentage change in labor required to produce one more unit of output.
   C. equal to the ratio of total product to the quantity of labor employed.
   D. a measure of the percentage change in output that can result when the quantity of labor is held constant.

7.   The point of inflection on the total product curve corresponds to the level of output where

   A. Stage II of production begins.
   B. average product is at a maximum.
   C. marginal product is at a maximum.
   D. All of the above are correct.

8.   The law of diminishing returns

   A. is reflected in the negatively sloped portion of the marginal product curve.
   B. is the result of specialization and division of labor.
   C. applies in both the short run and the long run.
   D. All of the above are correct.

9.   Stage II of production begins at the point

   A. of inflection of the total product curve.
   B. where average and marginal product are equal.
   C. where total product is at a maximum.
   D. where marginal product is at a maximum.

10.   The marginal revenue product of labor for a firm

   A. will increase if the price of the firm's output increases.
   B. is the firm's demand curve for labor.
   C. will decrease if the firm hires more labor.
   D. All of the above are correct.

11.   An isoquant that is

A. further from the origin represents greater output.
B. flatter represents the trade-offs between inputs that are poor substitutes.
C. negatively sloped represents input combinations associated with Stage I of production.
D. All of the above are correct.

12.   The absolute value of the slope of a convex isoquant

A. is equal to the marginal rate of technical substitution.
B. is equal to the ratio of the marginal products of the two inputs.
C. decreases from left to right.
D. All of the above are correct.

13.   The combination of inputs is optimal

A. at points of tangency between isoquants and isocosts.
B. if the marginal revenue product is equal to the marginal resource cost for all inputs.
C. if the marginal rate of technical substitution between every pair of inputs is equal to the ratio of the prices of those inputs.
D. All of the above are correct.

14.   An isocost line will be shifted further away from the origin

A. if the prices of both inputs increase.
B. if total cost increases.
C. if there is an advance in technology.
D. All of the above are correct.

15.   If isoquants are plotted on a graph with capital measured on the vertical axis and labor on the horizontal axis, then an increase in the wage rate will cause the isocost line

A. to become steeper and the optimal quantity of labor will decrease.
B. to become steeper and the optimal quantity of labor will increase.
C. to become flatter and the optimal quantity of labor will decrease.
D. to become flatter and the optimal quantity of labor will increase.

16.   A line that connects all points where the marginal rate of technical substitution is equal to the ratio of input prices is called the

A. input demand curve.
B. total product curve.
C. expansion path.
D. isocost line.

17. Suppose that three isoquants that represent 10, 20, and 30 units of output are plotted on a graph and a straight line is drawn from the origin through the isoquants. If the portion of the line between the isoquants that represent 10 and 20 units of output is longer than the portion of the line between the isoquants that represent 20 and 30 units of output, then the firm represented by these isoquants

    A. has engaged in product innovation.
    B. is experiencing increasing returns to scale.
    C. is experiencing decreasing returns to scale.
    D. will maximize profits by producing 10 units of output.

18. If the output elasticities of all inputs used by a firm are summed together, then the total

    A. will be greater than one if returns to scale are decreasing.
    B. will be equal to one if returns to scale are constant.
    C. will be less than one if returns to scale are increasing.
    D. All of the above are correct.

19. Which of the following is not a characteristic of production technologies that can be described by the Cobb-Douglas production function?

    A. The marginal product of an input divided by the average product of that input is constant.
    B. The exponents will sum to one if returns to scale are constant.
    C. Linear regression can be used to estimate the parameters of the function.
    D. All of the above are characteristics of the Cobb-Douglas production function.

20. If the marginal product of labor is 2, the marginal product of capital is 4, the wage rate is $3, the rental price of capital is $6, and the price of output is $1.50, then the firm should

    A. Increase output by hiring more labor, more capital, or both.
    B. Hold output constant, but hire more labor and less capital.
    C. Decrease output by reducing the quantity of capital, reducing the number of units of labor, or both.
    D. None of the above is correct.

21. Comparative advantage is the basis for

    A. efficient production.
    B. international trade.
    C. economies of scale.
    D. the capital-labor tradeoff.

22. A country that has an abundance of cheap labor will tend to

    A. import goods that are produced using a lot of labor.
    B. refrain from international trade entirely.
    C. export goods that are produced using a lot of labor.
    D. export goods that are produced using little labor.

23. Intra-industry trade refers to

   A. international trade in differentiated products.
   B. the exchange of information between firms in the same industry.
   C. the exchange of information between firms in different industries.
   D. barter between competing firms.

24. Which of the following acronyms refers to the use of computers to design new products?

   A. CDP
   B. ADP
   C. CAM
   D. CAD

25. By using computers to design and manufacture products, firms are able to

   A. reduce production costs.
   B. reduce the optimal lot size.
   C. reduce the time required to introduce new products.
   D. All of the above are correct.

Problems

Arcane Assemblies was formed in the mid-1980s as the result of an unlikely partnership between Arthur Rex and Bob Merlin. After a rocky start, the company began production of a computer interface enhancer called the Wizard Card. When installed in a computer, the Wizard Card intercepts commands entered from the keyboard and uses artificial intelligence to translate them into the commands that users really intended to enter in the first place.

The first versions of the product were quirky, with serious quality control problems, and Arcane Assemblies came close to bankruptcy. Fortunately, Merlin had another card up his sleeve and, after a long and intensive search, Arthur was able to find an investor willing to support its production. The investor, Holly Grail, has decided to take an active role in the business. She insists that production of the new version of the Wizard Card be planned using the methods of managerial economics. As a way to ensure that this is done, she hires a consulting engineer to analyze the alternative production methods available to the firm. The engineer identifies four types of circuit board assembly systems (A, B, C, and D) and determines the number of Wizard Cards that can be produced per month using the different combinations of labor (L) and capital (K) with each system. The results of the analysis are given in the table that follows.

When Holly presents the production information to Arthur and Merlin, they are initially unsure of how to proceed. A call to the local university yields a suggestion. Why not hire a student as an apprentice? Merlin finds the offer appealing, and the others agree. The following day, you find yourself working for Arcane Assemblies. Solve Problems 1 through 7 using this information.

Labor	Capital (K)			
(L)	A	B	C	D
1	9	6	0	0
2	38	18	9	0
3	51	55	38	24
4	62	96	88	69
5	69	117	128	138
6	70	127	160	180
7	70	132	186	210
8	70	133	206	235
9	70	133	211	245
10	70	133	211	250

1. Begin your analysis of the production possibilities table by calculating the average product (AP_L) and the marginal product (MP_L) of labor and the output elasticity of labor (E_L) for each of the four production systems. Enter these values in the tables below.

Production System A

L	1	2	3	4	5	6	7	8	9	10
AP_L										
MP_L										
E_L										

Production System B

L	1	2	3	4	5	6	7	8	9	10
AP_L										
MP_L										
E_L										

Production System C

L	1	2	3	4	5	6	7	8	9	10
AP_L										
MP_L										
E_L										

Production System D

L	1	2	3	4	5	6	7	8	9	10
AP_L										
MP_L										
E_L										

2. Next, plot the total product curves for each of the production systems in the graph below and then plot the average and marginal product curves for each of the production systems on the four graphs that follow.

Chapter 6: Problem 2

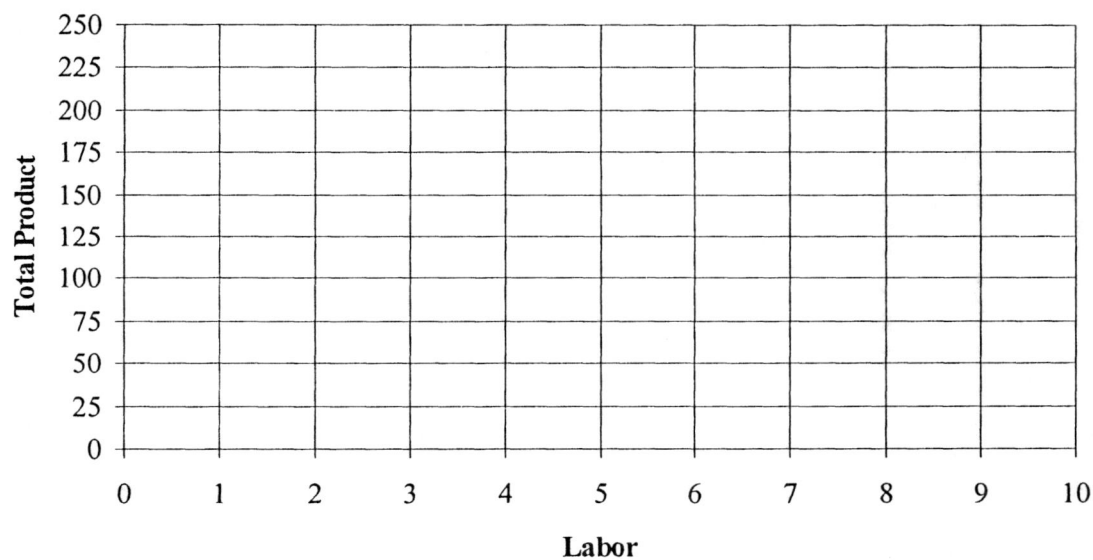

Chapter 6: Problem 2 - System A

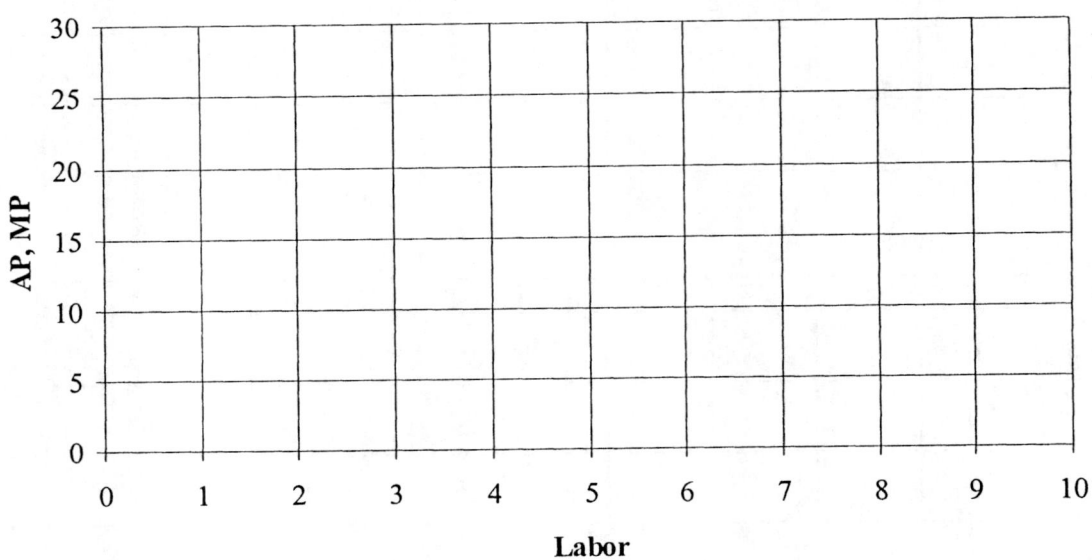

Chapter 6: Problem 2 - System B

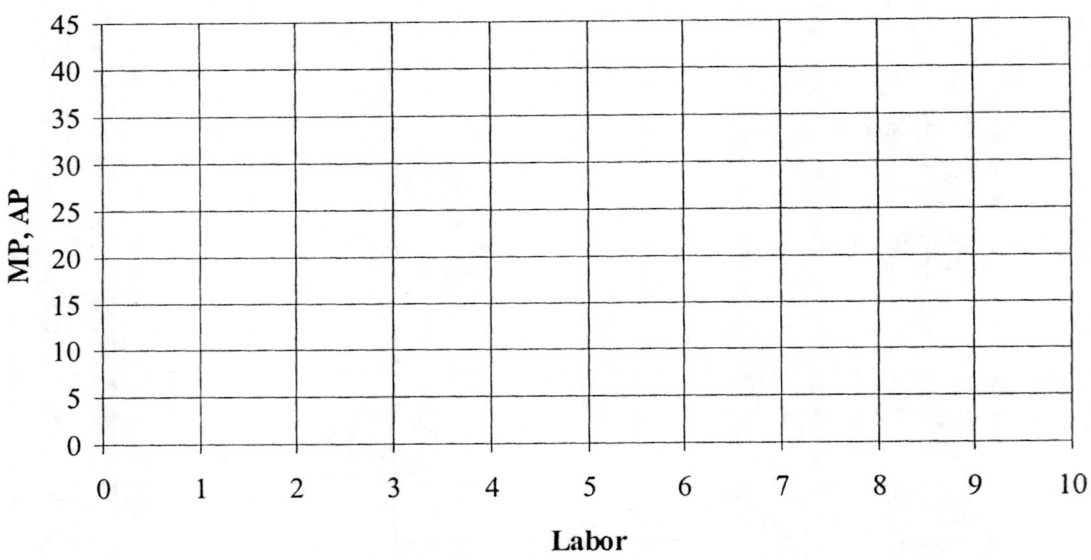

Chapter 6: Problem 2 - System C

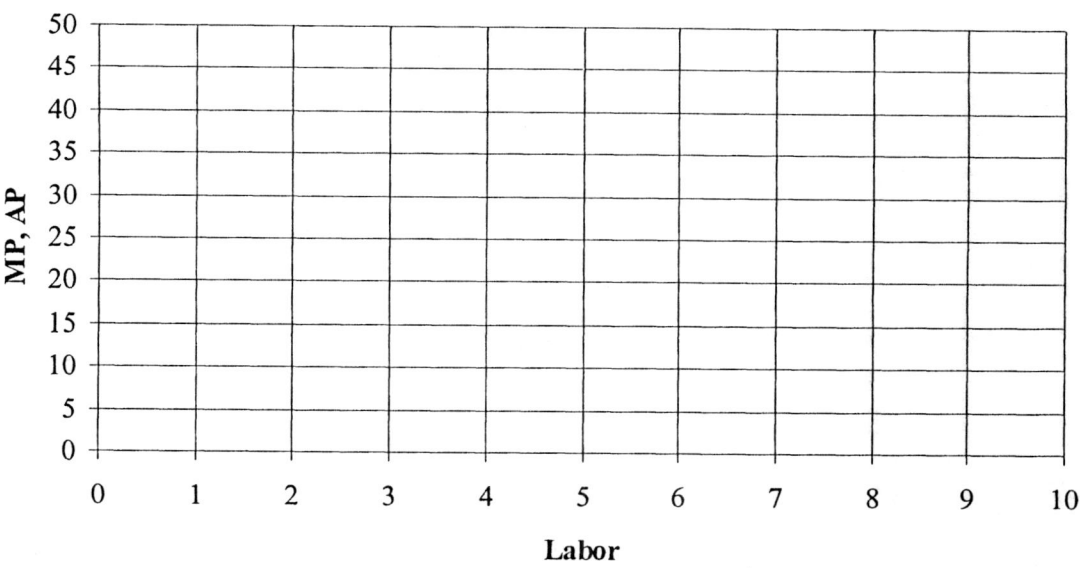

Chapter 6: Problem 2 - System D

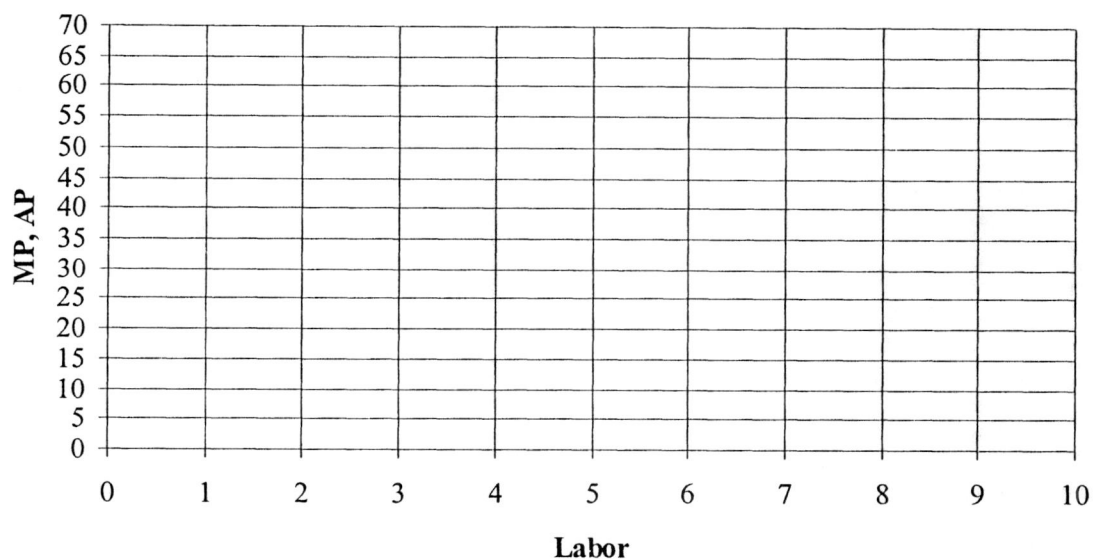

3. Determine the range of output that corresponds to Stage II of production for labor for each of the four production systems and enter this information in the table below. Assume that hiring more than 10 units of labor will not increase output for any of the production systems.

Stage II	Capital (K)			
	A	B	C	D
Begins				
Ends				

With preliminary analysis of the production possibilities completed, you are ready to consider costs and revenues. Arthur believes that Arcane Assemblies can sell as many Wizard Cards as it can produce at a price (net of materials costs and shipping) of $100. Holly's analysis of the local labor market indicates that any number of qualified workers can be hired for $1,800 per month. Finally, Merlin has determined the monthly rental cost of capital for the four production systems to be $8,000 for D, $5,000 for C, $1,000 for B, and zero for A. Production system A involves no capital utilization.

4. Calculate the marginal revenue product of labor for each of the production systems and enter their values in the table below.

Labor (L)	Capital (K)			
	A	B	C	D
1				
2				
3				
4				
5				
6				
7				
8				
9				
10				

5.   Plot the relevant portions of the four labor demand curves for each of the production systems on the graph below. Label the labor demand curves A, B, C, and D. Also plot the labor supply curve on the graph.

Chapter 6: Problem 5

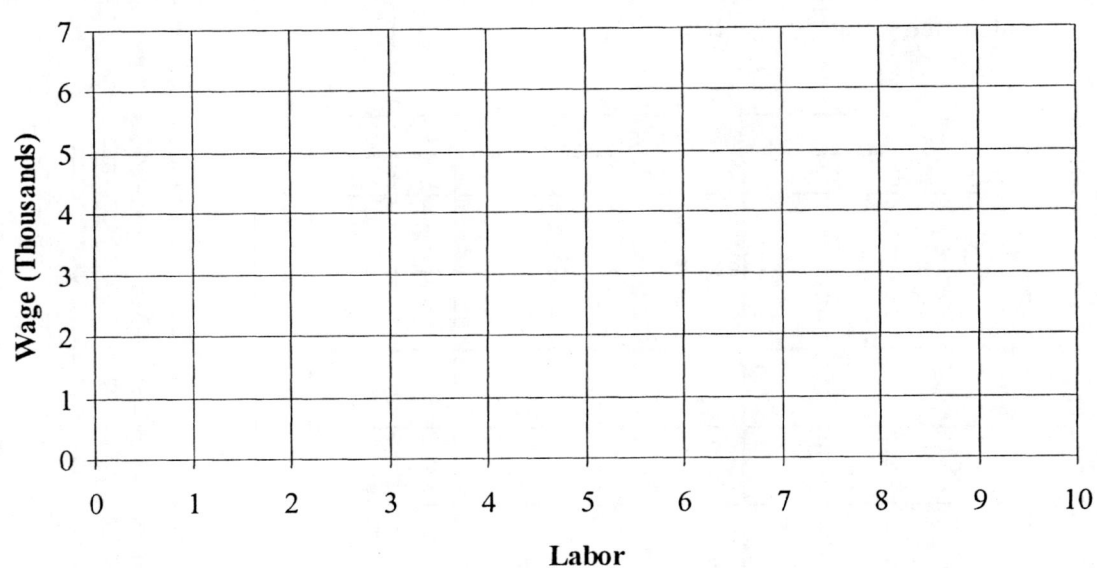

6.   From the graph in Problem 5, determine the number of workers that Arcane Assemblies should employ (L), the total cost of labor (wL), the total cost of production (TC), total product (Q), total revenue (TR), and total profit (π) for each production system and record the values in the table below. Which production system should Arcane Assemblies use and how many units of labor should it employ?

	Capital (K)			
	A	B	C	D
L				
wL				
TC				
Q				
TR				
π				

7.   Finally, show that the production system that was identified as optimal in Problem 6 is also optimal according to the general optimization principle by completing the following steps. First, determine the marginal product and marginal revenue product of capital for each of the four production systems. Assume that Arcane Assemblies employs the number of workers that was found to be optimal in Problem 6. Next, determine the marginal resource cost of each of the four production systems. Enter the values into the table below and then plot the values on the graph that follows. How are these values used to identify the optimal production system?

	Capital (K)			
	A	B	C	D
MP				
MRP				
MRC				

Chapter 6: Problem 7

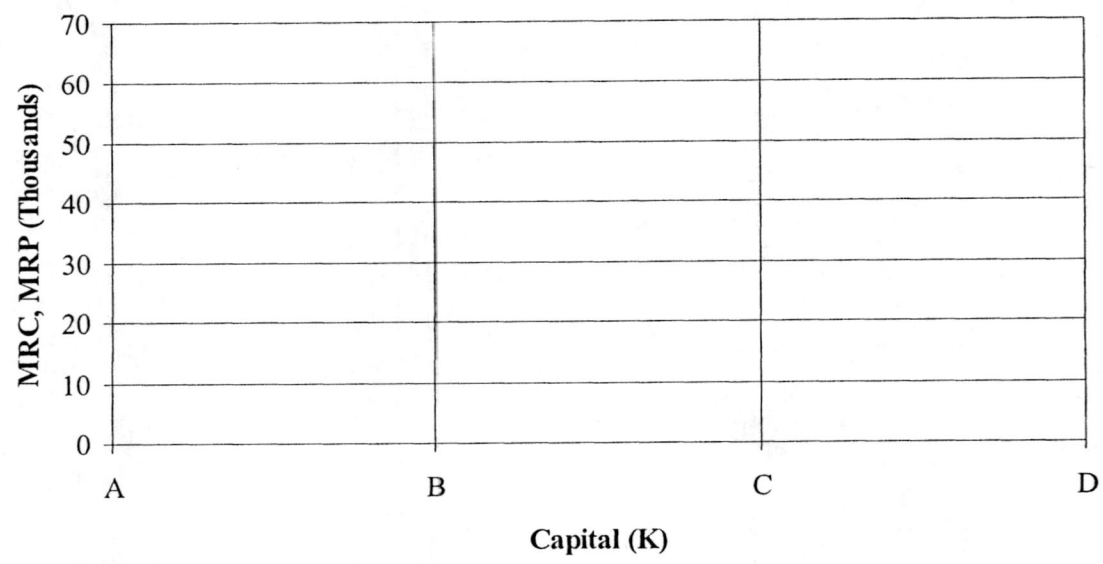

Byzantium Bakery is located on State Street in Yore Town, Pennsylvania. It is a small operation known for its opulently crusty loaves. The owner, Leo Constantius, makes a practice of hiring interns from two well-known cooking schools. They remain at Byzantium Bakery for a three-month internship and then go on to full-time positions in five-star restaurants. Yeast of Eden Cooking College (YECC) and Xavier Unleavened Polytechnic (XUP) both produce highly competent graduates, and Leo has found that productivity is higher if he hires interns from both schools rather than just one. Over the past few years, he has compiled the production possibilities table that is shown below, in which Y represents the number of YECC bakers and X represents the number of XUP bakers.

Y	Loaves of Bread per Hour (Q)							
7	9	21	31	40	48	55	60	64
6	11	22	31	39	46	52	56	59
5	12	22	30	37	43	48	51	53
4	12	21	28	34	39	43	45	48
3	11	19	25	30	34	37	39	40
2	9	16	21	25	28	30	30	29
1	5	12	16	19	21	22	21	19
0	0	7	10	12	13	13	11	8
X=>	0	1	2	3	4	5	6	7

Leo is not sure how to use the information in the table, so he calls up a crusty old economist that he knows at Yore Town University and asks for advice. The economist sends out a student who recently did a wonderful job as an apprentice with Arcane Assemblies. Welcome to your new assignment. Use this information to solve Problems 8 through 12.

8. Use the information in the table to construct an isoquant map. Plot isoquants for Q = 12, Q = 21, Q = 30, Q = 39, and Q = 48 on the graph below.

Chapter 6: Problem 8

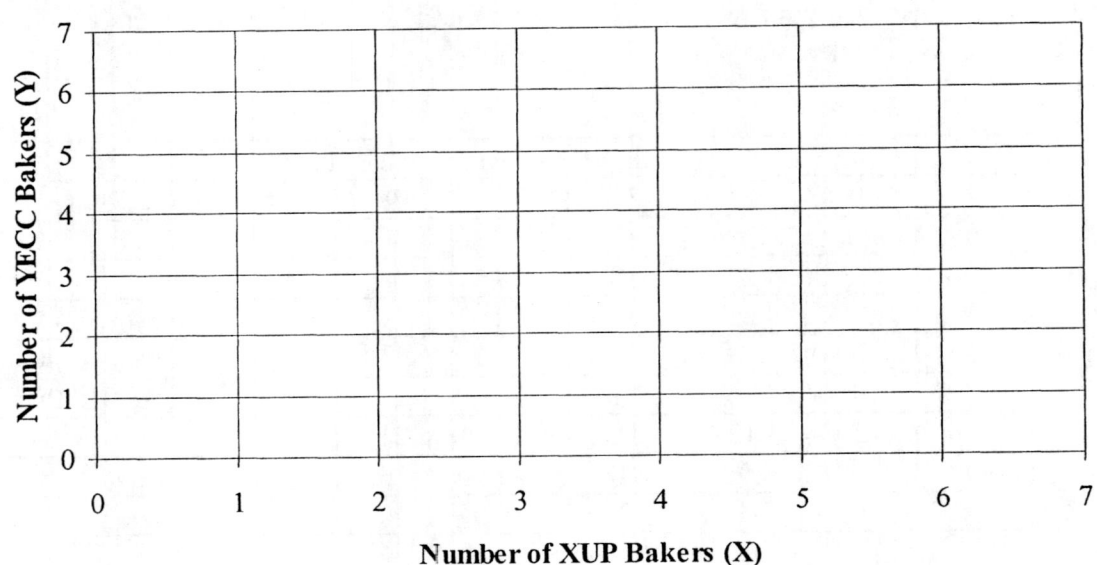

In the past, Leo has paid bakers from both colleges the same wage. Recently, however, the administration at XUP has insisted on a higher wage. The next group of YECC interns will charge $4 per hour while the XUP interns will charge $5 per hour. Leo wonders if he should stop hiring XUP interns entirely or, if he keeps on hiring both XUP and YECC interns, how many of each he should hire.

9. Plot five isocost lines on the graph with the isoquant map from Problem 8. Each of the isocost lines should pass through the one point on each isoquant that represents the optimal combination of bakers. Next, determine the optimal number of bakers from each school, Leo's total cost of bakers, and the vertical and horizontal intercepts of the isocost lines and enter these values in the table below.

	Q = 12	Q = 21	Q = 30	Q = 39	Q = 48
Optimal Y					
Optimal X					
Total Cost					
Y Intercept					
X Intercept					

10. Plot the expansion path and the ridge lines on the graph in Problem 8. If the only inputs used by Byzantium Bakery are the two types of bakers, what are returns to scale like for the firm along the expansion path?

11. Calculate the marginal rate of technical substitution (MRTS) in two ways for each of the five isoquants plotted on the graph in Problem 8. Begin at the optimal combination of X and Y on each isoquant. First, calculate the MRTS for a one unit decrease in X. Second, calculate it for a one unit decrease in Y. Enter your results in the table below.

MRTS	Q = 12	Q = 21	Q = 30	Q = 39	Q = 48
Decrease Y					
Decrease X					

12.   Is there a situation in which Leo should hire only YECC graduates? Is there a situation in which Leo should only hire XUP graduates? If Leo wants to produce 30 loaves per hour and the hourly cost of both types of graduates is the same, how many of each should Leo hire?

The Cimmerian Cutlery Company has estimated the following Cobb-Douglas production function using cross-sectional data on 14 firms in the cutlery industry:

$$\ln Q = 1.20 + 0.30 \ln K + 0.10 \ln L + 0.50 \ln S$$

$$(4.19) \qquad (2.85) \qquad (2.69)$$

$$R^2 = 0.91$$

where Q is the number of utensils produced per month (in thousands), K is the number of units of capital, L is the number of production workers employed, and S is the number of non-production support workers employed. The numbers in parenthesis below the estimated slope coefficients are t values. Use this information to solve Problems 13 through 17 below.

13.   If Cimmerian Cutlery employs 120 units of capital, 600 production workers, and 60 support workers, how many thousands of utensils will be produced per month according to the estimated function?

14.   Find the marginal product and average product of each of the inputs when the firm employs 120 units of capital, 600 production workers, and 60 support workers. Is the firm operating in Stage II of production for all of the inputs?

15.   Find the output elasticities of the three inputs. Determine the returns to scale in production. If the firm doubled the number of units of capital it employs, by what percentage would output increase? What if it doubled the number of units of production labor or of support workers? What if it doubled all inputs?

16. The rental cost of capital per day is $85, the hourly wage of production labor is $5, and the weekly salary of support workers is $285. Is Cimmerian Cutlery using the optimal combination of inputs? If the price per thousand units of cutlery is $200, is Cimmerian Cutlery producing the optimal quantity of output? If not, should it increase production or decrease production?

17. Are the estimated slope coefficients of the Cobb-Douglas production function statistically significant at the 5% level? At the 1% level? How much of the variation in Q does the estimated function explain?

Problems (calculus required)

18. Given: $Q = 20K^{0.3}L^{0.7}$, $C* = \$1,000$, $r = \$30$ and $w = \$10$. Determine the amount of labor and capital that maximizes output and determine the optimal amount of output. Calculate and interpret the Lagrangian multiplier.

19. Given: $Q = 20K^{0.3}L^{0.7}$, $r = \$30$ and $w = \$10$. Determine the amount of labor and capital that the firm should use to minimize the cost of producing 1,562 units of output and determine the optimal cost of production. Calculate and interpret the Lagrangian multiplier.

20.   Given: $Q = 20K^{0.2}L^{0.8}$, $r = \$7$, $w = \$32$, $K = 60$, and $P = \$2$. Determine the amount of labor that the firm should hire in order to maximize short-run profits. Also calculate the level of profit that the firm will realize.

True-False Answers

1	T	13	F	25	T	37	F	49	T
2	T	14	T	26	F	38	F	50	F
3	F	15	T	27	T	39	F	51	F
4	T	16	F	28	T	40	T	52	F
5	F	17	T	29	T	41	T	53	F
6	F	18	T	30	T	42	F	54	T
7	F	19	T	31	T	43	T	55	F
8	F	20	F	32	T	44	F	56	F
9	T	21	T	33	T	45	F	57	F
10	F	22	T	34	F	46	T	58	F
11	T	23	T	35	T	47	T	59	T
12	F	24	T	36	F	48	F	60	T

Multiple Choice Answers

1	D	6	A	11	A	16	C	21	B
2	B	7	C	12	D	17	B	22	C
3	B	8	A	13	D	18	B	23	A
4	C	9	B	14	B	19	D	24	D
5	D	10	D	15	A	20	D	25	D

Solutions to Problems

1.   The average product of labor (AP_L) is equal to the ratio of total product divided by the number of units of labor employed. Under Production System A, for example, total product is 9 ($Q = 9$) when one unit of labor is employed ($L = 1$), so $AP_L = = 9/1 = 9$. When two units of labor are employed ($L = 2$), total product is 38 ($Q = 38$) and $AP_L = 38/2 = 19$.

The marginal product of labor (MP_L) is equal to the change in total product divided by the change in the number of units of labor employed. Under Production System A, for example, total product is 9 (Q = 9) when one unit of labor is employed (L = 1) and 38 (Q = 38) when two units of labor are employed (L = 2), so the marginal product of the first unit of labor is (9 - 0)/(1 - 0) = 9 and the marginal product of the second unit of labor is (38 - 9)/(2 - 1) = 29.

The output elasticity of labor (E_L) is equal to the ratio of the marginal product of labor divided by the average product of labor. Under Production System A, for example, marginal product is 9 (MP_L = 9) and average product is also 9 (AP_L = 9) when one unit of labor is employed, so the output elasticity of labor is 9/9 = 1. When two units of labor are employed, marginal product is 29 (MP_L = 29) and average product is 19 (AP_L = 19) so the output elasticity of labor is 29/19 = 1.53.

Production System A

L	1	2	3	4	5	6	7	8	9	10
AP_L	9.00	19.00	17.00	15.50	13.80	11.67	10.00	8.75	7.78	7.00
MP_L	9.00	29.00	13.00	11.00	7.00	1.00	0.00	0.00	0.00	0.00
E_L	1.00	1.53	0.76	0.71	0.51	0.09	0.00	0.00	0.00	0.00

Production System B

L	1	2	3	4	5	6	7	8	9	10
AP_L	6.00	9.00	18.33	24.00	23.40	21.17	18.86	16.63	14.78	13.30
MP_L	6.00	12.00	37.00	41.00	21.00	10.00	5.00	1.00	0.00	0.00
E_L	1.00	1.33	2.02	1.71	0.90	0.47	0.27	0.06	0.00	0.00

Production System C

L	1	2	3	4	5	6	7	8	9	10
AP_L		4.50	12.67	22.00	25.60	26.67	26.57	25.75	23.44	21.10
MP_L		9.00	29.00	50.00	40.00	32.00	26.00	20.00	5.00	0.00
E_L		2.00	2.29	2.27	1.56	1.20	0.98	0.78	0.21	0.00

Production System D

L	1	2	3	4	5	6	7	8	9	10
AP_L			8.00	17.25	27.60	30.00	30.00	29.38	27.22	25.00
MP_L			24.00	45.00	69.00	42.00	30.00	25.00	10.00	5.00
E_L			3.00	2.61	2.50	1.40	1.00	0.85	0.37	0.20

2. The table given at the beginning of Problem 1 shows the relationship between the quantity of labor employed (L) and total product (Q) for each of four different types of capital (circuit board assembly systems A, B, C, and D). Average product is calculated by taking the ratio of total product to labor (Q/L) and marginal product is calculated by taking the ratio of the change in total product ($\Delta Q/\Delta L$).

Chapter 6: Problem 2

Chapter 6: Problem 2 - System A

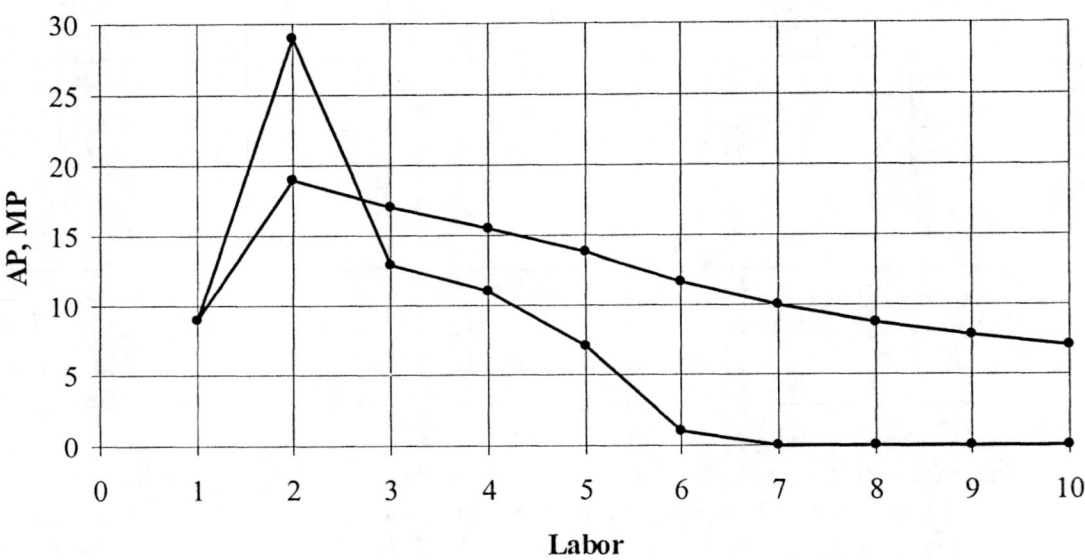

Chapter 6: Problem 2 - System B

Chapter 6: Problem 2 - System C

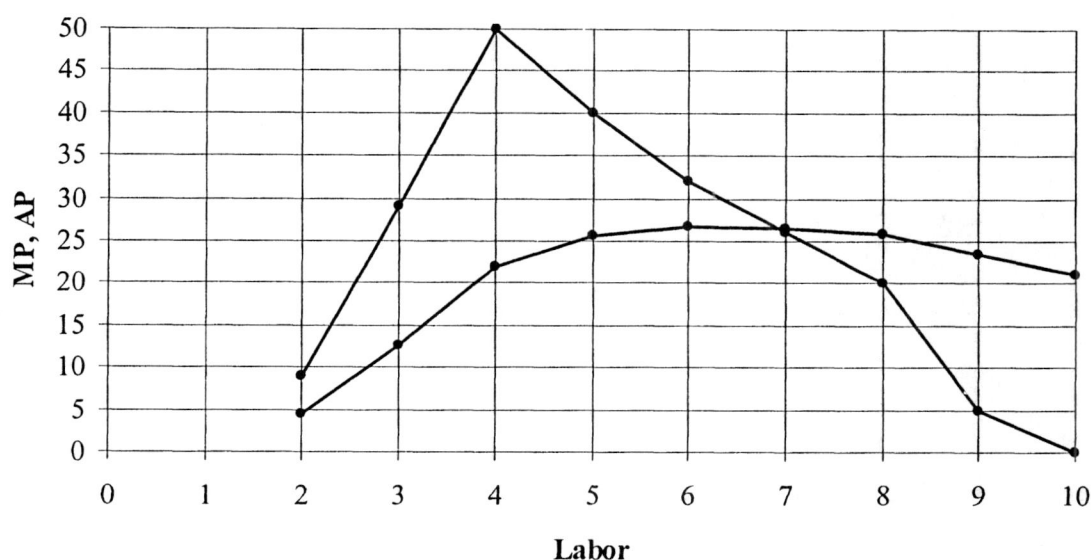

Chapter 6: Problem 2 - System D

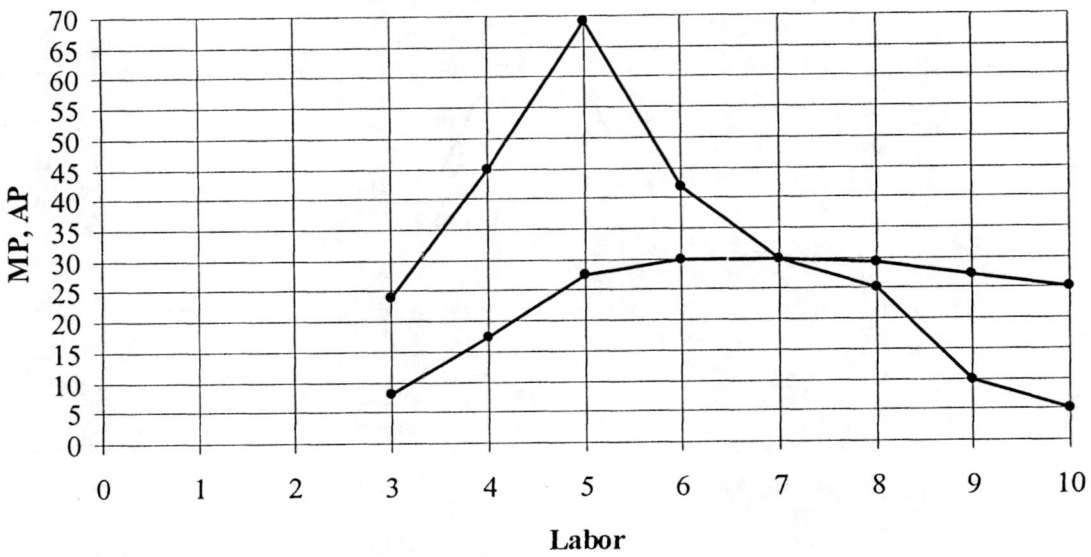

3. Stage II of production begins where the average product of the variable input is at a maximum, i.e., where the marginal and average product of the variable input are equal or where average product begins to decline. Stage II of production ends where total product is at a maximum, i.e., where marginal product is equal to zero or becomes negative. The levels of output at the beginning and end of Stage II can be identified from the tables in Problem 1 or the graphs in Problem 2.

Stage II	Capital (K)			
	A	B	C	D
Begins	38	96	186	210
Ends	70	133	211	250

4.	The marginal revenue product of labor is equal to the marginal product of labor multiplied times the marginal revenue of output. In this case, the marginal revenue of output is equal to price. The marginal revenue product is equal to marginal product multiplied by $100.

Labor (L)	Capital (K)			
	A	B	C	D
1	900	600	0	0
2	2,900	1,200	900	0
3	1,300	3,700	2,900	2,400
4	1,100	4,100	5,000	4,500
5	700	3,100	4,000	6,900
6	100	1,000	3,200	4,200
7	0	500	2,600	3,000
8	0	100	2,000	2,500
9	0	0	500	1,000
10	0	0	0	500

5. The relevant portions of the labor demand curves are found to the right of the point of intersection between average product and marginal product where marginal product is diminishing.

Chapter 6: Problem 5

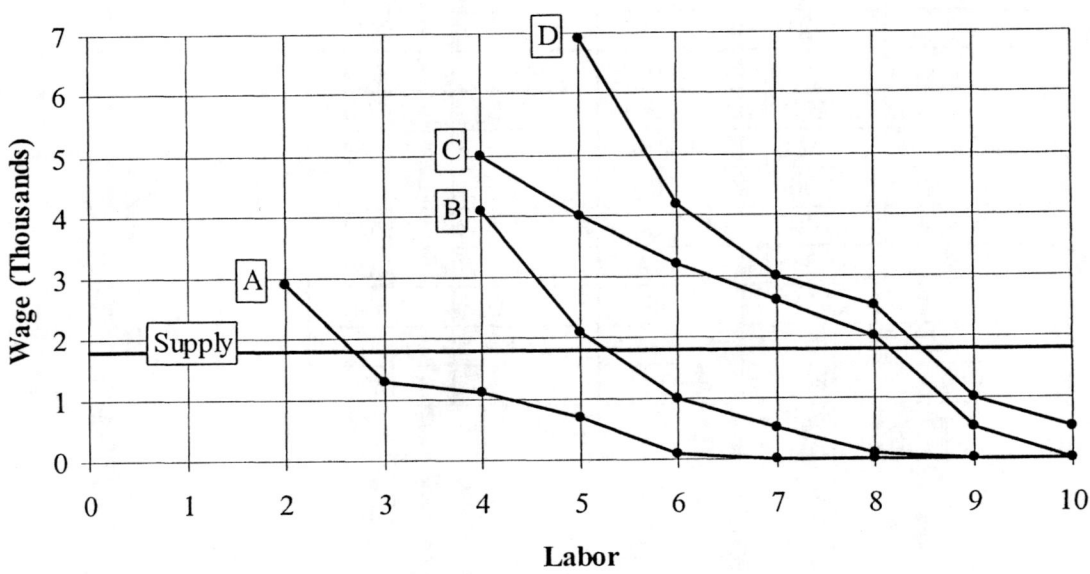

6. Arcane Assemblies should employ a number of workers such that the marginal revenue product (MRP_L) of labor is as close as possible to the marginal resource cost (MRC_L) of labor without being less than the marginal resource cost of labor. On the graph, this level of employment corresponds to points on the labor demand curves that are just above the horizontal labor supply curve. For example, under Production System A, $MRP_L = \$2,900$ when $L = 2$ and $MRP_L = \$1,300$ when $L = 3$. The optimal level of employment of labor is 2 because $MRC_L = \$1,800$.

The total cost of labor is equal to the optimal quantity of labor multiplied times the cost per unit of labor. For example, under Production System B, the optimal quantity of labor is 5 so total labor cost is (5)($\$1,800$) = $\$9,000$.

The total cost of production is equal to total labor cost plus the cost of capital. For example, under Production System B, total labor cost is $\$9,000$ and the cost of capital is $\$1,000$ so total cost is $\$10,000$.

Total product is determined by reference to the production possibilities table. For example, under Production System C, the optimal quantity of labor is 8 and the total product that corresponds to this quantity of labor under this production system is 206.

Total revenue is equal to the optimal total product multiplied by the price per unit of output. For example, under Production System C, the optimal total product is 206. The output price is $100, so total revenue is (206)($100) = $20,600.

Total profit is equal to total revenue minus total cost. For example, under Production System D, total revenue at the optimal total product of 235 is $23,500 and total cost is $22,400 so total profit is $23,500-$22,400 = $1,100.

Comparison of the profit alternatives available to Arcane Assemblies indicates that their profit will be maximized if they use Production System B and hire 5 units of labor.

	Capital (K)			
	A	B	C	D
L	2	5	8	8
wL	3,600	9,000	14,400	14,400
TC	3,600	10,000	19,400	22,400
Q	38	117	206	235
TR	3,800	11,700	20,600	23,500
π	200	1,700	1,200	1,100

7.   To show that the production system that was identified as optimal in Problem 6 is also optimal according to the general optimization principle, it must be demonstrated that the marginal revenue product of capital is as close as possible to the marginal resource cost of capital without being below the marginal resource cost given the number of units of labor employed optimally by the firm.

The marginal product of capital is equal to the change in total product due to a change in the production system while holding constant the number of units of labor employed. For example, the marginal product of Production System B when five units of labor are employed is the total product under Production System B (Q = 117) minus the total product under Production System A (Q = 69), or 117 - 69 = 48.

The marginal revenue product of capital is equal to the marginal product of capital multiplied by the price of output. For example, the marginal revenue product of Production System C when five units of labor are employed is the marginal product of Production System C (MP = 11) times the price of output (P = $100) or (11)($100) = $1,100.

The marginal resource cost of capital is equal to the change in cost that results from a change from a less expensive to a more expensive production system. For example, the marginal resource cost of Production System C is equal to the cost of capital for Production System C ($5,000) minus the cost of capital for Production System B ($1,000) or $5,000 - $1,000 = $4,000.

Finally, comparing the marginal revenue product and marginal resource cost of capital for each production system when five units of labor are employed indicates that Production System B is optimal because the marginal resource cost of capital ($1,000) is less than the marginal revenue product of capital ($4,800) and because the additional capital expenditures required to change to Production System C would yield a marginal cost ($4,000) greater than the associated marginal revenue ($1,100).

	Capital (K)			
	A	B	C	D
MP	69	48	11	10
MRP	6,900	4,800	1,100	1,000
MRC	0	1,000	4,000	3,000

Chapter 6: Problem 7

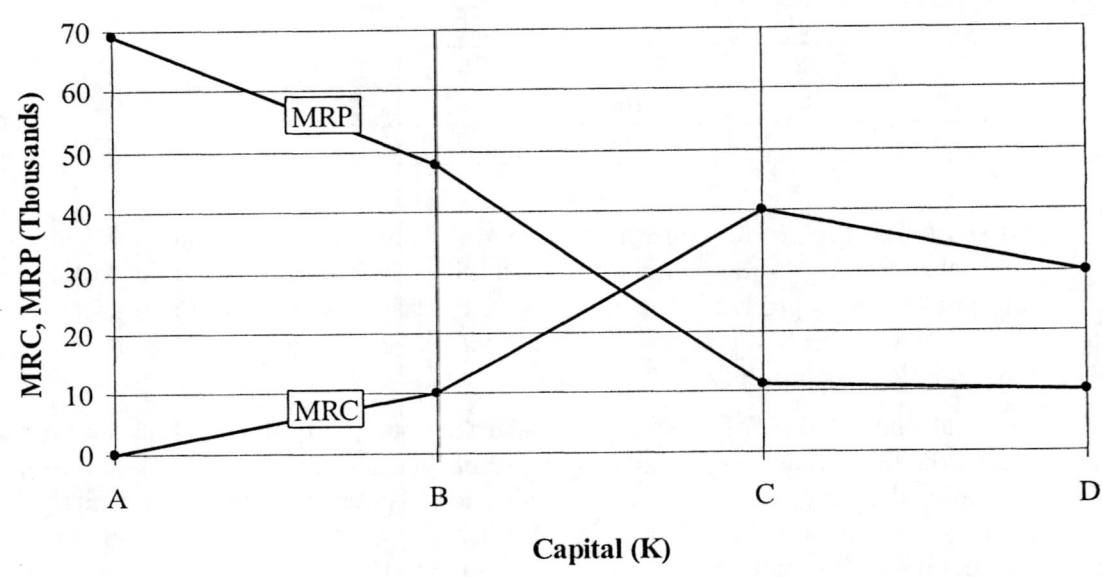

8.	The isoquant map is identified by locating the combinations of inputs that yield the same total product, plotting the points on the graph, and then connecting the points associated with the same level of output.

Chapter 6: Problem 8

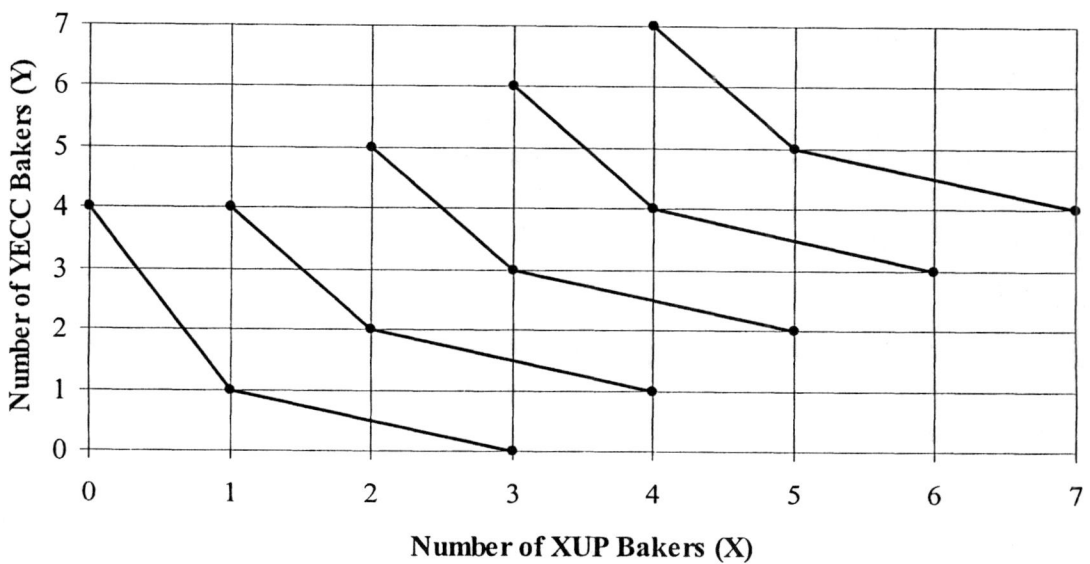

9.	There are several ways to solve this problem. Each begins by identifying the optimal combination of inputs on each isoquant. Once this is accomplished, the total cost of production is calculated and this value is used to determine the intercepts of the relevant isocost line.

One way to identify the minimum cost input combination on an isoquant is to calculate the total cost of production at every point. For example, when output is 39, there are three points on the isoquant. For Y = 6 and X = 3, total cost is $39. For Y = 4 and X = 4, total cost is $36. For Y = 3 and X = 6, total cost is $42. Thus, the minimum cost of producing 39 units of output is $36 and is accomplished using 3 YECC graduates and 3 XUP graduates.

A second way to identify the minimum cost input combination on an isoquant is to calculate the slope of the isocost line and then to visually identify the cost minimizing combinations of inputs on the graph. In this case, the slope of the isoquant is the negative of the ratio of the cost of the input measured on the vertical axis (the cost of YECC graduates, which is $4) divided by the price of the input measured on the horizontal axis (the cost of XUP graduates, which is $5) or -5/4 = -1.25.

A third way to identify the minimum cost input combination on an isoquant is to calculate the marginal rate of technical substitution (MRTS) between each adjacent combination of inputs along an isoquant and then to identify the point on each isoquant where the absolute value of the slope of the isocost is between the two marginal rates of technical substitution that are on either side of the point. The MRTS is equal to the absolute value of the change in the variable measured on the vertical axis divided by the change in the variable measured on the horizontal axis. For example, when output is 21, the MRTS between the point $Y = 7$, $X = 1$ and $Y = 4$, $X = 1$ is $(7 - 4)/(1 - 1)$ or infinity. Between $Y = 4$, $X = 1$ and $Y = 2$, $X = 2$ is $(4 - 2)/(1 - 2)$ or 2. Between $Y = 2$, $X = 2$ and $Y = 1$, $X = 4$ is $(2 - 1)/(2 - 4)$ or 0.5. Finally, between $Y = 1$, $X = 4$ and $Y = 1$, $X = 6$ is $(1 - 1)/(4 - 6)$ or zero. Thus, the optimal combination of inputs is $Y = 2$, $X = 2$ because the absolute value of the slope of the isocost (1.25) is between the two adjacent MRTS values (2 and 0.5) at this point.

Once the optimal points have been identified, total cost is calculated by multiplying the cost of each input by the number of units of the input used to optimally produce a given quantity of output. For example, the total cost of producing 21 units of output optimally is $(2)(\$4) + (2)(\$5)$ or $18.

Finally, the intercepts of the isocost lines are calculated by taking the ratio of the total cost divided by the cost of the relevant input. For example, the total cost of producing 21 units of output optimally is $18. The price of Y is $4. The vertical (or Y) intercept is 18/4 or 4.50. The price of X is $5. The horizontal (or X) intercept is 18/5 or 3.60.

	Q = 12	Q = 21	Q = 30	Q = 39	Q = 48
Optimal Y	1	2	3	4	5
Optimal X	1	2	3	4	5
Total Cost	$9	$18	$27	$36	$45
Y Intercept	2.25	4.5	6.75	9	11.25
X Intercept	1.8	3.6	5.4	7.2	9

10. Returns to scale are analyzed by dividing the percentage change in output by the percentage change in inputs. If this ratio is greater than one, returns to scale are increasing. If it is equal to one, returns to scale are constant. If it is less than one, returns to scale are decreasing. For example, when output increases from 12 to 21 and inputs increase from 1 to 2, the proportional change in output is $(21 - 12)/12 = 0.75$ and the proportional change in inputs is $(2 - 1)/1 = 1.00$. The ratio is $0.75/1.00$ or 0.75, which indicates that returns to scale are decreasing. When output increases from 21 to 30, the proportional changes in output and inputs are $(30 - 21)/21 = 0.43$ and $(3 - 2)/2 = 0.5$ and the ratio is $0.43/0.5 = 0.86$. Between 30 and 39, the ratio is $0.30/0.33 = 0.90$. Between 39 and 48, the ratio is $0.23/0.25 = 0.92$. Thus, between every pair of output levels on the expansion path, returns to scale are decreasing. Note that this not a situation one would be likely to encounter in reality.

11. The marginal rates of technical substitution (MRTS) between two points on an isoquant is equal to the absolute value of the change in the input measured on the vertical axis divided by the change in the input measured on the horizontal axis. For example, when output is equal to 39, the MRTS between $Y = 4$, $X = 4$ (the optimal combination of

inputs) and Y = 6, X = 3 is (4 - 6)/(4 - 3) or 2. Between the optimal combination and Y = 3, X = 6 is (4 - 3)/(4 - 6) or 0.50.

MRTS	Q = 12	Q = 21	Q = 30	Q = 39	Q = 48
Decrease Y	0.5	0.5	0.5	0.5	0.5
Decrease X	3	2	2	2	2

12.   Leo should hire only YECC graduates if the absolute value of the slope of the isocost line (i.e., the input price ratio) is greater than the MRTS at any point on an isoquant where X > 0. For example, if output is 12, the price of Y is $13 and the price of X is $4, then the absolute value of the slope of the isocost line is 3.25 (greater than the MRTS of 3) and only YECC graduates should be hired to produce this level of output. Conversely, if the absolute value of the slope of the isocost line is less than 0.5, for example if the price of Y is $1 and the price of X is $4, then the absolute value of the slope of the isocost line is 0.25 and only XUP graduates should be hired to produce 12 units of output.

If the price per unit of both types of graduates is the same, then the absolute value of the slope of the isocost line is 1. If Leo wants to produce 30 loaves per hour, then the MRTS between Y = 3, X = 3 and Y = 2, X = 4 is also 1. In this case, both of the points are equally optimal. Leo can use Y = 3, X = 3 (at a total cost of 3 + 3 = 6 times the input price) or Y = 2, X = 4 (at a total cost of 2 + 4 = 6 times the input price) with identical results.

13.   Substituting ln(120) = 4.79, ln(600) = 6.40, and ln(60) = 4.09 into the function yields ln Q = 5.32. Taking the antilog of this value yields Q = 204.38. An alternative way to solve this problem is to transform the estimated function back into a power function, substitute the values of the variables into the function, and then solve directly for Q. Since the antilog of 1.20 is 3.32, the power function is

$$Q = 3.32 \, K^{0.30} L^{0.10} S^{0.50}$$

Substituting the values into the function yields

$$Q = (3.32)(120^{0.30})(600^{0.10})(60^{0.50}) = 205.01$$

The difference between the two calculated values of Q is due to rounding.

14.   The marginal product of an input can be calculated very easily from a Cobb-Douglas function once the average product has been calculated. It is equal to the estimated coefficient of the input multiplied times the average product of the input. The average product of an input is equal to the ratio of total output divided by the number of units of the input employed. Using Q = 205, the average products of each of the three inputs are

AP of K = 205/120 = 1.71 so MP = (0.3)(1.71) = 0.51

AP of L = 205/600 = 0.34 so MP = (0.1)(0.34) = 0.03

AP of S = 205/60 = 3.42 so MP = (0.5)(3.42) = 1.71

With regard to the second part of the problem, the firm is operating in Stage II of production for all of the inputs. The marginal product is less than the average product and greater than zero for each input, which indicates that average product is declining and that total product is increasing.

15.   The output elasticities are equal to the estimated slope coefficients of a logarithmically transformed Cobb-Douglas function. A doubling of the number of units of an input is equivalent to a 100% increase in the employment of the input. The effect on output of a doubling is thus equal to 100% times the relevant output elasticity. Thus, a doubling of capital will yield a 30% increase in output, a doubling of production workers will yield a 10% increase, and a doubling of support workers will yield a 50% increase in output. A doubling of all inputs is equal to the sum of the effects of doubling each input individually; i.e., 30% + 10% + 50% = 90%. This value also indicates that returns to scale are decreasing, because a doubling of all inputs results in less than a doubling of output. The returns to scale for a Cobb-Douglas function can always be determined easily by summing the estimated slope coefficients. If the sum is less than one, then returns to scale are decreasing; if the sum is equal to one, they're constant; and if the sum is greater than one, they are increasing.

16.   If the combination of inputs employed by Cimmerian Cutlery is optimal, then the marginal production per dollar spent on each input should be equal. Calculating these values yields:

MP per dollar on K is 0.51/85 = 0.006

MP per dollar on L is 0.03/5 = 0.006

MP per dollar on S is 1.71/285 = 0.006

Since all are equal, the combination of inputs is optimal. If one of these ratios was larger than the others, it would indicate that a greater quantity of the corresponding input should be employed by the firm. If one ratio was smaller than the others, it would indicate that a smaller quantity of the corresponding input should be employed by the firm.

If the number of units produced by the firm is optimal, then the marginal revenue product (MRP) of each input should be equal to the price of the input. Assuming that the price of output is equal to marginal revenue, the MRP is equal to marginal product multiplied by price. Thus, the MRP of capital is $(0.51)(200) = \$102$, of production labor is $(0.03)(200) = \$6$, and of support labor is $(1.71)(200 = \$342$. In each case, the input price is below its MRP. This indicates that more of each input should be employed and more output should be produced if the firm is to maximize profits.

17.   The number of degrees of freedom (d.f.) used to identify the relevant value from the t table is n - k - 1, where n is the number of observations (n = 14) and k is the number of slope coefficients estimated (k=3). Thus, d.f. = 14 - 3 - 1 = 10. The table value for a test of significance at the 5% level is 2.228 and at the 1% level it is 3.169. Comparison of these values with the t ratios from the estimated equation indicates that all slope coefficients are significant at the 5% level, but only the coefficient for capital is significant at the 1% level.

The coefficient of determination (R^2) measures the proportion of the variation in Q that is explained by the estimated regression equation. In this case, 91% of the variation is explained.

18.   The first step is to set up the Lagrangian function:

$$Z = 20K^{0.3}L^{0.7} + \lambda(1000 - 30K - 10L)$$

The second step is to determine the first-order conditions:

$$\delta Z/\delta K = (0.3)(20)(L/K)^{0.7} - \lambda 30 = 0$$

$$\delta Z/\delta L = (0.7)(20)(K/L)^{0.3} - \lambda 10 = 0$$

$$\delta Z/\delta \lambda = 1000 - 30K - 10L = 0$$

The third step is to solve the system of partial derivatives that comprise the first-order conditions by a process of substitution. There are a number of ways to approach this process. We will begin by solving $\delta Z/\delta K = 0$ and $\delta Z/\delta L = 0$ for λ, setting them equal to each other so as to eliminate λ, and then solving for L.

$$(0.3)(2/3)(L/K)^{0.7} = \lambda = (0.7)(2)(K/L)^{0.3}$$

$$L = 7K$$

The next step is to substitute 7K for L in $\delta Z/\delta \lambda = 0$ and then to solve for K.

$$1000 - 30K - (10)(7K) = 0 \text{ so } K = 10.$$

With K determined, its value is substituted into the constraint to give L = 70. Next, both K and L are substituted into $\delta Z/\delta K = 0$ and it is solved to give $\lambda = 0.78$. Finally, the values of K and L are substituted into the production function to yield Q = 780.91.

The value of the Lagrangian multiplier measures the approximate change in the optimal Q that will result from a one unit increase in total cost.

19.   The first step is to set up the Lagrangian function:

$$Z = 30K + 10L + \lambda(1562 - 20K^{0.3}L^{0.7})$$

The second step is to determine the first-order conditions:

$$\delta Z/\delta K = 30 - \lambda(0.3)(20)(L/K)^{0.7} = 0$$

$$\delta Z/\delta L = 10 - \lambda(0.7)(20)(K/L)^{0.3} = 0$$

$$\delta Z/\delta \lambda = 1562 - 20K^{0.3}L^{0.7} = 0$$

The third step is to solve the system of partial derivatives that comprise the first-order conditions by a process of substitution. There are a number of ways to approach this process. We will begin by solving $\delta Z/\delta K = 0$ and $\delta Z/\delta L = 0$ for $1/\lambda$, setting them equal to each other so as to eliminate λ, and then solving for L.

$$(0.3)(2/3)(L/K)^{0.7} = 1/\lambda = (0.7)(2)(K/L)^{0.3}$$

$$L = 7K$$

The next step is to substitute 7K for L in $\delta Z/\delta \lambda = 0$ and then to solve for K.

$$1562 - 20K^{0.3}(7K)^{0.7} = 0 \text{ so } K = 20.$$

With K determined, its value is substituted into the constraint to give L = 140. Next, both K and L are substituted into $\delta Z/\delta K = 0$ and it is solved to give $\lambda = 1.28$. Finally, the values of K and L are substituted into the cost function to yield C = $2,000.

The value of the Lagrangian multiplier measures the approximate change in total cost that will result from a one-unit increase in output, i.e., the marginal cost of production.

20.   The profit function for the firm is

$$\pi = (2)(20K^{0.2}L^{0.8}) - 7K - 32L$$

Substitute in the value of K to get

$$\pi = (2)(20)(60^{0.2}L^{0.8}) - (7)(60) - 32L = 90.72L^{0.8} - 420 - 32L$$

Take the derivative with respect to L and set it equal to zero to get the first-order condition and then solve for L:

$$\delta\pi/\delta L = 72.57L^{-0.2} - 32 = 0 \text{ so } L = 60$$

Substitute this value of L into the production function to get Q = 1,200. Total revenue is $2,400. Total cost is $2,340. Total profit is $60.

CHAPTER 7

COST THEORY AND ESTIMATION

Learning Objectives

This chapter reviews the microeconomic theory of cost and explains how cost relationships can be estimated and used in decision making. When you have completed the material in this chapter you should understand the relationship between the production theory and cost theory and between empirically estimated production functions and their cost counterparts. More fundamentally, you should be conversant with the economic concept of cost and be able to distinguish it from accounting approaches to cost measurement. You should understand the relationships between total and unit cost curves in the short-run and the long-run, the relationship between cost and profit, the application of cost-profit-volume (breakeven) analysis, and the significance of operating leverage. Finally, you should understand how to use regression, engineering, and survival methods to estimate cost functions and you should be aware of the difficulties that are commonly encountered in the estimation of cost functions.

Summary of Notation and Formulas

(7-1) $\quad TC = TFC + TVC$

(7-2) $\quad AFC = \dfrac{TFC}{Q}$

(7-3) $\quad AVC = \dfrac{TVC}{Q}$

(7-4) $\quad ATC = \dfrac{TC}{Q} = AFC + AVC$

(7-5) $\quad MC = \dfrac{\Delta TC}{\Delta Q} = \dfrac{\Delta TVC}{\Delta Q}$

Equations 7-1 through 7-5 define the family of short-run cost functions. Equation 7-1 defines short-run total cost (TC) as total fixed cost (TFC) plus total variable cost (TVC). Equations 7-2, 7-3, and 7-4 define average fixed cost (AFC), average variable cost (AVC), and average total cost (ATC) as the ratio of the relevant total cost divided by output (Q). Equation 7-5 defines marginal cost (MC) as the change in short-run total cost or, equivalently, the change in total variable cost divided by the corresponding change in output.

(7-6) $\quad AVC = \dfrac{TVC}{Q} = \dfrac{wL}{Q} = \dfrac{w}{Q/L} = \dfrac{w}{AP_L}$

$$(7\text{-}7) \quad MC = \frac{\Delta TVC}{\Delta Q} = \frac{\Delta(wL)}{\Delta Q} = \frac{w}{\Delta Q/\Delta L} = \frac{w}{MP_L}$$

Equations 7-6 and 7-7 relate average variable cost and marginal cost to the average product of labor (AP_L), the marginal product of labor (MP_L), and the wage rate (w) in the case where labor is the only variable input and the wage rate is constant.

$$(7\text{-}8) \quad LAC = \frac{LTC}{Q}$$

$$(7\text{-}9) \quad LMC = \frac{\Delta LTC}{Q}$$

Equation 7-8 defines long-run average cost (LAC) as long-run total cost (LTC) divided by output (Q). Equation 7-9 defines long-run marginal cost (LMC) as the change in long-run total cost divided by the corresponding change in output.

$$(7\text{-}10) \quad C = aQ^b$$

$$(7\text{-}11) \quad \log C = \log a + b \log Q$$

Equations 7-10 and 7-11 define the learning curve as a power function and represent it in two forms. The second is the result of a logarithmic transformation applied to the first. The transformed equation can be estimated using linear regression analysis. The learning curve defines short-run average variable cost (C) as a function of the short-run average cost of the first unit of a commodity or service that was produced (a), the cumulative total number of units produced (Q), and a parameter that measures the rate at which average cost declines as the total number of units produced increases (b). Note that Q is not used in the same way here as it was previously. It does <u>not</u> represent units of output per time period. Instead, it represents the total number of units of output produced up to a point in time.

$$(7\text{-}13) \quad TR = (P)(Q)$$

$$(7\text{-}14) \quad TC = TFC + (AVC)(Q)$$

$$(7\text{-}15) \quad TR = TC$$

$$(7\text{-}16) \quad (P)(Q_B) = TFC + (AVC)(Q)$$

$$(7\text{-}17) \quad Q_B = \frac{TFC}{P - AVC}$$

$$(7\text{-}18) \quad Q_T = \frac{TFC + \pi_T}{P - AVC}$$

Equations 7-13 through 7-18 define the linear cost-volume-profit, or breakeven, analysis model. Equations 7-13 and 7-14 define linear total revenue (TR) and total cost (TC) functions in terms of a fixed commodity price (P), the number of units produced and sold (Q), total fixed cost (TFC), and a constant average variable cost (AVC). Equation 7-15 defines the breakeven condition of zero economic profit. Equation 7-16 restates the previous equation in terms of the definitions of total revenue and total cost and the breakeven quantity of output (Q_B). Equation

---

7-17 is obtained by solving the previous equation for the breakeven quantity. Equation 7-18 defines the cumulative total number of units (Q_T) that must be sold in order to attain a target level of profit. It is derived from Equation 7-17 by adding a specified target level of profit (π_T) to the numerator.

(7-19) $\quad DOL = \dfrac{\%\Delta\pi}{\%\Delta Q} = \dfrac{\Delta\pi/\pi}{\Delta Q/Q} = \dfrac{\Delta\pi}{\Delta Q}\dfrac{Q}{\pi}$

(7-20) $\quad DOL = \dfrac{\Delta Q(P-AVC)Q}{\Delta Q[Q(P-AVC)-TFC]} = \dfrac{Q(P-AVC)}{Q(P-AVC)-TFC}$

Equation 7-19 defines the degree of operating leverage (DOL) as the percentage change in profit ($\%\Delta\pi$) divided by the corresponding percentage change in output ($\%\Delta Q$). It then rewrites the definition by substituting point definitions for the percentage changes. Equation 7-20 rewrites the degree of operating leverage under the assumption that profit is a linear function of output; i.e., it assumes that total revenue and total cost are defined by Equations 7-13 and 7-14 so DOL is equal to the difference between total revenue and total variable costs [(Q)(P)-(Q)(AVC)] divided by total economic profit [(Q)(P)-(Q)(AVC)-TFC]. Note that this implies that DOL cannot be calculated if a firm is initially breaking even.

(7-22) $\quad TVC = aQ + bQ^2 + aQ^3$

(7-23) $\quad AVC = \dfrac{TVC}{Q} = a + bQ + CQ^2$

(7-24) $\quad MC = a + 2bQ + 3cQ^2$

(7-32) $\quad Q = \dfrac{-b}{2c}$

(7-36) $\quad Q = \dfrac{-b}{3c}$

Equations 7-22, 7-23, and 7-24 represent a cubic short-run total variable cost (TVC) function and the related average variable cost (AVC) and marginal cost (MC) functions. The parameters of these functions (a > 0, b < 0, and c > 0) can be estimated using regression analysis. Equations 7-32 and 7-36 define the value of Q when AVC is at a minimum and when MC is at a minimum, respectively.

(7-25) $\quad TVC = a + bQ$

(7-26) $\quad AVC = \dfrac{a}{Q} + b$

(7-27) $\quad MC = b$

Equations 7-25, 7-26, and 7-27 represent a linear short-run total variable cost (TVC) function and the related average variable cost (AVC) and marginal cost (MC) functions. The parameters of these functions (a and b > 0) can be estimated using regression analysis.

True-False Questions

T F 1.   The value of the inputs owned and used by a firm is an explicit cost.

T F 2.   The entrepreneur's opportunity cost is an implicit cost.

T F 3.   Economic cost is generally lower than accounting cost.

T F 4.   Accounting costs and explicit costs are the same.

T F 5.   Sunk costs are not relevant to managerial decisions.

T F 6.   In the short run, total cost is equal to zero when output is equal to zero.

T F 7.   In the long run, total cost is equal to zero when output is equal to zero.

T F 8.   Economic cost curves define the minimum economic costs of producing various levels of output.

T F 9.   Total variable cost is equal to short-run total cost minus total fixed cost.

T F 10. The average fixed cost curve is U-shaped.

T F 11. The law of diminishing returns is reflected in the downward-sloping portion of the short-run marginal cost curve.

T F 12. Average total cost is equal to marginal cost where marginal cost is at a minimum.

T F 13. If the long-run average cost curve slopes upward over some range of output, then the firm is experiencing increasing returns to scale over that range of output.

T F 14. The point of inflection of the short-run total variable cost function corresponds to the level of output where marginal cost is at a minimum.

T F 15. If marginal cost is greater than average total cost, then average total cost is rising.

T F 16. The vertical distance between the short-run average total and average variable cost curves is equal to marginal cost.

T F 17. The minimum short-run average total cost occurs at a level of output that is greater than that at which average variable cost is at a minimum.

T F 18. The slope of a ray drawn from the origin to any point on a total cost curve is equal to average total cost at that point.

T F 19. If a ray that is drawn from the origin to a point on a total cost curve is tangent to the total cost curve, then its slope is equal to the minimum average total cost of production.

T F 20. The point at which the marginal product of a variable input is at a maximum corresponds to the point at which marginal cost is at a maximum.

T F 21. The level of output at which the average product of a variable input is at a maximum corresponds to the level of output where short-run average total cost is at a minimum.

T F 22. All costs are variable costs in the long run.

T F 23. The long-run total cost curve is derived from the firm's expansion path.

T F 24. The long-run average cost curve is tangent to the lowest points on all possible short-run average total cost curves.

T F 25. Long-run average cost slopes downward over a range of output where a firm experiences decreasing returns to scale.

T F 26. If long-run marginal cost is greater than long-run average cost, then the firm is experiencing decreasing returns to scale.

T F 27. Long-run marginal cost is equal to short-run marginal cost at the level of output where the corresponding short-run average total cost curve is tangent to the long-run average cost curve.

T F 28. Industries where the long-run average cost curve has a positive slope over a wide range of output are referred to as natural monopolies.

T F 29. Industries in which small and large firms coexist successfully have long-run average cost curves that are nearly horizontal.

T F 30. Firms that produce more than one type of product cannot benefit from economies of scope.

T F 31. Learning curves slope upward.

T F 32. If a learning curve is represented by $C = aQ^b$, then $b > 0$.

T F 33. The brain drain refers to the emigration of highly skilled workers from their home countries.

T F 34. Cost-volume-profit analysis is used to determine the profit-maximizing level of output.

T F 35. The contribution margin per unit is equal to price minus short-run average variable cost.

T F 36. Breakeven output is equal to total fixed cost divided by the contribution margin per unit.

T F 37. The degree of operating leverage is equal to the ratio of the firm's total fixed cost to total variable cost.

T F 38. An increase in operating leverage results from the substitution of fixed costs for variable costs.

T F 39. Economic theory suggests that a cubic function is an appropriate form for an empirical short-run total variable cost curve.

T F 40. The survival technique is used to estimate short-run total variable cost functions.

T F 41. Logistics is also referred to as supply chain management.

T F 42. Just-in-time inventory management and globalization have contributed to the emergence and growth of logistics.

T F 43. Logistics refers to the rational assessment of supply and demand by consumers.

T F 44. While it may contribute to cost savings, logistics is not a source of competitive advantage.

T F 45. Logistics merges a firm's design and manufacturing functions into a centrally managed unit.

Multiple Choice Questions

1. Which of the following is a variable cost?

    A. Interest payments
    B. Raw materials costs
    C. Property taxes
    D. All of the above are variable costs.

2. Which of the following is an implicit cost?

    A. The salary earned by a corporate executive
    B. Depreciation in the value of a company-owned car as it wears out
    C. Property taxes
    D. All of the above are implicit costs.

3. If the output levels at which short-run marginal and average cost curves reach a minimum are listed in order from smallest to greatest, then the order would be

    A. AVC, MC, ATC
    B. ATC, AVC, MC
    C. MC, AVC, ATC
    D. AVC, ATC, MC

4. Learning curves represent the relationship between

    A. average variable cost and the number of units produced per time period.
    B. average variable cost and the cumulative number of units produced.
    C. total cost and technology.
    D. average variable cost and the rate of increase in technology.

5. If an input is owned and used by a firm, then its

    A. explicit cost is zero.
    B. implicit cost is zero.
    C. opportunity cost is zero.
    D. economic cost is zero.

6. Short-run marginal cost is equal to

    A. the change in total cost divided by the change in output.
    B. the change in total variable cost divided by the change in output.
    C. the cost per unit of the variable input divided by the marginal product of the variable input.
    D. all of the above.

7. Short-run average variable cost is equal to

 A. total variable cost divided by output.
 B. average total cost minus average fixed cost.
 C. the cost per unit of the variable input divided by the average product of the variable input.
 D. all of the above.

8. Which of the following short-run cost curves declines continuously?

 A. Average total cost
 B. Marginal cost
 C. Average fixed cost
 D. Average variable cost

9. The law of diminishing returns begins at the level of output where

 A. marginal cost is at a minimum.
 B. average variable cost is at a minimum.
 C. average fixed cost is at a maximum.
 D. None of the above is correct.

10. The long-run average cost curve is at a minimum at a level of output where

 A. the firm is experiencing constant returns to scale.
 B. it is equal to long-run marginal cost.
 C. the long-run average cost curve is tangent to the lowest point on a short-run average total cost curve.
 D. all of the above occur.

11. If a firm has a downward sloping long-run average cost curve, then

 A. it is experiencing decreasing returns to scale.
 B. it is experiencing decreasing returns.
 C. it is a natural monopoly.
 D. marginal cost is greater than average cost.

12. One reason that a firm may experience increasing returns to scale is that greater levels of output make it possible for the firm to

 A. employ more specialized machinery.
 B. obtain bulk purchase discounts.
 C. employ a greater division of labor.
 D. All of the above are correct.

13. One reason that a firm may experience decreasing returns to scale is that greater levels of output can result in

 A. a greater division of labor.
 B. an increase in meetings and paperwork.
 C. smaller inventories per unit of output.
 D. All of the above are correct.

14. Economies of scope refers to the decrease in average total cost that can occur when a firm

    A. produces more than one product.
    B. has monopoly power in world markets.
    C. controls the raw materials used as inputs.
    D. narrows the scope of its regional markets.

15. Breakeven analysis identifies the

    A. profit-maximizing level of output.
    B. level of output where economic profit is equal to zero.
    C. level of output where marginal revenue is equal to marginal cost.
    D. All of the above are correct.

16. Which of the following is not an assumption of linear breakeven analysis?

    A. Output price is constant
    B. Average variable cost is constant
    C. Average fixed cost is constant
    D. All of the above are assumptions of linear breakeven analysis.

17. The responsiveness or sensitivity of a firm's profits to changes in output is measured by a firm's

    A. operating leverage.
    B. contribution margin per unit.
    C. degree of operating leverage.
    D. returns to scale.

18. Which of the following values cannot be calculated at the firm's breakeven level of output?

    A. operating leverage.
    B. contribution margin per unit.
    C. degree of operating leverage.
    D. profit.

19. If a linear short-run variable cost function is estimated using cross-sectional data, then the corresponding marginal cost function will be

    A. U-shaped.
    B. upward-sloping.
    C. downward-sloping.
    D. horizontal.

20. The survival technique

    A. can be used to estimate short-run total variable cost functions.
    B. is based on a technical knowledge of a firm's production function.
    C. uses regression analysis in combination with time-series or cross-sectional data.
    D. None of the above is correct.

21. The process whereby firms reduce their production costs by taking advantage of international differences in the prices of inputs and international similarities in preferences is referred to as the

   A. strategic opportunity concept.
   B. new international economies of scale.
   C. global dictum.
   D. transnational cost theorem.

22. Which of the following would be referred to as "outsourcing?"

   A. Marketing products outside of a firm's home country
   B. Hiring temporary workers on a contract basis
   C. Subcontracting production to firms in other countries
   D. Identifying and implementing production innovations

23. When a firm designs a core product for the entire world that can be adapted in a number of ways to accommodate different types of markets, it is taking advantage of the

   A. strategic opportunity concept.
   B. new international economies of scale.
   C. global dictum.
   D. transnational cost theorem.

24. The Japanese cost-management system involves

   A. designing a product and then determining the cost of producing it.
   B. a new system of accounting for capital depreciation.
   C. determining how much a product should cost and then determining how it should be produced.
   D. minimizing international transportation costs.

25. The contribution margin per unit is equal to the

   A. price of a good.
   B. the difference between total revenue and total cost.
   C. difference between price and average total cost.
   D. difference between price and average variable cost.

Problems

Priscilla Diller quit her $60,000 per year job with South Central Construction to open her own company, Diller Didactic Consulting. She rented an office in the Peach Street Professional Building for $550 a month, hired a receptionist for $1,500 a month, and leased a computer from Silly Clone Systems for $130 per month.

At first, business was slow, so Priscilla paid $800 to use a mailing list and sent out 1,200 advertising brochures. The cost of postage and printing was $1.37 per brochure. Business improved immediately, and no further advertising has been necessary.

Priscilla's business improved so much that she hired two associates for $5,000 per month and installed them in the remaining two offices in the Peach Street Professional Building, and then she bought the building for $198,000. She replaced her one leased computer with three computers of the same type that she purchased from Silly Clone Systems for $22,000 and she talked her husband into quitting his $24,000 per year teaching job so that he could work for Diller Didactic as an executive secretary.

Use the preceding information to solve Problems 1 through 3.

1. What were the explicit, implicit, and relevant monthly costs of running Diller Didactic Consulting before business improved? What monthly revenue was required for the firm to break even?

2. What are the explicit, implicit, and relevant monthly costs of running Diller Didactic Consulting after business improved? What monthly revenue is required for the firm to break even?

3. Are any of Diller Didactic's past expenditures irrelevant to future business decisions; i.e., are any of them sunk costs? If so, which?

Eustachian Ducting of Erie, Pennsylvania, has hired Diller Didactic to advise them on their cost and production decisions. The owner of Eustachian Ducting tells Priscilla that he can get as many ducting jobs as he wants if he charges $50 per job. Priscilla decides to begin by estimating the firm's short-run total cost schedule. Her results are given in the following table, where Q is the number of jobs per day and TC is total cost per day.

Q	0	1	2	3	4	5	6
TC	60	75	80	90	120	180	300

Use this information to solve Problems 4 and 5.

4. Fill in the blanks in the table below with total fixed cost (TFC), total variable cost (TVC), total revenue (TR), and total profit (π). Plot the total cost curves and the total revenue curve on the graph that follows. How many jobs should Eustachian Ducting accept per day to maximize profits? How many jobs does the firm need per day to break even?

Q	TC	TFC	TVC	TR	π
0	60				
1	75				
2	80				
3	90				
4	120				
5	180				
6	300				

Chapter 7: Problem 4

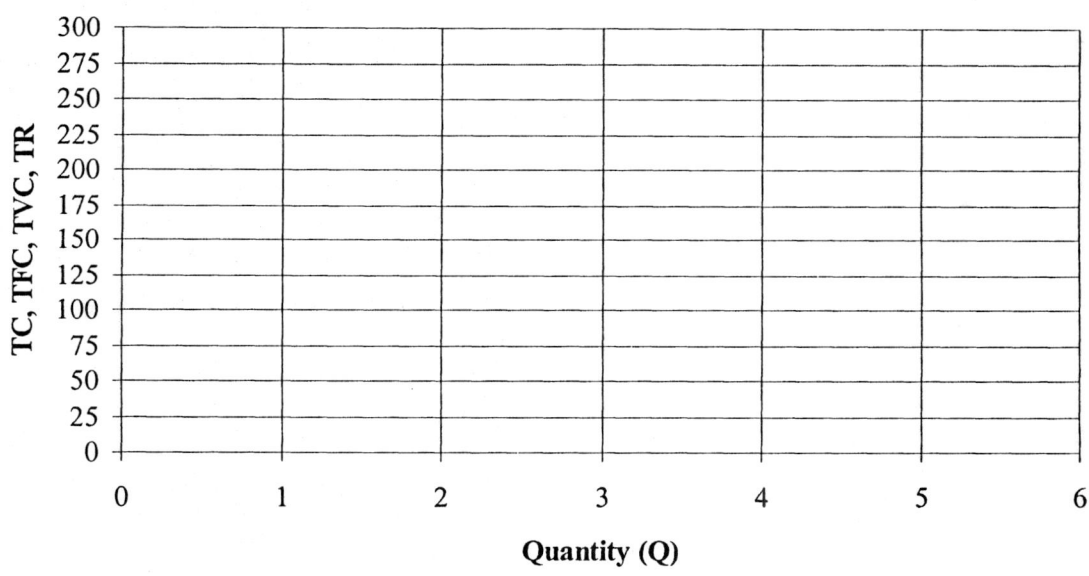

Quantity (Q)

5. Fill in the blanks in the table below with average fixed cost (AFC), average variable cost (AVC), average total cost (ATC), marginal cost (MC), and marginal revenue (MR). Plot the unit cost curves and marginal revenue on the graph that follows. Use unit costs and marginal revenue to determine the number of jobs per day that are required to break even, the number that will maximize profit, and the total profit that the firm will realize at this level of output.

Q	AFC	AVC	ATC	MC	MR
0					
1					
2					
3					
4					
5					
6					

Chapter 7: Problem 5

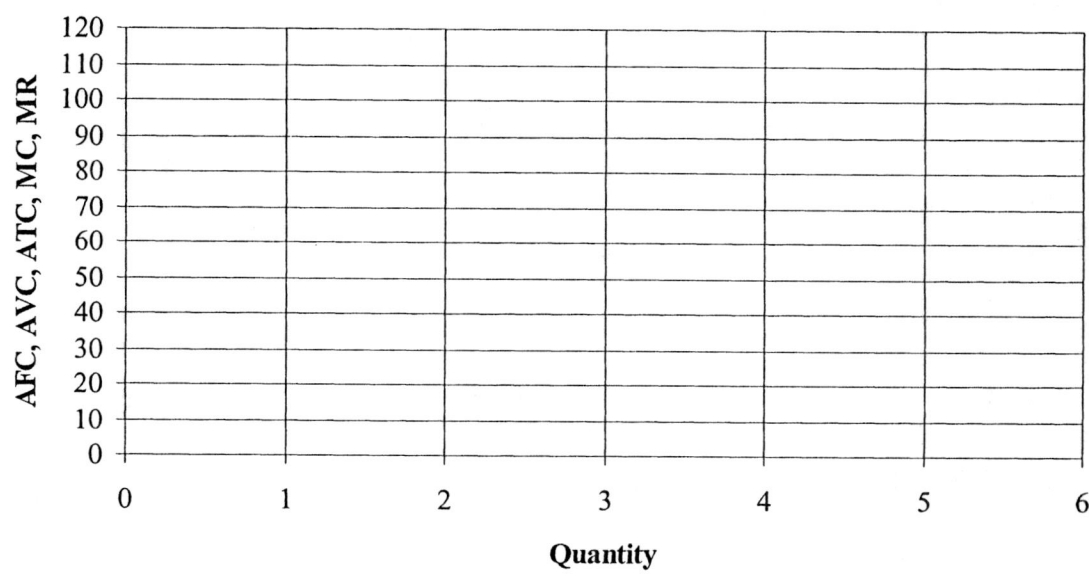

Field Research of Georgia is a genetic engineering company. Last year, the company received federal approval to produce a genetically engineered amphibian. This creature eats pond scum and secretes copious quantities of a tar-like substance, Ranatar, that has great commercial potential. The owner of Field Research has hired Diller Didactic Consulting to provide an economic analysis of the costs associated with the production of Ranatar.

Extensive consultation with engineers and technicians at Field Research yields the following results. If the wage rate (w) is $10,000 per week and the rental price of capital (r) is $20,000 per week, then cost-minimizing combinations of labor (L) and capital (K) for various rates of production (Q) measured in thousands of tons per month are as follows:

Q	10	20	40	60	100
K	3	6	10	18	45
L	6	10	20	24	35

Use this information to solve Problems 6 through 9.

6. Calculate the long-run total cost (LTC), average cost (LAC), and marginal cost (LMC). Also calculate the short-run total fixed cost (TFC), total variable cost (TVC), and average variable cost (AVC) under the assumption that capital is fixed. Enter these values (measured in $1,000s) in the table below. Plot LTC, LAC, and LMC on the graphs that follow. Describe returns to scale for this production function.

Q	LTC	TFC	TVC	AVC	LAC	LMC
10						
20						
40						
60						
100						

Chapter 7: Problem 6

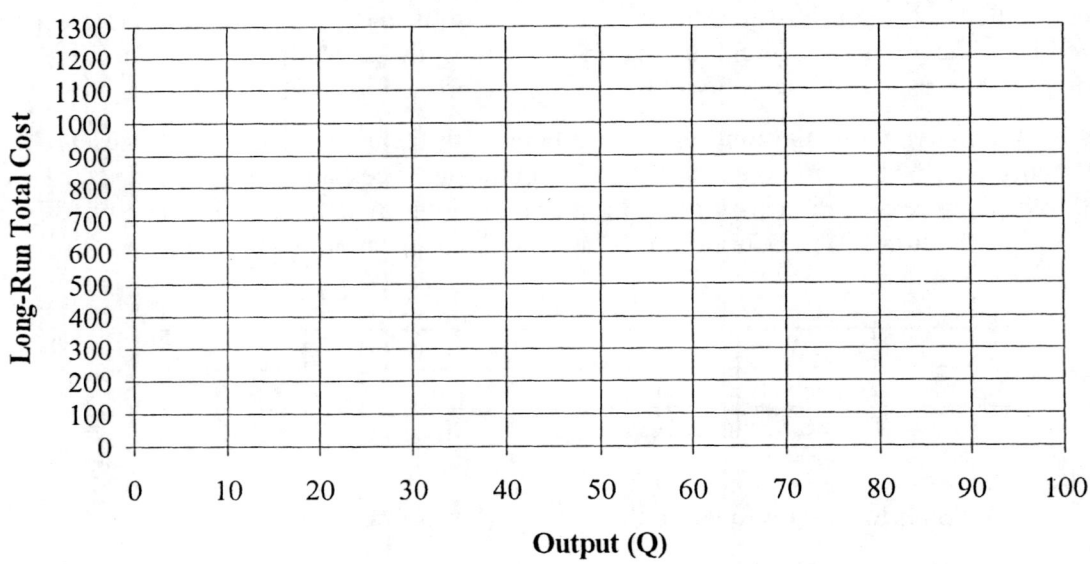

Chapter 7: Problem 6

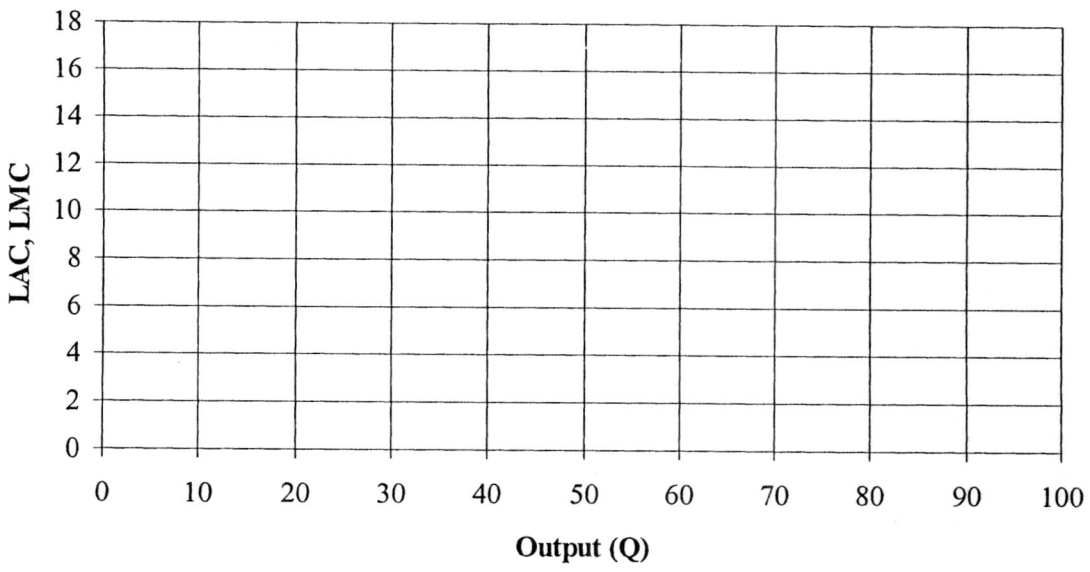

Output (Q)

7. Assume that the price per thousand tons of Ranatar is $13,000. Calculate the operating leverage (OL) and the degree of operating leverage (DOL) for each value of Q. For each of the values of TFC, assume that AVC is constant and calculate the breakeven level of production (Q_B). Enter these values in the table below. Plot each of the linear short-run total cost curves along with the total revenue curve on the graph that follows. What pattern is evident in the cost curves as TFC increases?

Q	OL	DOL	Q_B
10			
20			
40			
60			
100			

Chapter 7: Problem 7

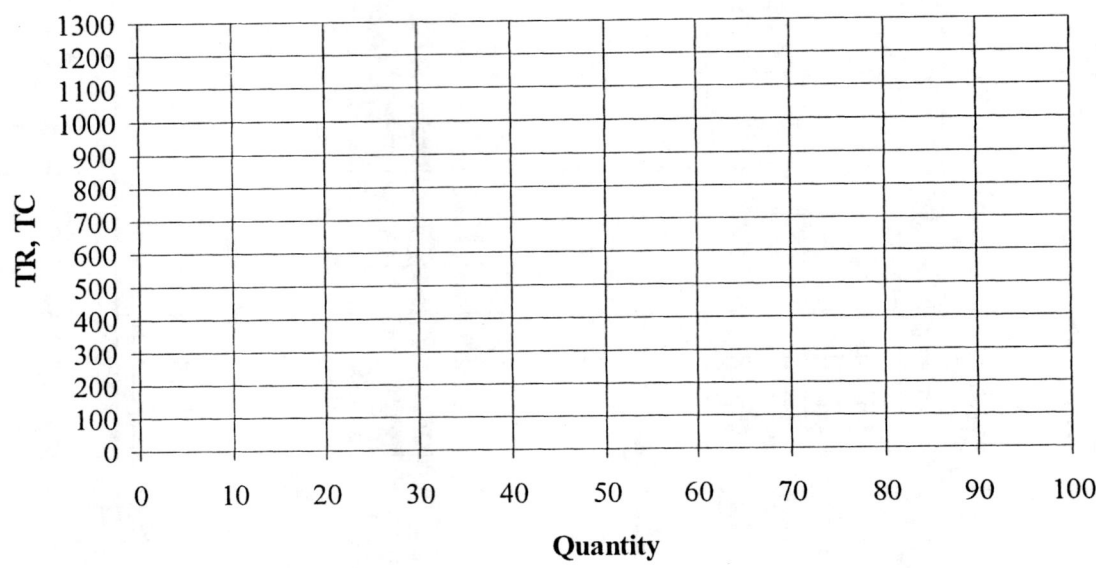

Quantity

8. Suppose that Field Research decides to build the production facility with K = 18 and that the price per 1,000 tons of Ranatar turns out to be $15,000. Assume that AVC is constant and calculate the degree of operating leverage for each level of output listed in the table below and enter them in the blank spaces in the table.

Q	25	50	75	100	125	150	175	200
DOL								

9. A few weeks after completing the work for Field Research, Diller Didactic gets a call from the owner. He says that the plant is currently producing 100,000 tons of Ranatar per month, that the degree of operating leverage is 1.6, and that profit is $1,000,000 per month. He wants to know what effect an increase in output to 120,000 tons will have on total profit. Priscilla is out of the office right now, so it is up to you to give them an answer. Using only the information given by the owner, calculate the predicted level of profit after the increase in output.

Silly Clone Manufacturing, a subsidiary of Silly Clone Computers, is preparing to produce a new computer chip. From past experience, Ed the production manager knows that the yield rate per batch of chips will increase and the cost per batch will decline over time. The yield rate is equal to the proportion of chips per batch that operate properly, so an increase in the yield rate will reduce unit cost. A reduction in the cost per batch will also contribute to a reduction in the cost per chip.

The first batch of chips have an average variable cost per unit of $20. Ed believes that AVC will decline at a rate defined by a learning curve coefficient of -0.50 per batch. Fred the marketing manager wants to price the chip aggressively to ensure strong penetration in the market. He suggests that a price of $10 per chip would be good place to start.

As the newest employee of Diller Didactic Consulting, you are asked to use this information to solve Problems 10 and 11.

10. Write out the learning curve function that is implied by Ed's description of the production process.

11. Calculate the AVC for each of the quantities listed in the table below and enter the values in the table. Plot the learning curve on the graph that follows. How many batches of chips will Silly Clone have to produce and sell before the contribution margin per unit rises to zero?

Q	1	2	3	4	5	6	7	8	9
AVC									

Chapter 7: Problem 11

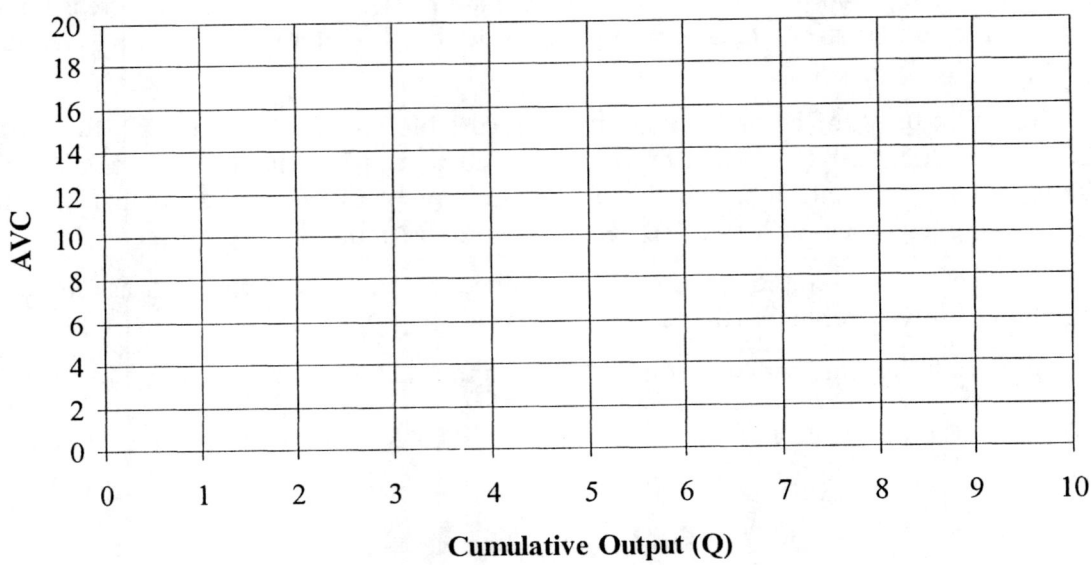

Cumulative Output (Q)

Magic Mushroom Farms, Inc. was founded by Tim O'Leary in 1965. The business has had its ups and downs since then, but has generally been highly successful. Recently, Tim's son Jim Bob took over the business. As a first step in the application of scientific management techniques, he has decided to estimate Magic Mushroom's total variable cost function.

Using seasonally adjusted deflated monthly time-series data for the past four years, Jim Bob obtained the following regression results:

$$TVC = 10.0\,Q - 2.8\,Q^2 + 0.3\,Q^3 + 0.05\,Q\,X$$

$$(4.03)\ (-2.78)\quad (1.68)\quad (3.79)$$

$$R^2 = 0.79$$

$$D\text{-}W = 1.79$$

TVC is total variable costs per month in hundreds of dollars, Q is monthly mushroom production in tons, and X is an index of input prices. Jim Bob has hired Diller Didactic Consulting to assist in the interpretation of his estimates and you have been assigned to the job. Use the information above to solve Problems 12 through 17.

12. Comment on the estimation results that Jim Bob obtained.

13. Assume that X = 100 and calculate TVC for the values of Q listed in the table below. What is the equation that defines average variable cost (AVC)? Calculate AVC and MC for the values of Q listed in the table. Enter your calculated values in the table and then plot TVC and the unit cost curves on the graphs that follow.

Q	TVC	AVC	MC
1			
2			
3			
4			
5			
6			
7			
8			
9			
10			

Chapter 7: Problem 13

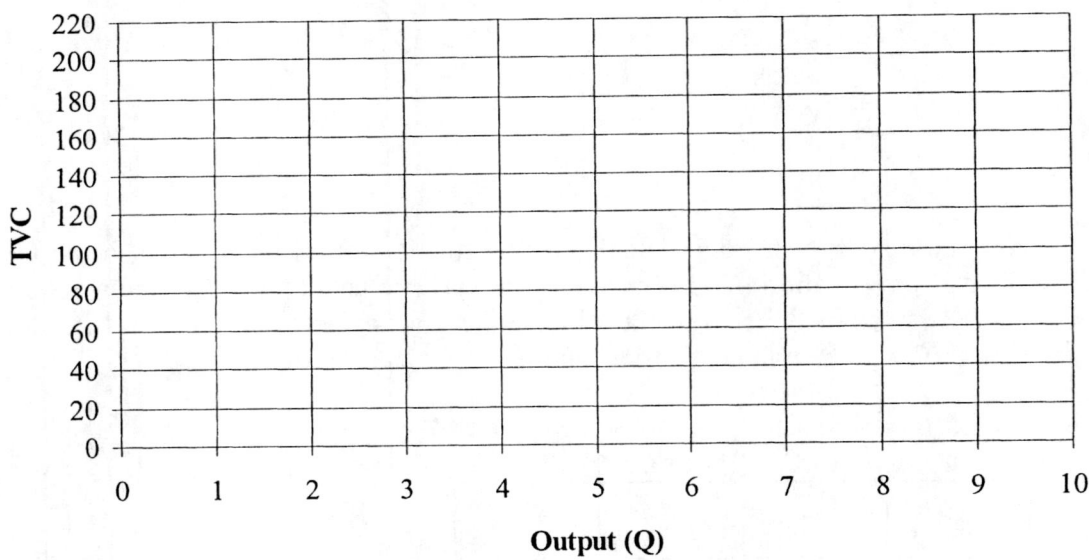

Chapter 7: Problem 13

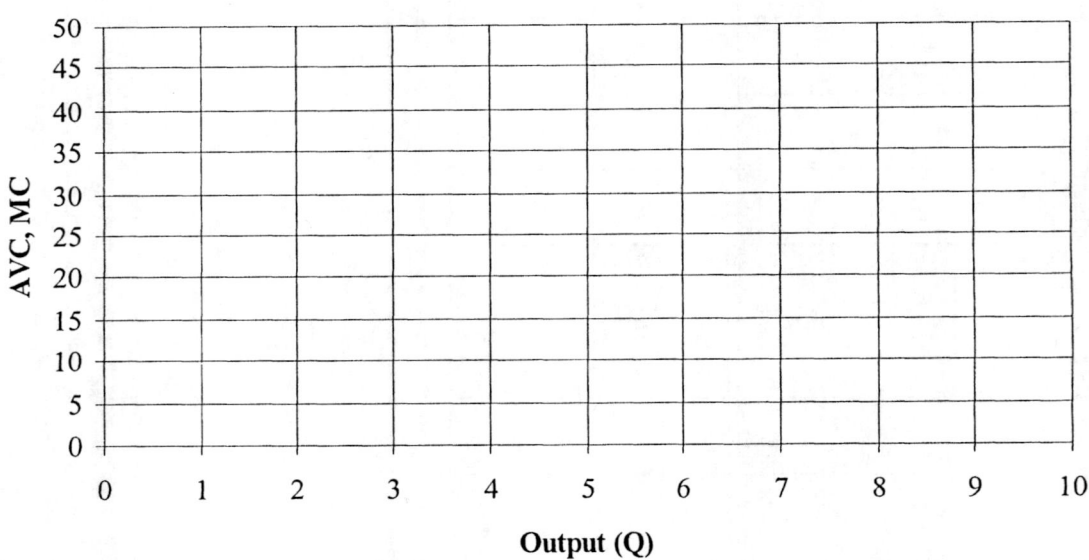

14. The index of input prices is expected to double over the next twelve months. Assume that X = 200 and calculate TVC for the values of Q listed in the table below. Calculate AVC and MC for the values of Q listed in the table. Enter your calculated values in the table and then plot TVC and the unit cost curves on the graphs from Problem 13. How did the increase in input prices influenced TVC? How did the increase influence the unit cost curves?

Q	TVC	AVC	MC
1			
2			
3			
4			
5			
6			
7			
8			
9			
10			

15. The mushroom market is highly competitive. The current market price is $2,000 per ton for any number of tons that Magic Mushroom can produce. Plot the total and marginal revenue functions on the graphs in Problem 13. The marginal cost function that corresponds to the estimated TVC function is:

$$MC = 10.0 - 5.6 \, Q + 0.9 \, Q^2 + 0.05 \, X$$

How many tons of mushrooms should be produced if $X = 100$? How many should be produced if $X = 200$?

Problems (calculus required)

16. Refer to the total variable cost function estimated by Jim Bob. Determine the level of output at which average variable cost is at a minimum when $X = 100$ and calculate the minimum average variable cost. Show that average variable cost is equal to marginal cost at this level of output.

17. Refer to the total variable cost function estimated by Jim Bob. Determine the level of output at which marginal cost is at a minimum when $X = 100$ and calculate the minimum marginal cost.

True-False Answers

1	F	10	F	19	T	28	F	37	F
2	T	11	F	20	F	29	T	38	T
3	F	12	F	21	F	30	F	39	T
4	T	13	F	22	T	31	F	40	F
5	T	14	T	23	T	32	F	41	T
6	F	15	T	24	F	33	T	42	T
7	T	16	F	25	F	34	F	43	F
8	T	17	T	26	T	35	T	44	F
9	T	18	T	27	T	36	T	45	F

Multiple Choice Answers

1	B	6	D	11	C	16	C	21	B
2	B	7	D	12	D	17	C	22	C
3	C	8	C	13	B	18	C	23	B
4	B	9	A	14	A	19	D	24	C
5	A	10	D	15	B	20	D	25	D

Solutions to Problems

1. The explicit costs of running Diller Didactic Consulting before business improved were the monthly office cost of $550, the receptionist's salary of $1,500, and the computer cost of $130. Total explicit cost was $2,180. The only implicit cost was Priscilla's opportunity cost of $60,000 per year or $5,000 per month. Total relevant monthly cost was $7,180 per month so $7,180 in monthly revenue was required for the firm to break even in economic terms.

2. The explicit costs of running Diller Didactic Consulting after business improved are the receptionist's salary of $1,500 and the associates' salaries of $10,000. Total explicit cost is $11,500. The implicit costs are Priscilla's opportunity cost of $60,000 per year or $5,000 per month, the opportunity cost of $550 each for the three offices that are now owned by the firm, the opportunity cost of $130 each for the three computers that are owned by the firm, and Willy Diller's opportunity cost of $24,000 per year or $2,000 per month. Total implicit cost is $9,040. Total relevant monthly cost is $20,540 per month so $20,540 in monthly revenue is required for the firm to break even in economic terms.

3. Several of Diller Didactic's past expenditures are irrelevant to future business decisions. First, consider the one-time advertising expense of $800 for the mailing list and $1,644 to print and send the advertising brochures. The decision to make this type of expenditure should be based on a comparison of its cost with a forecast of the benefits it will yield. However, once the expenditure is made, it becomes a sunk cost that is irrelevant to any future business decisions.

   The other two sunk costs involve the purchase of the office building and of the three computers. Again, the decision to purchase assets should be based on a comparison of their costs with forecasts of the benefits they will yield. But, once the assets are purchased, their prices are sunk costs that are not directly relevant to future business decisions. Business decisions should be based on the implicit value of an asset. In this case, the implicit value of a computer or an office building, reflected in its rental price, is determined by the market. The purchase price or book value is irrelevant.

4. TFC for any level of output is equal to TC when $Q = 0$. TVC is equal to TC - TFC. TR is equal to price times output; i.e., 50Q. Profit is equal to TR - TC. Profit is at a maximum ($\pi = 80$) when $Q = 4$. The firm must produce at least $Q = 2$ to avoid losses. This is the breakeven level of output in this case. Note that the firm would make zero profit if it produced $Q = 6$, but that this breakeven point represents a level of output beyond which the firm would make losses. When the total cost function is not linear, there can be two breakeven points.

Q	TC	TFC	TVC	TR	π
0	60	60	0	0	-60
1	75	60	15	50	-25
2	80	60	20	100	20
3	90	60	30	150	60
4	120	60	60	200	80
5	180	60	120	250	70
6	300	60	240	300	0

Chapter 7: Problem 4

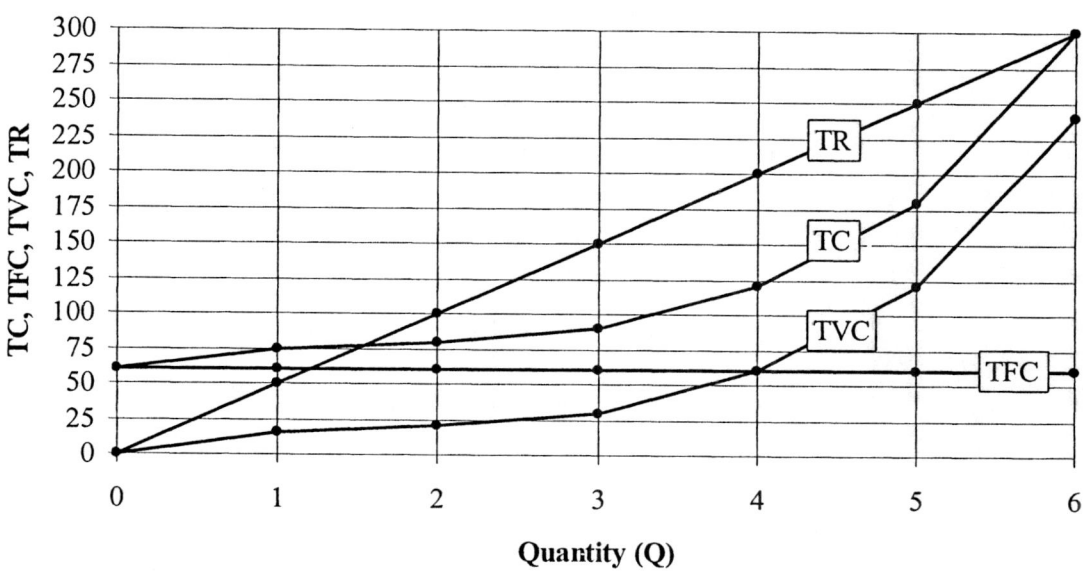

5. AFC is equal to TFC/Q. Thus, when Q = 2, AFC = 60/2. AVC is equal to TVC/Q, so when Q = 3, AVC = 30/3. ATC is equal to TC/Q, so when Q = 4, ATC = 120/4. MC is equal to the change in TC divided by the corresponding change in Q. MC between Q = 2 and Q = 3 is (90 - 80)/(3 - 2). MC is also equal to the change in TVC divided by the corresponding change in Q. MC between Q = 3 and Q = 4 is (60 - 30)/(4 - 3). Note that MC is plotted on a graph between the values of Q, so MC = 5 is plotted above Q = 1.5.

The firm breaks even when ATC is equal to average revenue. In this case, because price is constant, marginal revenue and average revenue are equal. The lower breakeven level of output occurs when output is increased from Q = 1 to Q = 2, because MR < ATC for Q = 1 and MR > ATC for Q = 2. The second breakeven level of output occurs at Q = 6, where MR = ATC.

Profit is maximized where an increase in output would cause MC to exceed MR. Thus, output should be increased up to Q = 4, because MC = 30 and MR = 50. However, output should not be increased to Q = 5, because MC = 60 and MR = 50. Profit per unit is equal to price minus average total cost (MR - ATC) and total profit is equal to profit per unit times the number of units produced. When Q = 4, profit per unit is 50 - 30 = 20 and total profit is 4(50 - 30) = 80.

Q	AFC	AVC	ATC	MC	MR
1	60	15	75	15	50
2	30	10	40	5	50
3	20	10	30	10	50
4	15	15	30	30	50
5	12	24	36	60	50
6	10	40	50	120	50

Chapter 7: Problem 5

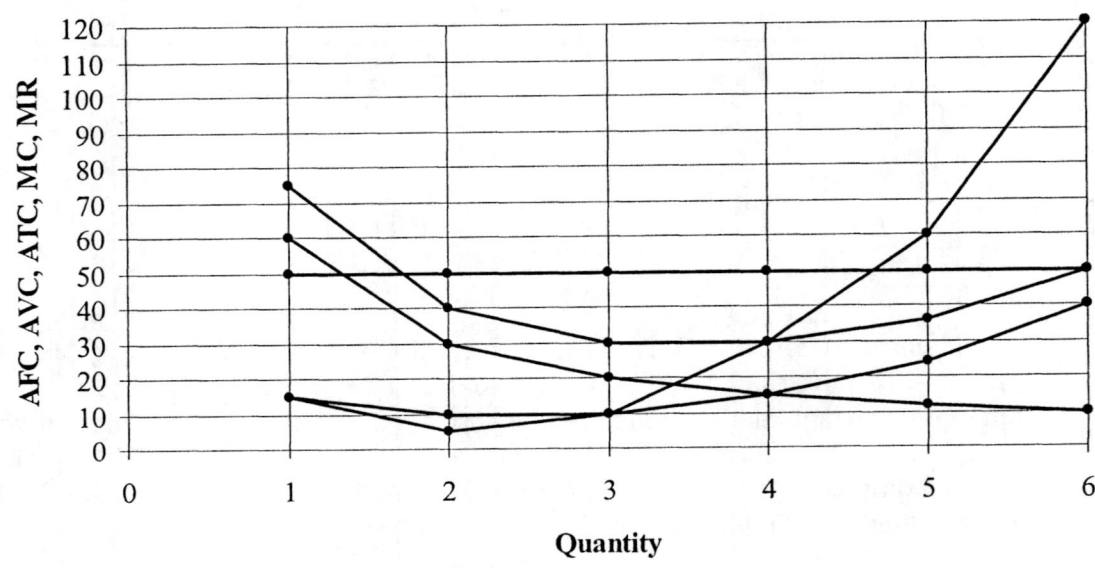

6. Returns to scale can be approximated by comparing the percentage change in input quantities with the percentage change in output due to changes in the scale of operation. The table that follows presents the percentage changes between adjacent scales and indicates the nature of returns to scale.

Between Q = 10 and Q = 40, returns to scale must be increasing because the percentage increase in Q is greater than the corresponding percentage increase in one input and is equal to the percentage change in the other. The reasoning is as follows. Assuming that the marginal product of each input is greater than zero at the optimum, then if both inputs were increased by 100%, then the percentage increase in output would have to be greater than 100%. This result is supported by the form of the long-run average cost curve, which slopes downward between Q = 10 and Q = 40.

Between Q = 40 and Q = 100, returns to scale are ambiguous because the percentage increase in one input is greater than the percentage increase in output while that of the other input is less than the increase in output. However, the long-run average cost curve is horizontal between Q = 40 and Q = 60, which suggests that returns to scale are constant over this range. Between Q = 60 and Q = 100, the long-run average cost curve slopes upward, which suggests that returns to scale are decreasing over this range. The results are ambiguous because the ratio of inputs is not constant along the expansion path that is used to derive the long-run cost curve.

ΔQ	%ΔQ	%ΔK	%ΔL	Returns to Scale
10 => 20	100%	100%	67%	Increasing
20 => 40	100%	67%	100%	Increasing
40 => 60	50%	80%	20%	Ambiguous
60 => 100	67%	150%	45%	Ambiguous

Q	LTC	TFC	TVC	AVC	LAC	LMC
10	120	60	60	6	12	12
20	220	120	100	5	11	10
40	400	200	200	5	10	9
60	600	360	240	4	10	10
100	1250	900	350	3.5	12.5	16.25

Chapter 7: Problem 6

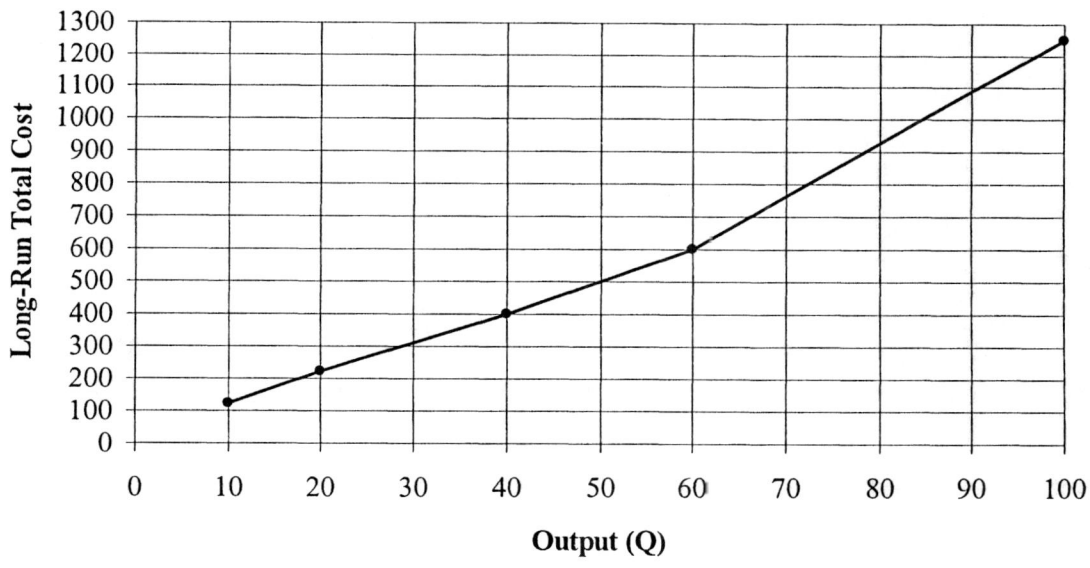

Chapter 7: Problem 6

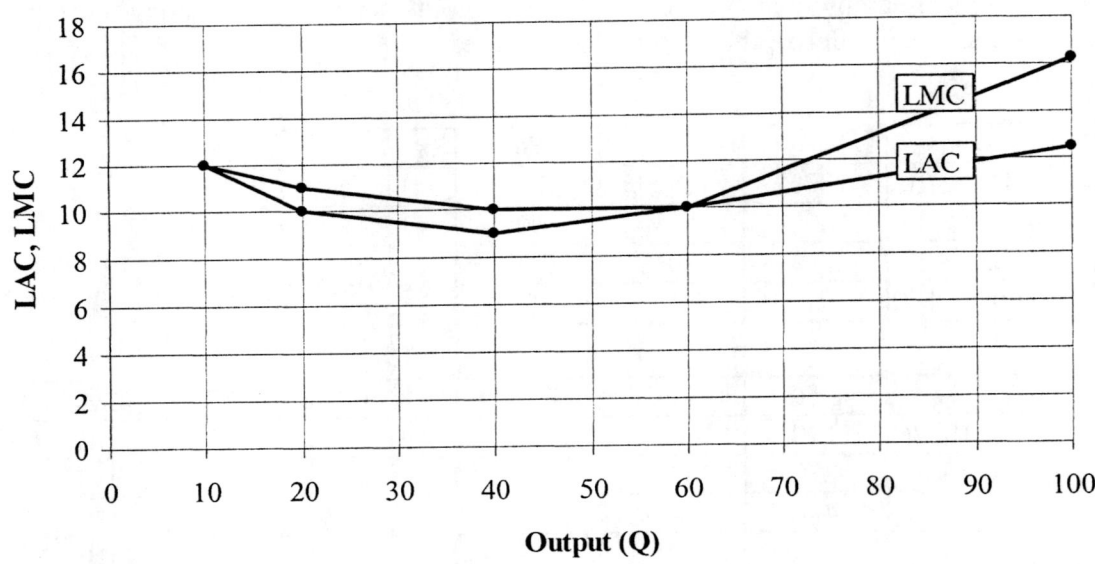

Long-run total cost (LTC) is equal to the sum of short-run total fixed cost (TFC = Kr) and total variable cost (TVC = Lw).

LTC = TFC + TVC = (K)(r) + (L)(w)

Long-run average cost (LAC) is equal to LTC/Q, long-run marginal cost (LMC) is equal to the change in LTC divided by the corresponding change in Q, and short-run average variable cost (AVC) is equal to TVC/Q.

For   Q = 10,   TFC = (3)(20) = 60,   TVC = (6)(10) = 60,   LTC = 60 + 60 = 120, LAC = 120/10 = 12, LMC = (120 - 0)/(10 - 0) = 12, and AVC = 60/10 = 6.

For   Q = 20,   TFC = (6)(20) = 120,   TVC = (10)(10) = 100,   LTC = 120 + 100 = 220, LAC = 220/20 = 11, LMC = (220 - 120)/(20 - 10) = 10, and AVC = 100/20 = 5.

For   Q = 40,   TFC = (10)(20) = 200,   TVC = (20)(10) = 200,   LTC = 200 + 200 = 400, LAC = 400/40 = 10, LMC = (400 - 220)/(40 - 20) = 9, and AVC = 200/40 = 5.

For   Q = 60,   TFC = (18)(20) = 360,   TVC = (24)(10) = 240,   LTC = 360 + 240 = 600, LAC = 600/60 = 10, LMC = (600 - 400)/(60 - 40) = 10, and AVC = 240/60 = 4.

For Q = 100, TFC = (45)(20) = 900, TVC = (35)(10) = 350, LTC = 900 + 350 = 1,250, LAC = 1,250/100 = 12.5, LMC = (1,250 - 600)/(100 - 60) = 16.3, and AVC = 350/100 = 3.5.

7.   Operating leverage (OL) is equal to total fixed cost divided by total variable cost (TFC/TVC). The formula that defines the degree of operating leverage (DOL) in terms of price (P), output (Q), TFC, and TVC is given below.

DOL = [Q(P - AVC)]/[Q(P - AVC) - TFC]

The formula that gives the breakeven level of output (Q_B) is given below.

Q_B = TFC/(P - AVC)

For Q = 10, P = 13, TVC = 60, AVC = 6, and TFC = 60, the calculations yield

OL = 60/60 = 1 and DOL = [10(13 - 6)]/[10(13 - 6) - 60] = 7

Q_B = 60/(13 - 6) = 8.6

For Q = 20, P = 13, TVC = 100, AVC = 5, and TFC = 120, the calculations yield

OL = 120/100 = 1.2 and DOL = [20(13 - 5)]/[20(13 - 5) - 120] = 4

Q_B = 120/(13 - 5) = 15

For Q = 40, P = 13, TVC = 200, AVC = 5, and TFC = 200, the calculations yield

OL = 200/200 = 1 and DOL = [40(13 - 5)]/[40(13 - 5) - 200] = 2.7

Q_B = 200/(13 - 5) = 25

For Q = 60, P = 13, TVC = 240, AVC = 4, and TFC = 360, the calculations yield

OL = 360/240 = 1.5 and DOL = [60(13 - 4)]/[60(13 - 4) - 360] = 3

Q_B = 360/(13 - 4) = 40

For Q = 100, P = 13, TVC = 350, AVC = 3.5, and TFC = 900, the calculations yield

OL = 900/350 = 2.6 and DOL = [100(13 - 3.5)]/[100(13 - 3.5) - 900] = 19

Q_B = 900/(13 - 3.5) = 94.7

As TFC increases, the linear cost curves become flatter because AVC decreases. At the same time, their intercepts increase because TFC defines the intercept. As a result of these two forces, the breakeven level of output increases as TFC increases.

Q	OL	DOL	Q_B
10	1.0	7.0	8.6
20	1.2	4.0	15.0
40	1.0	2.7	25.0
60	1.5	3.0	40.0
100	2.6	19.0	94.7

Chapter 7: Problem 7

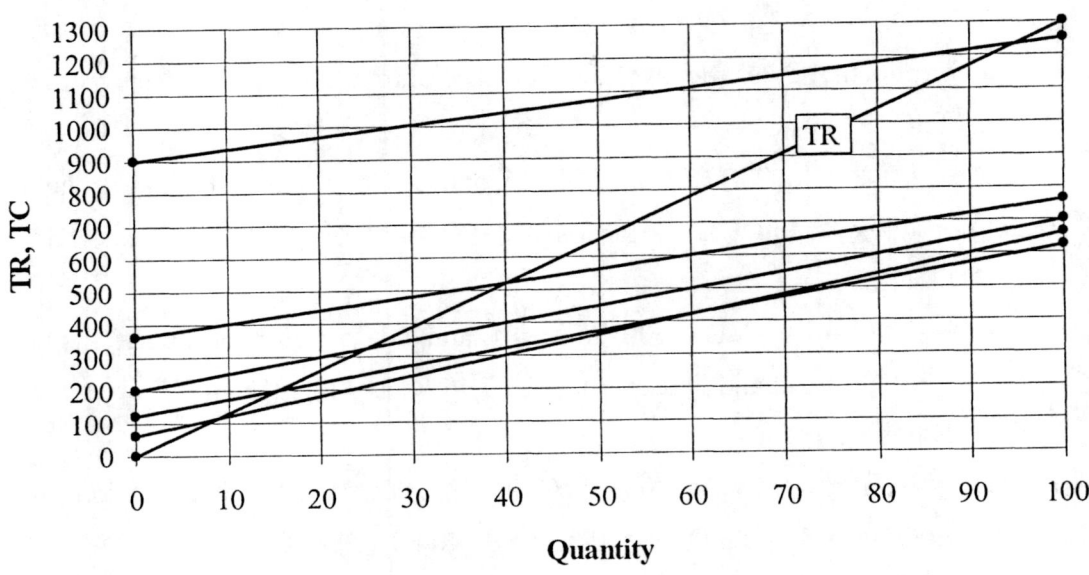

8. If Field Research builds the production facility with $K = 18$, then $TFC = 360$ and $AVC = 4$. If the price per 1,000 tons of Ranatar turns out to be \$15,000, then $P = 15$. The formula for the degree of operating leverage is

    $$DOL = [Q(15 - 4)]/[Q(15 - 4) - 360] = 11Q/(11Q - 360)$$

    For $Q = 50$, for example, $DOL = [(11)(50)]/[(11)(50) - 360] = 2.9$

Q	25	50	75	100	125	150	175	200
DOL	-3.2	2.9	1.8	1.5	1.4	1.3	1.2	1.2

9. The following information is given. $Q = 100$, $DOL = 1.6$, profit (π) is 1000, and output will increase to $Q = 120$. The general formula for DOL is given below.

    $$DOL = \%\Delta\pi/\%\Delta Q = (\Delta\pi/\Delta Q)(Q/\pi)$$

    This can solved for the change in profits and written as follows:

    $$\Delta\pi = (\%\Delta Q)(DOL)(\pi) = (\Delta Q)(DOL)(\pi/Q)$$

    The change in profit is thus:

    $$\Delta\pi = (120-100)(1.6)(1000/100) = 320$$

    The level of profit after the increase in Q is thus

    $$\pi + \Delta\pi = 1,000 + 320 = 1,320 \text{ or } \$1,320,000.$$

10. $AVC = 20Q^{-0.50}$

11. Note that the learning curve function (written in general terms as $AVC = aQ^b$) can be solved for Q as shown below.

$Q = (AVC/a)^{(1/b)}$

In this case, the solution value of Q for $AVC = P = 10$ is

$Q = (10/20)^{-2} = 4$

Q	1	2	3	4	5	6	7	8	9
AVC	20	14.1	11.5	10	8.9	8.2	7.6	7.1	6.7

Chapter 7: Problem 11

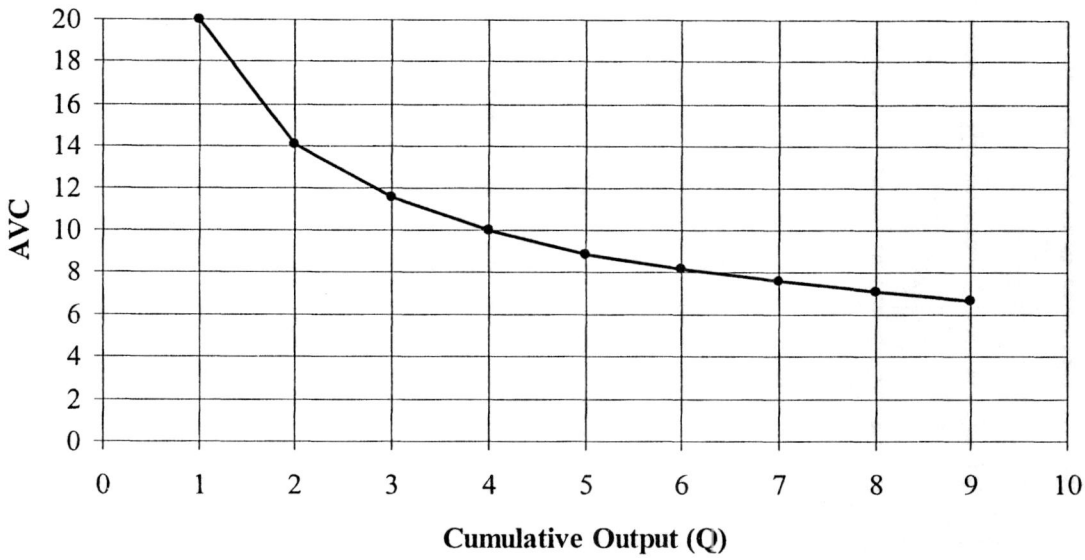

12. The estimates are based on four years of monthly data or 48 observations. The number of degrees of freedom for the t distribution is d.f. = n - k - 1 = 48 - 4 -1 = 43. The critical values of t at d.f. = 40 (which are approximately the same as those at d.f. = 43) are 1.684 (10%), 2.021 (5%), and 2.704 (1%). Thus, all coefficients save for that of the cubic term are significant at the 1% level. The cubic coefficient is borderline significant at the 10% level. The coefficient of determination (R^2) indicates that 79% of the variation in total variable cost is explained by the estimated equation. The Durbin-Watson test statistic is above the upper value from the table ($d_U = 1.72$) so there is no evidence of significant autocorrelation. All signs of the estimated coefficients are as expected. The estimated equation appears satisfactory.

13. TVC is calculated by substituting the appropriate values of Q and X into the estimated cost equation. Average variable cost (AVC) is TVC/Q. Marginal cost is the change in total variable cost divided by the corresponding change in Q. For example, if Q = 2 and X = 100,

$$TVC = (10.0)(2) - (2.8)(2^2) + (0.3)(2^3) + (0.05)(2)(100) = 21.2$$

$$AVC = 21.2/2 = 10.6$$

$$MC = (21.2 - 12.5)/(2 - 1) = 8.7$$

The equation that defines average variable cost is obtained by dividing TVC by Q.

$$AVC = 10.0 - 2.8\,Q + 0.3\,Q^2 + 0.05\,X$$

Q	TVC	AVC	MC
1	12.5	12.5	12.5
2	21.2	10.6	8.7
3	27.9	9.3	6.7
4	34.4	8.6	6.5
5	42.5	8.5	8.1
6	54.0	9.0	11.5
7	70.7	10.1	16.7
8	94.4	11.8	23.7
9	126.9	14.1	32.5
10	170.0	17.0	43.1

Chapter 7: Problem 13

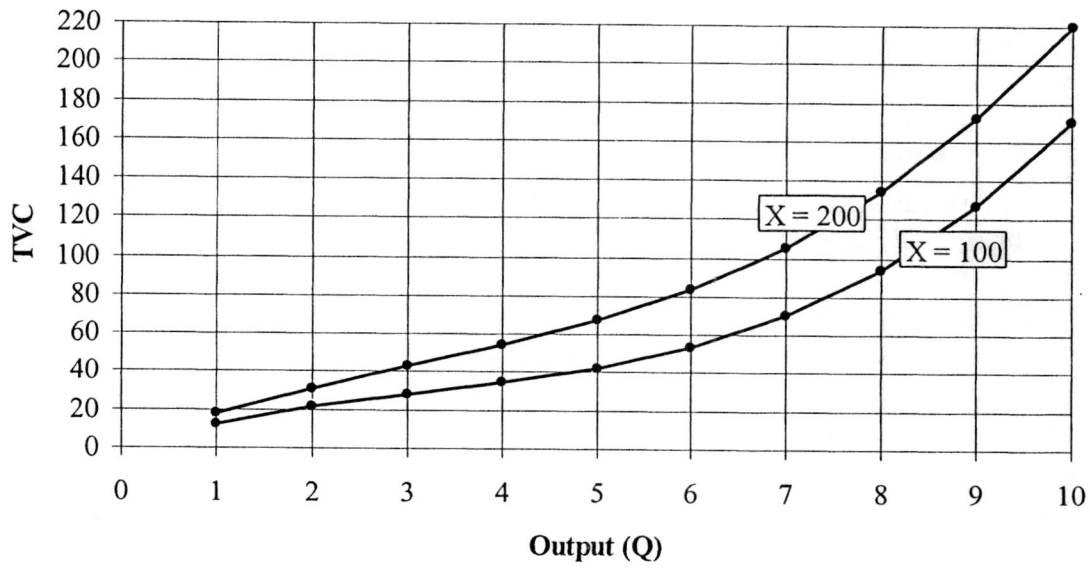

Chapter 7: Problem 13

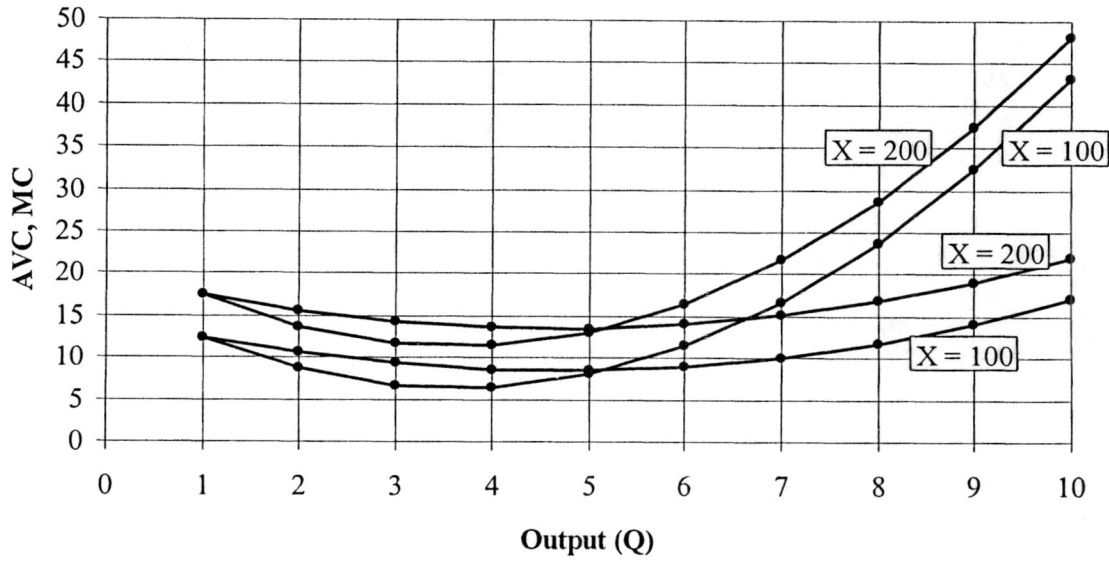

14. As in Problem 13, TVC is calculated by substituting the appropriate values of Q and X into the estimated cost equation. Average variable cost (AVC) is TVC/Q. Marginal cost is the change in total variable cost divided by the corresponding change in Q. For example, if $Q = 4$ and $X = 200$,

$TVC = (10.0)(4) - (2.8)(4^2) + (0.3)(4^3) + (0.05)(4)(200) = 54.4$

$AVC = 54.4/4 = 13.6$

$MC = (54.4 - 42.9)/(4 - 3) = 11.5$

The increase in input prices caused TVC to increase, pivoting the TVC curve upward. It caused the unit cost curves to shift upward.

Q	TVC	AVC	MC
1	17.5	17.5	17.5
2	31.2	15.6	13.7
3	42.9	14.3	11.7
4	54.4	13.6	11.5
5	67.5	13.5	13.1
6	84.0	14.0	16.5
7	105.7	15.1	21.7
8	134.4	16.8	28.7
9	171.9	19.1	37.5
10	220.0	22.0	48.1

15. The marginal cost (MC) function is derived from the total variable cost (TVC) function using calculus. MC is equal to the derivative (or partial derivative) of TVC.

If price is constant at $2,000 per ton, then the relevant marginal revenue is MR = 20. Setting this equal to MC for $X = 100$ yields:

$20 = 10.0 - 5.6 Q + 0.9 Q^2 + (0.05)(100)$ or

$0 = -5 + 5.6 Q + 0.9 Q^2$

This equation can be solved using the quadratic formula to yield $Q = -0.8$ and $Q = 7.0$. The second of these solutions is confirmed as the profit maximizing level of output by reference to the approximate MC values calculated in the table for Problem 13.

Setting MR = 20 equal to MC for $X = 200$ yields

$20 = 10.0 - 5.6 Q + 0.9 Q^2 + (0.05)(200)$ or

$0 = 5.6 Q - 0.9 Q^2$

This equation can be solved algebraically to yield $Q = 6.2$. This solution is confirmed as the profit maximizing level of output by reference to the approximate MC values calculated in the table for Problem 14.

16. The average variable cost function when $X = 100$ is

$AVC = 10.0 - 2.8\ Q + 0.3\ Q^2 + (0.05)(100)$

The level of output at which AVC is at a minimum is calculated by taking the derivative of the function, setting the derivative equal to zero, and then calculating the value of Q from this relationship. The minimum value of AVC and the corresponding value of MC are calculated by substituting the calculated value of Q into the appropriate equations.

$dAVC/dQ = -2.8 + 0.6Q = 0$ so $Q = 4.67$

$AVC = 15 - (2.8)(4.67) + (0.3)(4.67^2) = 8.5$

$MC = 15 - (5.6)(4.67) + (0.9)(4.67^2) = 8.5$

17. The level of output at which MC is at a minimum is calculated by taking the derivative of the function, setting the derivative equal to zero, and then calculating the value of Q from this relationship.

$dMC/dQ = -5.6 + 1.8\ Q = 0$ so $Q = 3.11$

The minimum MC for this value of Q is

$MC = 15 - (5.6)(3.11) + (0.9)(3.11^2) = 6.3$

CHAPTER 8

MARKET STRUCTURE: PERFECT COMPETITION, MONOPOLY, AND MONOPOLISTIC COMPETITION

Learning Objectives

The price of a commodity and the quantity traded of the commodity per time period depend on the characteristics of buyers, which are represented by the market demand function, the characteristics of sellers, which are represented by the production and cost functions, and the market structure. Market structure defines the way that sellers and buyers interact to determine equilibrium price and quantity. When you have completed the material in this chapter, you should have a fundamental understanding of the nature of three of the most important market structures: perfect competition, monopoly, and monopolistic competition, and of how these market structures operate to determine short-run and long-run equilibrium price and quantity.

Summary of Notation and Formulas

(8-1) $QD = 625 - 5P$

(8-2) $QS = 175 + 5P$

Equations 8-1 and 8-2 are mathematical expressions that represent linear market demand and market supply curves. They can be solved algebraically for the market equilibrium quantity and price by setting quantity demanded (QD) equal to quantity supplied (QS) as shown in the text. The general problem (where **a** and **-b** represent the intercept and slope of the demand curve and **c** and **d** represent the intercept and slope of the supply curve, respectively) and its solution are shown below.

Demand: $QD = a - bP$

Supply: $QS = c + dP$

Equilibrium: $QD = QS$

Substitution of the demand and supply curves into the equilibrium condition yields

$a - bP = c + dP$

This equation can be solved for the equilibrium price, which is

$$P^* = (a - c)/(b + d)$$

Equilibrium quantity is then determined by substituting the equilibrium price into either the demand or the supply curve to yield

$$Q^* = (cb + ad)/(b + d)$$

(8-3) $P = MR$

For a perfectly competitive firm (a "price-taker"), the market price (P) is identical to the firm's marginal revenue (MR).

True-False Questions

T F 1. Market structure refers to the competitive environment in which the buyers and sellers of a product operate.

T F 2. Economists define a market as a place where buyers go to purchase units of a commodity.

T F 3. A market structure is defined in terms of the number and sizes of buyers and sellers on a market, the type of product traded on the market, the mobility of resources, and the amount of knowledge economic agents have about market conditions.

T F 4. If a market is perfectly competitive, then the market demand curve must be infinitely price elastic.

T F 5. If the firms in an industry are **price takers**, then every firm in the industry faces a horizontal demand curve.

T F 6. Firms that sell commodities on markets that are imperfectly competitive face downward-sloping demand curves.

T F 7. Monopoly is a market structure in which there is only one buyer of a product for which there are no close substitutes.

T F 8. Oligopoly is a market structure in which there are few sellers of a product and additional sellers cannot easily enter the industry.

T F 9. Monopsony is a market structure in which there is a single buyer of a commodity or input for which there are no close substitutes.

T F 10. Under perfect competition, changes in market supply do not affect market price.

T F 11. Commodities that sell for the same price are referred to as homogeneous.

T F 12. Most commodities are traded on perfectly competitive markets.

T F 13. The combination of product homogeneity and perfect knowledge ensure that a single price will prevail on a perfectly competitive market.

T F 14. Product price on a competitive market is determined by the intersection of the market demand curve with the market supply curve.

T F 15. If a firm in a perfectly competitive industry charges a higher price than that charged by other firms in the industry it will be unable to sell any of its output.

T F 16. The demand curve faced by a perfectly competitive firm is horizontal.

T F 17. A perfectly competitive firm's demand curve is above its marginal revenue curve.

T F 18. If profit maximizing firms in a perfectly competitive industry are producing 14,000 units per day, but can only sell 12,000 units per day at the current market price of $23, then the market equilibrium price must be greater than $23.

T F 19. If profit maximizing firms in a perfectly competitive industry will produce 14,000 units per day if the market price is $23 and consumers will purchase 14,000 units per day if the market price is $20, then the market equilibrium quantity must be greater than 14,000.

T F 20. The **efficient market hypothesis** asserts that the price of a share of a firm's stock reflects the value implied by available information about the profitability of the firm.

T F 21. The only choice available to a perfectly competitive firm that is producing efficiently is what price to charge in order to maximize profits.

T F 22. Every profit-maximizing firm should produce a level of output where marginal revenue is equal to marginal cost.

T F 23. A perfectly competitive firm maximizes profit by producing a level of output where marginal cost is equal to price.

T F 24. If a perfectly competitive firm is producing a level of output where its marginal cost is greater than market price, it should raise its price.

T F 25. If a perfectly competitive firm is producing a level of output where price is equal to marginal cost and greater than average variable cost, then it should cease production in the short run.

T F 26. The **shut-down point** of a perfectly competitive firm is at the minimum point on its short-run average variable cost curve.

T F 27. The supply curve of a perfectly competitive firm is identical to the portion of its marginal cost curve that is above its average total cost curve.

T F 28. If a perfectly competitive firm is in long-run equilibrium, then it is earning an economic profit of zero.

T F 29. If a perfectly competitive firm is in long-run equilibrium, then market price is equal to short-run marginal cost, short-run average total cost, long-run marginal cost, and long-run average total cost.

T F 30. If firms in a perfectly competitive industry are earning economic profits greater than zero, then more firms will enter the industry.

T F 31. If more firms enter a perfectly competitive industry, market equilibrium price will increase.

T F 32. A perfectly competitive firm is in long-run equilibrium when all inputs are earning their opportunity costs.

T F 33. Depreciation of a country's currency tends to make imports more expensive.

T F 34. Appreciation of a country's currency tends to increase the demand for the country's exports.

T F 35. An increase the number of U.S. dollars required to purchase one British pound would be a depreciation of the U.S. dollar and an appreciation of the British pound.

T F 36. An increase in the U.S. demand for British products would tend to cause an appreciation of the British pound.

T F 37. A monopolist's marginal revenue is below market price.

T F 38. A natural monopoly is one that results from exclusive control of a crucial natural resource.

T F 39. All monopoly power that is based on barriers to entry is subject to decay in the long run except that based on government franchise.

T F 40. Monopolists always make economic profits.

T F 41. Monopolists are **price takers**.

T F 42. If a monopolist earns $5,000 when it sells 100 units of output and $5,025 when it sells 101 units of output, then the marginal revenue of the 101st unit is $25.

T F 43. If a monopolist has a linear demand curve, then it has a linear marginal revenue curve.

T F 44. A profit-maximizing monopolist will never produce a quantity that corresponds to a point on the inelastic portion of its demand curve.

T F 45. A monopolist will shut down in the short run if price is everywhere less than average total cost.

T F 46. A monopolist that is earning a profit in the short run can be expected to earn at least as much profit in the long run.

T F 47. If a monopolist is in short-run equilibrium, it must be in long-run equilibrium.

T F 48. In general, if a perfectly competitive industry is taken over by a monopolist, it will charge a lower price and produce a larger quantity of output.

T F 49. When compared to perfect competition, monopoly results in a **deadweight loss**.

T F 50. The difference between the total amount that consumers would be willing to pay for a given level of consumption and the amount that they actually have to pay is called **consumers' surplus**.

T F 51. Most markets are either perfectly competitive or monopolized.

T F 52. If a firm is small, produces a differentiated good for which there are many close substitutes, and it is easy to enter and exit the industry, then the firm is a monopolistic competitor.

T F 53. Monopolistic competition is most common in the manufacturing sector.

T F 54. The short-run supply curve for a monopolistically competitive firm is identical to the upward-sloping portion of the firm's marginal cost curve above average variable cost.

T F 55. Monopolistically competitive firms are price takers.

T F 56. Monopolistically competitive firms face a downward-sloping demand curve.

T F 57. If an imperfectly competitive firm has a linear demand curve, then its marginal revenue curve has the same price intercept as its demand curve.

T F 58. If an imperfectly competitive firm has a linear demand curve, then its marginal revenue curve has a quantity intercept that is half that of the demand curve.

T F 59. As more firms enter a monopolistically competitive industry, the market supply curve shifts to the right.

T F 60. As firms leave a monopolistically competitive industry, the remaining firms' demand curves shift to the right and become less elastic.

T F 61. If a monopolistically competitive firm is in long-run equilibrium, then its short-run average total cost curve is tangent to its demand curve.

T F 62. A market that is monopolistically competitive will tend to have fewer firms than would be the case if the same market was perfectly competitive.

T F 63. Monopolistically competitive firms operate with excess capacity.

T F 64. In the long run, monopolistically competitive firms earn zero economic profit.

T F 65. Product variation is the result of quality control problems.

T F 66. Monopolistically competitive firms attempt to minimize selling expenses.

T F 67. Selling expenses include any marketing expenditures that are intended to increase the demand for a product.

T F 68. A firm should increase expenditures on marketing and product variation up to the point where an additional dollar spent generates a marginal revenue of no less than one dollar.

T F 69. One problem with the theory of monopolistic competition is that it is difficult to define a market and to identify the firms that comprise it.

T F 70. In most cases, a monopolistically competitive market can be adequately approximated by the perfectly competitive model or the oligopoly model.

Multiple Choice Questions

1.   Which of the following is not a type of market structure?

A. Competitive monopoly
B. Oligopoly
C. Perfect competition
D. All of the above are types of market structures.

2.   If the market demand curve for a commodity has a negative slope then the market structure must be

A. perfect competition.
B. monopoly.
C. imperfect competition.
D. The market structure cannot be determined from the information given.

3.   If a firm sells its output on a market that is characterized by many sellers and buyers, a homogeneous product, unlimited long-run resource mobility, and perfect knowledge, then the firm is a

A. a monopolist.
B. an oligopolist.
C. a perfect competitor.
D. a monopolistic competitor.

4.   If a firm sells its output on a market that is characterized by a single seller and many buyers of a homogeneous product for which there are no close substitutes and barriers to long-run resource mobility, then the firm is

A. a monopolist.
B. an oligopolist.
C. a perfect competitor.
D. a monopolistic competitor.

5.   If a firm sells its output on a market that is characterized by many sellers and buyers, a differentiated product, and unlimited long-run resource mobility, then the firm is

A. a monopolist.
B. an oligopolist.
C. a perfect competitor.
D. a monopolistic competitor.

6.   If a firm sells its output on a market that is characterized by few sellers and many buyers and limited long-run resource mobility, then the firm is

A. a monopolist.
B. an oligopolist.
C. a perfect competitor.
D. a monopolistic competitor.

7.   If one perfectly competitive firm increases its level of output, market supply

A. will increase and market price will fall.
B. will increase and market price will rise.
C. and market price will both remain constant.
D. will decrease and market price will rise.

8.   Which of the following markets comes close to satisfying the assumptions of a perfectly competitive market structure?

A. The stock market.
B. The market for agricultural commodities such as wheat or corn.
C. The market for petroleum and natural gas.
D. All of the above come close to satisfying the assumptions of perfect competition.

9.   A perfectly competitive firm should reduce output or shut down in the short run if market price is equal to marginal cost and price is

A. greater than average total cost.
B. less than average total cost.
C. greater than average variable cost.
D. less than average variable cost.

10.   The market demand curve for a perfectly competitive industry is QD = 12 - 2P. The market supply curve is QS = 3 + P. The market will be in equilibrium if

A. P = 6 and Q = 9.
B. P = 5 and Q = 2.
C. P = 4 and Q = 4.
D. P = 3 and Q = 6.

11.   Which of the following is <u>not</u> a barrier to entry that typically results in monopoly?

A. The firm controls the entire supply of a raw material.
B. Production of the industry's product is subject to economies of scale over a broad range of output.
C. Production of the industry's product requires a large initial capital investment.
D. The firm holds an exclusive government franchise.

12.   In the short run, a monopolist will shut down if it is producing a level of output where marginal revenue is equal to short-run marginal cost and price is

A. greater than average total cost.
B. less than average total cost.
C. greater than average variable cost.
D. less than average variable cost.

13.   A **natural monopoly** refers to a monopoly that is defended from direct competition by

A. economies of scale over a broad range of output.
B. a government franchise.
C. control over a vital input.
D. a patent or copyright.

14. When a perfectly competitive industry is in long-run equilibrium, all firms in the industry

    A. earn zero economic profits.
    B. produce a level of output where short-run marginal cost is equal to short-run average total cost.
    C. produce a level of output where long-run marginal cost is equal to long-run average cost.
    D. All of the above are correct.

15. The short-run supply curve of a perfectly competitive firm

    A. is equal to that portion of the short-run marginal cost curve that is above the average variable cost curve.
    B. is equal to that portion of the short-run marginal cost curve that is above the average total cost curve.
    C. is equal to that portion of the short-run average total cost curve that is above the average variable cost curve.
    D. None of the above is correct.

16. The long-run supply curve of a perfectly competitive firm

    A. is equal to that portion of the long-run marginal cost curve that is above the relevant short-run average variable cost curve.
    B. is equal to that portion of the long-run marginal cost curve that is above the relevant short-run average total cost curve.
    C. is equal to that portion of the long-run average total cost curve that is above the relevant short-run average variable cost curve.
    D. None of the above is correct.

17. A depreciation of the U.S. dollar relative to foreign currencies will make

    A. foreign imports less expensive in the United States.
    B. U.S. exports less expensive in foreign countries.
    C. the demand for U.S. exports decrease.
    D. All of the above are correct.

18. The value of the U.S. dollar on the foreign exchange market will tend to

    A. increase if there is an increase in the demand for U.S. exports by foreign countries.
    B. decrease if there is an increase in the demand for foreign imports by the United States.
    C. decrease if monetary authorities intervene on the foreign exchange market by selling U.S. dollars for foreign currencies.
    D. All of the above are correct.

19.   A monopolized market is in long-run equilibrium when

   A. zero economic profit is earned by the monopolist.
   B. production takes place where price is equal to long-run marginal cost and long-run average cost.
   C. production takes place where long-run marginal cost is equal to marginal revenue and price is not below long-run average cost.
   D. All of the above are correct.

20.   A monopolist produces 14,000 units of output and charges $14 per unit. Its marginal revenue is $8, its marginal cost is $7 and rising, its average total cost is $10, and its average variable cost is $9. The monopolist should

   A. increase output, which will result in an increase in the firm's positive economic profit.
   B. increase output, which will reduce the firm's economic losses.
   C. shut down, which will reduce the firm's economic losses.
   D. decrease output, which will result in an increase in the firm's positive economic profit.

21.   Which of the following types of firms is most likely to be a monopolistic competitor?

   A. A local telephone company.
   B. An automobile manufacturer.
   C. A restaurant.
   D. All of the above are likely to be monopolistic competitors.

22.   Which of the following is a differentiated product?

   A. A hamburger.
   B. A shirt.
   C. An automobile.
   D. All of the above are differentiated products.

23.   Which of the following is not a characteristic of monopolistic competition?

   A. Few sellers.
   B. A differentiated product.
   C. Easy entry into and exit from the industry.
   D. All of the above are characteristics of monopolistic competition.

24.   The demand curve faced by a monopolistically competitive firm is

   A. perfectly elastic.
   B. elastic.
   C. unit elastic.
   D. inelastic.

25. If an imperfectly competitive firm is producing a level of output where marginal cost is equal to marginal revenue, marginal revenue is below average variable cost, and price is equal to average total cost, then the firm

    A. should shut down.
    B. should decrease output, but should not shut down.
    C. should increase output.
    D. None of the above is correct.

26. If an imperfectly competitive firm is producing a level of output where marginal cost is equal to marginal revenue, marginal revenue is below average variable cost, and price is equal to average total cost, then the firm is <u>not</u>

    A. in long-run equilibrium.
    B. in short-run equilibrium.
    C. minimizing short-run average total cost.
    D. breaking even.

27. Product variation refers to

    A. an activity undertaken by a firm to increase demand.
    B. a problem with quality control that tends to decrease demand.
    C. an activity undertaken by a firm to make demand more price inelastic.
    D. None of the above is correct.

28. Which of the following is <u>not</u> a criticism of the theory of monopolistic competition?

    A. It is difficult to define a monopolistically competitive market and to determine the firms and products that comprise it.
    B. When product differentiation is slight, each firm's demand curve is nearly horizontal so the perfectly competitive solution provides an adequate approximation to the monopolistically competitive solution.
    C. When there are strong brand preferences and few producers of many differentiated products, or when there are many producers but only a few compete as rivals for any given consumer, then the oligopoly solution provides an adequate approximation to the monopolistically competitive solution.
    D. All of the above are correct.

29. Which of the following industries is most likely to be monopolistically competitive?

    A. The automobile industry
    B. The steel industry
    C. The car repair industry
    D. The electrical generating industry

30. Marginal revenue is equal to price for which one of the following types of market structure?

    A. Monopoly
    B. Perfect competition
    C. Monopolistic competition
    D. Oligopoly

Problems

Resorts Unlimited, Ltd. is considering the construction of a new health spa in the resort town of Frangipani, Idaho. If built, the spa will employ a large number of unskilled workers from the area. The spa will require 600,000 hours of unskilled labor per year. The cost of unskilled labor is a major factor in determining whether or not the spa will be profitable, so Resorts Unlimited hires an economic consulting firm to analyze wage rates. The firm has estimated the following market demand and supply curves for annual hours (in millions) of unskilled labor in Frangipani.

$$QD = 30 - 4P$$

$$QS = 5 + P$$

One source of unskilled labor in the Frangipani area is the Frangipani campus of Idaho College. The consultants have found that an annual contribution of $1 million to the college will allow an expansion that will contribute 1 million hours of unskilled labor to the Frangipani labor market. Use this information to solve Problems 1 through 3.

1. Plot the estimated market demand and supply curves on the graph below. Algebraically calculate the equilibrium price and quantity and compare your calculated value with the point of intersection on the graph.

Chapter 8: Problem 1

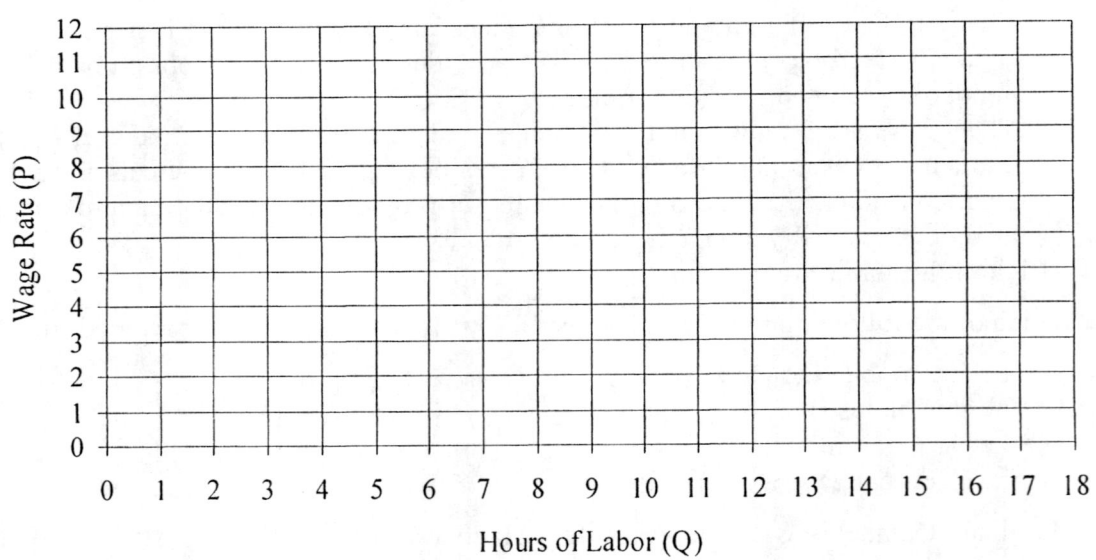

2. Determine the effect on equilibrium price and quantity if the spa is built and 600,000 hours of unskilled labor are employed by the spa. How will this affect other employers of unskilled labor in Frangipani? How will it affect total expenditures on unskilled labor in Frangipani?

3. Assume that the spa is built, 600,000 hours of unskilled labor are employed by the spa, and $1 million is contributed annually to Idaho College. Plot the new supply and demand curves on the graph from Problem 1. Algebraically calculate the new equilibrium price and quantity. How will the contribution affect other employers of unskilled labor in Frangipani? How will it affect total expenditures on unskilled labor in Frangipani? How will the $1 million contribution influence the spa's annual expenditures on unskilled labor? Should the contribution be made?

Emma Carson is the chief microbiologist in charge of fungus research at Etna Labs. She has determined that a variety of smut found only in the Amazon rain forest has extraordinary medicinal properties. Unfortunately, the region in which the smut occurs is scheduled to be razed in order to make way for a shopping mall. Fortunately, Emma has found a way to culture this smut in the laboratory. The marginal cost of producing the patented Etna Smut Culture Kit is $10. The estimated annual demand for the kits for medical research and pharmaceutical production (in thousands) is

QD = 100 - 2P

Use this information to solve Problems 4 and 5.

4. Plot the demand curve, the marginal cost curve, and the marginal revenue curve on the graph below. Algebraically determine the profit-maximizing price that Etna should charge for Smut Culture Kits, the number they can expect to sell, and their total revenue.

Chapter 8: Problem 4

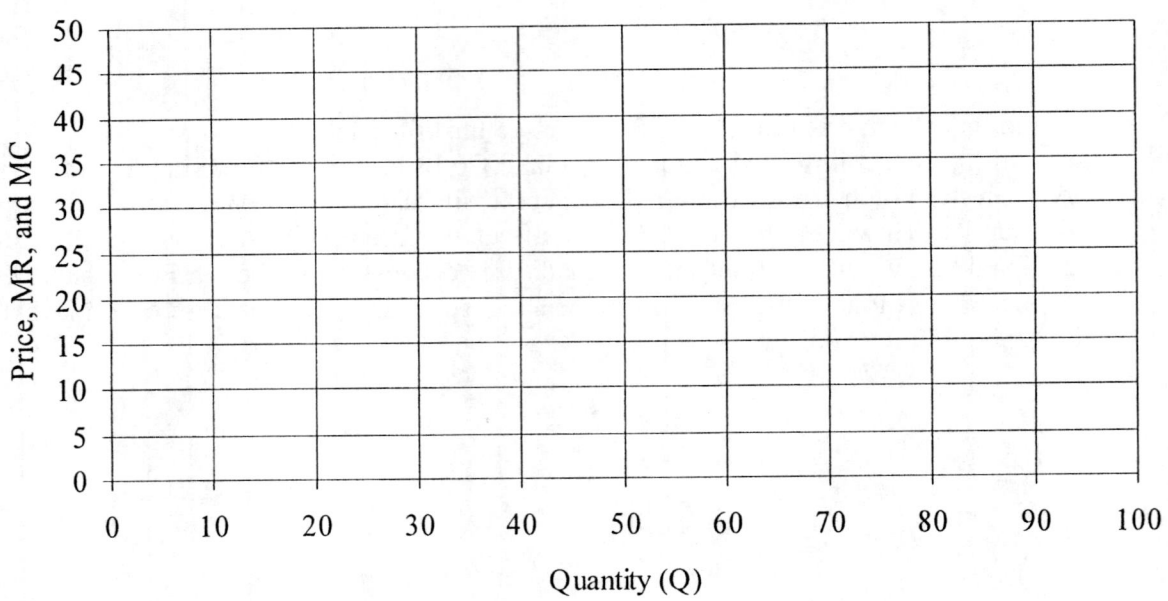

Construction of the shopping mall in the Amazon has been blocked by an environmental organization's Save Our Smut (SOS) campaign. The land has been sold by the mall developer and is now being used for large scale smut farming. The availability of raw smut has had a substantial impact on the demand for cultured smut, and so the demand for Smut Culture Kits has declined. The demand curve for the kits is now

$$QD = 40 - 2P$$

5. Plot the new demand curve and marginal revenue curve on the graph from Problem 4. Algebraically determine the profit-maximizing price that Etna should charge for Smut Culture Kits, the number they can expect to sell, and their total revenue.

Betty Joe Conundrum is the president of Menacing Faces, a company that manufactures injection molded rubber masks. The company is planning to demolish its old factory and to build a new one. An engineering study was conducted to determine production costs for three different factories. Total predicted monthly production costs (in $1,000s per month) for various output levels (in 1,000s of units per month) for each of the three factories are presented in the table below.

Use this information to solve Problems 6 to 8.

Q	TC (Plant 1)	TC (Plant 2)	TC (Plant 3)
0	5	8	13
1	7	11	18
2	8	13	21
3	11	14	23
4	17	17	24
5	27	23	27
6	42	33	33
7	63	48	43
8	93	69	58
9	137	99	79
10	201	143	109

6. Calculate long-run total, average, and marginal cost for Menacing Faces and enter them in the table below. Plot the total and unit cost values on the graphs that follow.

Q	LTC	LAC	LMC
0			
1			
2			
3			
4			
5			
6			
7			
8			
9			
10			

Chapter 8: Problem 6

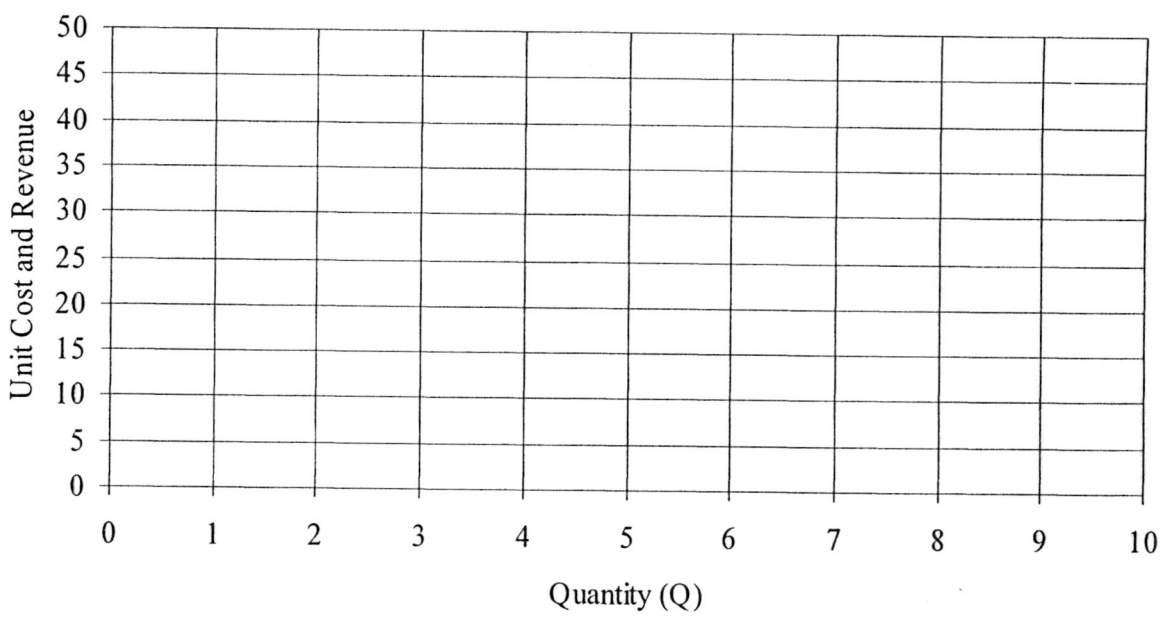

Chapter 8: Problem 6

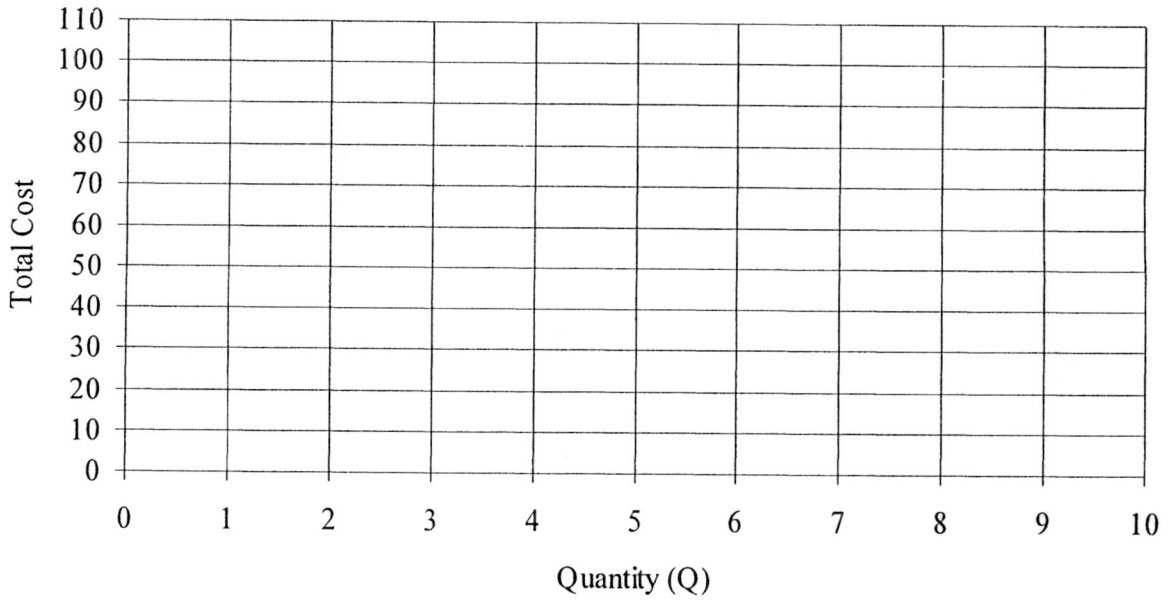

7.   Assume that Menacing Faces is a monopolist and that the demand curve for its output is

QD = 23.5 - 0.5P

Calculate average revenue, total revenue, and marginal revenue from the demand curve and enter them in the table below. Plot marginal revenue and average revenue on the unit cost graph from Problem 6. Determine long-run equilibrium quantity, price, and profit. Which one of the factories should Betty Joe build?

Q	AR	TR	MR
0			
1			
2			
3			
4			
5			
6			
7			
8			
9			
10			

8. Now assume that Menacing Faces is a perfect competitor. At what price and output will Betty Joe be indifferent between the small and the mid-sized factory? At what price and output will she be indifferent between the mid-sized and the large factory? If she builds the mid-sized or large plant, what will happen in the long run?

9. Ruby Davino owns a small firm that assembles and tests electronic components that are used in a variety of different products. The industry in which Davino's firm operates is very competitive. All of the firms in the industry use the same technology and all have the same input costs. The production costs for Davino's firm (in $1,000s per month) are listed in the table below. Output is measured in thousands of units per month. Calculate the short-run average total, average variable, and marginal cost and enter them into the table. Plot the unit cost curves on the graph that follows Problem 11.

Q	TC	ATC	AVC	MC
0	6.0			
1	9.0			
2	11.0			
3	12.6			
4	14.8			
5	18.5			
6	23.7			
7	31.5			
8	43.4			
9	60.3			
10	86.3			

10. Refer to the information given in Problem 9. Assuming that the current plant size is optimal, what is the long-run equilibrium price and output for Davino's firm? If total monthly industry demand at this price is 450 thousand units, then approximately how many firms will comprise the industry when it is in long-run equilibrium? What price corresponds to the **shutdown point** for the firms?

11. Refer to the information given in Problem 9. Assume that the industry consists of 100 firms and that the industry demand curve is $QD = 820 - 100P$, where quantity is measured in hundreds of thousands per month and the price per thousand units is measured in thousands of dollars. Plot the industry supply curve and the industry demand curve on the second graph below. What is the equilibrium price and quantity?

Chapter 8: Problem 11

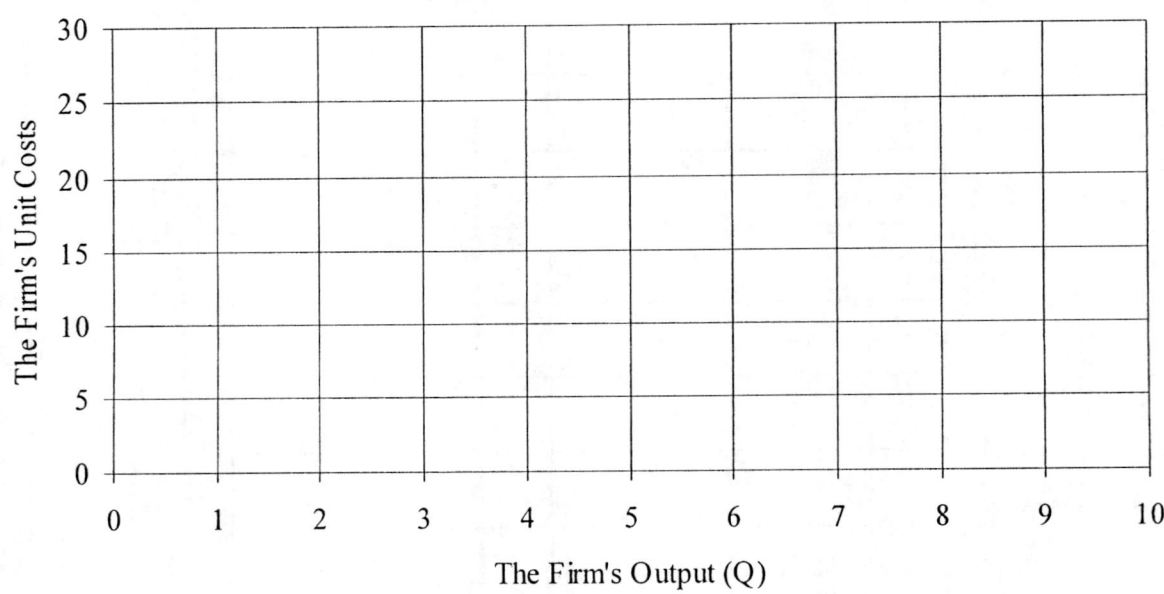

The Firm's Unit Costs

The Firm's Output (Q)

Chapter 8: Problem 11

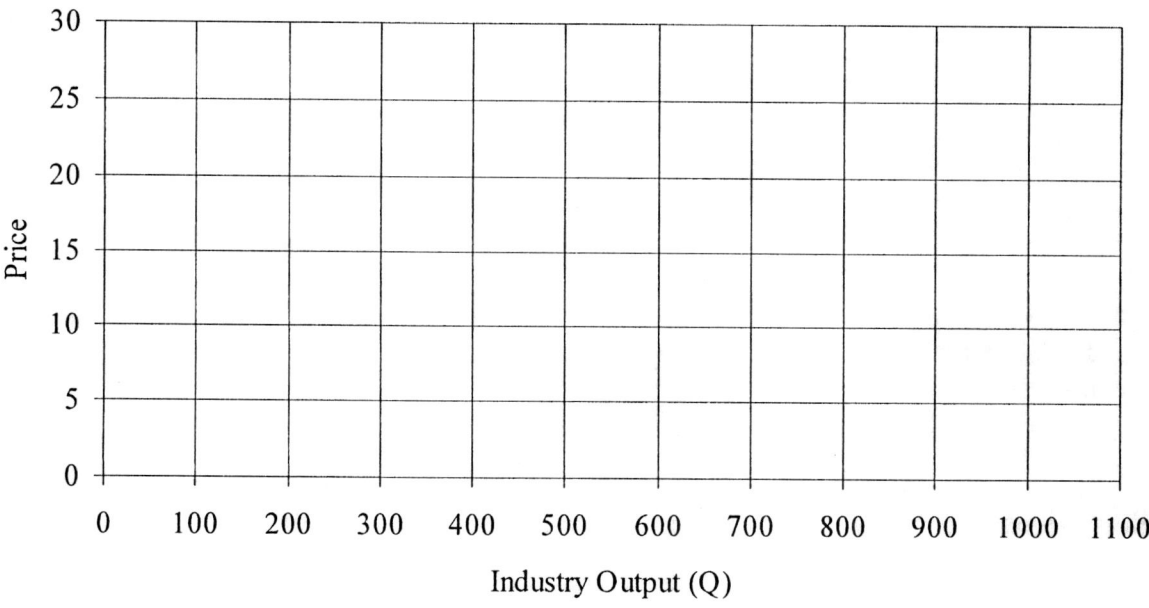

Industry Output (Q)

12. Refer to the information given in Problem 11. Assume that the industry demand curve has shifted to QD = 1070 - 100P. Plot the new industry demand curve on the graph for Problem 11. What is the new short-run equilibrium price and quantity? What quantity of output per month will Davino's firm produce in the short run? How much profit will Davino's firm earn in the short run? How many firms will be in the industry after adjustment to long-run equilibrium?

13.	Refer to the information given in Problem 11. Assume that the industry demand curve has shifted to QD = 570 - 100P. Plot the new industry demand curve on the graph for Problem 11. What is the new short-run equilibrium price and quantity? What quantity of output per month will Davino's firm produce in the short run? How much profit will Davino's firm earn in the short run? How many firms will be in the industry after adjustment to long-run equilibrium?

Beautiful Baguette's Bakery is a monopolistically competitive firm located in Cleveland, Colorado. The demand for its output, where quantity is in hundreds of loaves and price is in dollars, is defined below.

$$Q^d = 14 - 1.4\,P$$

The firm's marginal cost is $2 per loaf when production is less than or equal to 600 loaves per week. Between 600 and 800 loaves per week, marginal cost rises linearly to $4 per loaf. The firm is unable to produce more than 800 loaves per week. Use this information to solve Problems 14 through 16 below.

14.	Plot the demand, marginal revenue, and marginal cost curves on the graph below.

Chapter 8: Problem 14

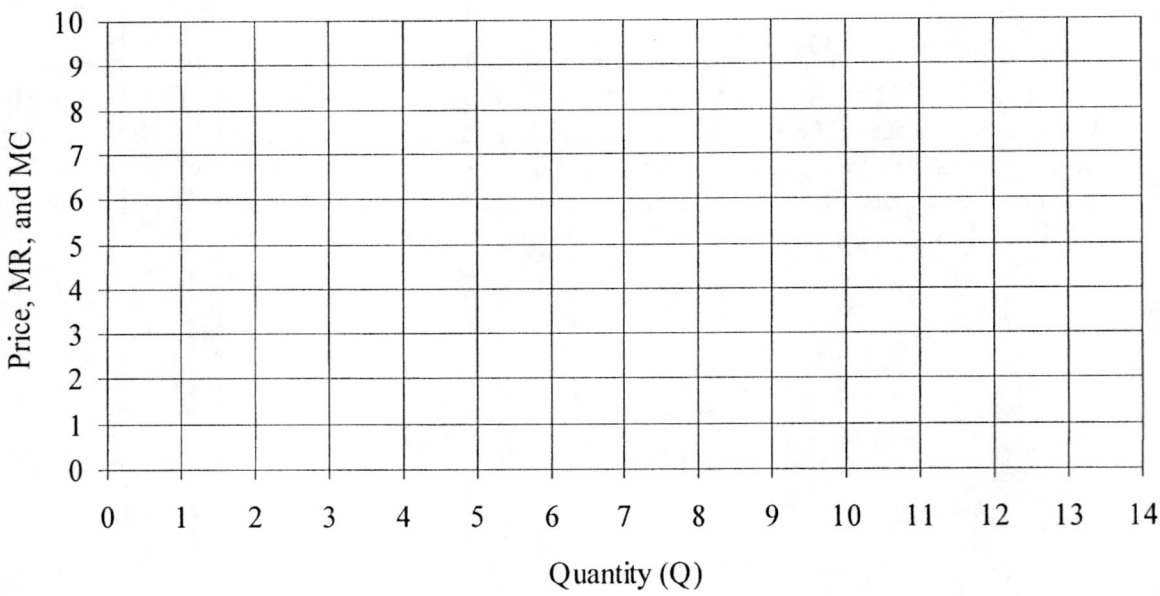

15. Calculate the firm's profit maximizing level of output and the price per loaf that corresponds to this level of output.

16. If the graph you plotted in Problem 1 represents long-run equilibrium for the firm and the firm is making positive economic profits at the equilibrium level of output, what will happen when the "industry" adjusts to long-run equilibrium? How would this long-run adjustment be represented on the graph?

17. The cost curves drawn on the graph below represent the long-run marginal and average costs of a monopolistically competitive firm. Draw in the linear demand curve and marginal revenue curve that would cause the firm and the "industry" to be in long-run equilibrium. Identify the firm's long-run equilibrium price and quantity, compare it to competitive equilibrium, and use the graph to explain the meaning of "excess capacity" as the term is applied to monopolistically competitive firms.

Chapter 8: Problem 17

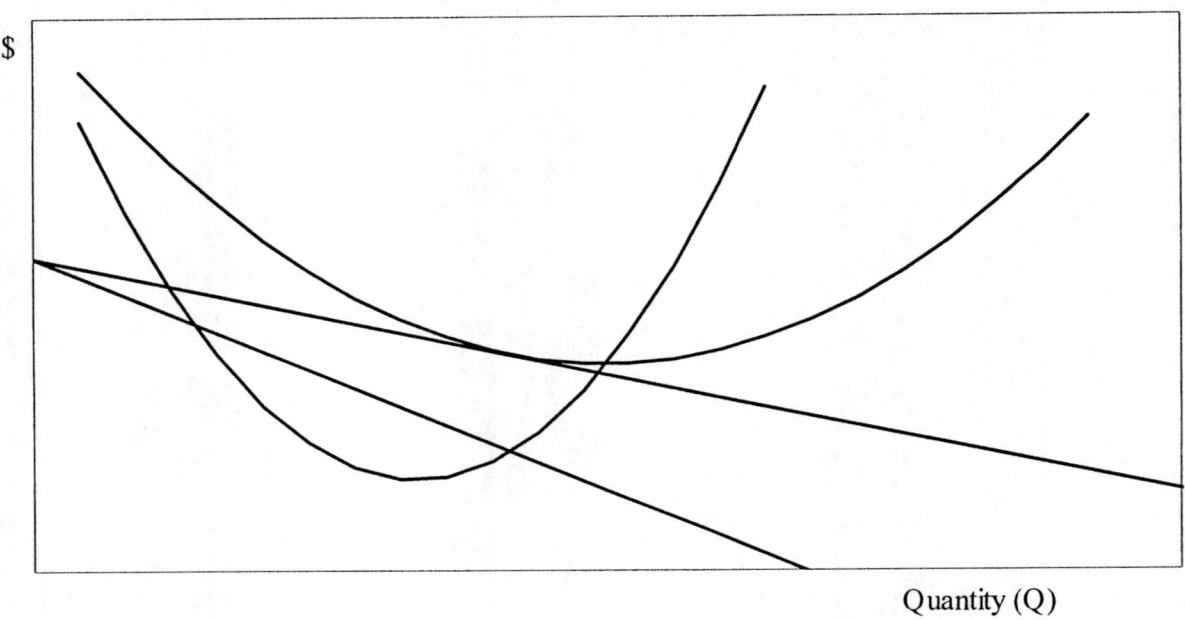

Quantity (Q)

Problems (calculus required)

18. The market demand curve faced by an imperfectly competitive firm is

$QD = 401 - 5 P$

The firm's total cost curve is

$TC = 5 + 45 Q - 10 Q^2 + Q^3$

Calculate the firm's profit maximizing level of output and the corresponding price, total revenue, total cost, and profit.

19.   A competitive firm has the following total cost function

$$TC = 100 + 50\,Q - 5\,Q^2 + 0.20\,Q^3$$

If the market price is $10, how many units of output should the firm produce? What total revenue, total cost, and profit will the firm earn?

20.   Refer to the total cost function given in Problem 15. If the market price is $90, how many units of output should the firm produce? What total revenue, total cost, and profit will the firm earn?

True-False Answers

1	T	15	T	29	T	43	T	57	T
2	F	16	T	30	T	44	T	58	T
3	T	17	F	31	F	45	F	59	F
4	F	18	F	32	T	46	T	60	T
5	T	19	F	33	T	47	F	61	T
6	T	20	T	34	F	48	F	62	F
7	F	21	F	35	T	49	T	63	T
8	T	22	T	36	T	50	T	64	T
9	T	23	T	37	T	51	F	65	F
10	F	24	F	38	F	52	T	66	F
11	F	25	F	39	T	53	F	67	T
12	F	26	T	40	F	54	F	68	T
13	T	27	F	41	F	55	F	69	T
14	T	28	T	42	T	56	T	70	T

Multiple Choice Answers

1	A	7	C	13	A	19	C	25	D
2	D	8	D	14	D	20	A	26	C
3	C	9	D	15	A	21	C	27	A
4	A	10	D	16	B	22	D	28	D
5	D	11	C	17	B	23	A	29	C
6	B	12	D	18	D	24	B	30	B

Solutions to Problems

1. The market equilibrium price (P*) is calculated by setting quantity demanded (QD) equal to quantity supplied (QS) and then solving for P.

    $30 - 4P = 5 + P$

    $30 - 5 = (4 + 1)P$

    $P* = 25/5 = 5$

    The market equilibrium quantity (Q*) is calculated by substituting the equilibrium price into either the demand curve or the supply curve and then solving for Q.

    $Q* = 30 - (4)(5) = 10$

    $Q* = 5 + 5 = 10$

Chapter 8: Problem 1

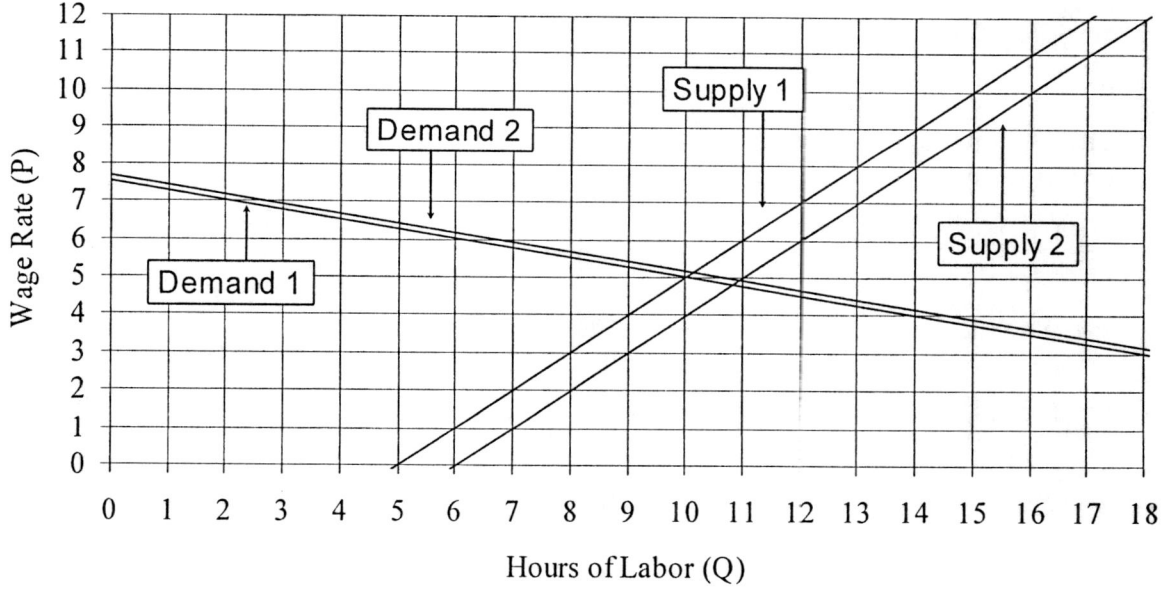

2. If the spa is built and an additional 600,000 hours of unskilled labor are employed, the demand curve will shift to the right by 0.6 million. The new demand curve is

    $QD = 30.6 - 4P$

    The new market equilibrium price is calculated by setting quantity demanded (QD) equal to quantity supplied (QS) and then solving for P.

    $30.6 - 4P = 5 + P$

$30.6 - 5 = (4 + 1) P$

$P* = 25.6/5 = 5.12$

The new market equilibrium quantity (Q*) is calculated by substituting the equilibrium price into either the demand curve or the supply curve and then solving for Q.

$Q* = 30.6 - (4)(5.12) = 10.12$

$Q* = 5 + 5.12 = 10.12$

If the spa is built, it will spend $(0.6)(5.12) = \$3.072$ million on labor. Other employers will spend $(10.12 - 0.6)(5.12) = \$48.7424$ million on labor. Currently, other employers hire 10 million hours at $5 an hour for a total of $50 million. Total expenditures on unskilled labor will increase from $50 to $51.8144 million and employment will increase from 10 to 10.12 million hours if the spa is built.

3. If $1 million is contributed to the college, supply will increase by 1 million hours. The new supply curve is

$QS = 6 + P$

The new market equilibrium price is calculated by setting quantity demanded (QD) equal to quantity supplied (QS) and then solving for P.

$30.6 - 4 P = 6 + P$

$30.6 - 6 = (4 + 1) P$

$P* = 24.6/5 = 4.92$

The new market equilibrium quantity (Q*) is calculated by substituting the equilibrium price into either the demand curve or the supply curve and then solving for Q.

$Q* = 30.6 - (4)(4.92) = 10.92$

$Q* = 6 + 4.92 = 10.92$

If the spa is built and the contribution is made, the spa will spend $(0.6)(4.92) = \$2.952$ million on labor. Other employers will spend $(10.92 - 0.6)(4.92) = \$50.7744$ million on labor. Other employers currently hire 10 million hours at $5 an hour for a total of $50 million, so they will hire more labor and their expenditures will increase. Total expenditures on unskilled labor will increase from $50 to $53.7264 million and employment will increase from 10 to 10.92 million hours if the spa is built.

If the spa is built and no contribution is made, the spa will spend a total of $3.072 million on unskilled labor. If the spa is built and the contribution is made, the spa will spend $2.952 million on labor. Since the saving due to the contribution is less than $1 million, the contribution should not be made.

4. The profit-maximizing level of output is calculated by setting marginal revenue equal to marginal cost and then solving for quantity. Marginal revenue is calculated by algebraically inverting the demand curve and then doubling its slope. The demand curve is inverted by solving for P.

$$P = (100 - Q)/2 = 50 - 0.5\,Q$$

Marginal revenue (MR) is obtained by doubling the slope.

$$MR = 50 - Q$$

Setting marginal revenue equal to marginal cost yields the profit-maximizing quantity.

$$50 - Q = 10$$

$$Q^* = 50 - 10 = 40$$

The corresponding profit-maximizing price is calculated by substituting the optimal quantity into the inverted demand curve and solving.

$$P^* = 50 - (0.5)(40) = 30$$

Total revenue (TR) is equal to the optimal price times the optimal quantity.

$$TR = (30)(40) = 1200$$

Chapter 8: Problem 4

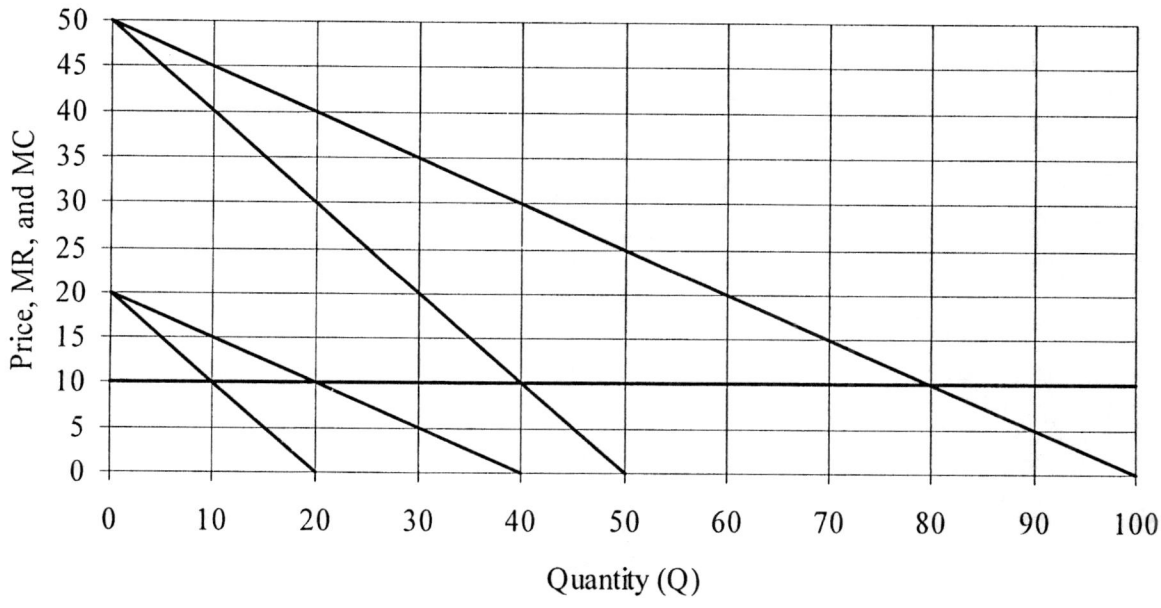

5. The profit-maximizing level of output is calculated by setting marginal revenue equal to marginal cost and then solving for quantity. Marginal revenue is calculated by algebraically inverting the demand curve and then doubling its slope. The demand curve is inverted by solving for P.

$$P = (40 - Q)/2 = 20 - 0.5 Q$$

Marginal revenue (MR) is obtained by doubling the slope.

$$MR = 20 - Q$$

Setting marginal revenue equal to marginal cost yields the profit-maximizing quantity.

$$20 - Q = 10$$

$$Q^* = 20 - 10 = 10$$

The corresponding profit-maximizing price is calculated by substituting the optimal quantity into the inverted demand curve and solving.

$$P^* = 20 - (0.5)(10) = 15$$

Total revenue (TR) is equal to the optimal price times the optimal quantity.

$$TR = (15)(10) = 150$$

6. Long-run total cost (LTC) is equal to the lowest total cost of the three factories at each level of output. Long-run average cost (LAC) is equal to long-run total cost divided by output (Q). Long-run marginal cost is equal to the change in total cost divided by the corresponding change in output.

Q	LTC	LAC	LMC
0	5	-	-
1	7	7.0	2
2	8	4.0	1
3	11	3.7	3
4	17	4.3	6
5	23	4.6	6
6	33	5.5	10
7	43	6.1	10
8	58	7.3	15
9	79	8.8	21
10	109	10.9	30

Chapter 8: Problem 6

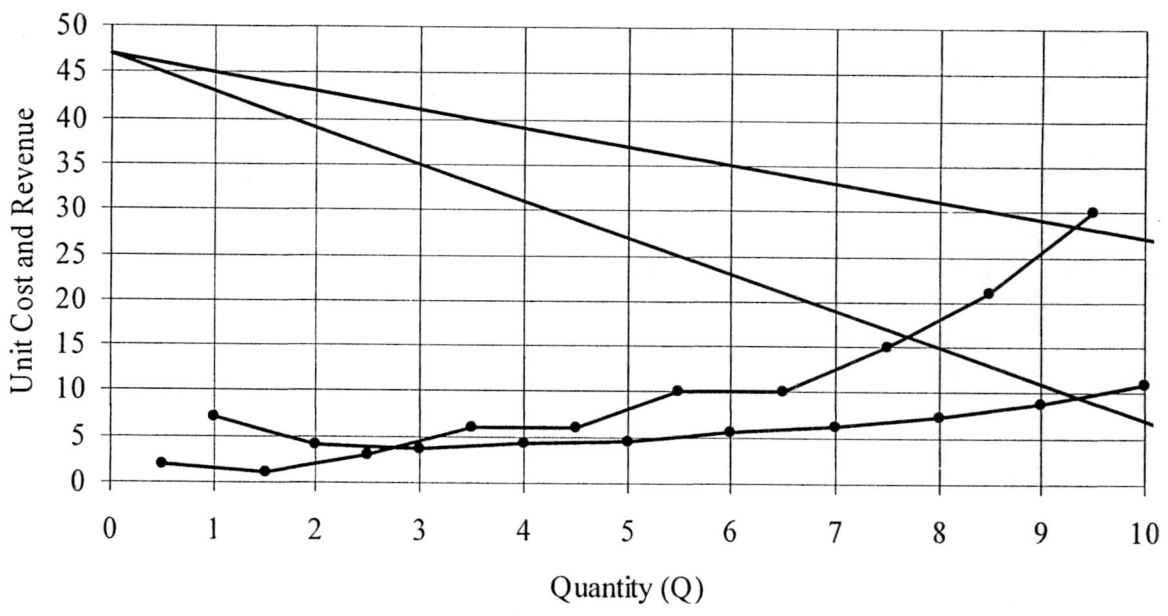

Chapter 8: Problem 6

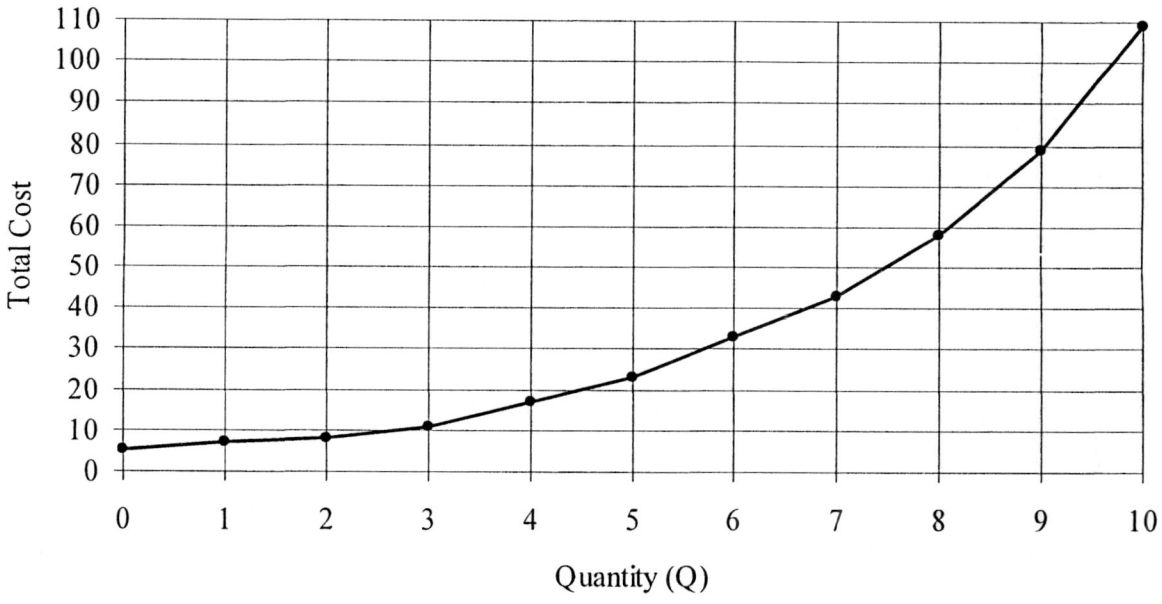

7. Average revenue (AR), or unit price, is calculated from quantity by inverting the demand curve and then substituting the values of Q into the function. The inverted function is calculated by solving the demand curve for P.

$$P = (23.5 - Q)/0.5 = 47 - 2Q$$

Total revenue is equal to average revenue multiplied by output.

$$TR = (P)(Q) = (47 - 2Q)(Q) = 47Q - 2Q^2$$

Marginal revenue (MR) is equal to the inverted demand function with the slope doubled.

$$MR = 47 - 4Q$$

The optimal long-run level of output ($Q^* = 8$) is found where LMC is equal to MR (LMC = MR = 15). Factory 3 is the optimal choice for production of this quantity. The optimal price is found by substituting $Q^* = 8$ into the inverted demand function. This yields $P^* = 47 - (2)(8) = 31$. Profit is equal to total revenue minus total cost $(31)(8) - 58 = 190$.

Q	AR	TR	MR
0	-	0	-
1	45	45	43
2	43	86	39
3	41	123	35
4	39	156	31
5	37	185	27
6	35	210	23
7	33	231	19
8	31	248	15
9	29	261	11
10	27	270	7

8. Total cost is identical for the small and mid-sized factories at Q = 4. This level of output will be optimal if marginal revenue is equal to 3. Total cost is identical for the mid-sized and large factories at Q = 6. This level of output will be optimal if marginal revenue is equal to 6.

If the mid-sized plant or large plant is built, Menacing Faces will ultimately go out of business. The long-run average cost curve slopes upward, so a firm with a small factory will be able to charge a lower price than a firm with a larger factory. As firms enter the industry, they will cause market price to fall and firms with larger factories will be unable to compete. They will consequently be forced to leave the industry.

9. Average total cost (ATC) is equal to total cost (TC) divided by output (Q). Average variable cost (AVC) is equal to total variable cost (TVC) divided by output. Total variable cost is equal to total cost less total fixed cost (TFC). Total fixed cost is equal to

total cost when Q = 0, i.e., TFC = 6.0. Marginal cost (MC) is equal to the change in total cost divided by the change in output.

Q	TC	ATC	AVC	MC
0	6.0	-	-	-
1	9.0	9.0	3.0	3.0
2	11.0	5.5	2.5	2.0
3	12.6	4.2	2.2	1.6
4	14.8	3.7	2.2	2.2
5	18.5	3.7	2.5	3.7
6	23.7	4.0	3.0	5.2
7	31.5	4.5	3.6	7.8
8	43.4	5.4	4.7	11.9
9	60.3	6.7	6.0	16.9
10	86.3	8.6	8.0	26.0

10.   A competitive firm is in long-run equilibrium when it is earning zero economic profits. This corresponds to the minimum point on the average total cost curve, where average total cost and marginal cost are equal. This occurs at a price of P = 3.7 and a quantity of Q = 4.5. If total industry demand for the components is 450 thousand (Q = 450), then the industry must be comprised of 450/4.5 = 100 firms. Recall that marginal cost is graphed between units. The shutdown point corresponds to the minimum point on the average variable cost curve; i.e., a price of P = 2.2 and a quantity of Q = 3.5. If price falls below this level, the firm will minimize losses by producing no output (Q = 0).

11. The equilibrium price and quantity is found at the intersection of the demand curve with the industry marginal cost curve. This occurs at $P = 3.7$ with 450 thousand units of output.

Chapter 8: Problem 11

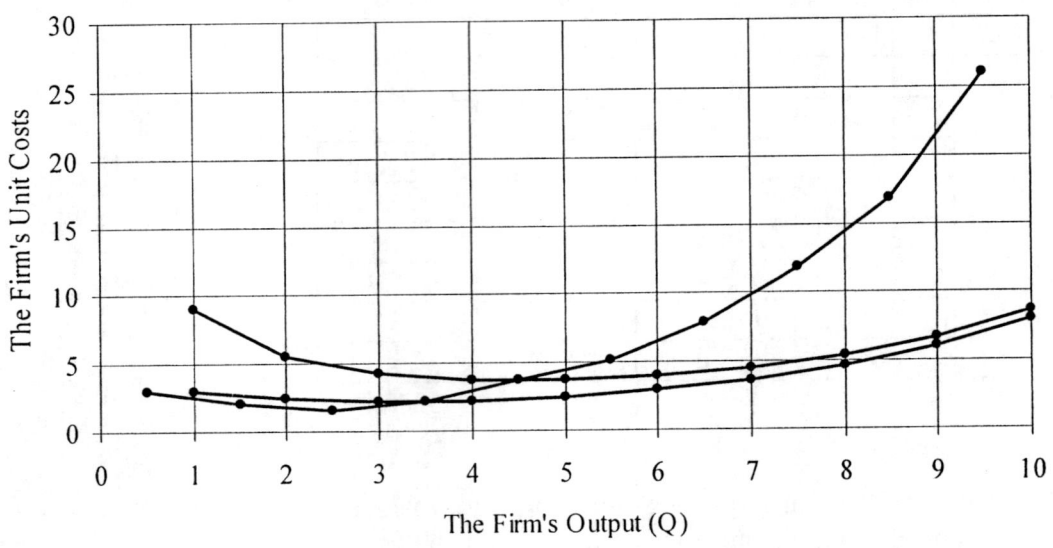

Chapter 8: Problem 11

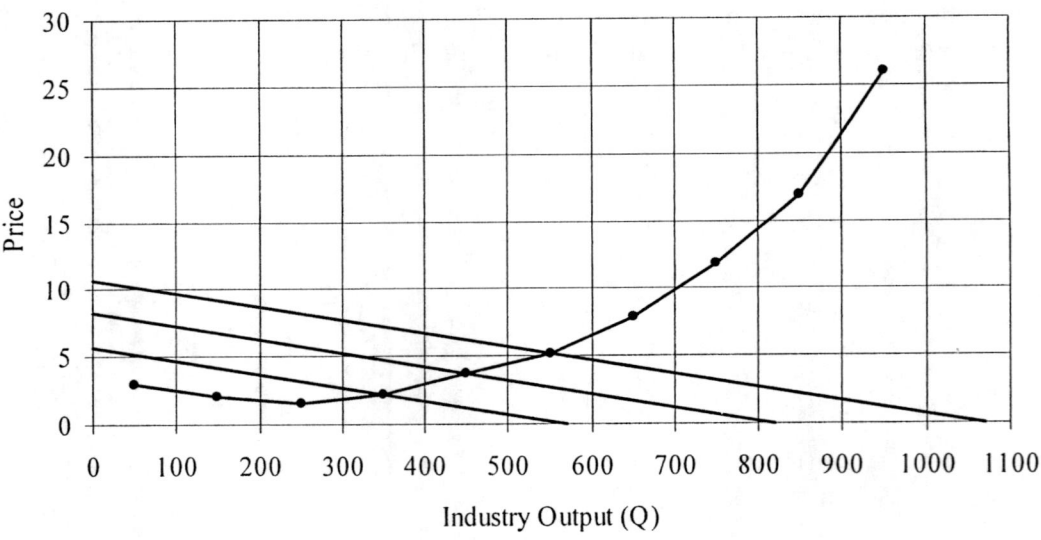

12.   The new short-run equilibrium price and quantity is found at the intersection of the new demand curve with the industry marginal cost curve. This occurs at P = 5.2 with 550 thousand units of output. Davino's firm will produce Q = 5.5 per month and will earn profit equal to approximately (5.5)(5.2 - 3.85) = 7.425. Average total cost (ATC = 3.85) is approximated by the midpoint between ATC for Q = 5 and ATC for Q = 6.

The number of firms in the industry after price falls to the long-run equilibrium level of P = 3.7 is determined by substituting P=3.7 into the demand curve to determine total industry production and then dividing this figure by the optimal output for each firm. This yields a total industry output of 700 thousand units. Since each firm will produce Q = 4.5, the total number of firms will be approximately 700/4.5 = 156 firms.

13.   The new short-run equilibrium price and quantity is found at the intersection of the new demand curve with the industry marginal cost curve. This occurs at P = 2.2 with 350 thousand units of output. Davino's firm will produce Q = 3.5 per month and will earn profit equal to approximately (3.5)(2.2-3.95) = -6.125. Since P = 2.2 corresponds to the shutdown point, losses will actually be equal to total fixed cost, TC = 6. Because this is the shutdown point, the firm is indifferent between producing Q = 3.5 and producing Q = 0.

The number of firms that will be in the industry after price rises to the long-run equilibrium level of P = 3.7 is determined by substituting P = 3.7 into the demand curve.

QD = 570 - (100)(3.7) = 200

Total industry output will be 200 thousand units. Since each firm will produce Q = 3.5 in long-run equilibrium, the total number of firms will be approximately 200/3.5 = 57 firms.

14. Marginal revenue is derived from the demand curve as follows by halving both coefficients of the demand curve. Since demand is $Q^d = 14 - 1.4P$, marginal revenue is $Q = 7 - 0.7MR$ in inverted form or $MR = 10 - 1.43Q$ in standard form.

Chapter 8: Problem 14

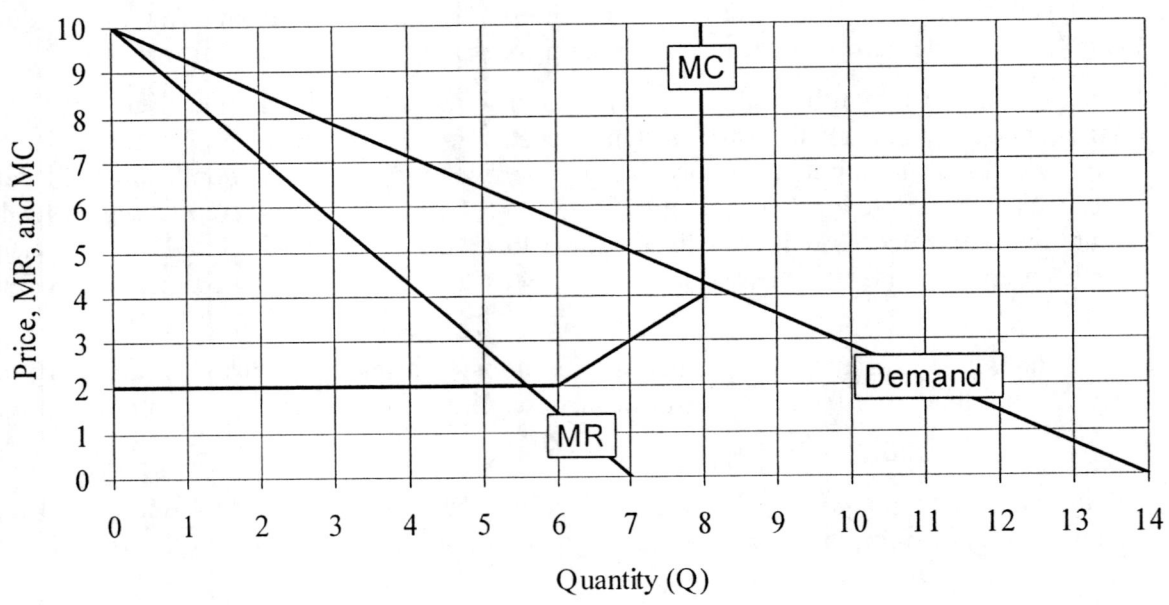

15. If marginal cost is $2 and is set equal to marginal revenue, then the solution indicates that the profit-maximizing level of output (Q) is 5.6 or 560 loaves per week. If 5.6 is substituted into the demand function, the corresponding value of P can be calculated. $Q^d = 5.6 = 14 - 1.4P$ implies that P = $6.

16. Adjustment to long-run equilibrium in the presence of economic profits will involve the entry of new monopolistic competitors into the "industry". The increased availability of substitutes will decrease the demand for bread produced by Beautiful Baguette's Bakery and will also cause the demand curve to become more elastic. This would be represented on the graph by a leftward shift in the demand curve combined with a flattening of the curve.

17. At long-run equilibrium, the monopolistic competitor's demand curve is tangent to the long-run average cost curve at a level of output where marginal revenue intersects the long-run marginal cost curve. This level of output (Q) is less than that which would minimize long-run average cost and, therefore, less than the level of output that a competitive firm would produce in long-run equilibrium. The monopolistic competitor has excess capacity in the sense that the plant used to produce the optimal level of output is smaller, and involves a higher unit cost, than would be the case under perfect competition. The price charged (P) is also higher than the competitive price.

Chapter 8: Problem 17

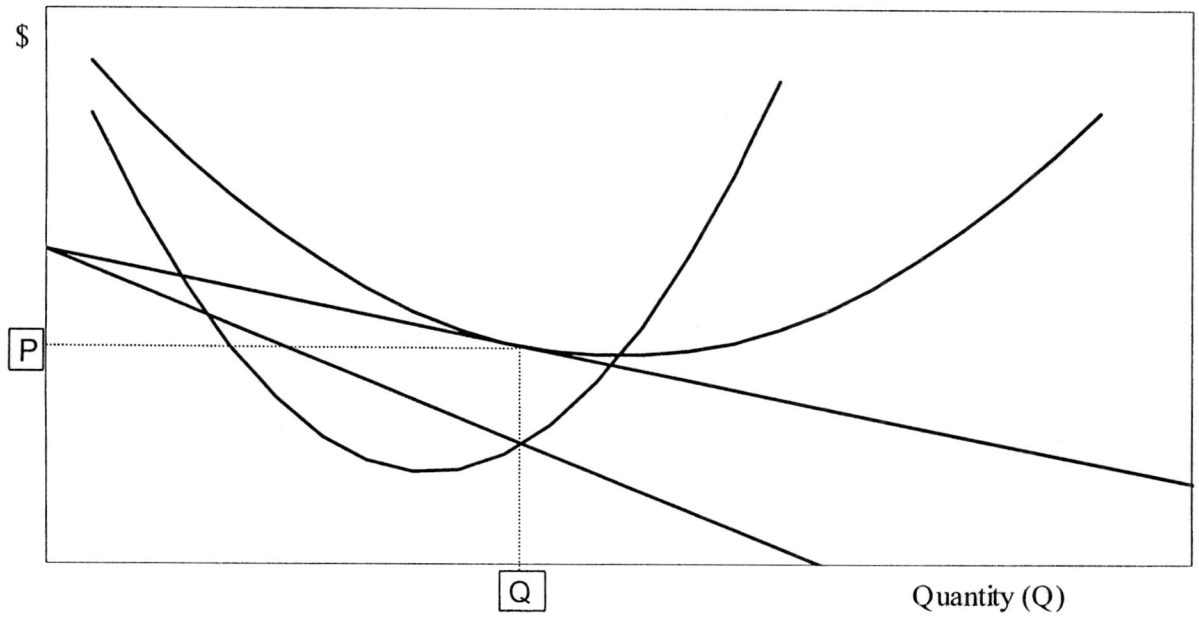

18.   There are two equivalent ways to solve this problem. One is to calculate marginal revenue (MR) and marginal cost (MC) functions, set them equal to each other, and solve for the optimal level of output (Q). The second is to set up the profit function, set its derivative equal to zero, and solve for the optimal level of output. We will begin with the second method and then show that it is equivalent to the first.

Total revenue is derived by multiplying the inverse of the demand function by Q. The inverse is derived by solving the demand function for P.

$$P = (401 - Q)/5 = 80.2 - 0.2\,Q$$

$$TR = PQ = (80.2 - 0.2\,Q)(Q) = 80.2\,Q - 0.2\,Q^2$$

Profit (π) is equal to total revenue minus total cost.

$$\pi = (80.2\,Q - 0.2\,Q^2) - (5 + 45\,Q - 10\,Q^2 + Q^3)$$

The derivative of the profit function is then set equal to zero.

$$d\pi/dQ = (80.2 - 0.4\,Q) - (45 - 20\,Q + 3\,Q_2) = 0$$

Notice that the first part of the derivative is the derivative of the total revenue function, which is marginal revenue, and that the second part is the derivative of the total cost function, which is marginal cost, so the derivative of the profit function can be written as follows.

$$d\pi/dQ = dTR/dQ - dTC/dQ = MR - MC = 0$$

Thus, setting the derivative of the profit function equal to zero is exactly equivalent to setting marginal revenue equal to marginal cost.

Collecting terms in the derivative of the profit function yields the following quadratic function.

$35.2 + 19.6 \, Q - 3 \, Q^2 = 0$

The solution of a quadratic function can be determined by application of the **quadratic formula**.

If a quadratic equation is written in the following form:

$aX^2 + bX + c = 0$

then the two solutions to the equation are defined by

$$X = \frac{-b \pm \sqrt{b^2 - 4ac}}{2a}$$

In this case a = -3, b = 19.6, and c = 35.2. Substituting these values into the quadratic formula yields:

$$X = \frac{-(19.6) \pm \sqrt{(19.6)^2 - 4(-3)(35.2)}}{2(-3)}$$

The solutions are Q = -1.47, which yields Profit = -32.39, and Q = 8, which yields Profit = 391.8. Clearly, the first solution is not a maximum. The second solution is established as a maximum by taking the second derivative and determining its sign. It should be negative. The second derivative is

$d^2\pi/dQ^2 = 19.6 - 6 \, Q = 19.6 - (6)(8) = -28.4$

This value is negative, so Q = 8 is the profit maximizing solution. Total revenue is 628.8, total cost is 237, and profit is 391.8.

19.   There are two equivalent ways to solve this problem. One is to calculate the marginal cost (MC) function, set it equal to price, and then solve for the optimal level of output (Q). The second is to set up the profit function, set its derivative equal to zero, and solve for the optimal level of output. We will begin with the second method and then show that the two are equivalent.

Total revenue is equal to price times output.

$$TR = PQ = 10\ Q$$

Profit is equal to total revenue minus total cost.

$$\pi = (10\ Q) - (100 + 50\ Q - 5\ Q^2 + 0.2\ Q^3)$$

The derivative of the profit function is then set equal to zero.

$$d\pi/dQ = (10) - (50 - 10\ Q + 0.6\ Q^2) = 0$$

Notice that the first part of the derivative is the derivative of the total revenue function, which is equal to price for a competitive firm, and that the second part is the derivative of the total cost function, which is marginal cost, so the derivative of the profit function can be written as follows.

$$d\pi/dQ = dTR/dQ - dTC/dQ = P - MC = 0$$

Thus, setting the derivative of the profit function equal to zero is exactly equivalent to setting price (or marginal revenue) equal to marginal cost.

Collecting terms in the derivative of the profit function yields the following quadratic function.

$$-40 + 10\ Q - 0.6\ Q^2 = 0$$

The function is solved by application of the **quadratic formula**. In this case a = -0.6, b = 10, and c = -40. Substituting these values into the quadratic formula yields

$$X = \frac{-(10) \pm \sqrt{(10)^2 - 4(-0.6)(-40)}}{2(-0.6)}$$

The solutions are Q = 6.67, which yields Profit = -203.7, and Q = 10, which yields Profit = -200. Clearly, the first solution is not a maximum. The second solution appears to be a maximum. Its second derivative is negative.

$$d^2\pi/dQ^2 = 10 - 1.2\ Q = 10 - (1.2)(10) = -2$$

However, the firm can reduce its losses to -100 by producing no output at all. Average variable cost at Q = 10 is:

$$AVC = TVC/Q = (50Q - 5Q^2 + 0.2Q^3)/Q = (500 - 500 + 200)/10 = 20$$

Because the loss-minimizing level of production occurs where the price is below AVC, the firm should produce Q = 0. At this level of output, total revenue is equal to zero, total cost is equal to 100, and profit is equal to -100.

20. If P = 90 and TC is the same as in Problem 17, then the profit function and its derivative are

$$\pi = (90\,Q) - (100 + 50\,Q - 5\,Q^2 + 0.2\,Q^3)$$

$$d\pi/dQ = (90) - (50 - 10\,Q + 0.6\,Q^2) = 0$$

Collecting terms in the derivative of the profit function yields the following quadratic function.

$$40 + 10\,Q - 0.6\,Q^2 = 0$$

The function is solved by application of the **quadratic formula**. In this case a = -0.6, b = 10, and c = 40. Substituting these values into the quadratic formula yields

$$X = \frac{-(10) \pm \sqrt{(10)^2 - 4(-0.6)(40)}}{2(-0.6)}$$

The solutions are Q = -3.33, which yields Profit = -170.37, and Q = 20, which yields Profit = 1,100. Clearly, the first solution is not a maximum. The second solution is established as a maximum by taking the second derivative and determining its sign. It should be negative. The second derivative is

$$d^2\pi/dQ^2 = 10 - 1.2\,Q = 10 - (1.2)(20) = -14$$

This value is negative, so Q = 20 is the profit maximizing solution. Total revenue is 1800, total cost is 700, and profit is 1100.

CHAPTER 9

OLIGOPOLY AND FIRM ARCHITECTURE

Learning Objectives

The price of a commodity and the quantity traded of the commodity per time period depend on the characteristics of buyers, which are represented in aggregate by the market demand function, the characteristics and behavior of firms, represented by production and cost functions and by their organizational architecture, and the market structure. Market structure defines the way that sellers and buyers interact to determine equilibrium price and quantity, focusing in particular on the amount of market power each has and the way it is exerted. When you have completed the material in this chapter, you should have a fundamental understanding of the nature of a market structure that is less competitive than perfect competition or monopolistic competition and more competitive than monopoly and of the ideal firm architecture for the environment it presents. This market structure, oligopoly, describes the operation of most of the world's major corporations. A study of the way oligopolists interact to determine equilibrium price and quantity will provide you with important insights into the operation of markets that are characterized by strategic behavior and a small number of rival firms.

True-False Questions

T F 1.   A duopoly is an oligopoly in which several firms duel for consumer demand.

T F 2.   A differentiated oligopoly is a form of market organization where several different large firms produce a homogeneous commodity.

T F 3.   Oligopoly is the prevalent form of market organization in the manufacturing sectors of industrial nations.

T F 4.   A market may be organized as an oligopoly if there are many producers of a product, but transportation costs limit the number that compete directly on a local market.

T F 5.   Oligopolistic markets are characterized by rivalries between firms that arise because the actions of each firm in an industry have an effect on the other firms in the industry.

T F 6.   Limit pricing refers to the oligopolistic practice of charging a price so low that new firms are discouraged from entering the industry.

T F 7.   The sources of oligopoly are generally the same as for monopoly, i.e., barriers to entry.

T F 8.   Concentration ratios measure the total number of firms required to produce the total output of an industry.

T F 9.   The Herfindahl index is equal to the sum of the market shares of all firms in an industry.

T F 10. If the concentration ratio for an industry is small, then the Herfindahl index is likely to be large.

T F 11. An oligopolistic industry is likely to have a large concentration ratio and a large Herfindahl index.

T F 12. The theory of contestable markets holds that an industry without barriers to entry or exit will operate as if it is perfectly competitive.

T F 13. The Cournot model is defined as a non-oligopolistic model.

T F 14. Firms described by the Cournot model assume that their rivals will keep their rates of production constant.

T F 15. Reference to the "Cournot" model is derived by merging "Course" and "not" into a single word and is a response to the question "Is this firm a monopolist?"

T F 16. The Cournot model focuses on interdependence among firms.

T F 17. An industry that can be described by the Cournot model will produce total output that is the same as that produced by a perfectly competitive industry, however they will charge a higher price.

T F 18. The kinked demand curve model describes a monopolistically competitive market.

T F 19. The kinked demand curve model provides an explanation of price rigidity in the face of changes in costs.

T F 20. The kinked demand curve model describes a demand curve that is very elastic for price cuts and less elastic for price increases.

T F 21. The marginal revenue curve associated with the kinked demand curve is vertical at the current market price.

T F 22. Oligopolists prefer to avoid engaging in nonprice competition.

T F 23. Collusion is illegal in the United States, but is legal in many other parts of the world.

T F 24. A cartel is an organization of colluding oligopolists.

T F 25. Cartels tend to self-destruct because each member has an incentive to cheat.

T F 26. Price leadership is an example of tacit collusion.

T F 27. The dominant-firm price leadership model describes a market structure in which a dominant firm is the price maker and all other firms are price takers.

T F 28. There is no general theory of oligopoly.

T F 29. The sector in which the size of the largest firms has grown most is banking.

T F 30. The sales maximization model assumes that firms will always continue to increase output until marginal revenue is equal to zero.

T F 31. If a firm with marginal cost equal to $2 faces a demand curve defined as $QD = 100 - 5P$, then revenue is at a maximum when price is $10.

T F 32. If a firm with marginal cost equal to $2 faces a demand curve defined as $QD = 100 - 5P$, then profit is at a maximum when price is $10.

T F 33. The movement towards globalization has been slowed by changes in the telecommunications and transportation industries.

T F 34. Firms in the entertainment and communications industry have grown and globalized by means of mergers.

T F 35. A firm's architecture is defined by the buildings and furnishings that it owns.

T F 36. Successful firms concentrate on their core competencies and outsource all other activities.

T F 37. In order to compete successfully in global markets, firms should sacrifice agility for the economies of scale associated with large production facilities.

T F 38. The steel industry is comprised of virtual corporations.

T F 39. A virtual corporation is a temporary network of independent companies.

T F 40. Relationship enterprises are more limited and temporary than virtual corporations.

T F 41. Porter's strategic framework describes a structure based on five forces.

T F 42. Porter's strategic framework describes the strategies that firms should follow to maximize profits.

T F 43. According to Porter's strategic framework, profits will be lower in industries where suppliers have a high degree of bargaining power.

T F 44. If a firm produces a unique product and inspires a brand loyalty, it will tend to have higher profits.

T F 45. The creative company relies on six sigma to increase the efficiency of production.

Multiple Choice Questions

1.   The market for automobiles is an example of

   A. monopolistic competition.
   B. duopoly.
   C. differentiated oligopoly.
   D. pure oligopoly.

2.   If an industry is comprised of four firms and their market shares are 40%, 30%, 20%, and 10%, then the Herfindahl index for the industry is

   A. 100
   B. 200
   C. 3,000
   D. 10,000

3.   The Herfindahl index will be largest for an industry that is

A. a monopoly.
B. perfectly competitive.
C. a duopoly.
D. monopolistically competitive.

4.   The Herfindahl index will be smallest for an industry that is

A. a monopoly.
B. perfectly competitive.
C. a duopoly.
D. a differentiated oligopoly.

5.   According to the Cournot model, a firm will

A. assume that rival firms will keep their production constant.
B. produce the quantity where marginal revenue equals marginal cost.
C. respond to changes in production by rival firms by adjusting its production.
D. All of the above are correct.

6.   According to the Bertrand model, a firm will assume that rival firms will

A. keep their rates of production constant.
B. keep their prices constant.
C. match price cuts but not price increases.
D. match price increases but not price cuts.

7.   According to the kinked demand curve model, a firm will assume that rival firms will

A. keep their rates of production constant.
B. keep their prices constant.
C. match price cuts but not price increases.
D. match price increases but not price cuts.

8.   The refrigerator industry is an example of

A. monopolistic competition.
B. monopoly.
C. oligopoly.
D. perfect competition.

9.   The petroleum industry is an example of

A. monopolistic competition.
B. pure oligopoly.
C. duopoly.
D. differentiated oligopoly.

10.   The kinked demand curve model assumes that

A. firms match price increases, but not price cuts.
B. demand is more elastic for price cuts than for price increases.
C. changes in marginal cost can never lead to changes in market price.
D. None of the above is correct.

11. Which of the following is <u>not</u> a form of nonprice competition?

    A. Advertising
    B. Quality of service
    C. Product quality
    D. All of the above are forms of nonprice competition.

12. A cartel that gives each member the exclusive right to operate in a particular geographic area is a

    A. market-sharing cartel.
    B. centralized cartel.
    C. price leadership cartel.
    D. None of the above is correct.

13. A cartel that operates like a multiplant monopolist is a

    A. market-sharing cartel.
    B. centralized cartel.
    C. price leadership cartel.
    D. None of the above is correct.

14. Under the dominant-firm price leadership model,

    A. all firms but the dominant firm are price takers.
    B. the dominant firm acts as the residual monopolistic supplier.
    C. the demand curve faced by the dominant firm is flatter than the market demand curve.
    D. All of the above are correct.

15. Oligopolistic firms can earn positive economic profits

    A. in the short run, but not in the long run.
    B. in the short run and in the long run.
    C. in the long run, but not in the short run.
    D. in neither the short run nor the long run.

16. Which of the following forms of market organization assumes that entry and exit of firms is costless?

    A. Differentiated oligopoly
    B. Duopoly
    C. Monopolistic competition
    D. Pure oligopoly

17. The harmful effects of oligopoly include all of the following <u>except</u>

    A. Economies of scale result in a small number of large firms that spend more of research and development.
    B. Price is greater than long-run marginal and average cost.
    C. Production does not generally take place at the lowest point on the long-run average cost curve.
    D. All of the above are harmful effects of oligopoly.

18. The sales maximization model assumes that imperfectly competitive firms will produce a level of output where

    A. marginal revenue is equal to zero.
    B. marginal revenue is equal to marginal cost.
    C. marginal revenue is equal to zero if profit is satisfactory.
    D. they will break even.

19. One reason that most economists do not support government industrial and trade policies is that the outcomes of these policies cannot

    A. have a positive effect on a country's industries.
    B. be accurately predicted.
    C. help a country to overcome a comparative disadvantage.
    D. prevent a country from losing a comparative advantage.

20. The growth of global oligopolists has been encouraged by

    A. the development of new transportation and telecommunications technologies.
    B. the globalization of tastes.
    C. reductions in barriers to international trade and investment.
    D. All of the above.

21. In which of the sectors listed below has the growth in concentration has been most pronounced during the past decade?

    A. Agriculture.
    B. Mining.
    C. Banking.
    D. Home construction.

22. Firms in which of the following industries have used mergers and acquisitions to grow and globalize?

    A. Telecommunications
    B. Entertainment and communications media
    C. Consumer products
    D. All of the above.

23. Compared to relationship enterprises, virtual corporations are more likely to be

    A. lasting and stable.
    B. short term and temporary.
    C. global in scope.
    D. oligopolistic.

24. When several independent firms form a temporary network to take advantage of a short-term business opportunity, the result is called a

    A. collaborative firm.
    B. relationship enterprise.
    C. virtual corporation.
    D. cartelized partnership.

25. The ideal firm architecture includes all of the following except:

    A. A focus on core competencies
    B. The integration of physical and virtual systems
    C. A hierarchical, top down management structure
    D. Smaller, more flexible production facilities

26. Porter's strategic framework identifies forces that influence an industry's

    A. intensity of competition and profitability.
    B. rate of growth.
    C. popularity among consumers.
    D. potential as an exporter within the global economy.

27. Which of the following is **not** a force identified by Porter's strategic framework?

    A. Threat of entry
    B. Intensity of rivalry
    C. Government tax policy
    D. Bargaining power of buyers

28. The knowledge economy is characterized by a reliance on

    A. innovation and creativity.
    B. a customer-centric approach.
    C. efficiency in production.
    D. All of these answers are correct.

29. An emphasis on design innovation is typical of

    A. the knowledge economy.
    B. the virtual corporation.
    C. relationship enterprises.
    D. the creative firm.

30. CENCOR is an acronym for a design strategy that consists of the following parts:

    A. Collaborate, evaluate, celebrate, occlude, and rationalize
    B. Calibrate, explore, create, organize, and realize
    C. Create, evoke, circumvent, officiate, and redeem
    D. Calculate, erect, consign, offer, and return

Problems

1. An oligopolist has the following linear marginal cost curve: $MC = 1 + 0.5\,Q$

    At prices below \$5, the firm faces the following demand curve: $Q = 9 - P$

    At prices above \$5, the firm faces the following demand curve: $Q = 24 - 4\,P$

    Plot the firm's kinked demand curve and marginal revenue curve and the firm's marginal cost curve on the graph below.

Chapter 9: Problem 1

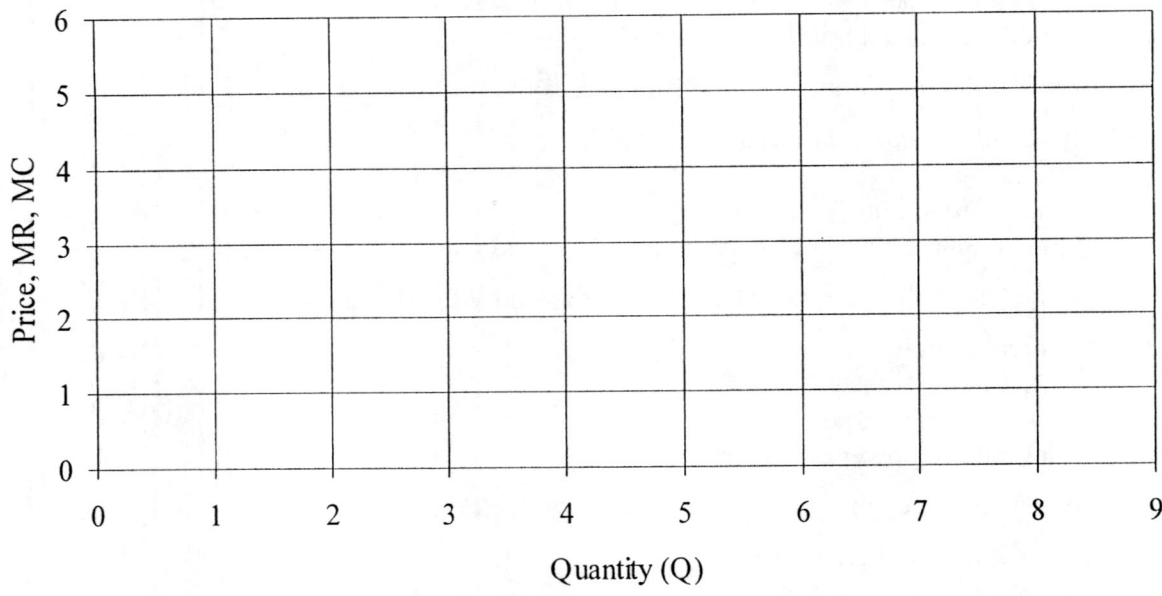

Within what range of marginal cost will the firm maintain the same price and level of output?

The managers of General House and Westing Electric, two competing firms that sell products that are virtually identical, have decided to form a secret agreement. They intend to cooperate in setting prices and to adjust their output accordingly. They have the following cost curves:

General House: MC = 1/2 + Q   ATC = 1/2 + 1/2 Q

Westing Electric: MC = 1/2 + Q/3   ATC = 1/2 + Q/6

They face the following industry demand curve: Q = 16 - 2 P

Use this information to solve Problems 2 and 3.

2. Plot the industry demand, marginal revenue, marginal cost, and average total cost on the graph below. Use the graph to determine industry price and output under the assumption that each firm is maximizing profit without cooperating with the other (that the industry is competitive) and then calculate each firm's total revenue, total cost and profit.

Chapter 9: Problem 2

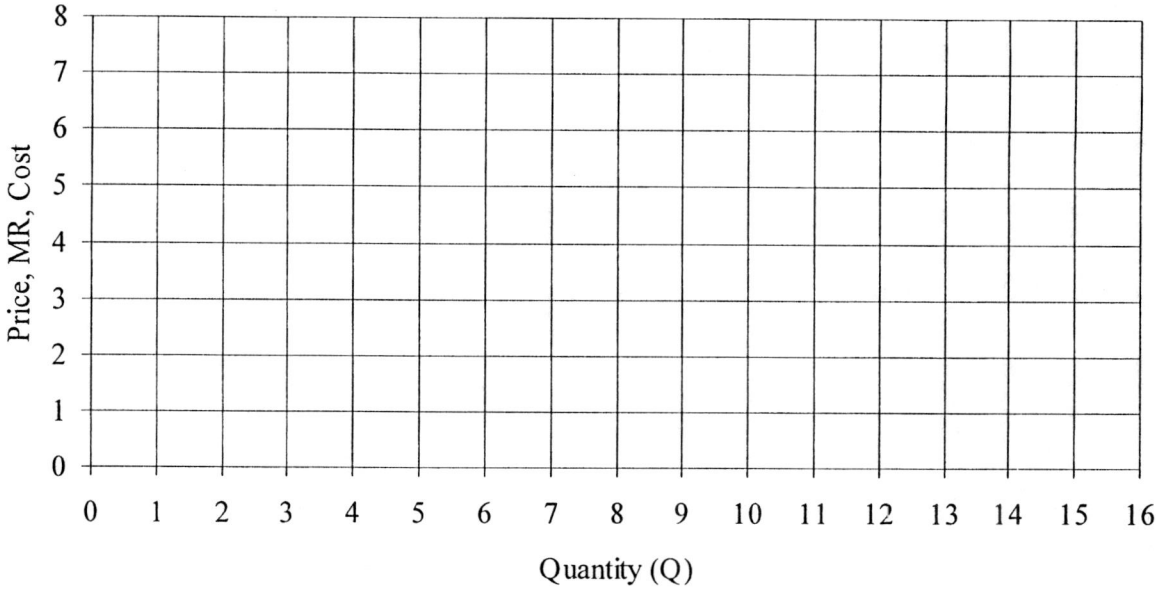

3. Now assume that the two firms decide to behave as a centralized cartel. Determine industry price and output and then calculate each firm's total revenue, total cost and profit. Are both of the firms better off than they were when they were competing? Why or why not?

4.   The graph that follows represents several features of a market that is dominated by a price leader. Market demand, the horizontal sum of the followers' marginal cost curves, and the leading firm's marginal cost curve are shown. Based on the curves plotted on the graph, draw in the price leader's demand and marginal revenue curve and identify the equilibrium market price, total output, and the division of total output between the leader and the followers. Label the graph carefully.

Chapter 9: Problem 4

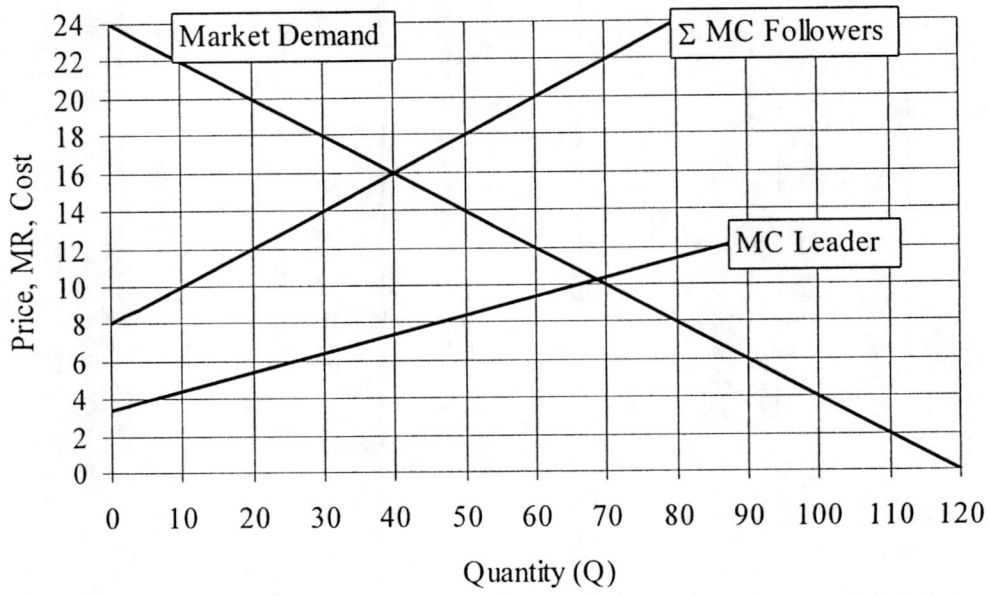

5. Ferrous Scrounge is the manager of a firm that recycles metal scrap. The firm's average cost is equal to $140 per ton. It faces the following linear demand curve: Q = 500 - 2P.

Derive the firm's profit function and plot it on the graph below.

Chapter 9: Problem 5

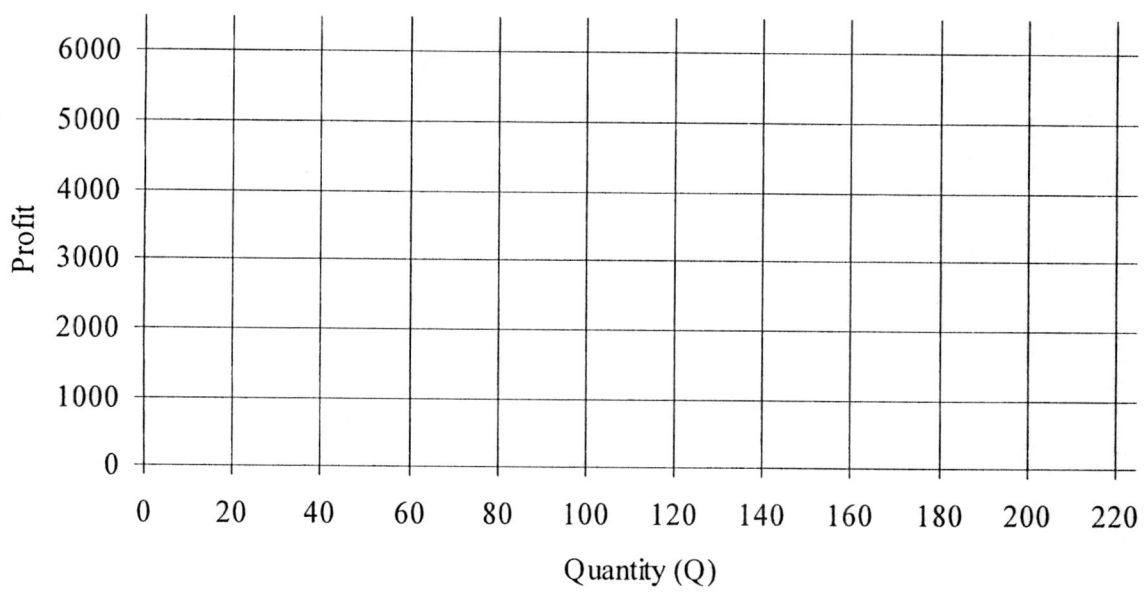

What is the firm's profit-maximizing price and output? What will the firm's profit be at this level of output?

If Ferrous Scrounge decides to maximize sales, what price will be charged and what level of output will be produced? What will the firm's profit be at this level of output?

If Ferrous Scrounge decides to maximize sales subject to the constraint that profit may be no less than 1,345.5, what price will be charged and what level of output will be produced?

6.   The City of Erie, Pennsylvania, is considering the development of lake shore ferry facilities that would transport the public across Lake Erie to Canada. The inverse demand curve for ferry service is defined as follows: $P = 60 - 0.01Q$

Erie has obtained bids from two ferry operators. Firm 1 has a marginal cost per passenger of $10. Firm 2 has a marginal cost per passenger of $14.

Your task is to predict the price and quantity that will prevail if both ferry operators are given access to the facilities. Assume that they will operate as a Cournot duopoly.

Derive and graph the firms' reaction functions, determine the number of passengers each firm will serve, and compute the market price.

Chapter 9: Problem 6

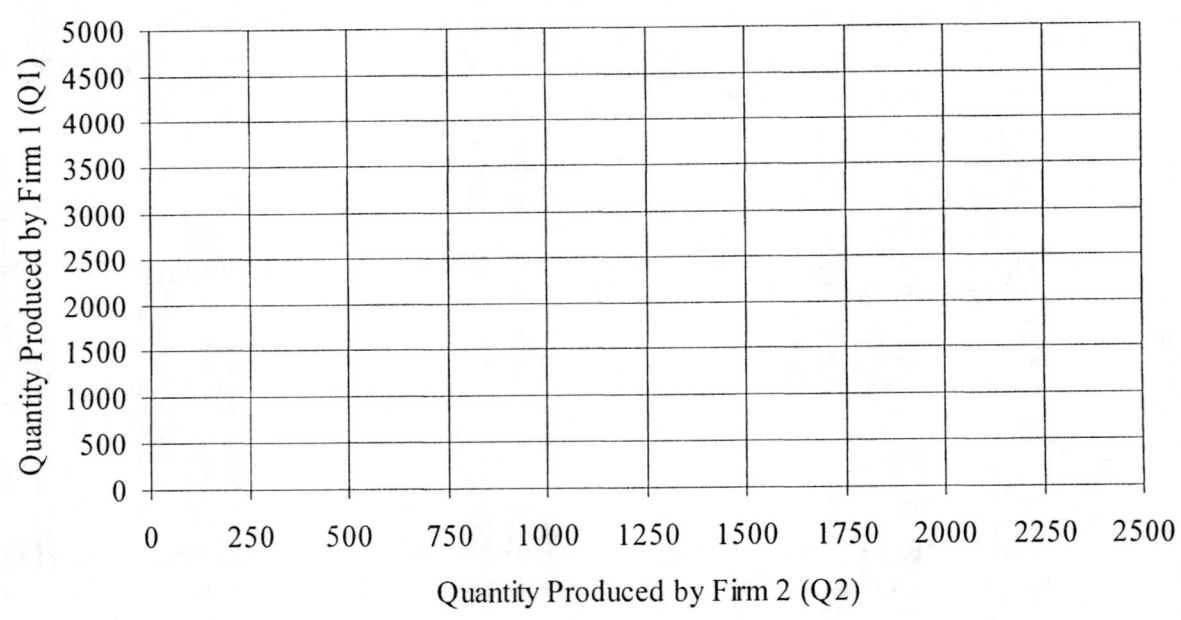

True-False Answers

1	F	10	F	19	T	28	T	37	F
2	F	11	T	20	F	29	T	38	F
3	T	12	T	21	T	30	F	39	T
4	T	13	F	22	F	31	T	40	F
5	T	14	T	23	T	32	F	41	T
6	T	15	F	24	T	33	F	42	F
7	T	16	T	25	T	34	T	43	T
8	F	17	F	26	T	35	F	44	T
9	F	18	F	27	T	36	T	45	F

Multiple Choice Answers

1	C	7	C	13	B	19	B	25	C
2	C	8	C	14	D	20	D	26	A
3	A	9	B	15	B	21	C	27	C
4	B	10	D	16	C	22	D	28	C
5	D	11	D	17	A	23	B	29	D
6	B	12	A	18	C	24	C	30	B

Solutions to Problems

1. At prices below \$5, the firm's marginal revenue curve is

   $Q = 4.5 - 0.5\ MR$ or $MR = 9 - 2\ Q$

   At prices above \$5, the firm's marginal revenue curve is

   $Q = 12 - 2\ MR$ or $MR = 6 - 0.5\ Q$

   The "kink" in the marginal revenue curve corresponds to the level of output where the two demand curves intersect. This level of output is found by inverting the two demand curves and then setting them equal to each other as follows.

   $Q = 9 - P$ becomes $P = 9 - Q$

   $Q = 24 - 4\ P$ becomes $P = 6 - 0.25\ Q$

   Equating them yields $9 - Q = 6 - 0.25\ Q$ which implies $Q = 4$

   Thus, from $Q = 0$ to $Q = 4$, the demand curve and marginal revenue curve for prices above \$5 will prevail and when Q is greater than 4, the demand curve and marginal revenue curve for prices above \$5 will be appropriate. At $Q = 4$, marginal revenue will be vertical between $MR = 9 - (2)(1) = 1$ and $MR = 6 - (0.5)(4) = 4$. Thus, any level of marginal cost between 1 and 4 will keep output constant at $Q = 4$. Notice that marginal cost is $MC = 1 + (0.5)(4) = 3$, so $Q = 4$ and $P = \$5$ in this case.

Chapter 9: Problem 1

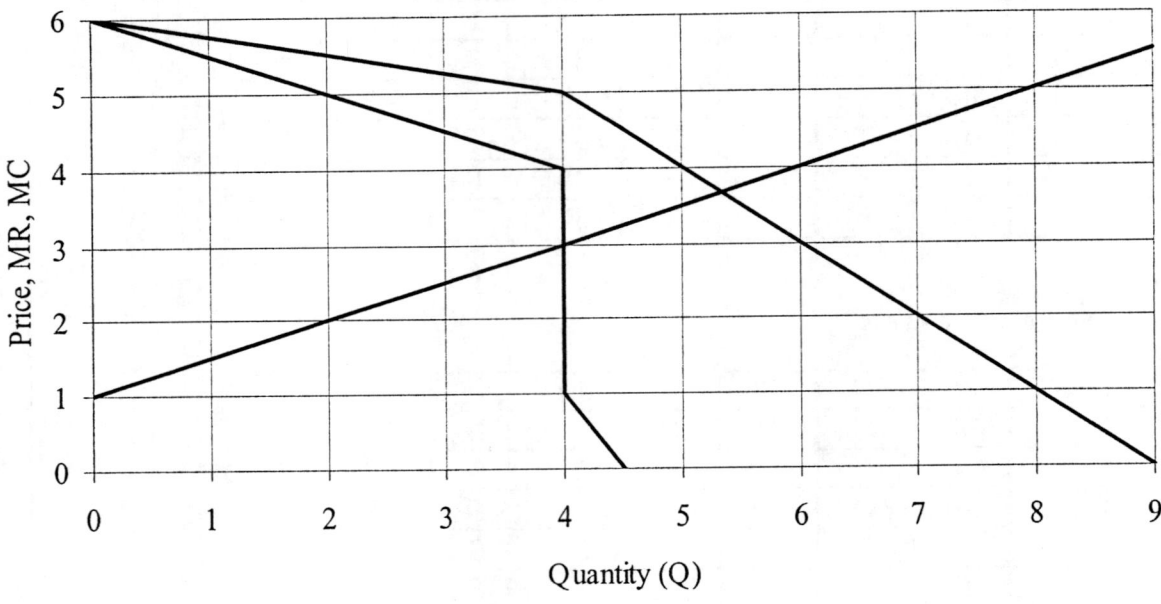

Quantity (Q)

2. The marginal revenue curve is derived by halving the coefficients of the demand curve, which yields $Q = 8 - MR$ or $MR = 8 - Q$. The industry cost curves are derived by horizontally summing the firms' cost curves as follows. First, the cost curves are solved for Q (or inverted) and then they are summed. This yields the following:

For GH: $Q = -0.5 + MC$ and $Q = -1 + 2\,ATC$

For WE: $Q = -1.5 + 3\,MC$ and $Q = -3 + 6\,ATC$

Industry MC: $Q = -2 + 4\,MC$ so $MC = 0.5 + 0.25\,Q$

Industry ATC: $Q = -4 + 8\,ATC$ so $ATC = 0.5 + 0.125\,Q$

Note that, for a competitive industry, the horizontal sum of the firms' marginal cost curves define the industry's supply curve. Thus, competitive equilibrium price can be calculated by setting the industry MC (supply) function equal to the industry demand curve as follows:

$-2+4P = 16-2P$, which implies that $P = 3$ and $Q = 10$

When price is equal to 3, GH will maximize profit by producing $Q = -0.5 + 3 = 2.5$ and We will maximize profit by producing $Q = -1.5 + (3)(3) = 7.5$. GH will have total costs equal to $(Q)(ATC) = (2.5)[0.5 + (0.5)(2.5)] = 4.375$ and so will earn a profit equal to $PQ - TC = (3)(2.5) - 4.375 = 3.125$. WE will have total costs equal to $(Q)(ATC) = (7.5)[0.5 + (7.5/6) = 13.125$ and so will earn a profit equal to $PQ - TC = (3)(7.5) - 13.125 = 9.375$. Thus, at the competitive equilibrium, total industry revenue is \$30, total industry cost is \$17.50, and total industry profit is \$12.50.

Chapter 9: Problem 2

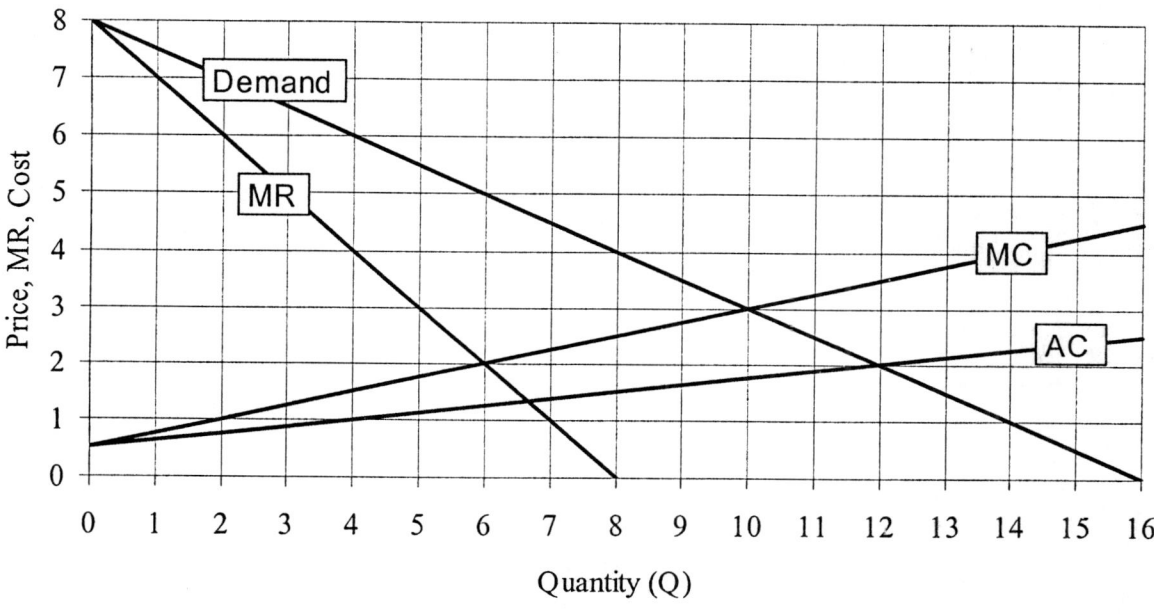

3.   If the firms behave as a centralized cartel, they will produce a level of output where marginal revenue (not demand) is equal to the sum of their marginal costs. This level of output is calculated by setting the industry MC function equal to marginal revenue as follows:

$0.5 + 0.25Q = 8 - Q$ which implies that $Q = 6$ and $MR = MC = 2$

The industry price is found by substituting the quantity into the industry demand curve:

$6 = 16 - 2P$ which implies that $P = 5$

At $MC = 2$, GH will produce $Q = 1.5$ with total revenue of $PQ = (5)(1.5) = 7.50$, total cost of $(Q)(ATC) = (1.5)[0.5 + (1.5/2)] = 1.875$, and profit of $TR - TC = 7.50 - 1.875 = 5.625$.

We will produce $Q = 4.5$ with total revenue of $PQ = (5)(4.5) = 22.50$, total cost of $(Q)(ATC) = (4.5)[0.5 + (4.5/6)] = 5.625$, and profit of $TR - TC = 22.50 - 5.625 = 16.875$.

Industry revenue is $PQ = (5)(6) = 30$, industry cost is $(Q)(ATC) = (6)[0.5 + (6)(0.125)] = 7.50$, and industry profit is $TR - TC = 30 - 7.50 = 22.50$.

Both of the firms are better off than they were prior to forming a agreement to act as a centralized cartel because both are experiencing higher levels of profit than before.

---

4. The leader's demand curve is equal to the horizontal difference between the sum of the followers' marginal cost curves and the market demand curve. The leader's marginal revenue curve is derived from the leader's demand curve in the usual way. The leader identifies the level of output (QL) that will maximize profit (where the leader's marginal cost is equal to the leader's marginal revenue) given the presence of the competitive followers and then charges the price (P) implied by that quantity. The followers are left to determine their own profit-maximizing levels of output (QL), which corresponds to the competitive solution of MC = P.

Chapter 9: Problem 4

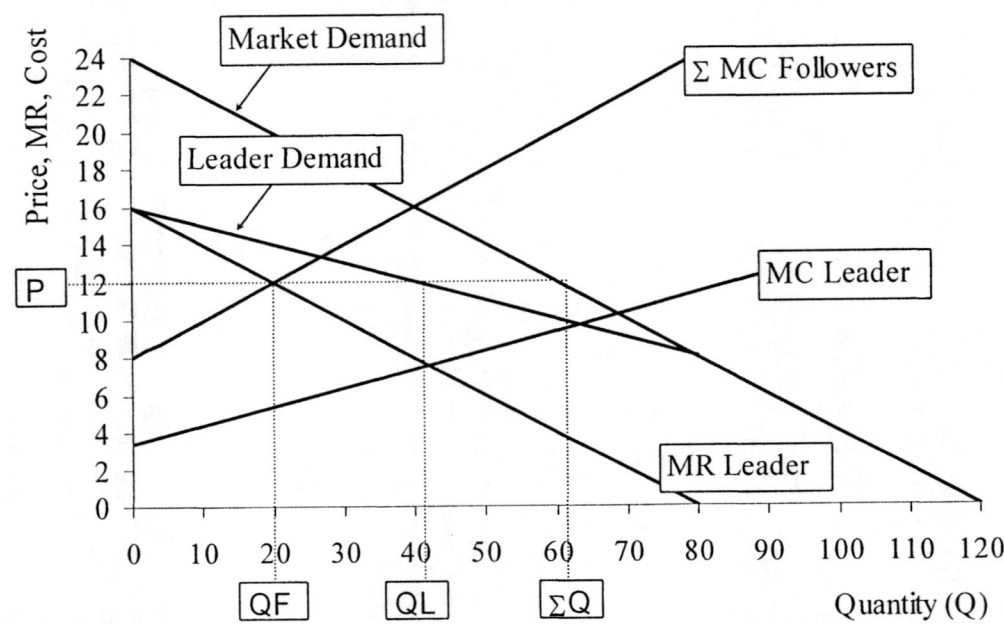

5. The firm's inverse demand function is P = 250 - 0.5Q. Total revenue is TR = 250Q - 0.5Q². The profit function is $\pi = 250Q - 0.5Q^2 - 140Q = 110Q - 0.5Q^2$.

The firm's marginal revenue function is MR = 250 - Q. Setting MR = MC yields

250 - Q = 140

The profit-maximizing level of output is Q = 110 and the corresponding price is

P = 250 - (0.5)(110) = 195.

Profit is $\pi = (110)(110) - (0.5)(110^2) = 6,050$.

Sales will be at a maximum at a level of output where MR = 0. Setting MR = 0 yields

MR = 250 - Q = 0 so Q = 250.

The corresponding price is P = 250 - (0.5)(250) = 125.

Profit is $\pi = (110)(250) - (0.5)(250^2) = -3{,}750$.

The profit-constrained sales maximization solution is found by setting the profit function equal to 1,345.5 and solving for the corresponding levels of output. This is accomplished by application of the **quadratic formula**.

If a quadratic equation is written in the form

$$aX^2 + bX + c = 0$$

then the two solutions to the equation are defined by

$$X = \frac{-b \pm \sqrt{b^2 - 4ac}}{2a}$$

In this case a = -0.5, b = 110, and c = -1345.5. Substituting these values into the quadratic formula yields

$$X = \frac{-(110) \pm \sqrt{(110)^2 - 4(-0.5)(1345.5)}}{2(-0.5)}$$

The solutions are Q = 13 and Q = 207. The second of these is the constrained sales maximization solution. The price that corresponds to Q = 207 is P = 146.5.

Chapter 9: Problem 5

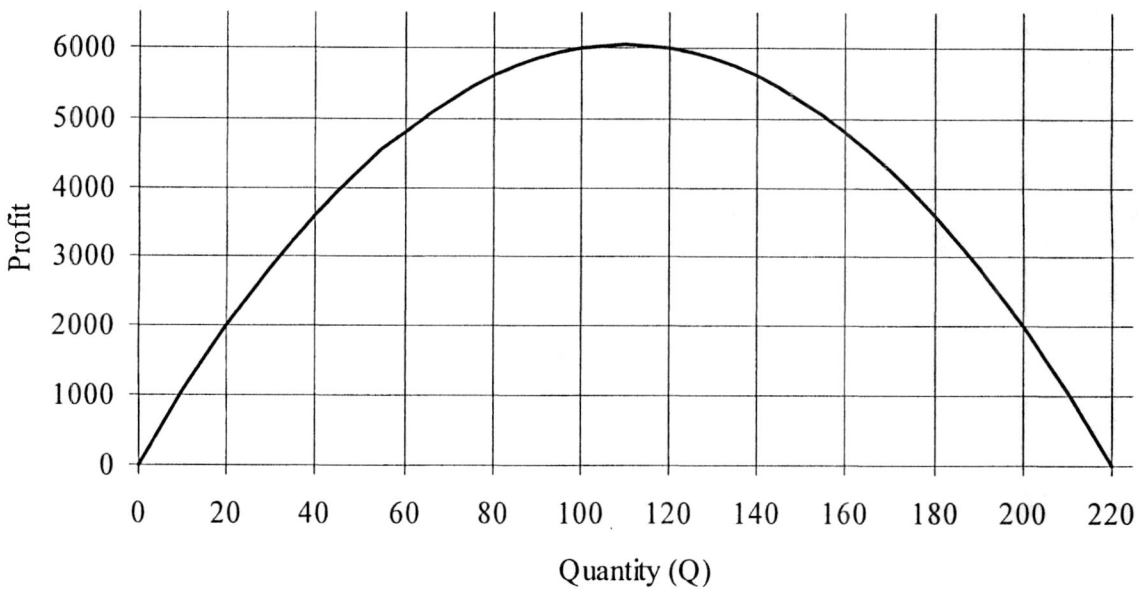

6. Derive the marginal revenue function for each firm and set it equal to marginal cost as follows:

$MR1 = 60 - 0.01 \ Q2 - 0.02 \ Q1 = 10$

$MR2 = 60 - 0.01 \ Q1 - 0.02 \ Q2 = 14$

Reaction function for firm 1: $Q1 = (60 - 0.01 \ Q2 - 10)/0.02 = 2500 - 0.50 \ Q2$

Reaction function for firm 2: $Q2 = (60 - 0.01 \ Q1 - 14)/0.02 = 2300 - 0.50 \ Q1$

Solve the reaction functions simultaneously for the quantities:

$Q1 = 2500 - (0.50)(2300 - 0.50 \ Q1) = 1350 + 0.25 \ Q1 \Rightarrow Q1 = 1350/0.75 = 1800$

$Q2 = 2300 - (0.50)(1800) = 1400$

Market price is found by substituting quantity into the demand function:

$P = 60 - (0.01)(Q1 + Q2) = 60 - (0.01)(3200) = \$28$

Chapter 9: Problem 6

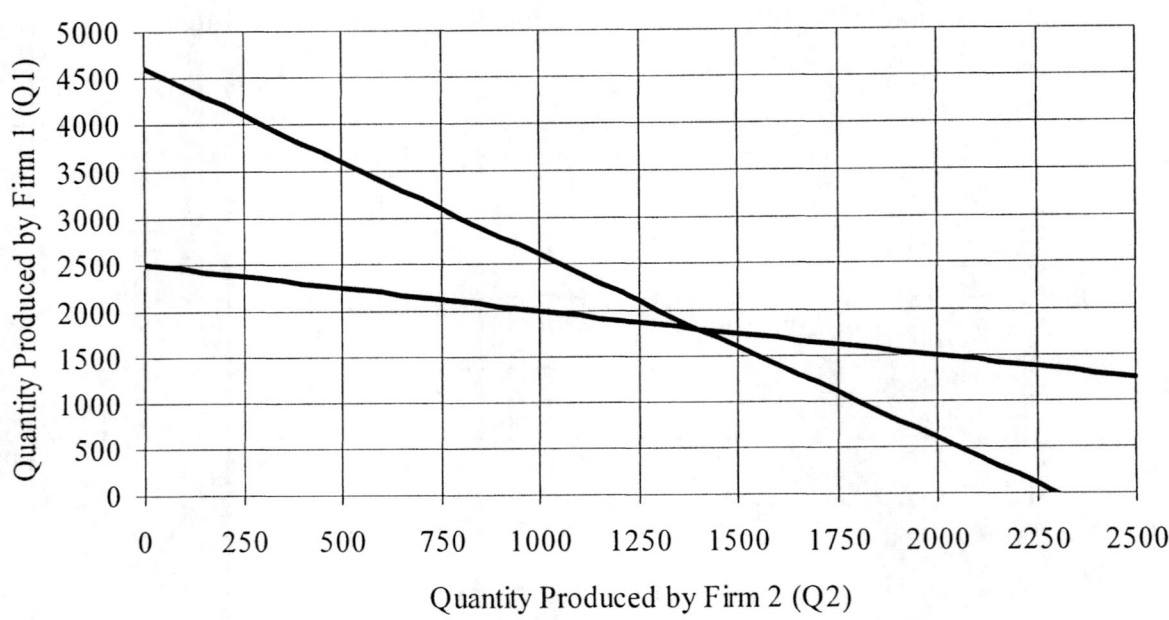

CHAPTER 10

GAME THEORY AND STRATEGIC BEHAVIOR

Learning Objectives

The mathematical models of oligopoly presented in the previous chapter focus on the determination of price and output on markets where firms are interdependent. Game theory provides an alternative way to analyze the strategic behavior of interdependent firms. When you have completed the material in this chapter, you will know how to formulate and analyze a decision-making problem using the methods and tools of game theory. Your knowledge of the prisoners' dilemma, Nash equilibrium, and of decision-making in simultaneous, repeated, and sequential game situations will provide important insights into the formulation of strategy by corporations in a global competitive environment.

True-False Questions

T F 1. Game theory can be used to analyze nonprice competition in oligopolistic markets.

T F 2. Game theory is particularly useful in analyzing multiple-move decision-making situations.

T F 3. One criticism of game theory is that, by considering only the best outcome of each strategy, it views the world in an excessively optimistic light.

T F 4. Strategic behavior refers to decisions made in the long run, but not the short run.

T F 5. Game theory is concerned with identifying optimal strategies in conflict situations.

T F 6. A table that gives the profits that will result from all possible combinations of a firm's available strategies and its opponent's available responses is called a payoff matrix.

T F 7. Dominant strategy refers to the behavior of the price leader in an industry with a dominant firm.

T F 8. One of the postulates of game theory is that a firm will always have a single dominant strategy.

T F 9. A Nash equilibrium results when every firm in an industry chooses a strategy that is optimal given the strategies chosen by its competitors.

T F 10. The prisoners' dilemma is a situation where each player chooses a dominant strategy but each could do better if both chose different strategies.

T F 11. The prisoners' dilemma refers to a situation in which both players cooperate in determining a strategy.

T F 12. A tit-for-tat strategy makes it possible for firms to cooperate without colluding.

T F 13. A tit-for-tat strategy cannot be successfully employed in repeated games.

T F 14. A firm that establishes a reputation for aggressive and irrational behavior may be attempting to establish a credible threat to its competitors.

T F 15. While game theory is useful in analyzing the behavior of individual oligopolists, it does not apply to the behavior of nations that are engaged in competitive behavior.

T F 16. Strategic behavior recognizes that, under oligopoly, one firm's decision does not affect other firms.

T F 17. A defining characteristic of oligopoly is that all firms in an industry typically consider the reactions of competitors when they formulate strategy.

T F 18. Game theory is primarily concerned with the study of games like roulette and dice.

T F 19. When two children fight over a piece of cake, it is an example of a zero-sum game.

T F 20. Game theory can be used to predict the behavior of nations in conflict.

T F 21. When two movie theater chains pay for advertisements proposing that people should "go out and see a show tonight," their expenditures are strategies in a zero-sum game where profit is the payoff.

T F 22. If the payoffs in a game are measured in terms of market share, then duopolists are engaged in a nonzero-sum game.

T F 23. A firm's dominant strategy is superior or equivalent to any other available strategy.

T F 24. A rational firm will select a dominant strategy, if one exists.

T F 25. Game theory predicts that players will always have a dominant strategy.

T F 26. A dominant strategy equilibrium is always a Nash equilibrium.

T F 27. A Nash equilibrium is always a dominant strategy equilibrium.

T F 28. If a player's optimal strategy depends on the behavior of rival players, then that player must have a dominant strategy.

T F 29. The prisoners' dilemma provides an explanation for price wars among oligopolists.

T F 30. The prisoners' dilemma is unable to explain the seeming inability of most commodity cartels to maintain high prices.

T F 31. Firms in a cartel "cheat" by selling more output than they are supposed to.

T F 32. A credible threat is one that is not believable.

T F 33. Reputation is a source of credible threat.

T F 34. Excess capacity is an example of a credible threat that can act as a deterrent to entry by rivals.

T F 35. Tit-for-tat is a strategy that cannot be applied in repeated games.

T F 36. Decision trees represent strategies and outcomes in the form of a branching diagram.

T F 37. The technique of backward induction involves starting at the beginning of a decision tree and working through to the end.

T F 38. Sequential games can be solved using the technique of backward induction.

T F 39. The strategy of being the first to enter a new market may result in a "first mover" advantage.

T F 40. Government industrial policies and strategies can be cescribed using game theory.

Multiple Choice Questions

1.   A firm that considers the potential reactions of its competitors when it makes a decision

   A. is referred to as a price leader.
   B. is engaged in strategic behavior.
   C. is engaged in collusion.
   D. is referred to as a barometric firm.

2.   Which of the following is an example of strategic behavior?

   A. A firm builds excess capacity to discourage the entry of competitors.
   B. A firm adopts the pricing behavior of a dominant firm under the assumption that other firms will do likewise.
   C. Firms in an industry increase advertising expenditures to avoid losing market share.
   D. All of the above are examples of strategic behavior.

3.   Which one of the following is <u>not</u> a part of every game theory model?

   A. Players
   B. Payoffs
   C. Probabilities
   D. Strategies

4.   In game theory, a choice that is optimal for a firm no matter what its competitors do is referred to as

   A. the dominant strategy.
   B. the game-winning choice.
   C. super optimal.
   D. a gonzo selection.

5.   Which of the following circumstances in an industry will result in a Nash equilibrium?

   A. All firms have a dominant strategy and each firm chooses its dominant strategy.
   B. All firms have a dominant strategy, but only some choose to follow it.
   C. All firms have a dominant strategy, and none choose it.
   D. None of the above is correct.

6.   Which of the following describes a Nash equilibrium?

   A. A firm chooses its dominant strategy, if one exists.
   B. Every competing firm in an industry chooses a strategy that is optimal given the choices of every other firm.
   C. Market price results in neither a surplus nor a shortage.
   D. All firms in an industry are earning zero economic profits.

7. A prisoners' dilemma is a game with all of the following characteristics except one. Which one is not present in a prisoners' dilemma?

   A. Players cooperate in arriving at their strategies.
   B. Both players have a dominant strategy.
   C. Both players would be better off if neither chose their dominant strategy.
   D. The payoff from a strategy depends on the choice made by the other player.

8. Which of the following legal restrictions, if enforced effectively, would be likely to solve a prisoners' dilemma type of problem for the firms involved?

   A. A law that prevents a cartel from enforcing rules against cheating.
   B. A law that makes it illegal for oligopolists to engage in collusion.
   C. A law that prohibits firms in an industry from advertising their services.
   D. All of the above would be likely to solve a prisoners' dilemma for the firms.

9. Until recently, medical doctors and lawyers have been prohibited from engaging in competitive advertising. If the prisoners' dilemma applies to this situation, then the presence of this restriction would be likely to

   A. increase profits earned by individuals in these professions.
   B. reduce profits earned by individuals in these professions.
   C. have no effect on the profits earned by individuals in these professions.
   D. increase the profits of some and reduce the profits of other individuals in these professions.

10. Which one of the following conditions is required for the success of a tit-for-tat strategy?

   A. Demand and cost conditions must change frequently and unpredictably.
   B. The number of oligopolists in the industry must be relatively small.
   C. The game can be repeated only a small number of times.
   D. Firms must be unable to detect the behavior of their competitors.

11. An oligopolist may engage in short-run behavior that results in lower profits if

   A. it leads to a Nash equilibrium.
   B. it is a dominant strategy.
   C. it is not involved in a repeated game.
   D. it lends credibility to the firm's threats.

12. A firm may decide to increase its scale so that it has excess production capacity because, by doing so, it is able to

   A. minimize its average cost of production.
   B. establish a credible deterrent to the entry of competing firms.
   C. take advantage of a dominant strategy in a prisoners' dilemma.
   D. attain a Nash equilibrium and avoid repeated games.

13. Game theory is concerned with

   A. predicting the results of bets placed on games like roulette.
   B. the choice of an optimal strategy in conflict situations.
   C. utility maximization by firms in perfectly competitive markets.
   D. the migration patterns of caribou in Alaska.

14. Which of the following is an example of a game theory strategy?

    A. You scratch my back and I'll scratch yours.
    B. If the shoe fits, wear it.
    C. Monkey see, monkey do.
    D. None of the above.

15. In game theory, a situation in which one firm can gain only what another firm loses is called a

    A. nonzero-sum game.
    B. prisoners' dilemma.
    C. zero-sum game.
    D. cartel temptation.

16. Which of the following is a nonzero-sum game?

    A. Prisoners' dilemma
    B. Chess
    C. Competition among duopolists when market share is the payoff
    D. All of the above.

17. Which of the following is a zero-sum game?

    A. Prisoners' dilemma
    B. Chess
    C. A cartel member's decision regarding whether or not to cheat
    D. All of the above.

18. A plan of action that considers the reactions of rivals is an example of

    A. accounting liability.
    B. strategic behavior.
    C. accommodating behavior.
    D. risk management.

19. In game theory, the outcome or consequence of a strategy is referred to as the

    A. payoff.
    B. penalty.
    C. reward.
    D. end-game strategy.

20. A strategy that is best regardless of what rival players do is called

    A. first-mover advantage.
    B. a Nash equilibrium strategy.
    C. tit-for-tat.
    D. a dominant strategy.

21.   A game that involves interrelated decisions that are made over time is a

A. sequential game.
B. repeated game.
C. zero-sum game.
D. nonzero-sum game.

22.   A game that involves multiple moves in a series of identical situations is called a

A. sequential game.
B. repeated game.
C. zero-sum game.
D. nonzero-sum game.

23.   Sequential games can be solved using

A. tit-for-tat.
B. dominated strategies.
C. backward induction.
D. risk averaging.

24.   Industrial policy

A. is strategic behavior that takes place at the national level.
B. may be accomplished by protecting and subsidizing selected industries.
C. is intended to provide competitive advantage to selected firms.
D. All of the above.

25.   A firm that is threatened by the potential entry of competitors into a market builds excess production capacity. This is an example of

A. a prisoners' dilemma.
B. collusion.
C. a credible threat.
D. tit-for-tat.

Problems

1.   Two surgeons who specialize in elective plastic surgery must decide whether or not to advertise their services. Each believes that advertising will increase profits by $10 thousand per month provided that the other does not advertise, in which case the surgeon who does not advertise will experience a $5 thousand decrease in profits. If both surgeons advertise, then each believes that profits will decline by $1 thousand per month. If neither advertises, of course, profits will remain as they are. Use this information to construct a payoff matrix. Determine each surgeon's optimal strategy. Is this a prisoners' dilemma? How would you expect the surgeons to react to a law prohibiting advertising? Why?

2.   Two amusement parks that are located on either side of a highway are considering promotional advertising campaigns to stimulate demand. If both parks advertise, then both will experience a $20 thousand increase in profits. If Park A advertises and Park B does not, then Park A will experience a $10 thousand dollar increase in profits and Park B will experience a $5 thousand increase in profits. If Park B advertises and Park A does not, then Park A will experience a $30 thousand increase in profits and Park B will experience a $10 thousand increase in profits. If neither park advertises, then profits will remain constant. Use this information to construct a payoff matrix. Determine each park's optimal strategy. Is this a prisoners' dilemma? Does either park have a dominant strategy? Is there a Nash equilibrium and, if there is, what is it? How is the concept of credible threat relevant to this game?

3. A firm (Firm 1) is considering the introduction of a discount on its products. If Firm 1 and all of the other firms in the industry discount their products, then all of the firms will experience a $20 thousand increase in profits. If Firm 1 introduces discounts and the other firms do not, then Firm 1 will experience a $20 thousand increase in profits and the other firms will experience a $10 thousand increase in profits. If the other firms introduce discounts and Firm 1 does not, then Firm 1 will experience a $10 thousand increase in profits and the other firms will experience a $20 thousand increase in profits. If none of the firms introduce discounts, then profits will remain unchanged. Use this information to construct a payoff matrix. Determine the optimal strategies. Is this a prisoners' dilemma? Is there a dominant strategy?

Alaphortu Manufacturing produces a sonic cleaning device, the Dentoplexor, that is used by dentists to remove plaque from teeth. The firm has not been profitable in recent years. Its low stock valuation made it possible for Phoryu, Inc., a Japanese firm, to acquire a controlling interest and undertake a merger. The new company, Alaphortu Phoryu (**Firm A**), is considering two possible strategies for the future. The first is to invest in a promotion and brand-building campaign in order to expand the market share of the Dentoplexor (**Promote**). The second is to discontinue the product entirely and repurpose the manufacturing capacity in a more profitable application (**Leave**).

The Dentoplexor's primary competitor is the Dentotome, produced by the Bytme Corporation (**Firm B**). Bytme, too, is considering two strategies. The first is to introduce a new product, the Dentozapper (**New**), which uses laser beams to clean teeth. The second is to update the Dentotome (**Update**) by making it more compact and powerful.

4.   The decision tree below represents the payoffs associated with sequential decisions by the two firms described above, with Firm A moving first. Determine the Nash equilibrium strategies and payoffs for the two firms.

	Firm A	Firm B
New	-$10	$30
Update	$25	$40
New	$0	$60
Update	$0	$50

5.   The decision tree below has the same payoffs as that shown above, but it has Firm B moving first. Determine the Nash equilibrium strategies and payoffs for the two firms in this case.

	Firm A	Firm B
Promote	-$10	$30
Leave	$0	$60
Promote	$25	$40
Leave	$0	$50

6.   Does the order of play make a difference in the example above? Comment on the concept of first-mover advantage using this problem as an example.

The Fermay Corporation has decided to build a new factory in Eastern Europe that will allow it to become the dominant regional supplier of small personal appliances. It has yet to decide whether the production capacity of the factory should equal or exceed projected demand. Excess capacity will allow the firm to increase supply and drive prices down if a competitor attempts to enter the market, but it is less efficient, so profits will be lower.

A second firm, Fermbe, has developed a strategic plan that will place it in direct competition with Fermay. It has not yet decided whether or not to execute the plan, however.

The decision tree that follows represents the situation described above as a three-stage sequential game. Fermay (**Firm A**) must decide whether to construct a factory with the capacity to produce more than the projected market demand (**Excess**) or not (**Equal**). Fermbe must then decide whether to follow its strategic plan and enter the market (**Enter**) or not (**Cancel**). Finally, in the third stage, Fermay must decide whether it will increase output and force prices down (**Increase**) or not (**Constant**).

7. Fermbe has hired you as a consultant to analyze the decision tree below. Determine the optimal strategies and payoffs for each firm and make your recommendations to Fermbe.

	Firm A	Firm B
Increase	$20	-$20
Constant	$30	$40
Increase	$30	$0
Constant	$95	$0
Increase	$10	$5
Constant	$40	$40
Increase	$55	$0
Constant	$100	$0

Fermay has just made a public commitment to build its new factory with excess capacity, with the announced goal of being "able to supply regional demand as it continues to grow and develop over time." You receive a phone call from Fermbe questioning your conclusions. You explain that, based on the decision tree analysis, this decision is inconsistent with rational, profit-maximizing behavior. It suggests that, if Fermay is behaving irrationally in this case, it may be prepared to use its excess capacity to force prices down and drive its competitors out of business, even though that would not be rational behavior, either.

8.   If Fermbe is convinced that Fermay will increase output if it enters the market, how will it affect the strategies that will be selected and the payoffs that will be realized by the two firms? What is your recommendation in this case? Comment on the concepts of reputation and credible threat using this problem as an example.

True-False Answers

1	T	9	T	17	T	25	F	33	T
2	F	10	T	18	F	26	T	34	T
3	F	11	F	19	T	27	F	35	F
4	F	12	T	20	T	28	F	36	T
5	T	13	F	21	F	29	T	37	F
6	T	14	T	22	F	30	F	38	T
7	F	15	F	23	T	31	T	39	T
8	F	16	F	24	T	32	F	40	T

Multiple Choice Answers

1	B	6	B	11	D	16	A	21	A
2	D	7	A	12	B	17	B	22	B
3	C	8	C	13	B	18	B	23	C
4	A	9	A	14	A	19	A	24	D
5	A	10	B	15	C	20	D	25	C

Solutions to Problems

1. The payoff matrix is given below.

		Doctor B	
		Advertise	Don't Advertise
Doctor A	Advertise	(-1,-1)	(10,-5)
	Don't Advertise	(-5, -10)	(0, 0)

The optimal decision for each surgeon is to advertise. This is a dominant strategy. If one surgeon does not advertise, then the other can increase profits by advertising. If one surgeon advertises, then the other can reduce losses by advertising. Thus, regardless of what the other surgeon does, advertising is optimal.

This is a prisoners' dilemma because both surgeons would be better off if no one advertised, but neither can trust the other to refrain from advertising.

A law that prohibits advertising should be welcomed by the surgeons. Compared to the dominant solution, in which both advertise and make losses of $1 thousand per month, each would be better off.

2. The payoff matrix is given below.

		Park B	
		Advertise	Don't Advertise
Park A	Advertise	(20,20)	(10,5
	Don't Advertise	(30,10)	(0,0)

Park A does not have a dominant strategy. Instead, its optimal strategy depends on the choice made by Park B. If Park B chooses to advertise, then Park A should not advertise because the payoff will be 30 instead of 20. If Park B decides not to advertise, then Park A should advertise because the payoff will be 10 instead of zero. Park B does have a dominant strategy. If Park A chooses to advertise, then Park B should advertise because the payoff will be 20 instead of 5. If Park A chooses not to advertise, then again Park B should advertise because the payoff will be 10 instead of zero. Thus, advertising is a dominant strategy for Park B.

This is not a prisoners' dilemma, because the players could not improve their payoffs by cooperating.

This game has a Nash equilibrium. Park B has a dominant strategy, which is to advertise. Park A will not advertise, since that is its preferred strategy when Park B advertises.

The issue of credible threat is relevant to this game because Park B will be better off if both parks advertise, but Park A will not advertise if Park B does. If Park A is convinced that Park B will advertise only if Park A advertises, then Park A will advertise. However, it would be irrational for Park B to not advertise. The credibility issue, then, involves Park B convincing Park A that it will act irrationally if Park A does not advertise.

3.   The payoff matrix is given below.

		Other Firms	
		Discount	No Discount
Firm 1	Discount	(20,20)	(20,10)
	No Discount	(10,20)	(0,0)

The optimal (and dominant) strategy for Firm 1 and for all of the other firms is to discount.

This is not a prisoners' dilemma because cooperation cannot improve upon the payoff that results from the dominant strategy.

4.   The Nash equilibrium is determined by backward induction, beginning with the choice by Firm B between New and Update. Firm A will then choose between Promote (assuming that B will choose Update) and Leave (assuming that B will choose New). The optimal strategy is for Firm A to choose Promote and Firm B to choose Update, as shown below, with payoffs of $25 and $40, respectively.

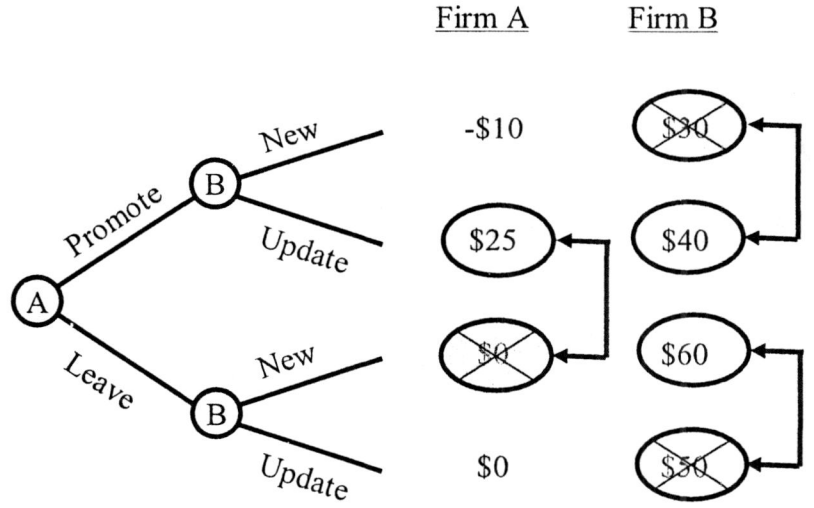

5. The Nash equilibrium is again determined by backward induction, this time beginning with the choice by Firm A. The optimal strategy is for Firm A to choose Leave and Firm B to choose New, as shown below, with payoffs of $0 and $60, respectively.

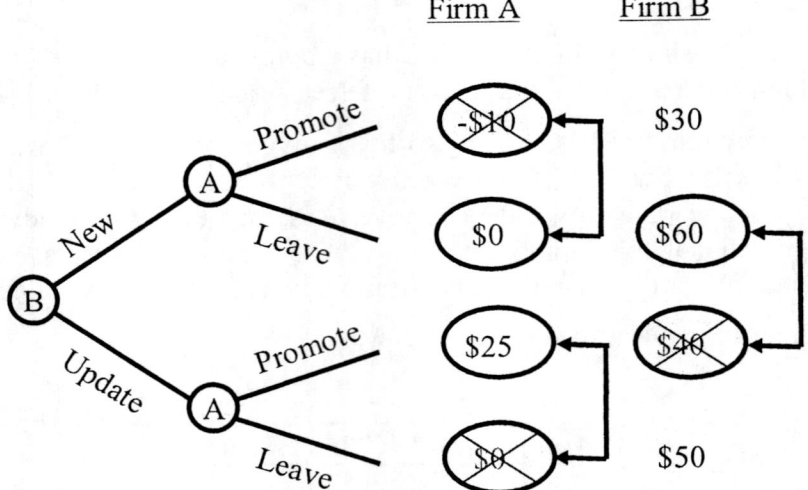

6. The order of play does make a difference in the optimal strategy by each firm and in the payoff each firm will receive. If Firm A goes first, it realizes a payoff of $25 versus $0 if Firm B goes first. If Firm B goes first, it gets $60 versus $40 if Firm A goes first. This example illustrates a case in which first-mover advantage consists of the higher payoff that will be captured by the first firm to make a strategic decision.

7. Using backward induction, begin with the choice by Firm A between Increase and Constant. In every case, Constant is the preferred strategy. It is dominant. Next, consider choice by Firm B between Enter and Cancel given That Firm A will choose Constant, where Enter is the dominant strategy. Finally, Firm A will compare Excess and Equal, given that Firm B will choose Enter, and will choose Equal. The optimal strategies are for Firm A to choose Equal, Firm B to choose Enter, and then for Firm A to choose constant. Your recommendation to Firm B should be to enter the market. The diagram that follows represents the derivation of this solution.

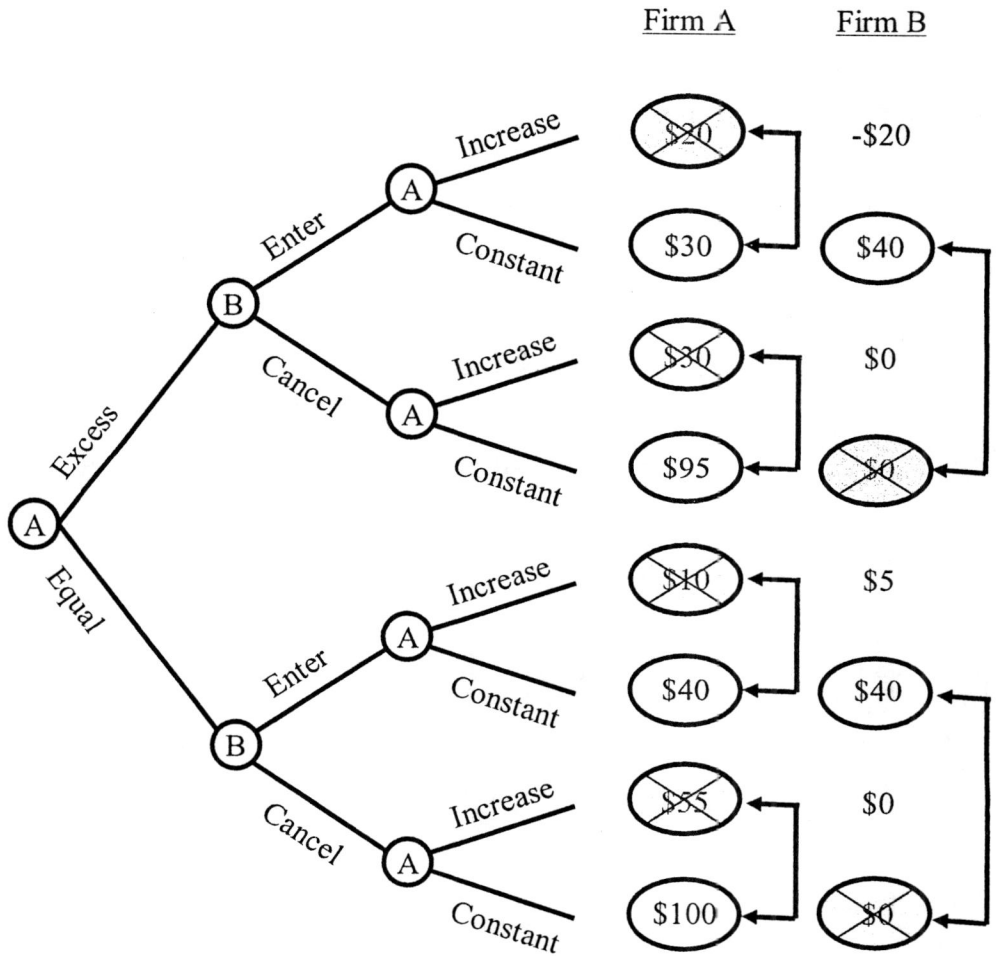

8. If Firm B believes that Firm A will respond to entry by increasing output, then its optimal strategy changes, as shown in the diagram below.

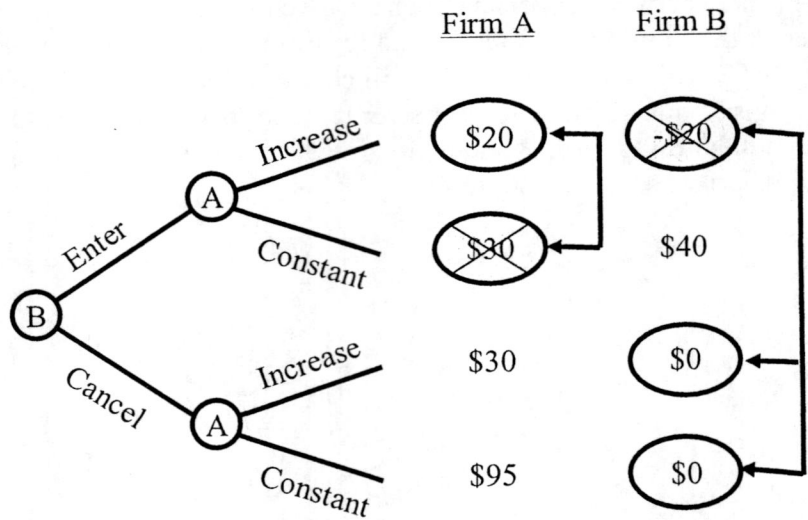

If Firm B enters the market, it will expect a payoff of -$20 versus a payoff of $0 if it does not enter the market. The rational strategy for Firm B, in that case, is to choose Cancel. If Firm B chooses Cancel, however, Firm A will have no reason to choose Increase. It will choose Constant, and will get a payoff of $95. The only way for Firm B to know for sure whether or not Firm A is bluffing is to call the bluff, a choice that could be very costly to Firm B. By behaving irrationally with regard to capacity, Firm A has become unpredictable. Your recommendation has to be for Firm B not to enter the market.

By choosing to behave in an irrational manner, Firm A has created a reputation for irrational competitive behavior. Because of this reputation, the excess production capacity is a credible threat. The result of this gambit by Firm A is that it ends up with a payoff of $95, which is far better than the $40 payoff it would have received by following the rational strategy that would have resulted in the Nash equilibrium.

CHAPTER 11

PRICING PRACTICES

Learning Objectives

The theoretical models of market structure that were presented in the previous two chapters assume that firms produce a single product on a single market and that the circumstances that determine optimal behavior are precisely known. While a knowledge of these models is fundamental to the understanding of the behavior of firms in a market economy, actual pricing practices must contend with additional complexities which are addressed in this chapter. When you have completed a careful study of this chapter, you should understand the ways in which firms maximize profits when they engage in the production of multiple products that are interdependent in terms of production costs and demand, how firms can employ price discrimination to enhance their profitability, how firms with semiautonomous divisions employ transfer pricing as part of their overall profit maximization strategy, and how information about the price elasticity of demand can be used to determine the optimal markup by firms that employ cost-plus pricing.

Summary of Notation and Formulas

(11-1) $MR_A = \dfrac{\Delta TR_A}{\Delta Q_A} + \dfrac{\Delta TR_B}{\Delta Q_A}$

(11-2) $MR_B = \dfrac{\Delta TR_B}{\Delta Q_B} + \dfrac{\Delta TR_A}{\Delta Q_B}$

Equations 11-1 and 11-2 are mathematical expressions that define the marginal revenue for product A (MR_A) and for product B (MR_B) when the two goods are produced by the same firm and the demand functions for the two goods are interdependent. Equation 11-1 defines MR_A as the sum of the change in total revenue from the sale of A (TR_A) divided by the corresponding change in the quantity of A (Q_A) plus the change in total revenue from the sale of B (TR_B) divided by the corresponding change in the quantity of A (Q_A). Equation 11-2 defines MR_B as the sum of the change in total revenue from the sale of B (TR_B) divided by the corresponding change in the quantity of B (Q_B) plus the change in total revenue from the sale of A (TR_A) divided by the corresponding change in the quantity of B (Q_B). Note that the second term in each of these two equations would be equal to zero if the demand functions for the two goods were independent.

(11-3) $m = \dfrac{P-C}{C}$

(11-4) $P = C(1+m)$

Equations 11-3 and 11-4 define the relationship between the markup on cost (m), the cost-plus price (P), and the fully allocated average cost (C).

(11-5) $\quad MR = P\left(1 + \dfrac{1}{E_P}\right)$

(11-6) $\quad P = \dfrac{MR}{1 + 1/E_P} = \dfrac{MR}{(E_P + 1)/E_P} = MR\dfrac{E_P}{E_P + 1}$

Equations 11-5 and 11-6 define the relationship between marginal revenue (MR), price (P), and the price elasticity of demand (E_P).

(11-7) $\quad P = C\dfrac{E_P}{E_P + 1}$

(11-8) $\quad m = \dfrac{E_P}{E_P + 1} - 1$

Equation 11-7 defines the optimal cost-plus price (P) as a function of the fully-allocated average cost (C), and the price elasticity of demand (E_P). Equation 11-8 defines the optimal markup (m) as a function of the price elasticity of demand.

True-False Questions

T F 1. If two goods produced by a single firm are substitutes in consumption, then an increase in the price of one will cause a decrease in demand for the other.

T F 2. If two goods produced by a single firm are complements in consumption, then a decrease in the price of one will cause an increase in demand for the other.

T F 3. If two goods (A and B) produced by a single firm are substitutes in consumption, then the change in total revenue from the sale of B divided by the corresponding change in the quantity of A will be positive.

T F 4. If two goods (A and B) produced by a single firm are complements in consumption, then the change in total revenue from the sale of B divided by the corresponding change in the quantity of A will be positive.

T F 5. If a firm has idle plant capacity, then it should produce additional products even if the marginal cost of doing so exceeds marginal revenue.

T F 6. Additional products should be introduced by a single-plant firm in order of decreasing profitability up to the point where the marginal revenue of the least profitable product is equal to its marginal cost.

T F 7. A single-plant firm that produces more than one product will charge the same price for every product that it produces.

T F 8. A single-plant multi-product firm will produce a quantity of each product such that the marginal cost of each product is the same.

T F   9.   A single-plant, multi-product, imperfectly competitive firm with excess plant capacity should continue to introduce new products until the price of the last product introduced is equal to its marginal cost or until all capacity is employed.

T F   10. An example of joint production with fixed proportions is petroleum refining.

T F   11. Joint production is the result of production interdependence.

T F   12. The optimal level of output where products are jointly produced in variable proportions occurs where the marginal cost of production is equal to the vertical summation of the marginal revenues of the individual products.

T F   13. If the optimal level of output where products are jointly produced in fixed proportions occurs where the marginal revenue for one product is negative, then the firm will maximize profit by disposing of some or all of the output of that product rather than by selling it.

T F   14. Products that are produced jointly in fixed proportions are substitutes in production.

T F   15. If products are produced jointly in fixed proportions, then their product transformation curves are right angles.

T F   16. If the product transformation curves for two goods produced jointly are straight lines, then the two goods are perfect substitutes in production.

T F   17. Price discrimination is illegal under U.S. law.

T F   18. Price discrimination refers to charging different prices for a product when price differences are not justified by differences in cost.

T F   19. A letter mailed to New York from Los Angeles costs less if it is sent first class than if it is sent by overnight mail, which proves that the U.S. Postal Service is engaging in price discrimination.

T F   20. First-degree price discrimination would allow a firm to charge the maximum possible price for every unit sold.

T F   21. If a firm that does not price discriminate begins to practice first-degree price discrimination, its profit will increase by an amount equal to consumers' surplus.

T F   22. A firm that is engaging in third-degree price discrimination will charge a lower price to buyers with less elastic demand curves.

T F   23. Perfectly competitive firms can engage in second-degree price discrimination.

T F   24. Price discrimination is most effective if all consumers have the same price elasticity of demand.

T F   25. A firm that sells on two markets and engages in third-degree price discrimination will increase the quantity sold on each market until marginal revenue is the same on both markets and is equal to marginal cost.

T F   26. A firm that sells on two markets and engages in third-degree price discrimination will adjust the quantity sold on each market until the same price holds on both markets.

T F   27. Persistent dumping refers to the practice of international price discrimination.

T F 28. Dumping occurs when a firm charges a higher price for a product on foreign markets than on domestic markets.

T F 29. Export subsidies are a form of dumping.

T F 30. A firm that is selling a product at a lower price on foreign markets for the purpose of driving foreign producers out of business is engaging in persistent dumping.

T F 31. The occasional sale of a commodity at a lower price on foreign markets is referred to as sporadic dumping.

T F 32. The harassment thesis holds that the threat of filing a dumping complaint against a foreign producer discourages the producer from aggressively competing in the domestic market.

T F 33. Persistent dumping and sporadic dumping may be desirable if benefits to domestic consumers exceed the losses experienced by domestic producers.

T F 34. Transfer pricing refers to the determination of prices of intermediate products sold by one semiautonomous division of a firm and purchased by another semiautonomous division of the same firm.

T F 35. Tax laws require that transfer prices be established, but they have little effect on the operation of a firm.

T F 36. Under cost-plus pricing, the more price elastic the demand is for a product, the higher the markup should be.

T F 37. Incremental analysis states that a firm should take an action if the resulting change in revenue exceeds the corresponding change in cost.

T F 38. Prestige pricing refers to setting a high product price in order to capitalize on snob appeal.

T F 39. Skimming refers to the practice of introducing several variations on a basic product and charging different prices for each.

T F 40. Value pricing refers to price cutting.

Multiple Choice Questions

1. Carolina Berries manufactures many varieties of jams and jellies. An increase in the price of their strawberry jam can be expected to

    A. increase the demand for their strawberry jelly because the two are complements.
    B. increase the demand for their strawberry jelly because the two are substitutes.
    C. decrease the demand for their strawberry jelly because the two are complements.
    D. decrease the demand for their strawberry jelly because the two are substitutes.

2. The Nintari Company produces video game playing machines and a second firm, Necsega, owns exclusive rights to manufacture games that can be used with the Nintari game machine. Both of these imperfectly competitive firms are maximizing profits. If Nintari buys Necsega and nothing else changes, then profits will be maximized if Nintari

   A. decreases the prices of game machines and games.
   B. does not change the prices of game machines or games.
   C. increases the prices of game machines and games.
   D. None of the above is correct.

3. Icarus Medical Supplies produces patented adhesives that are used to reassemble broken bones. Pindrop Medical Products manufactures patented pins that are also used to reassemble broken bones. Both of these imperfectly competitive firms are maximizing profit. If Icarus merges with Pindrop, then the merged firm will maximize profits if it

   A. decreases the prices of pins and adhesives.
   B. does not change the prices of pins or adhesives.
   C. increases the prices of pins and adhesives.
   D. None of the above is correct.

4. A single-plant, multi-product firm will introduce additional products

   A. in order of diminishing price elasticities of demand.
   B. until the marginal revenue from the last product introduced is equal to zero.
   C. until 100% of unused plant capacity is employed.
   D. None of the above is correct.

5. The optimal output of joint products that are produced in fixed proportions is found where

   A. the vertical sum of the marginal revenue from each product is equal to marginal cost.
   B. the horizontal sum of the marginal revenue from each product is equal to marginal cost.
   C. the marginal revenue from each product is equal to the marginal cost of producing each product.
   D. the marginal cost is equal to the corresponding price of each product.

6. The optimal combination of joint products that are produced in variable proportions is found where

   A. the marginal revenue from each product is equal to the marginal cost of producing each product.
   B. the isorevenue line is tangent to the product transformation curve.
   C. the isorevenue line is tangent to the relevant total cost curve.
   D. None of the above is correct.

7.   Which of the following is not an example of price discrimination?

   A. It costs more to make a long-distance phone call during the day than it does late at night.
   B. A ticket to the zoo costs less for a child than it does for an adult.
   C. Regular gasoline costs less than premium gasoline.
   D. All of the above are examples of price discrimination.

8.   A firm will realize the highest level of profit if it is able to engage in

   A. first-degree price discrimination.
   B. second-degree price discrimination.
   C. third-degree price discrimination.
   D. The answer cannot be determined without additional information.

9.   A grocery store that offers one can of soup for $0.35 and three cans for $1.00 is engaging in

   A. first-degree price discrimination.
   B. second-degree price discrimination.
   C. third-degree price discrimination.
   D. The answer cannot be determined without additional information.

10. A movie theater that charges a lower price for matinees than for evening showings is engaging in

   A. first-degree price discrimination.
   B. second-degree price discrimination.
   C. third-degree price discrimination.
   D. The answer cannot be determined without additional information.

11. A firm that is engaging in price discrimination will

   A. charge a higher price to consumers with a higher price elasticity of demand.
   B. charge a higher price to consumers with a lower price elasticity of demand.
   C. earn lower profits than a similar firm that does not engage in price discrimination.
   D. generally be a perfectly competitive firm.

12. Persistent dumping refers to the practice of

   A. international price discrimination.
   B. charging a lower price on foreign markets where demand is more price elastic.
   C. taking advantage of the segmentation of markets that results from domestic restrictions on imports.
   D. All of the above are correct.

13. A firm that is selling a product at or below cost on foreign markets in order to drive foreign producers out of business is engaging in

   A. international price discrimination.
   B. persistent dumping.
   C. predatory dumping.
   D. sporadic dumping.

14.   If there is no external market for an intermediate product, then the transfer price should be set equal to

   A. the marginal cost of producing the optimal quantity of the intermediate product.
   B. the marginal cost of producing the final product.
   C. the selling price of the final product.
   D. None of the above is correct.

15.   If the external market for an intermediate product is perfectly competitive, then the transfer price should be set equal to

   A. the market price of the final product.
   B. the competitive market price of the intermediate product.
   C. the marginal cost of the final product.
   D. None of the above is correct.

16.   If the external market for an intermediate product is imperfectly competitive, then the transfer price should be set equal to

   A. the market price of the intermediate product.
   B. the marginal cost of producing the optimal quantity of the intermediate product.
   C. the market price of the final product.
   D. None of the above is correct.

17.   A firm charges $14 for a product. If the markup is 40%, then the fully allocated average cost is

   A. $19.60
   B. $10.00
   C. $8.40
   D. None of the above is correct.

18.   A firm produces a product with a fully allocated average cost equal to $20. If the price elasticity of demand for the product is -5, then the product price should be set at

   A. $25.
   B. $24.
   C. $23.
   D. $22.

19.   Setting a high price when a product is first introduced and then gradually lowering its price over time is referred to as

   A. value pricing.
   B. skimming.
   C. price lining.
   D. prestige pricing.

20.   Developing a product to sell at a predetermined price is called

   A. value pricing.
   B. skimming.
   C. price lining.
   D. prestige pricing.

21. A pricing practice that involves charging a fixed fee plus a per unit price for a good or service is referred to as

   A. bundling.
   B. skimming.
   C. a two-part tariff.
   D. first degree price discrimination.

22. A tying agreement requires buyers of a product to

   A. purchase another product needed in the use of the first product.
   B. purchase a minimum number of units.
   C. refrain from exporting the product to certain countries.
   D. All of the above are true of a tying agreement.

23. A pricing practice that requires buyers to purchase packages of different goods and does not make the goods available separately is called

   A. value pricing.
   B. bundling.
   C. a two-part tariff.
   D. skimming.

24. A firm has two products and two customers. Customer 1 is willing to pay $5 for Product A and $3 for Product B. Customer 2 is willing to pay $7 for Product A and $4 for Product B. Can the firm increase revenue by bundling and, if so, how much should be charged for the bundle?

   A. The firm cannot increase profits by bundling.
   B. The firm can increase profits by bundling. The bundle should sell for $12.
   C. The firm can increase profits by bundling. The bundle should sell for $10.
   D. The firm can increase profits by bundling. The bundle should sell for $7.

25. A firm has two products and two customers. Customer 1 is willing to pay $9 for Product A and $4 for Product B. Customer 2 is willing to pay $7 for Product A and $5 for Product B. Can the firm increase revenue by bundling and, if so, how much should be charged for the bundle?

   A. The firm cannot increase profits by bundling.
   B. The firm can increase profits by bundling. The bundle should sell for $12.
   C. The firm can increase profits by bundling. The bundle should sell for $10.
   D. The firm can increase profits by bundling. The bundle should sell for $7.

Problems

Gnomus Knurling Company specializes in the application of ornamental knurling to garden tools. The tools are produced by other firms and then delivered to Gnomus for processing. Gnomus has equipment that allows it to knurl in any of five different styles (designated as styles A, B, C, D, and E). The demand curves for the five styles of knurling have been estimated and are listed below, where Q_i represents the number of garden tools knurled with style i per week in hundreds and P_i represents the price per knurl job associated with style i.

$Q_A = 6 - 0.6\, P_A$

$Q_B = 8 - P_B$

$Q_C = 10 - 2\, P_C$

$Q_D = 12 - 3\, P_D$

$Q_E = 12 - 4\, P_E$

Use this information to solve Problems 1 and 2.

1. Gnomus has a constant marginal cost of $3 per knurl job regardless of which style, or combination of styles, it produces. Determine the number of knurl jobs of each style Gnomus should do and the price it should charge for each style. Use the graph below to show the optimal levels of production and price. Your graph should be similar in format to Figure 11-1 in the text.

Chapter 11: Problem 1

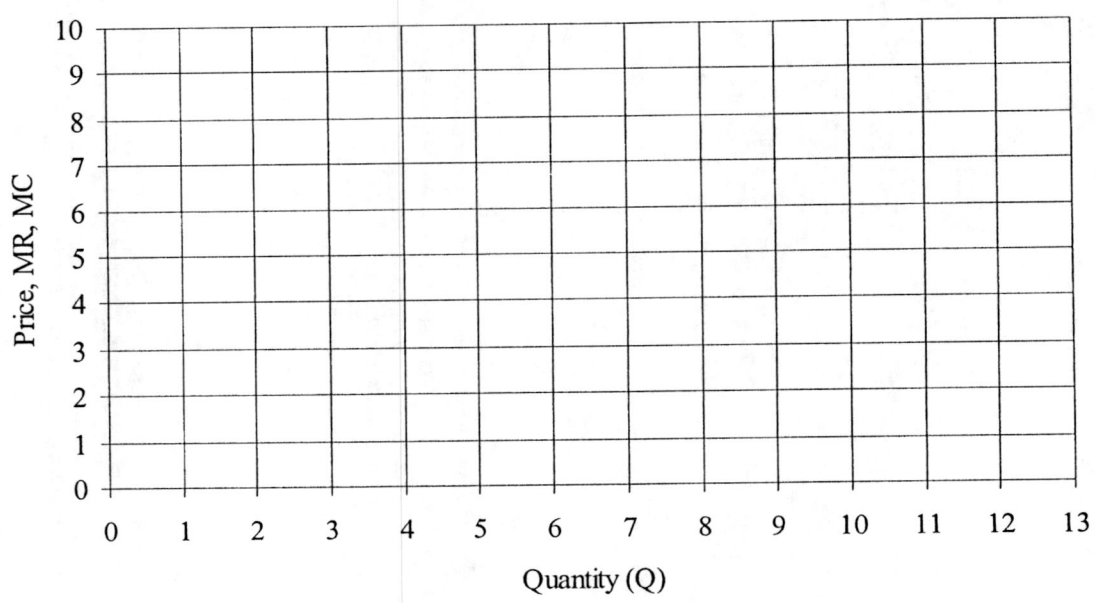

2.   A shortage of qualified knurlers has prompted Gnomus to increase its hourly wage rate. As a result, its marginal cost has risen to $4 per knurl job. Determine the number of knurl jobs of each style Gnomus should perform and the price it should charge for each style. Use the graph below to show the optimal levels of production and price.

Chapter 11: Problem 2

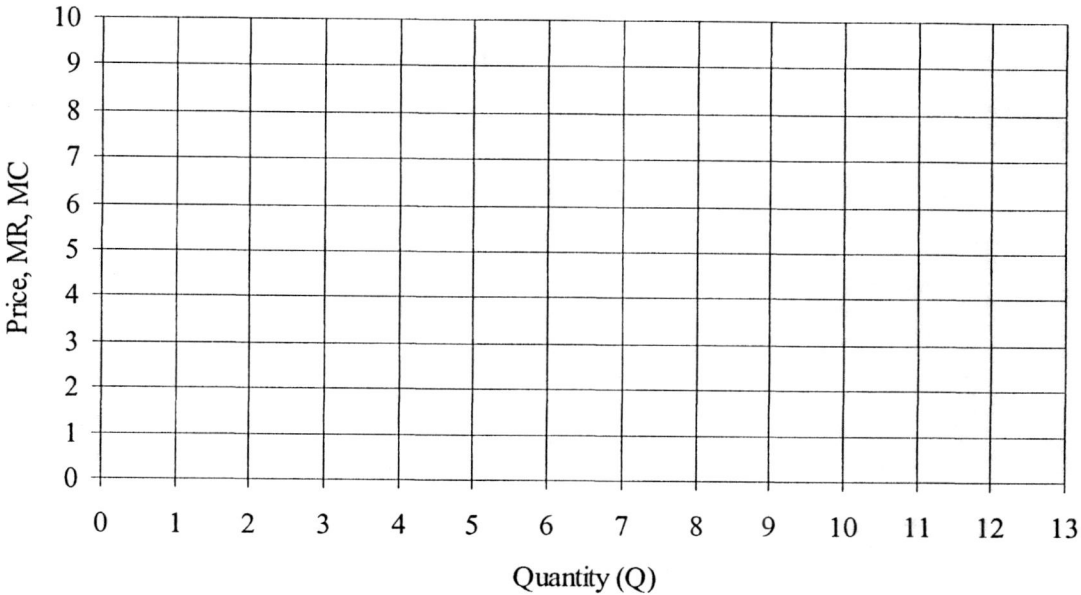

Amazon Pharmaceuticals is a company that extracts a variety of medicinal substances from plants that are indigenous to the Amazon Basin. One of its most successful products, RU18, is used to reduce the risk of organ rejection that is associated with certain types of implantation procedures. RU18 is extracted from a species of Amazonian liverwort. A byproduct of the extraction process, RU21, is a distilled palliative that is used to support exploratory bimanual operations. RU18 and RU21 are jointly produced in fixed proportions, with one unit of each derived from each specimen of the liverwort that is processed. The estimated demand functions for RU18 and RU21 are defined below. Use this information to solve Problems 3 and 4.

$Q_{RU18} = 16 - 2\ P_{RU18}$

$Q_{RU21} = 10 - 2\ P_{RU21}$

3.	The marginal cost of harvesting and processing the liverworts that yield RU18 and RU21 is

$MC = 3 + 0.5\,Q$

Determine the quantities of RU18 and RU21 that Amazon Pharmaceuticals should produce and sell and the prices that should be charged for the two products. Show the solution on the graph below. Your graph should be similar in format to Figure 11-2 in the text.

Chapter 11: Problem 3

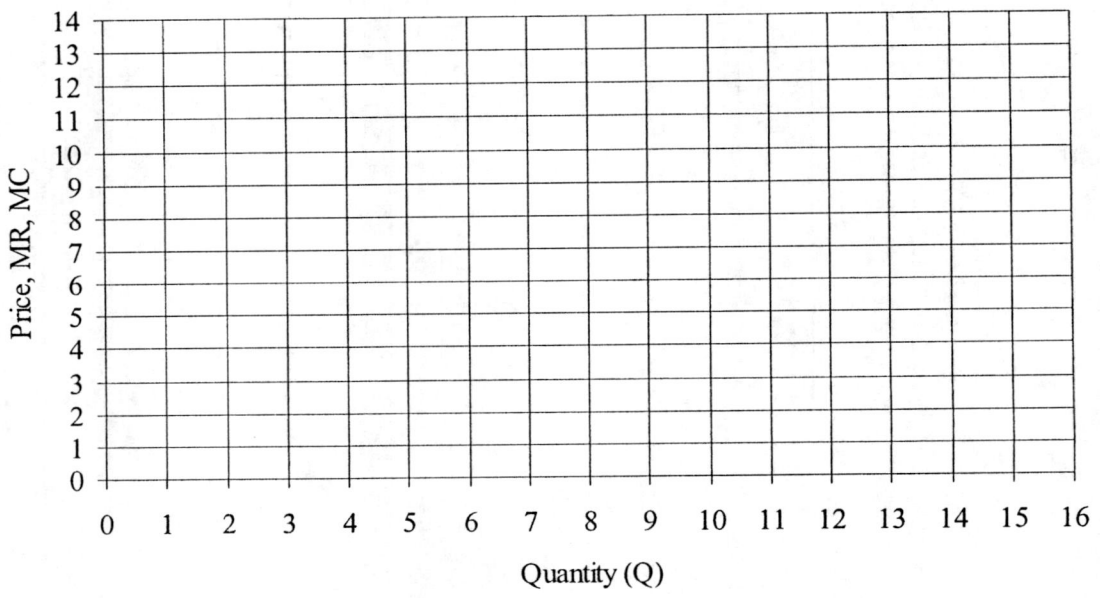

Price, MR, MC

Quantity (Q)

4. The discovery of readily accessible groves of the liverworts that are used to produce RU18 and RU21 causes the marginal cost of harvesting to decrease. It is now defined as

$$MC = 1 + Q/6$$

Determine the quantities of RU18 and RU21 that Amazon Pharmaceuticals should produce and sell now and the prices that it should charge for the two products. Show your solution on the graph below.

Chapter 11: Problem 4

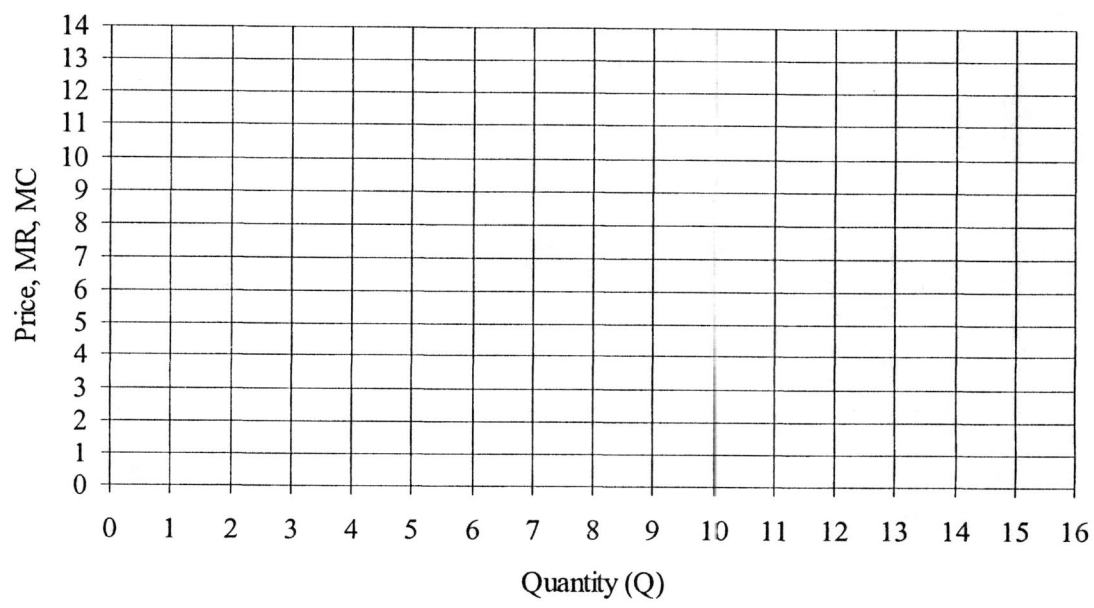

5. Wilbur Daedalus, owner and manager of Icarus Solariums, has estimated the demand for tanning services and has found that there are peak periods when demand is relatively high (evenings, weekends, and holidays) and there are off-peak periods when demand is relatively low (weekdays). His demand estimates, where Q represents the number of tanning sessions per month in hundreds and P is the price per session, are

Peak periods: $Q_P = 10 - P_P$

Off-peak periods: $Q_O = 8 - 1.6 P_O$

The marginal cost of a tanning session is equal to \$1 during both peak and off-peak periods. What price should Wilbur charge during peak periods? During off-peak periods? How many sessions per month can be expected at these prices? Plot the total market demand, marginal revenue, and marginal cost curve on the graph below.

Chapter 11: Problem 5

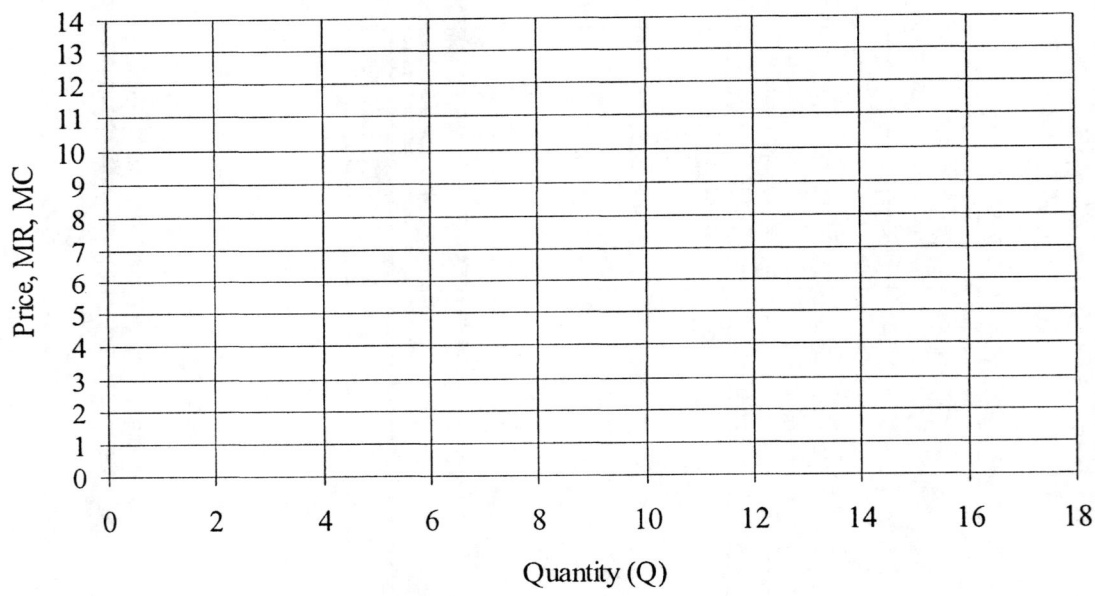

The Invincible Computer Company (ICC) is comprised of three semiautonomous divisions. The component division is located in Korea, the assembly division is located in Mexico, and the marketing division is located in the United States. Components are manufactured in Korea and are purchased by the assembly plant in Mexico. The assembled computers are purchased by the marketing division in the United States and are then sold to the final users.

The external demand function faced by the marketing division is

$$Q_M = 160 - 2\,P_M$$

The marginal cost functions of the three divisions of the firm, exclusive of transfer costs, are

Components: $MC_C = 7.5 + 0.05\,Q_C$

Assemblies: $MC_A = 0.25\,Q_A$

Marketing: $MC_M = 7.0 + 0.01\,Q_M$

Use this information to solve Problems 6 and 7.

6.   There are currently no external markets for either the components used by ICC or for the assembled computers. Plot final market demand, marginal revenue, and ICC's marginal cost function (label it MC_1) on the graph that follows. Determine the quantity of output the firm should produce and the price it should charge. Also determine the transfer prices of components and assemblies.

Chapter 11: Problem 6

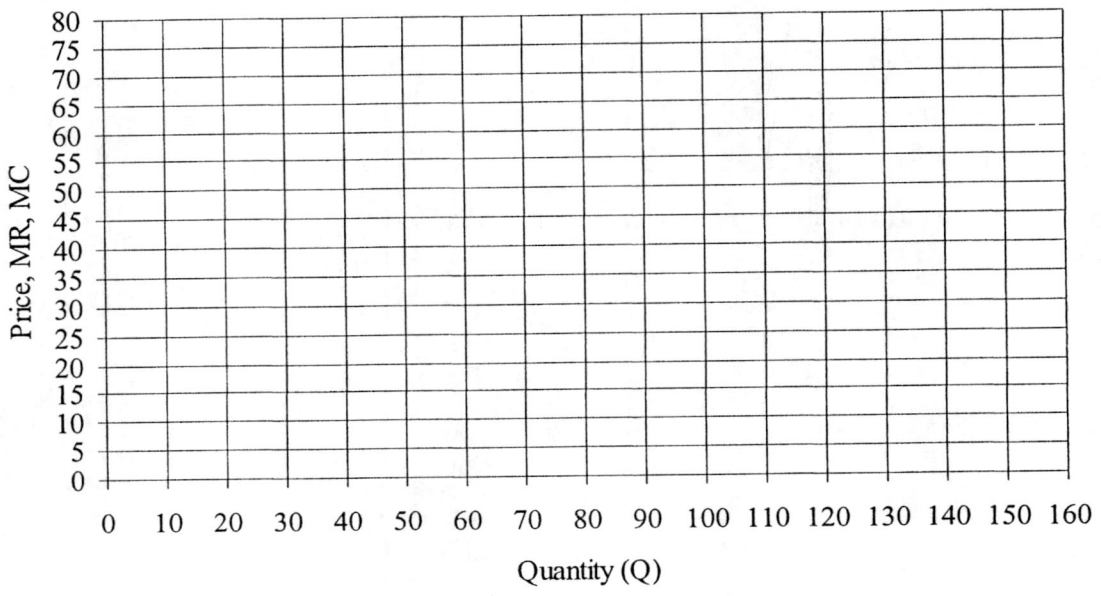

7.   The production of computer components, and the demand for components, has vastly expanded. The market for components has become perfectly competitive. The competitive price for components, P_C, is $20. On the graph you used for Problem 6, plot the new ICC marginal cost function (MC_2). Determine the quantity of output the firm should produce and the price it should charge. Also determine the transfer prices and the levels of output of components and assemblies.

True-False Answers

1	F	9	T	17	F	25	T	33	T
2	T	10	F	18	T	26	F	34	T
3	F	11	T	19	F	27	T	35	F
4	T	12	F	20	T	28	F	36	F
5	F	13	T	21	T	29	T	37	T
6	T	14	F	22	F	30	F	38	T
7	F	15	T	23	F	31	T	39	F
8	T	16	T	24	F	32	T	40	T

Multiple Choice Answers

1	B	6	B	11	B	16	B	21	C
2	A	7	C	12	D	17	B	22	A
3	C	8	A	13	C	18	A	23	B
4	D	9	B	14	A	19	B	24	A
5	A	10	C	15	B	20	C	25	B

Solutions to Problems

1. The first step in solving Problems 1 and 2 is to determine the inverse demand functions and the associated marginal revenue functions. These functions are given below.

$P_A = 10 - (5/3) Q_A$ $MR_A = 10 - (10/3) Q_A$

$P_B = 8 - Q_B$ $MR_B = 8 - 2 Q_B$

$P_C = 5 - 0.5 Q_C$ $MR_C = 5 - Q_C$

$P_D = 4 - (1/3) Q_D$ $MR_D = 4 - (2/3) Q_D$

$P_E = 3 - 0.25 Q_E$ $MR_E = 3 - 0.5 Q_E$

The second step is to determine the optimal level of output for each of the five different styles by setting the relevant marginal revenue function equal to marginal cost and then solving for output. The results of this calculation are given below.

$3 = 10 - (10/3) Q_A$ implies that $Q_A = 2.1$

$3 = 8 - 2 Q_B$ implies that $Q_B = 2.5$

$3 = 5 - Q_C$ implies that $Q_C = 2$

$3 = 4 - (2/3) Q_D$ implies that $Q_D = 1.5$

$3 = 3 - 0.5 Q_E$ implies that $Q_E = 0$

The third step is to determine the price that should be charged for each style by substituting the output level into the inverse demand function. Note that style E will not be produced. The results of this calculation are given below.

$P_A = 10 - (5/3)(2.1) = 6.5$

$P_B = 8 - 2.5 = 5.5$

$P_C = 5 - (0.5)(2) = 4$

$P_D = 4 - (1/3)(1.5) = 3.5$

Finally, the demand and marginal revenue curves are plotted on the graph. Note that they are plotted in order of declining profitability. If only one style could be produced, it would be style A. If only two styles could be produced, they would be styles A and B. And so on.

Chapter 11: Problem 1

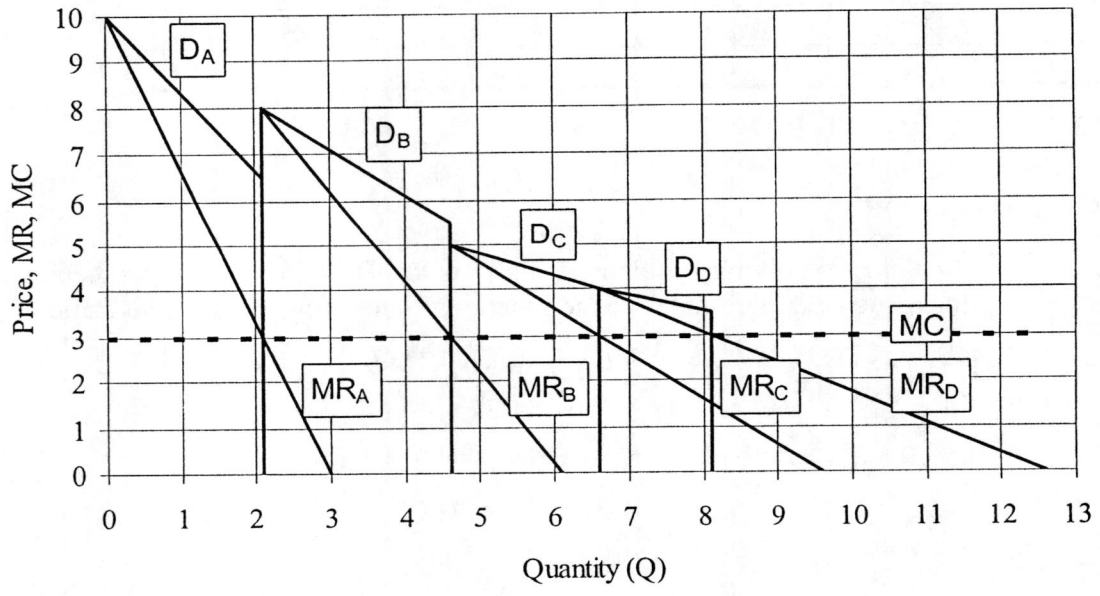

2. Following the same procedure employed in Problem 1, the optimal quantities of each style are calculated by setting each marginal revenue function equal to the marginal cost of $4 and then the price of each style is calculated by substituting the optimal quantity into the inverted demand function. The results of these calculations are given below.

$Q_A = 1.8$ and $P_A = 7$

$Q_B = 2$ and $P_B = 6$

$Q_C = 1$ and $P_C = 4.5$

$Q_D = 0$ so style D will not be produced

$Q_E = -2$ so style E will not be produced

Chapter 11: Problem 2

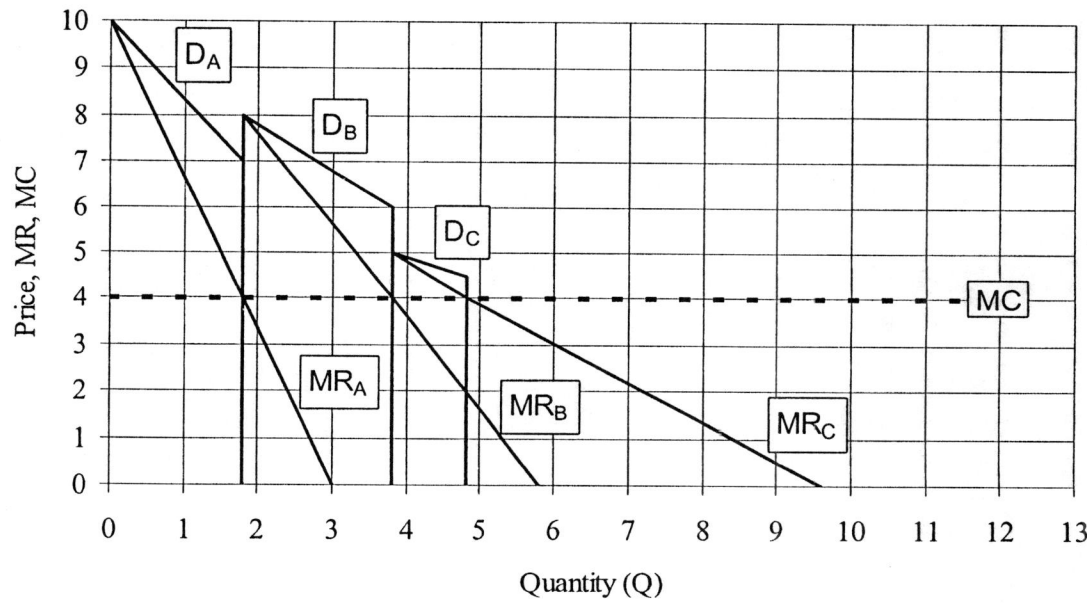

3. The first step in solving Problems 3 and 4 is to determine the inverse demand functions and the associated marginal revenue functions. These functions are given below.

$P_{RU18} = 8 - 0.5\, Q_{RU18}$ $\qquad\qquad$ $MR_{RU18} = 8 - Q_{RU18}$

$P_{RU21} = 5 - 0.5\, Q_{RU21}$ $\qquad\qquad$ $MR_{RU21} = 5 - Q_{RU21}$

The second step is to construct the total marginal revenue curve by vertically summing the marginal revenue functions of the two joint products. Since the number of each product is equal to the number of liverworts processed, the subscript on Q can be dropped in this calculation.

Total MR $= MR_{RU18} + MR_{RU21} = 8 - Q + 5 - Q = 13 - 2Q$

Note that the total marginal revenue function constructed above is only valid so long as both of the component marginal revenue values are nonnegative; i.e., from $Q = 0$ to $Q = 5$. If Q is greater than 5, the total marginal revenue curve is equal to the marginal revenue curve for RU18.

The third step is to set marginal cost equal to total marginal revenue and then solve for the optimal Q. This calculation is carried out below.

$3 + 0.5\,Q = 13 - 2\,Q$ which implies that $Q = 4$

Since this level of output is less than $Q = 5$, the quantities of RU18 and RU21 that should be offered for sale by the firm are also equal to four and the appropriate prices can be determined by substituting $Q = 4$ into the two inverted demand functions. This calculation is carried out below.

$P_{RU18} = 8 - (0.5)(4) = 6$

$P_{RU21} = 5 - (0.5)(4) = 3$

Chapter 11: Problem 3

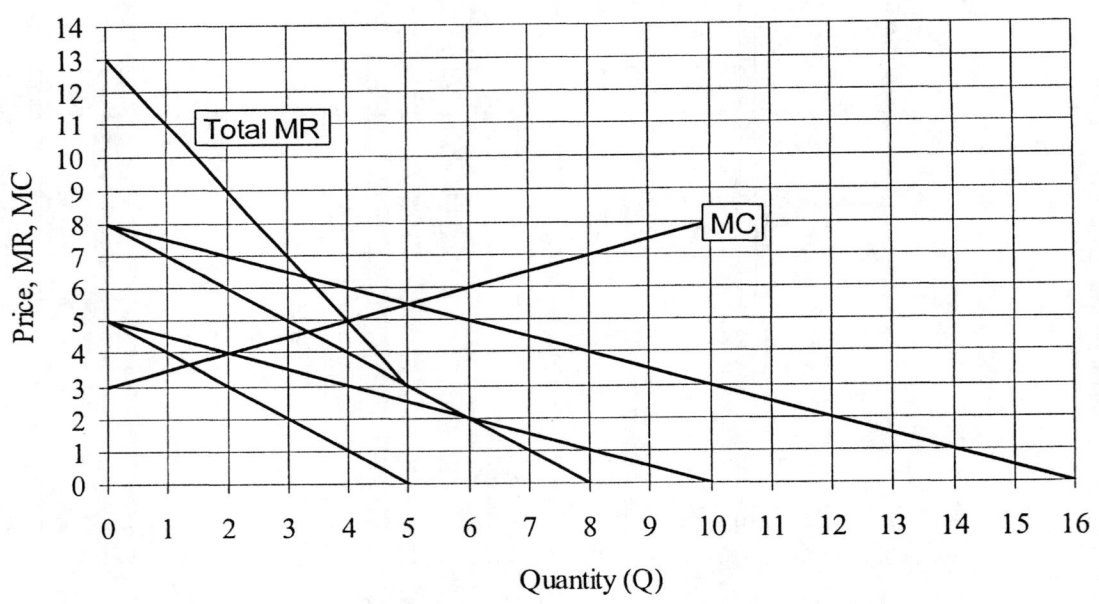

4.   Following the same procedure used to solve Problem 3, marginal cost is set equal to total marginal revenue and then solved for Q.

$1 + (1/6) Q = 13 - 2 Q$, which implies that $Q = 5.5$

This is not the optimal level of output, however, because the marginal revenue for RU21 is negative at this level of output. Consequently, marginal cost must be set equal to the marginal revenue of RU18 only to determine the optimal level of output.

$1 + (1/6) Q = 8 - Q$, which implies that $Q = 6$

This determines the quantity of RU18 that should be offered for sale the firm. The price of RU18 is determined by substituting this quantity into the inverted demand function as follows:

$P_{RU18} = 8 - (0.5)(6) = 5$

The price that should be charged for RU21 is that which corresponds to a marginal revenue of zero. To determine this level of output, the marginal revenue function for RU21 is set equal to zero and solved.

$MR_{RU21} = 5 - Q_{RU21} = 0$, which implies that $Q_{RU21} = 5$

The additional unit of RU21 that could be produced from the quantity of liverworts that is processed is not offered for sale. It is disposed of to keep price at the optimal level. Finally, the price that will be charged for RU21 is found by substituting the output level into the inverse demand function.

$P_{RU21} = 5 - (0.5)(5) = 2.5$

Chapter 11: Problem 4

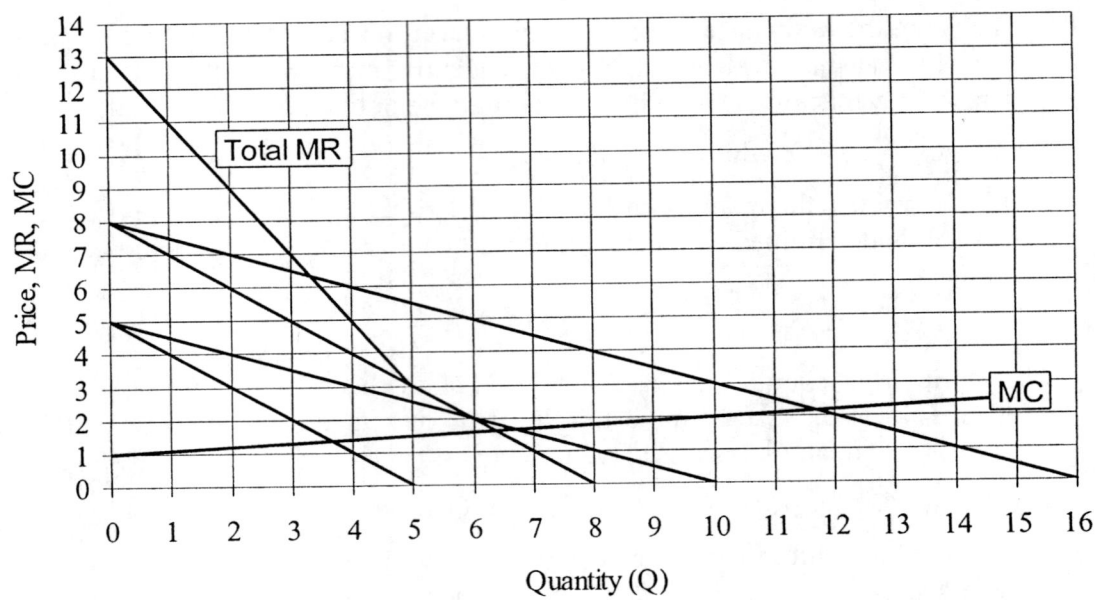

5. The first step in solving this type of problem is to determine the inverse demand functions and the corresponding marginal revenue functions for the two separable markets.

Peak periods: $P_P = 10 - Q_P$ $MR_P = 10 - 2\,Q_P$

Off-peak periods: $P_O = 5 - 0.625\,Q_O$ $MR_O = 5 - 1.25\,Q_O$

Next, the total market demand and marginal revenue functions must be calculated by horizontally summing the demand functions. This is accomplished by adding together the corresponding functions for the two markets. From P = 10 down to P = 5, total market demand is identical to the demand function for peak time periods. From P = 5 (and Q = 5) down to P = 0, total market demand is the horizontal sum of peak period and off-peak period demand functions:

$Q = 18 - 2.6\,P$ which implies that $P = 6.9231 - 0.3846\,Q$ and $TR = PQ = 6.9231\,Q - 0.3846\,Q^2$

Similarly, from MR = 10 down to MR = 5 (and Q = 2.5), the total marginal revenue function is based on the peak-period demand function. When output is above 2.5, the total marginal revenue function is based on the total market demand function, and is equal to

$MR = 6.9231 - 0.7692\,Q$

The optimal level of total output is determined by setting marginal cost equal to total market marginal revenue. In this case the solution is trivial. However, if the marginal cost function was more complex, the procedure would be the same. The optimal level of total output would be determined and then used to calculate the corresponding level of marginal cost. This, in turn, would be substituted into the marginal revenue functions for each market to determine the output on each market and then the output levels would be substituted into the inverse demand functions to determine the prices.

Setting marginal cost equal to total market marginal revenue yields

$1 = 6.9231 - 0.7692 Q$, which implies that $Q = 7.7$

Substituting the marginal cost into the marginal revenue functions for the individual markets yields

Peak periods: $MR_P = 10 - 2 Q_P = 1$ which implies that $Q_P = 4.5$

Off-peak periods: $MR_O = 5 - 1.25 Q_O = 1$ which implies that $Q_O = 3.2$

Note that these quantities sum to $Q = 7.7$. Finally, the prices on each market are determined by substituting the levels of output into the inverted demand functions.

Peak periods: $P_P = 10 - (4.5)$, which implies that $P_P = 5.5$

Off-peak periods: $P_O = 5 - (0.625)(3.2)$, which implies that $P_O = 3$

Chapter 11: Problem 5

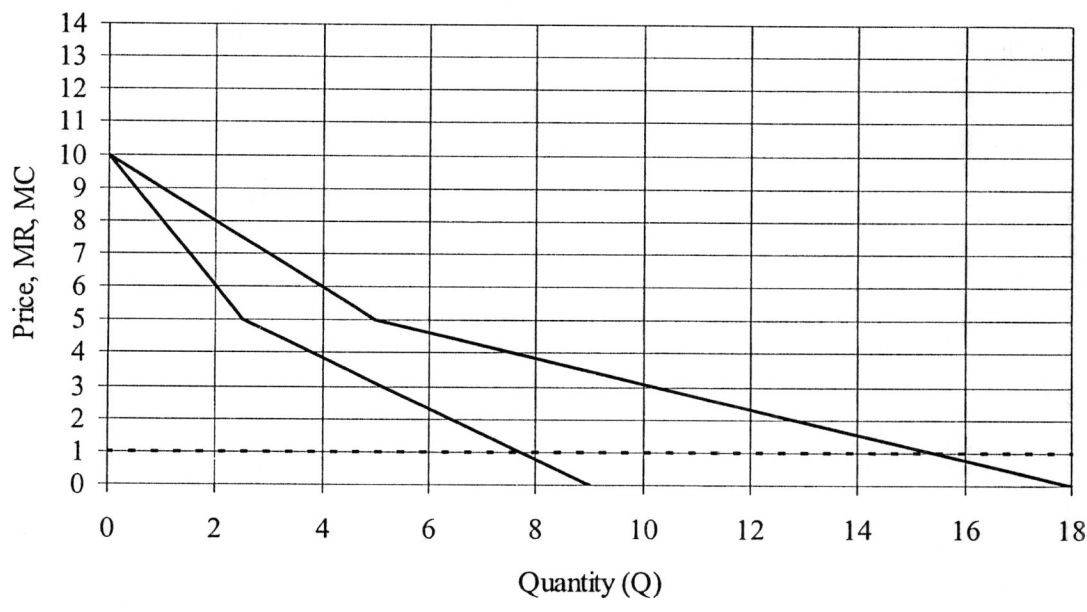

6.   The first step in solving Problems 6 and 7 is to derive the inverse of the market demand function and the corresponding marginal revenue function.

$P = 80 - 0.5\,Q$

$MR = 80 - Q$

Second, the total marginal cost function for ICC (MC) is calculated by vertically summing the marginal cost function for components, assembled computers, and marketing.

$MC = MC_C + MC_A + MC_M = 14.5 + 0.31\,Q$

The optimal level of output by the firm is calculated by setting the marginal cost function for the firm equal to the marginal revenue function.

$14.5 + 0.31\,Q = 80 - Q$, which implies that $Q = 50$

The optimal price is determined by substituting the output level into the inverse of the demand function.

$P = 80 - (0.5)(50) = 55$

The transfer price of components (P_C) when they are sold to the assembly division in Mexico is calculated by substituting the optimal level of component production ($Q_C=50$) into the marginal cost function for components.

$P_C = 7.5 + (0.05)(50) = 10$

The transfer price of assembled computers (P_A) when they are sold to the marketing division in the United States is calculated by substituting the optimal level of assembly production ($Q_A = 50$) into the marginal cost function for components and then adding the transfer cost of components.

$P_A = (0.25)(50) + 10 = 22.5$

Chapter 11: Problem 6

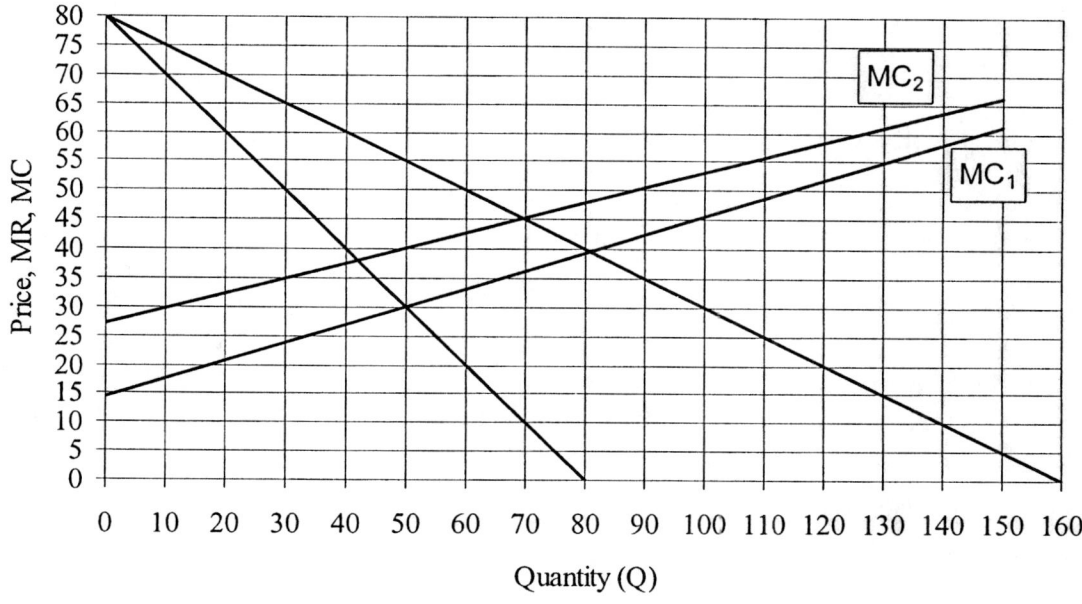

7.   The total marginal cost function for ICC (MC) is calculated by vertically summing the competitive price of components with the marginal costs of assembled computers and marketing. The competitive price of components is the appropriate transfer price.

$$MC = P_C + MC_A + MC_M = 27 + 0.26\,Q$$

The optimal level of output by the firm is calculated by setting the marginal cost function for the firm equal to the marginal revenue function.

$27 + 0.26\,Q = 80 - Q$, which implies that $Q = 42$

The optimal price is determined by substituting the output level into the inverse of the demand function, which yields $P = 80 - (0.5)(42) = 59$

The total output of components (Q_C) is calculated by setting the marginal cost of component production equal to the competitive price of components $(P_C = 20)$.

$P_C = 20 = 7.5 + 0.05\,Q_C$, which implies that $Q_C = 250$

Note that 42 components are sold to ICC and the remaining 208 are sold on the open market.

The transfer price of assembled computers (P_A) when they are sold to the marketing division in the United States is calculated by substituting the optimal level of assembly production $(Q_A = 42)$ into the marginal cost function for components and then adding the transfer cost of components.

$$P_A = (0.25)(42) + 20 = 30.5$$

Chapter 12

Regulation and Antitrust: The Role of Government in the Economy

Learning Objectives

When you finish reading this chapter, you should understand and be able to distinguish between the economic theory of regulation and the public interest theory of regulation. You should understand the concept of market failure and the government responses to market failure in the case of externalities and natural monopoly. You should be able to list the major pieces of antitrust legislation, identify their major provisions, explain how they have been enforced, and contrast the arguments in favor of regulation of industries with those of the deregulation movement. Finally, you should be able to identify the mechanisms used to regulate international trade and the effects of such regulations.

True-False Questions

T F 1. The economic theory of regulation holds that regulation is a response by government to cases in which markets cannot efficiently allocate resources.

T F 2. Licenses and patents are examples of regulations that act as barriers to entry and thereby limit competition.

T F 3. The public interest theory of regulation holds that government regulation is intended to correct problems due to monopoly power and externalities.

T F 4. Externalities refer to the side effects of production or consumption that cause private and social costs to differ.

T F 5. If the production of a good gives rise to external diseconomies, then less of the good is being produced than is socially optimal.

T F 6. If the consumption of a good gives rise to external economies, then less of the good is being consumed than is socially optimal.

T F 7. According to the public interest theory of regulation, the presence of external effects justifies government intervention.

T F 8. Government can correct for external diseconomies of production by subsidizing production.

T F 9. Government can correct for external diseconomies of consumption by taxing consumption.

T F 10. Government regulation of an activity that produces an externality can be expected to yield a socially optimal result only if the private and social benefits and costs of the activity can be accurately determined.

T F 11. Natural monopolies exist because of government regulation.

T F 12. A firm with an average total cost curve that has a negative slope at the level of output required to supply the entire market is a natural monopoly.

T F 13. Regulation that guarantees a normal rate of return on investment gives public utilities a strong incentive to keep costs down.

T F 14. If regulators set rates too high, then public utilities will tend to underinvest in fixed assets.

T F 15. Political pressure on appointees to public utility regulatory commissions tend to result in rate changes that are larger than necessary to obtain the socially optimal results.

T F 16. The two basic statutes of antitrust legislation are the Sherman and Clayton Acts.

T F 17. The two basic statutes of antitrust legislation prohibit monopolization, restraints of trade, and unfair competition.

T F 18. The first federal antitrust law enacted was the Clayton Act.

T F 19. A trust is an organizational structure that allows firms in an oligopolistic industry to operate as a cartel.

T F 20. A tying contract requires that sellers charge a price that is tied to the quantity of output produced.

T F 21. Interlocking directorates refers to a situation in which the same individual is on the board of directors of two or more competing corporations.

T F 22. Most antitrust suits filed in the United States are initiated by either the Department of Justice or the Federal Trade Commission (FTC).

T F 23. Price collusion among firms is clearly and unequivocally prohibited by antitrust laws.

T F 24. The Justice Department will generally challenge a horizontal merger if the postmerger Herfindahl index is less than 1,000.

T F 25. Conscious parallelism refers to the adoption of similar policies by oligopolists as a response to their recognized interdependence.

T F 26. Predatory pricing refers to the case in which a firm produces a level of output where marginal cost is equal to marginal revenue and charges a price such that demand exceeds supply.

T F 27. The purpose of deregulation is to increase competition and efficiency.

T F 28. An import tariff is a direct restriction on the quantity of a particular good that can be imported during a given time period.

T F 29. An import tariff and an import quota both have the effect of protecting domestic producers from foreign competition.

T F 30. Voluntary export restraints have the same effects as import tariffs, except that the positive revenue effects are realized by the exporting country rather than the importing country.

T F 31. Taxes on consumption, such as those used in European countries, encourage saving and investment.

T F 32. The U.S. taxes labor income and capital income, which discourages work and investment.

T F 33. Taxes and subsidies have no effect on business decisions.

T F 34. Taxes and subsidies have an adverse effect on economic efficiency.

T F 35. Businesses can reduce their tax liabilities by shifting production from low tax countries to high tax countries.

Multiple Choice Questions

1. Which one of the following types of government regulation does not limit competition and create artificial market power?

    A. Licensing regulations
    B. Patents
    C. Copyrights
    D. All of the above limit competition and create artificial market power.

2. Which of the following is not a law designed to protect the consumers of products?

    A. Warranty Act of 1975
    B. Federal Trade Commission Act of 1914
    C. 1990 Nutrition Labeling Act
    D. All of the above are designed to protect the consumers of products.

3. If an increase in output by a firm imposes uncompensated costs on other firms, these costs are referred to as

    A. external diseconomies of production.
    B. external economies of production.
    C. external diseconomies of consumption.
    D. external economies of consumption.

4. If an increase in output by a firm confers uncompensated benefits to other firms, these benefits are referred to as

    A. external diseconomies of production.
    B. external economies of production.
    C. external diseconomies of consumption.
    D. external economies of consumption.

5. If the consumption expenditures of some individuals impose uncompensated costs on other individuals, these costs are referred to as

    A. external diseconomies of production.
    B. external economies of production.
    C. external diseconomies of consumption.
    D. external economies of consumption.

6.	If the consumption expenditures of some individuals confer uncompensated benefits on other individuals, these benefits are referred to as

	A.	external diseconomies of production.
	B.	external economies of production.
	C.	external diseconomies of consumption.
	D.	external economies of consumption.

7.	Government regulation of natural monopolies typically sets the market price so that the level of output corresponds to the point of intersection between long-run

	A.	marginal cost and marginal revenue.
	B.	marginal cost and demand.
	C.	average cost and marginal revenue.
	D.	average cost and demand.

8.	Natural monopolies will produce a socially optimal level of output if government subsidies ensure an economic profit of zero and the market price is set by regulators at the point of intersection between long-run

	A.	marginal cost and marginal revenue.
	B.	marginal cost and demand.
	C.	average cost and marginal revenue.
	D.	average cost and demand.

9.	Which of the following is not a complication encountered by public utility regulatory commissions when they set rates?

	A.	It is difficult to determine the economic value of a public utility's fixed assets.
	B.	Public utilities typically engage in price discrimination, so many different rates must be determined.
	C.	The services provided by public utilities are typically jointly produced, so the allocation of costs among different services is difficult or impossible.
	D.	All of the above are problems that are encountered when regulatory commissions set rates.

10.	The Averch-Johnson effect refers to

	A.	the inefficiencies that result when regulators set public utility rates too high or too low.
	B.	the tendency toward natural monopoly in firms that have downward-sloping long-run average cost curves.
	C.	the 9 to 12 month time lag between recognition of a need for rate revision and action by regulatory commissions.
	D.	All of the above are correct.

11.	Most antitrust actions have been settled by means of

	A.	dissolution and divestiture.
	B.	an injunction.
	C.	a consent decree.
	D.	fines and jail sentences.

12. Which of the following is <u>always</u> illegal?

   A. Price discrimination
   B. Collusion
   C. Monopoly
   D. Interlocking directorates

13. Which of the following industries was <u>not</u> deregulated during the 1970s and 1980s?

   A. Airlines
   B. Electricity generation and distribution
   C. Telecommunications
   D. Banking

14. Which of the following <u>do not</u> protect domestic producers from foreign competition?

   A. Import tariffs
   B. Import quotas
   C. Voluntary export restrictions
   D. All of the above protect domestic producers from foreign competition.

15. Which of the following will <u>not</u> result from the imposition of an import tariff on a commodity?

   A. The supply of the commodity will increase.
   B. The price of the commodity will increase.
   C. Domestic production of the commodity will increase.
   D. All of the above will result from an import tariff.

Problems

Etch-A-Ketch Boat cleaning uses an acid solution to clean the hulls of boats. The market for boat cleaning services is perfectly competitive, so Etch-A-Ketch is a price taker. The market supply and demand functions for these services are defined below, where price (P) is in thousands of dollars and quantity (Q) is in hulls cleaned per day. Use this information to answer Problems 1 and 2.

Supply: $Q = 2 P$

Demand: $Q = 16 - 2 P$

1. Plot the market supply and demand curves on the graph below. Determine the market equilibrium price and quantity of boat cleaning services.

Chapter 12: Problem 1

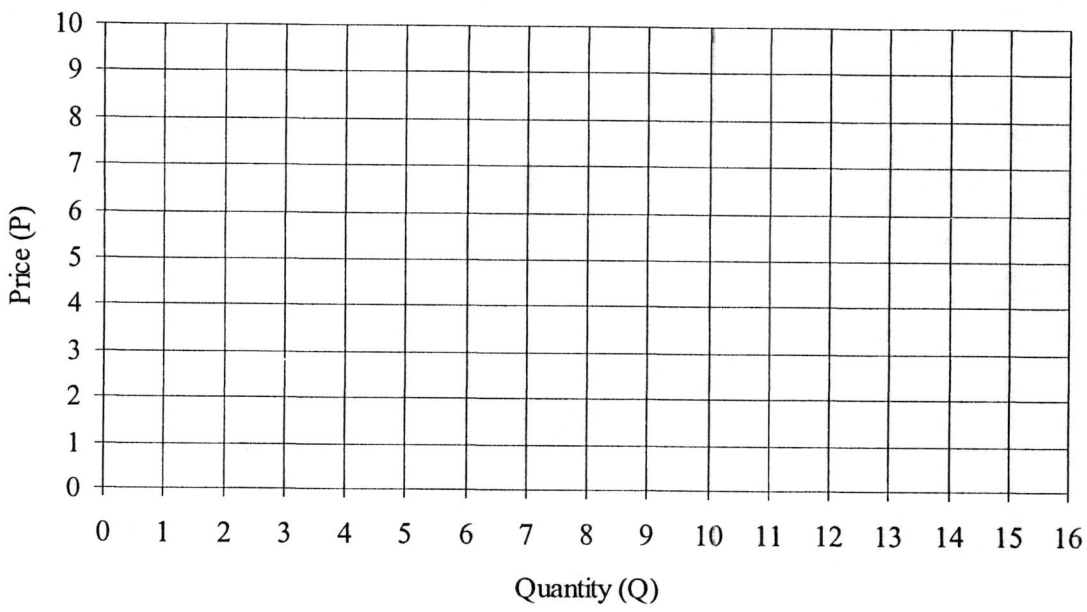

2. An employee of Etch-A-Ketch has filed a civil suit claiming that acid solutions are a health hazard to the public. The court has determined that hull-cleaning results in a social cost of $2,000 per hull over and above the market price. If a tax is used to impose the social cost on Etch-A-Ketch and all the other boat cleaners, what will the new equilibrium price and quantity be and how much will the boat cleaners pay in taxes? Plot the effect of the tax on the graph from Problem 1.

A college education contributes to individual well-being by enhancing earning opportunities and by providing intellectual enrichment. The market for college educations is perfectly competitive. The market supply and demand functions for college educations are given below, where the price (P) is defined in tens of thousands of dollars per college education and quantity (Q) is measured in hundreds of thousands of college educations completed per year. Use this information to answer Problems 3 and 4.

Supply: $Q = -0.5 + 0.5\,P$

Demand: $Q = 12 - 2\,P$

3.   Plot the market supply and demand curves on the graph below. Determine the market equilibrium price and quantity of college educations.

Chapter 12: Problem 3

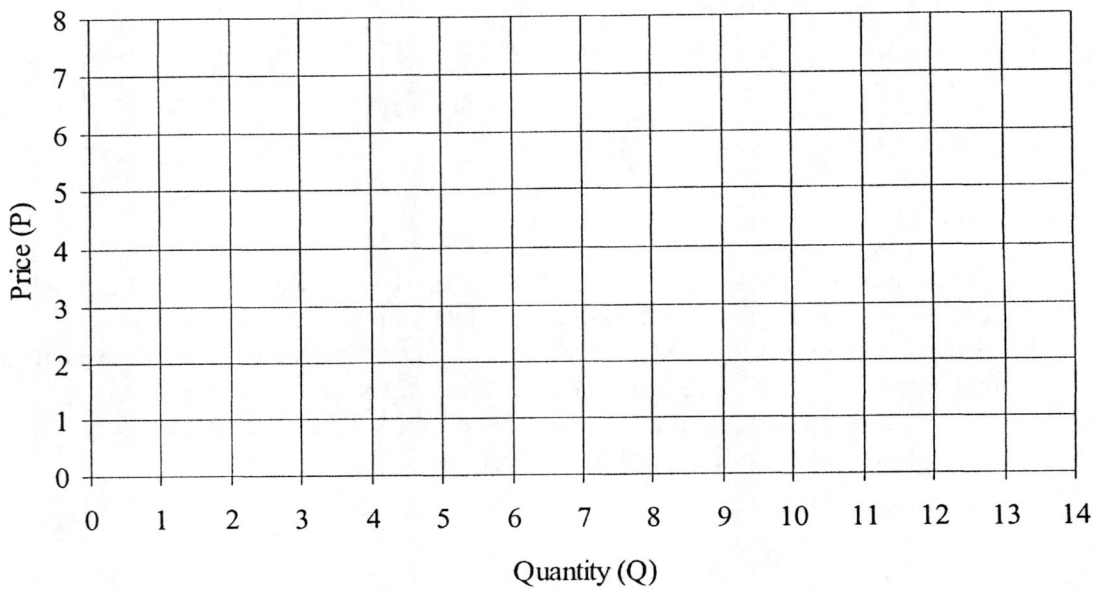

4. College educations provide social benefits that exceed their private benefits. A college educated individual is more likely to be a healthy, productive citizen. Suppose that an appropriate measure of the social benefit of a college education is $1,000 greater than its private cost. If a subsidy to students is used to compensate for the social cost value of college educations, what will the new equilibrium price and quantity be and how much will the government pay in subsidies? Plot the effect of the subsidy on the graph from Problem 3.

True-False Answers

1	F	8	F	15	F	22	F	29	T
2	T	9	T	16	T	23	T	30	T
3	T	10	T	17	T	24	F	31	T
4	T	11	F	18	F	25	T	32	T
5	F	12	T	19	T	26	F	33	F
6	T	13	F	20	F	27	T	34	T
7	T	14	F	21	T	28	F	35	F

Multiple Choice Answers

1	D	4	B	7	D	10	A	13	B
2	D	5	C	8	D	11	C	14	D
3	A	6	D	9	D	12	B	15	A

Solutions to Problems

1. The equilibrium price is calculated by setting the market supply and demand functions equal to each other and then solving for P. Equilibrium quantity is calculated by substituting the equilibrium price into either the supply or the demand function.

   $2 P = 16 - 2 P$, which implies that $P = 4$

   $Q = 2 P = (2)(4) = 8$

Chapter 12: Problem 1

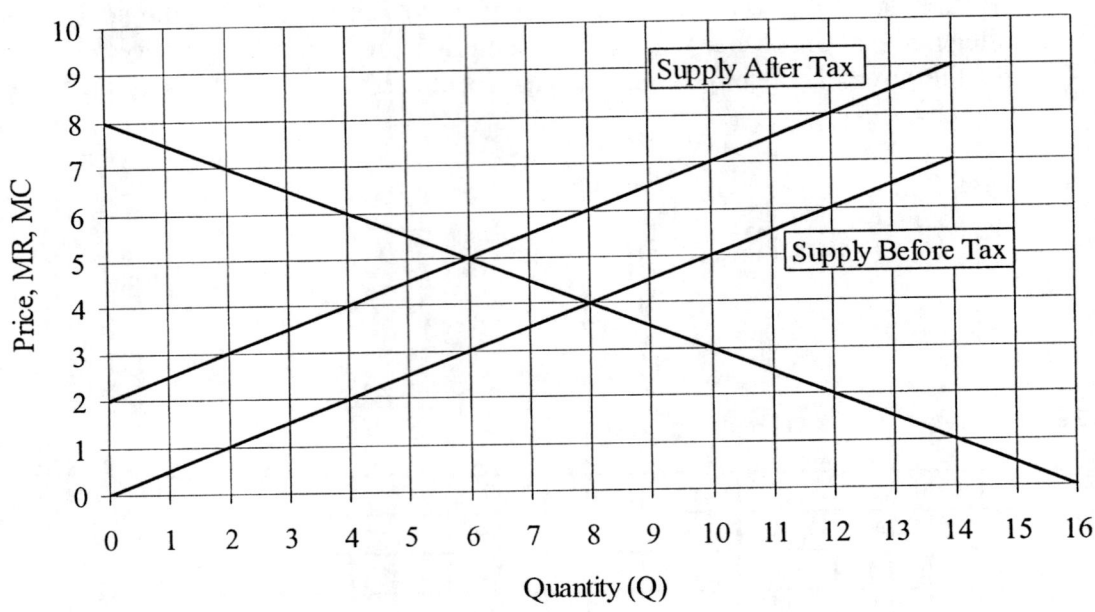

2. A $2,000 tax will shift the supply curve upward by $2,000. To see the effect of this shift on the supply function, the function is inverted and then 2,000 is added to the right side of the function.

    $Q = 2P$ becomes $P = 0.5Q$ after inversion

    $P = 0.5Q$ becomes $P = 2 + 0.5Q$ when the tax is added

    $P = 2 + 0.5Q$ becomes $Q = -4 + 2P$ when it is returned to its original form

    The new equilibrium price and quantity are found by application of the same procedure used in Problem 1.

    $-4 + 2P = 16 - 2P$, which implies that $P = 5$

    $Q = -4 + 2P = -4 + (2)(5) = 6$

    The amount of tax collected is $(2)(6) = 12$.

3. The equilibrium price is calculated by setting the market supply and demand functions equal to each other and then solving for P. Equilibrium quantity is calculated by substituting the equilibrium price into either the supply or the demand function.

    $-0.5 + 0.5P = 12 - 2P$, which implies that $P = 5$

    $Q = 12 - 2P = 12 - (2)(5) = 2$

Chapter 12: Problem 3

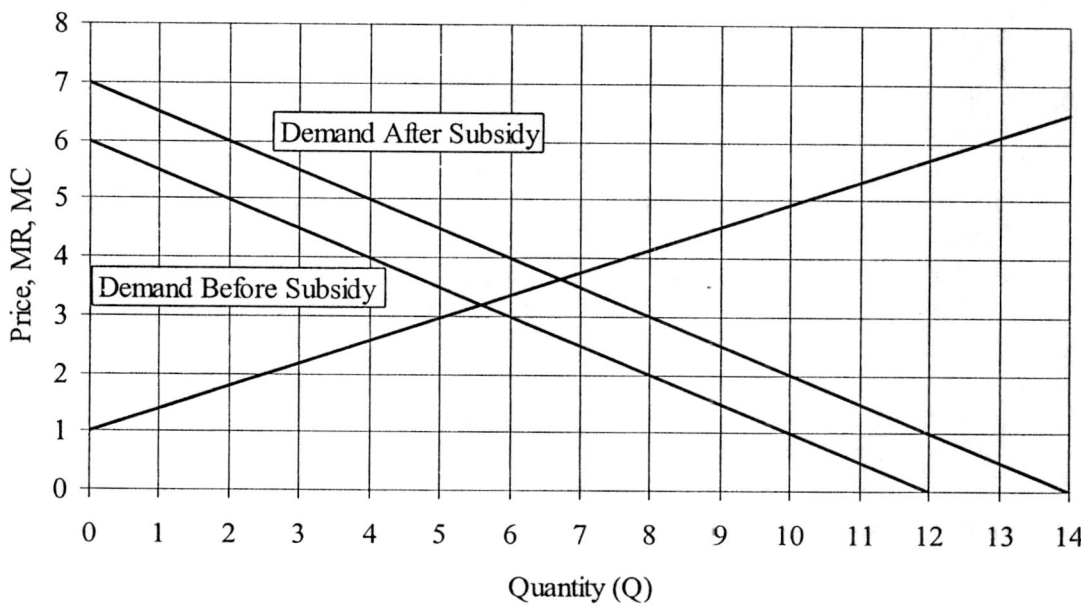

4. A $1,000 subsidy paid to students will shift the demand curve upward by $1,000. To see the effect of this shift on the demand function, the function is inverted and then 1,000 is added to the right side of the function.

Q = 12 - 2 P becomes P = 6 - 0.5 Q after inversion

P = 6 - 0.5 Q becomes P = 7 - 0.5 Q when the subsidy is added

P = 7 - 0.5 Q becomes Q = 14 - 2 P when it is returned to its original form

The new equilibrium price and quantity are found by application of the same procedure used in Problem 3.

-0.5 + 0.5 P = 14 - 2 P, which implies that P = 5.8

Q = 14 - 2 P = 14 - (2)(5.8) = 2.4

The amount of subsidy paid to students is (1)(2.4) = 2.4.

CHAPTER 13

RISK ANALYSIS

Learning Objectives

When you finish working through this chapter, you should be able to define and distinguish between risk and uncertainty and you should understand how to apply the methods that have been developed to support decisions made in their presence. Specifically, you should understand how to calculate and interpret expected profit, the variance, the standard deviation, and the coefficient of variation given a probability distribution of payoffs, how to distinguish between decision makers who are risk averters, risk neutral, or risk seekers in terms of the marginal utility of money, the risk-return tradeoff function, the risk-adjusted discount rate, and the certainty-equivalent coefficient, how to construct and interpret a decision tree, and how to apply the maximin and minimax regret criteria when uncertainty is present. In addition you should be able to define and explain the relevance of simulation, diversification, and hedging to decision making in the presence of risk.

Summary of Notation and Formulas

$$(13\text{-}1) \quad E(\pi) = \bar{\pi} = \sum_{i=1}^{n} \pi_i P_i$$

Equation 13-1 is a mathematical expression that defines expected profit ($E(\pi)$ or $\bar{\pi}$) in terms of the profit the firm expects to realize in state of nature i (π_i) and the probability of state of nature i (P_i) for each of n states of nature.

$$(13\text{-}2') \quad d_i = \pi_i - \bar{\pi}$$

$$(13\text{-}3') \quad \sigma^2 = \sum_{i=1}^{n} (\pi_i - \bar{\pi})^2 P_i$$

$$(13\text{-}4') \quad \sigma = \sqrt{\sigma^2}$$

$$(13\text{-}5') \quad Z = \frac{\pi_i - \bar{\pi}}{\sigma}$$

Equations 13-2', 13-3', 13-4', and 13-5' define the deviation of profit in state of nature i from expected profit (d_i), the variance of profit (σ^2), the standard deviation of profit (σ), and the Z value of profit in state of nature i.

$$(13\text{-}6') \quad v = \frac{\sigma}{\bar{\pi}}$$

Equation 13-6' defines the coefficient of variation of profit as the standard deviation of profit divided by expected profit.

$$(13\text{-}9) \quad \textit{Value of the firm} = \sum_{t=1}^{n} \frac{\pi_t}{(1+r)^t}$$

$$(13\text{-}10) \quad NPV = \sum_{t=1}^{n} \frac{R_t}{(1+k)^t} - C_0$$

Equation 13-9 represents the discounted present value of a firm in terms of n future profit levels at time period t (π_t) and the relevant discount rate. Equation 13-10 defines the risk-adjusted net present value of an investment project that has an initial cost of C_0 and yields n future net cash flows at time period t (R_t). The net cash flows in this equation are discounted by the risk-adjusted discount rate (k) which is larger than r for a risk averse decision maker.

$$(13\text{-}11) \quad NPV = \sum_{t=1}^{n} \frac{\alpha R_t}{(1+r)^t} - C_0$$

$$(13\text{-}12) \quad \alpha = \frac{R_t^*}{R_t}$$

Equation 13-11 defines the risk-adjusted value of an investment project. The net cash flows in this equation are adjusted by the certainty-equivalent coefficient (α) which is less than one for a risk averse investor. Equation 13-12 defines the certainty equivalent coefficient as the ratio of two values. The denominator of the ratio is the expected net value in time t (R_t) and the numerator (R_t^*) is a value that, if available with certainty, would provide the decision maker with a level of utility identical to that provided by the (risky) denominator.

True-False Questions

T F 1. When there is only one possible outcome to a decision, risk or uncertainty is present.

T F 2. Risk refers to a situation in which the probability of each possible outcome to a decision is unknown or meaningless.

T F 3. A payoff matrix shows the profit that would be earned under certainty, risk, and uncertainty so the decision maker can choose which is best.

T F 4. Decisions made under risk require a decision maker to choose both a strategy and a state of nature.

T F 5. A list of all possible states of nature and their probabilities is referred to as a probability distribution.

T F 6. If the probability that the economy will be in recession is 0.40, then the probability that the economy will not be in a recession must be 0.60.

T F 7. The expected profit of a strategy is equal to the level of profit realized from the outcome with the highest level of probability.

T F 8. The expected value of a strategy is a measure of risk.

T F 9. The normal probability distribution is an example of a discrete probability distribution.

T F 10. The Z value for a particular outcome is equal to the difference between the outcome and the expected outcome measured in terms of standard deviations.

T F 11. Z values cannot be negative or zero.

T F 12. All normal distributions have a mean equal to zero.

T F 13. If a person's total utility more than doubles when their wealth doubles, then that person is a risk averter.

T F 14. The expected value of a fair game is zero.

T F 15. If a person is risk averse, then they will only play games that have an expected value that is negative.

T F 16. A lower risk-adjusted discount rate should be used to evaluate an investment project that involves a higher level of risk.

T F 17. The riskier a project is, the smaller its certainty equivalent will be.

T F 18. A certainty equivalent coefficient of one is used if the decision maker is risk neutral.

T F 19. A decision tree shows a sequence of decisions and their outcomes under all states of nature.

T F 20. Branches coming out of circles on decision trees show alternative courses of action that can be selected by decision makers.

T F 21. Test marketing is an example of simulation.

T F 22. The maximin criterion is a method of dealing with uncertainty.

T F 23. The maximin criterion is applied by first selecting the best outcome from each strategy and then identifying the strategy that has the lowest of the best outcomes.

T F 24. The maximin and minimax regret criteria always lead to the same conclusion, but they identify it using different methods.

T F 25. In general, uncertainty can be eliminated by gathering additional information.

T F 26. Diversification provides a way of reducing risk and uncertainty.

T F 27. Investments in foreign-currency-denominated assets can be hedged by using the forward market in currencies.

T F 28. Hedging refers to the practice of making foreign investments.

T F 29. Hedging eliminates all risks associated with foreign investments.

T F 30. A forward contract is an agreement to purchase or sell at a price specified today for delivery at a future date.

T F 31. The principal-agent problem applies to the relationship between managers (the principals) and stockholders (the agents).

T F 32. Golden parachutes can overcome the principal-agent problem.

T F 33. The principal-agent problem exists because decision-makers and owners may have different goals.

T F 34. An auction is a market in which potential sellers compete to sell their products.

T F 35. An English auction is a sequential, ascending-bid auction.

Multiple Choice Questions

1.   A situation in which a decision maker knows all of the possible outcomes of a decision and also knows the probability associated with each outcome is referred to as

   A. certainty.
   B. risk.
   C. uncertainty.
   D. strategy.

2.   Which of the following methods of selecting a strategy is consistent with risk averting behavior?

   A. If two strategies have the same expected profit, select the one with the smaller standard deviation.
   B. If two strategies have the same standard deviation, select the one with the smaller expected profit.
   C. Select the strategy with the larger coefficient of variation.
   D. All of the above are correct.

3.   Which one of the following does <u>not</u> measure risk?

   A. Coefficient of variation
   B. Standard deviation
   C. Expected value
   D. All of the above are measures of risk.

4.   If a person's utility doubles when their income doubles, then that person is risk

   A. averse.
   B. neutral.
   C. seeking.
   D. There is not enough information given in the question to determine an answer.

5.   Strategy A has an expected value of 10 and a standard deviation of 3. Strategy B has an expected value of 10 and a standard deviation of 5. Strategy C has an expected value of 15 and a standard deviation of 10. Which one of the following statements is true?

   A. A risk averse decision maker will always prefer A to B, but may prefer C to A.
   B. A risk neutral decision maker will always prefer C to A or B.
   C. A risk seeking decision maker will always prefer C to A or B.
   D. All of the above are correct.

6. The coefficient of variation measures

   A. the risk per unit of expected payoff.
   B. the risk-adjusted expected value.
   C. the payoff per unit of risk.
   D. a decision maker's risk-return tradeoff.

7. A situation in which a decision maker must choose between strategies that have more than one possible outcome when the probability of each outcome is unknown is referred to as

   A. diversification.
   B. certainty.
   C. risk.
   D. uncertainty.

8. If a decision maker is risk averse, then the best strategy to select is the one that yields the

   A. highest expected payoff.
   B. lowest coefficient of variation.
   C. highest expected utility.
   D. lowest standard deviation.

9. Circumstances that influence the profitability of a decision are referred to as

   A. strategies.
   B. a payoff matrix.
   C. states of nature.
   D. the marginal utility of money.

10. The marginal utility of money diminishes for a decision maker who is

    A. a risk seeker.
    B. risk neutral.
    C. a risk averter.
    D. in a situation of uncertainty.

11. A strategy that yields an expected monetary payoff of zero is called a

    A. risk-neutral strategy.
    B. fair game.
    C. zero-sum game.
    D. certainty equivalent.

12. A risk-return tradeoff function

    A. shows the minimum expected return required to compensate an investor for accepting various levels of risk.
    B. slopes upward for a risk averse decision maker.
    C. is horizontal for a risk neutral decision maker.
    D. All of the above are correct.

13. If the market interest rate is 10% and a decision maker's risk adjusted discount rate is 12%, then the decision maker

    A. is risk averse.
    B. has a certainty-equivalent coefficient that is greater than one.
    C. is risk neutral.
    D. None of the above is correct.

14. Fred is willing to pay $1 for a lottery ticket that has an expected value of zero. This proves that Fred

    A. is risk averse.
    B. has a certainty-equivalent coefficient that is equal to one.
    C. is risk neutral.
    D. None of the above is correct.

15. The analysis of a complex decision situation by constructing a mathematical model of the situation and then performing a large number of iterations in order to determine the probability distribution of outcomes is called

    A. sensitivity analysis.
    B. expected utility analysis.
    C. simulation.
    D. a decision tree.

16. A payoff matrix presents all the information required to determine the optimal strategy using the

    A. expected value criterion.
    B. the maximin criterion.
    C. the utility maximization criterion.
    D. simulation criterion.

17. Which of the following is not a way to deal with decision making under uncertainty?

    A. Simulation
    B. Diversification
    C. Acquisition of additional information
    D. Application of the maximin criterion

18. A matrix that, for each state of nature and strategy, shows the difference between a strategy's payoff and the best strategy's payoff is called

    A. a maximin matrix.
    B. a minimax regret matrix.
    C. a payoff matrix.
    D. an expected utility matrix.

19.   The sequence of possible managerial decisions and their expected outcome under each set of circumstances can be represented and analyzed by using

   A. the minimax regret criterion.
   B. a decision tree.
   C. a payoff matrix.
   D. simulation.

20.   According to a survey carried out by Gitman and Forrester that was published in 1977, the most common way for businesses in the United States to deal with risk in capital budgeting decisions is by

   A. ignoring it.
   B. using the certainty equivalent method.
   C. using the risk-adjusted discount rate method.
   D. using the expected utility method.

21.   A futures contract

   A. is a type of bond that specifies the amount of interest that must be paid on a loan at a future point in time.
   B. is an agreement to buy or sell a commodity at a specified price at a specified point in time.
   C. is a partnership agreement between two parties that determines their future business relationship.
   D. None of the above is correct.

22.   Hedging refers to an investment strategy that is used to

   A. control risk from variations in currency prices.
   B. prevent losses due to corporate bankruptcies.
   C. ensure the highest possible rate of return.
   D. prevent foreign competition in domestic capital markets.

23.   Asymmetric information refers to circumstances in which

   A. both parties to a transaction have identical amounts of information.
   B. neither party to a transaction has any relevant information.
   C. one party to a transaction has more information than the other party.
   D. the riskiness of a transaction is greater than its expected return.

24.   The tendency for low-quality cars to drive high quality cars out of the used car market is an example of

   A. hedging.
   B. adverse selection.
   C. portfolio analysis.
   D. moral hazard.

25. A person with health insurance is more likely to become ill and visit a doctor than is someone without health insurance. One reason is that a person with health insurance is less likely to take precautions that will prevent illness. This is an example of

A. propinquity.
B. a futures contract.
C. hedging.
D. moral hazard.

26. The principal-agent problem may result if

A. a firm is owned and operated by the same person.
B. managers make decisions that are not in the best interest of owners.
C. a firm compensates managers based on the profitability of the firm.
D. All of these answers are correct.

27. One way to correct a potential principal-agent problem is for stockholders to

A. offer managers "golden parachutes" in the event of a takeover.
B. empower managers to make the decisions they feel are best.
C. ensure that there is no explicit linkage between managers' compensation and the profitability of the firm.
D. All of these answers are correct.

28. Which of the following is a sequential, ascending bid auction?

A. Dutch auction
B. First-price sealed bid auction
C. Second-price sealed bid auction
D. English auction

29. Which of the following is a descending bid auction?

A. Dutch auction
B. First-price sealed bid auction
C. Second-price sealed bid auction
D. English auction

30. The winner's curse refers to

A. the reaction of losers in an English auction to the winner.
B. a tax imposed on the winners of English auctions.
C. paying an amount that exceeds the true value of an item at auction.
D. a Dutch auction in which the winner is obliged, by tradition, to berate the auctioneer.

Problems

The Devi Gallery is a showroom for avant-garde art work that is located in New York City. The owner, Devi Mohr, is an artist with a keen business sense. In addition to her own work, she displays art taken on consignment and pieces that she purchases on her annual business trips to Europe. She is currently considering the purchase of works by two European artists. One is a relative unknown and the other is a mature artist of some stature. She must choose between the two and will base her decision on the following assessment of their potential value.

Abozzo Alla Prima is a vigorous young Italian artist noted for his anamorphic images of kitchen appliances. His set of six oil paintings can be purchased for $5,000 at the current exchange rate. Devi feels that the probability (P) distribution of potential profits (π) from the purchase of Abozzo's paintings (in $1,000s) in the United States is as follows:

π	-4	1	3	5
P	0.2	0.4	0.3	0.1

Kitsh Ecorche is a Parisian who has established a reputation as a master of drollery. She offers a set of signed and numbered velvet paintings entitled "The Vivisectionists Play Poker with Elvis" for $10,000. While Devi would not ordinarily be interested in this type of art, she has heard rumors that Ecorche's frenetic lifestyle is taking its toll on her health and that, as they say, it is only a matter of time. If Ecorche expires, her work may increase substantially in value. Devi believes that the probability distribution of potential profits (in $1,000s) from Ecorche's prints is as follows:

π	-2	4	32
P	0.6	0.35	0.05

Use this information to solve Problems 1, 2, 3, and 4.

1. Calculate the expected profit for each of the art works. Which should be selected on the basis of the expected value criterion?

2.   Calculate the standard deviation of profit for each of the art works. Which is the riskier of the two?

3.   Use the coefficient of variation to determine which of the two art works is preferable.

4.   Devi has estimated that her utility of profit function (where profits are measured in $1,000s) is

$$U = 20\pi - 0.1\pi^2$$

Use this utility function to calculate the expected utility of each of the art works. Which of the two does Devi prefer? Is she a risk seeker, a risk averter, or risk neutral?

5.   The VOX-Strummer Mutual Investment Fund has an expected annual rate of return of 12.4% with a standard deviation of 8%. If the return on investment has a normal probability distribution, what is the probability that the rate of return will be negative? What is the probability that the rate of return will exceed 6%? What is the probability that it will exceed 20%?

Tammany Manufacturing Company is considering two alternative projects. Only one can be chosen. Each is expected to last for five years. The cash flows associated with each project (in $1,000s) are listed in the table below. The initial cost is paid at the onset of the project. The remaining cash flows will be realized at the end of each of five years.

Project	Cost	Year 1	Year 2	Year 3	Year 4	Year 5
A	100	60	50	40	30	20
B	120	10	30	50	70	90

6.   Calculate the net present value of each project using a discount rate of 8%. Which project is preferred?

7.   Calculate the risk-adjusted net present value of each project. The risk-free discount rate is 8%. The risk premium on Project A is 2% and the risk premium on Project B is 4%. Which project is preferred?

8. Calculate the risk-adjusted net present value of each project. The risk-free discount rate is 8%. The risk premium coefficients for both projects are as follows:

Year 1	Year 2	Year 3	Year 4	Year 5
1	0.95	0.9	0.85	0.8

Which project is preferred?

9. Rural Township in Chambers County has a waste disposal problem. Their local landfill is getting full and the need to find an alternative can no longer be ignored. Three alternatives are under consideration. One possibility is to hire a New Jersey firm to haul away all of the trash in the land fill so that it can be filled in again. A second possibility is to start a recycling program that will allow the township to sell some types of waste, to compost other types, and to hire a New Jersey firm to haul away the rest. The third alternative is to find a new land fill area and to obtain the necessary permits to use it.

Each alternative involves costs, some of which are subject to risk. If the first alternative is selected and the land fill is emptied, there will be a one-time cost of $5.3 million. If the second alternative is selected, the cost will depend on the degree of compliance by residents with recycling regulations and on the market value of the recycled materials. There is a 20% chance that the present value of the costs of recycling will be $3.2 million, a 60% chance that the costs will be $4.8 million, and a 20% chance that the costs will be $7 million. If the third alternative is selected, the cost to purchase land and set up a new land fill area will be $3 million if the necessary permits can be obtained. There is a 40% chance that legal fees and impact studies will cost $1 million and the new land fill will be permitted, in which case the total cost will be $4 million. There is a 40% chance that the legal fees and impact studies will cost $1.5 million and the land fill will be permitted, in which case the total cost will be $4.5 million. There is a 20% chance that the legal fees and impact studies will cost $1.5 million and the land fill will not be permitted, in which case one of the other alternatives must be selected.

Use this information to construct a decision tree and to determine the best alternative using the expected value method.

10. The Widows and Orphans Investment Company is considering three investment projects. Their net payoffs, in millions of dollars, under each of four states of nature are listed in the table below. Determine the optimal strategy using the maximin criterion. Calculate the regret matrix and then determine the optimal strategy using the minimax regret criterion. Which one of these strategies would you recommend?

Project	States of Nature			
	Disastrous	Not Good	Good	Great
A	-4	-1	3	20
B	1	3	4	6
C	0	0	5	12

True-False Answers

1	F	8	F	15	F	22	T	29	F
2	F	9	F	16	F	23	F	30	T
3	F	10	T	17	T	24	F	31	F
4	F	11	F	18	T	25	F	32	T
5	T	12	F	19	T	26	T	33	T
6	T	13	F	20	F	27	T	34	F
7	F	14	T	21	F	28	F	35	T

Multiple Choice Answers

1	B	7	D	13	A	19	B	25	D
2	A	8	C	14	D	20	C	26	B
3	C	9	C	15	C	21	B	27	A
4	B	10	C	16	B	22	A	28	D
5	D	11	B	17	A	23	C	29	A
6	A	12	D	18	B	24	B	30	C

Solutions to Problems

1. The expected value of profit is calculated by multiplying each level of profit by its associated probability and then summing the products. The tables that follow show the calculations involved. The expected value of profits from the paintings by Abozzo Alla Prima is $1,000. The expected value of profits from the prints by Kitsh Ecorche is $1,800. On the basis of the expected value criterion, the prints by Ecorche should be purchased because they offer the higher expected value of profits.

π	-4	1	3	5
P	0.2	0.4	0.3	0.1
(P)(π)	-0.8	0.4	0.9	0.5

π	-2	4	32
P	0.6	0.35	0.05
(P)(π)	-1.2	1.4	1.6

2. The standard deviation of profits is calculated in a series of steps which are shown in the tables below. First, the deviation of each level of profit from its expected value (d) is calculated. Second, each deviation is squared. Third, each squared deviation is multiplied by its probability. Fourth, these values are summed and, finally, the square root of the sum is taken. The standard deviation of profits (in thousands of dollars) from the paintings by Abozzo Alla Prima is equal to 2.793, the square root of 7.8. The standard deviation of profits (in thousands of dollars) from the prints by Kitsh Ecorche is equal to 7.843, the square root of $50. The Ecorche prints are riskier than the Alla Prima paintings because the potential profits from the former are more variable.

π	-4	1	3	5
P	0.2	0.4	0.3	0.1
d	-5	0	2	4
d^2	25	0	4	16
(P)(d^2)	5	0	1.2	1.6

π	-2	4	32
P	0.6	0.35	0.05
d	-3.8	2.2	30.2
d^2	14.44	4.84	912.04
(P)(d^2)	8.7	1.7	45.6

3. The coefficient of variation is equal to the standard deviation of profits divided by the expected value of profits. The coefficient of variation of the paintings by Abozzo Alla Prima is 2,793/1,000, which is equal to 2.8. The coefficient of variation of the prints by Kitsh Ecorche is 7,483/1,800, which is equal to 4.2. The paintings by Alla Prima should be purchased because they have the lower coefficient of variation.

4. The expected utility of profits is calculated in a series of steps which are shown in the tables below. First, the levels of profit (in $1,000s) are converted to utility values. Second, each utility value is multiplied by its associated probability. Finally, these values are summed. The expected utility of profits from the paintings by Abozzo Alla Prima is 19.1. The expected utility of profits from the prints by Kitsh Ecorche is 30.1. On the basis of expected utility, the paintings by Ecorche should be purchased because they offer the higher expected utility.

Devi is a risk averter, because the marginal utility of profit decreases as profit increases. This can be seen by comparing the utility from $1,000 in profit (U = 19.9) with the utility of $2,000 in profits (U = 39.6). The marginal utility of the first thousand is 19.9. The marginal utility of the second thousand is 39.6 - 19.9 = 19.7, which is lower.

π	-4	1	3	5
P	0.2	0.4	0.3	0.1
U	-81.6	19.9	59.1	97.5
(P)(U)	-16.32	7.96	17.73	9.75

π	-2	4	32
P	0.6	0.35	0.05
U	-40.4	78.4	537.6
(P)U)	-24.24	27.44	26.88

5. The probability that the rate of return (X) will be negative is equal to the probability that the rate of return will be less than zero (X < 0). The first step in calculating this probability is to convert X = 0 into the corresponding Z value as follows:

Z = (0 - 12.4)/8 = -1.55

The table value for Z = 1.55 is 0.4394. The probability that Z will be less than -1.55 is equal to 0.5 - 0.4394 = 0.0606. This is also the probability that X will be less than zero.

The first step in calculating the probability that the rate of return will be greater than 6% (X > 6) is to convert X = 6 into the corresponding Z value as follows:

Z = (6 - 12.4)/8 = -0.80

The table value for Z = 0.80 is 0.2881. The probability that Z will be greater than -0.80 is equal to 0.5 + 0.2881 = 0.7881. This is also the probability that X will be greater than 6.

The first step in calculating the probability that the rate of return will be greater than 20% (X > 20) is to convert X = 20 into the corresponding Z value as follows:

$$Z = (20 - 12.4)/8 = 0.95$$

The table value for Z = 0.95 is 0.3289. The probability that Z will be greater than 0.95 is equal to 0.5 - 0.3289 = 0.1711. This is also the probability that X will be greater than 20.

6. The general setup for calculation of the net present value (NPV) of each project is given below.

$$NPV = -Cost + PVIF_{i,1}\pi_1 + PVIF_{i,2}\pi_2 + PVIF_{i,3}\pi_3 + PVIF_{i,4}\pi_4 + PVIF_{i,5}\pi_5$$

For a discount rate of 8%, the net present value of Project A is

$$NPV_A = -100 + (0.9259)(60) + (0.8573)(50) + (0.7938)(40) + (0.7350)(30) + (0.6806)(20) = 65.833$$

The net present value of project B is

$$NPV_B = -120 + (0.9259)(10) + (0.8573)(30) + (0.7938)(50) + (0.7350)(70) + (0.6806)(90) = 67.372$$

Project B has the higher positive net present value and so it is preferred. Note that, if both projects had a negative net present value, neither project would be desirable.

7. The general set up for calculation of the net present values is the same as in Problem 6. However, in this problem Project A will be discounted at 10% and Project B will be discounted at 12%.

$$NPV_A = -100 + (0.9091)(60) + (0.8264)(50) + (0.7513)(40) + (0.6830)(30) + (0.6209)(20) = 58.826$$

$$NPV_B = -120 + (0.8929)(10) + (0.7972)(30) + (0.7118)(50) + (0.6355)(70) + (0.5674)(90) = 43.986$$

Project A has the higher risk-adjusted net present value and so it is preferred.

8. The general setup for calculation of the net present values is the same as in Problem 6. However, in this problem each net cash flow must be multiplied by the relevant risk premium coefficient.

$$NPV_A = -100 + (0.9259)(1)(60) + (0.8573)(0.95)(50) + (0.7938)(0.90)(40) + (0.7350)(0.85)(30) + (0.6806)(0.80)(20) = 55.48$$

The net present value of project B is

$$NPV_B = -120 + (0.9259)(1)(10) + (0.8573)(0.95)(30) + (0.7938)(0.90)(50) + (0.7350)(0.85)(70) + (0.6806)(0.80)(90) = 42.15$$

Project A has the higher risk-adjusted net present value and so it is preferred.

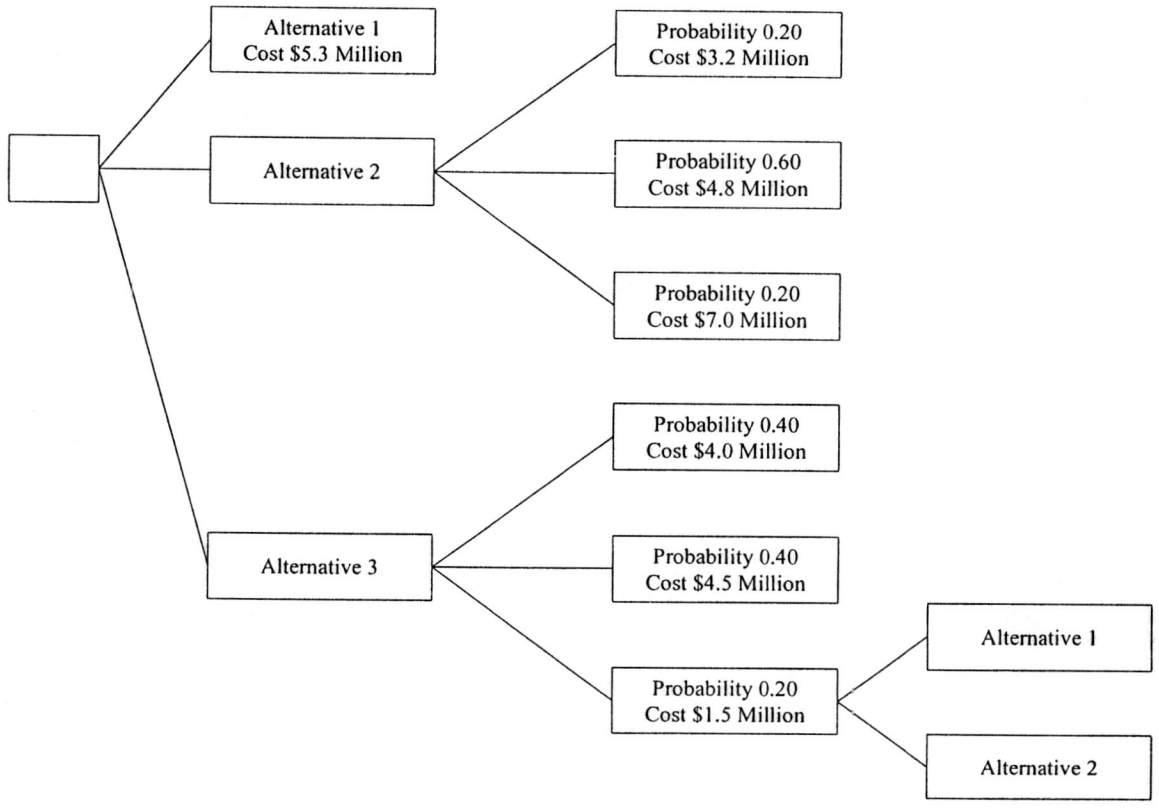

9.   Refer to the decision tree diagram above. Alternative 1 has a certain cost of $5.3 million. Alternative 2 has an expected cost that is calculated below:

$$(0.20)(3.2) + (0.60)(4.8) + (0.20)(7) = 4.92$$

Thus, Alternative 2 is preferred to Alternative 1.

Alternative 3 has an expected cost that will be calculated below. First, however, consider the situation in which expenses are incurred for a new land fill but a permit to create the new land fill is not granted. This forces the Township to choose between Alternatives 1 and 2. Thus, the cost of this eventuality is $1.5 million **plus** the expected cost of Alternative 1, or a total of $6.42.

$$(0.40)(4.0) + (0.40)(4.5) + (0.20)(1.5 + 4.92) = 4.684$$

Thus, Alternative 3 is preferred. If the new land fill doesn't work out, then Alternative 2 will be pursued.

10.   The maximin solution is determined in two steps. First, the minimum payoff for each project is identified. The minimum payoffs are -4, 1, and 0 for Projects A, B, and C, respectively. Second, the project with the largest minimum payoff is identified as the maximin solution. This is Project B with a minimum payoff of 1.

The minimax regret solution is determined in three steps. First, the regret matrix is calculated by subtracting the largest payoff for a given state of nature from all payoffs associated with that state of nature. For example, in the state of nature labeled "Great", the largest payoff is 20. This value is subtracted from 20, 6, and 12 for projects A, B, and C, respectively, to yield the regret associated with a project if this state of nature occurs. After this operation is carried out for each state of nature, the following regret matrix results:

Project	States of Nature			
	Disastrous	Not Good	Good	Great
A	5	4	2	0
B	0	0	1	14
C	1	3	0	8

The minimax regret solution is Project A, which has a maximum regret of 5. Projects B and C have maximum regret values of 14 and 8, respectively.

The preferred solution depends on the attitude of the investor towards risk. The maximin solution is conservative. It assumes that the worst will occur and seeks to minimize exposure to unfortunate consequences. The minimax regret solution indicates a less conservative attitude towards risk. In this problem it focuses on the large payoff of Project A relative to the other projects in state of nature "Great" rather than on the negative payoffs associated with Project A in states of nature "Disastrous" and "Not Good". If the Widows and Orphans Investment Company is averse to risk, then the maximin solution, Project B, would be preferred.

CHAPTER 14

LONG-RUN INVESTMENT DECISIONS: CAPITAL BUDGETING

Learning Objectives

When you have completed this chapter you should have a broad understanding of the capital budgeting process. You will have a basic knowledge of the methods used to evaluate alternative investment projects, the methods used to calculate the composite cost of capital, and the importance of capital in determining the international competitiveness of firms.

Summary of Notation and Formulas

(14-1) $NPV = \sum_{t=1}^{n} \frac{R_t}{(1+k)^t} - C_0$

Equation 14-1 defines the net present value (NPV) of a project in terms of the initial investment (C_0), the net cash flow in time period t (R_t) for each of n time periods, and the risk-adjusted discount rate (k).

(14-2) $\sum_{t=1}^{n} \frac{R_t}{(1+k^*)^t} = C_0$

Equation 14-2 defines the internal rate of return (IRR or k*) as the discount rate that equates the present value of future net cash flows with the initial investment associated with a project. Note that this equation implies that the net present value of a project is zero if the discount rate is equal to the internal rate of return.

(14-3) $PI = \dfrac{\sum_{t=1}^{n}[R_t/(1+k)^t]}{C_0}$

Equation 14-3 defines the profitability index (PI) as the discounted value of the future net cash flows from a project divided by the initial investment associated with the project. For projects that have a net present value greater than zero, this ratio will be greater than one.

(14-4) $k_d = r(1-t)$

Equation 14-4 defines the after-tax cost of borrowed funds (k_d) in terms of the market interest rate (r) and the marginal tax rate (t).

(14-5) $k_e = r_f + r_p$

(14-6) $k_e = r_f + p_1 + p_2$

Equations 14-5 and 14-6 define the cost of equity capital (k_e) in terms of a risk free rate of return (r_f) and a risk premium (r_p). Equation 14-6 separates the risk premium from Equation

---

14-5 into two components. The first component (p_1) is the added risk that is associated with debt issued by a firm when compared with risk-free debt issued in the form of government treasury bills. The second component (p_2) is the added risk that is associated with holding stocks issued by the firm rather than holding bonds issued by the firm.

$$(14\text{-}7) \quad P = \sum_{t=1}^{\infty} \frac{D}{(1+k_e)^t}$$

$$(14\text{-}8) \quad P = \frac{D}{k_e}$$

$$(14\text{-}9) \quad P = \frac{D}{k_e - g}$$

$$(14\text{-}10) \quad k_e = \frac{D}{P} + g$$

Equations 14-7 and 14-8 are equivalent representations of the present value of a firm (P) in terms of the firm's constant future dividend rate (D) for the indefinite future and the investor's required rate of return (k_e). Equation 14-9 represents the present value of a firm that has dividends that are expected to increase annually at a fixed rate (g) and Equation 14-10 is the equity cost of capital implied by the previous equation, i.e., the cost of equity capital implied by the dividend valuation model.

$$(14\text{-}11) \quad k_e = r_f + \beta(k_m - r_f)$$

Equation 14-11 defines the equity cost of capital according to the capital asset pricing model (CAPM) in terms of the risk-free rate of return (r_f), the average return on all common stocks (K_m), and the beta coefficient (β). The beta coefficient is a measure of the risk differential between the common stock of the firm and the common stock of all firms.

$$(14\text{-}12) \quad k_c = w_d k_d + w_e k_e$$

Equation 14-12 defines the weighted or composite cost of capital (k_c) in terms of the proportion of debt capital (w_d), the cost of debt capital (k_d), the proportion of equity capital (w_e), and the cost of equity capital (k_e).

True-False Questions

T F 1. Investment decisions involve costs and revenues that extend over a number of years.

T F 2. One of the reasons that capital budgeting is so important is that major capital investment projects are generally irreversible.

T F 3. A firm should continue to increase its level of capital investment so long as the rate of return on the least profitable investment project that the firm undertakes is less than the marginal cost of capital.

T F 4. In calculating net cash flows, depreciation is treated as a cost.

T F 5. In general, a firm should undertake a project only if its net present value is positive.

T F 6. In general, a firm should undertake any project that has an internal rate of return that is positive.

T F 7. If the internal rate of return is used to discount all cash flows associated with a project, the net present value of the project will be equal to zero.

T F 8. Calculation of the internal rate of return incorporates the implicit assumption that net cash flows from a project can be reinvested at the internal rate of return.

T F 9. If the net present value method and the internal rate of return method yield contradictory results, the latter should be followed rather than the former.

T F 10. A house that is owned by an individual is referred to as human capital, whereas a house that is owned by a corporation is referred to as non-human capital.

T F 11. The profitability per dollar invested is referred to as the profitability index.

T F 12. One problem with the profitability index is that it ignores the time value of money.

T F 13. In the absence of capital rationing, a firm should undertake all projects with a profitability index greater than zero.

T F 14. One advantage of using internal funding to support investment projects is that the firm experiences no economic cost of capital for internal funding.

T F 15. The cost of debt should generally be figured on an after-tax basis.

T F 16. The difference between the external and internal cost of raising equity capital is due to flotation costs.

T F 17. The cost of raising equity capital should generally be figured on an after-tax basis.

T F 18. The rate of return that stockholders require to invest in a firm is the cost of equity capital.

T F 19. The cost of debt is generally greater than the cost of equity capital.

T F 20. The difference between the rate of return on debt issued by the government and the rate of return on equity capital is referred to as a risk premium.

T F 21. According to the dividend valuation model, the price of a share of stock will increase if the rate of return required by investors increases.

T F 22. The capital asset pricing model determines the beta coefficient for a firm by regressing the variability in the firm's common stock against the variability in an index of all common stocks.

T F 23. A firm with a beta coefficient that is equal to zero has the same degree of risk as a broad-based portfolio of stocks.

T F 24. A firm with a beta coefficient that is equal to two is twice as risky as a broad-based portfolio of stocks.

T F 25. Firms generally use only one of the three equity capital valuation methods.

T F 26. The risk encountered by a firm when raising funds by issuing debt is greater than the risk from issuing common stock.

T F 27. The risk encountered by an investor when holding debt is greater than the risk from holding common stock.

T F 28. The composite cost of capital reflects the debt to equity ratio preferred by the firm.

T F 29. During most of the 1980s, the cost of capital in the United States was below the cost of capital in Japan.

T F 30. According to the 1977 study by Gitman and Forrester, the single most commonly used capital budgeting technique among the firms surveyed was the internal rate of return method.

Multiple Choice Questions

1. The process of planning expenditures that will influence the operation of a firm over a number of years is called

    A. investment.
    B. capital budgeting.
    C. net present valuation.
    D. dividend valuation.

2. Which of the following is not an example of a capital investment project?

    A. Replacement of worn out equipment
    B. Expansion of production facilities
    C. Development of employee training programs
    D. All of the above are examples of capital investment projects.

3. A firm is considering three investment projects which we will refer to as A, B, and C. Each project has an initial cost of $10 million. Investment A offers an expected rate of return of 16%, B of 8%, and C of 12%. The firm's cost of capital is 6% if it borrows $10 million, 10% if it borrows $20 million, and 15% if it borrows $30 million. Which project(s) should the firm invest in?

   A. Just A, because it offers the highest rate of return and is the only investment that has a rate of return higher than 15%
   B. All three should be undertaken, because the rate of return on B is above 6%, on C is above 10%, and on A is above 15%.
   C. Only A and C should be undertaken because both have rates of return that are greater than 10%.
   D. None of the above is correct.

4. Which of the following is <u>not</u> an appropriate way to measure cash flows?

   A. Treat depreciation as a negative cash flow
   B. Consider only incremental costs and revenues
   C. Consider only after-tax cash flows
   D. All of the above are appropriate ways to measure cash flows.

5. The net present value of a project is equal to

   A. the present value of all net cash flows that result from the project.
   B. the present value of all revenues minus the present value of all costs that result from the project.
   C. the present value of all future net cash flows that result from the project minus the initial investment required to start the project.
   D. All of the above are correct.

6. The net present value method and the internal rate of return method will always yield the same decision when

   A. a single project is evaluated.
   B. mutually exclusive projects are evaluated.
   C. a limited number of projects must be selected from a large number of opportunities.
   D. All of the above are correct.

7. Which of the following is <u>not</u> a form of capital as the term is used in economics?

   A. Houses owned by individuals
   B. Factories owned by businesses
   C. Education
   D. Money

8. In cases where capital must be rationed, a firm should rank projects according to their

   A. net present values.
   B. internal rates of return.
   C. profitability indexes.
   D. external rates of return.

9. Which of the following is an internal source of investment funding?

    A. Issuing bonds
    B. Sale of stocks
    C. Undistributed profits
    D. All of the above are internal sources.

10. A firm can borrow at an interest rate of 10%. Its marginal tax rate is 40%. What is its cost of debt?

    A. 10%
    B. 14%
    C. 6%
    D. None of the above is correct.

11. The method of raising funds for capital investment that involves the greatest risk to the firm is

    A. borrowing by selling bonds.
    B. relying on retained profits.
    C. issuing common stock.
    D. raising the dividend rate.

12. Which of the following sources of funds for capital investment involves a tax adjustment to determine the cost of capital?

    A. Retained profits
    B. Issuing debt
    C. Issuing common stock
    D. All of the above involve a tax adjustment.

13. Assume that the risk-free interest rate is 6% and that a firm can issue bonds at an interest rate of 9%. Assume further that the difference between the average yield on stocks and the average yield on corporate bonds is 4%. What is the risk premium associated with the firm's cost of equity capital?

    A. 15%
    B. 13%
    C. 7%
    D. 4%

14. Assume that investors require a rate of return of 10% to invest in a firm that pays a dividend of $2 per year. The price of the firm's stock is currently based on the assumption that the firm's dividend will remain constant. By how much will the price of the firm's stock increase if the firm begins to grow at a rate of 2% per year and is expected to continue to do so indefinitely?

    A. $25
    B. $20
    C. $10
    D. $5

15.　　The beta coefficient is associated with

　　A.　the capital asset pricing model.
　　B.　the dividend valuation model.
　　C.　the risk-free rate plus premium model.
　　D.　the tax-adjusted cost of debt.

16.　　Assume that the risk-free rate is 5% and that the rate of return on a balanced portfolio of common stocks is 9%. If a firm has a beta coefficient of 2, then its risk premium is

　　A.　18%
　　B.　10%
　　C.　8%
　　D.　4%

17.　　A firm must raise $10 million dollars in funding for a capital investment project. $2 million will be raised by issuing debt with an interest rate of 10% while the remainder will be raised by issuing stocks that will yield a return of 12%. The firm's marginal tax rate is 30%. What is the firm's composite cost of capital?

　　A.　15%
　　B.　12%
　　C.　11%
　　D.　10%

18.　　The debt to equity ratio that is selected by a firm depends

　　A.　on the attitude of the firm towards risk.
　　B.　the cost of debt and the cost of equity capital.
　　C.　the nature of the firm's business.
　　D.　All of the above are correct.

19.　　The review of projects after they have been implemented is called

　　A.　capital budgeting.
　　B.　a postaudit.
　　C.　blame spreading.
　　D.　context correlation.

20.　　According to the Gitman and Forrester study published in 1977, the two most commonly used capital budgeting techniques are

　　A.　net present value and profitability index.
　　B.　internal rate of return and payback period.
　　C.　net present value and average rate of return.
　　D.　profitability index and average rate of return.

Problems

1. The Hard Rock Coffee Company is anticipating a major expansion of its franchised coffee outlets into Europe and the Pacific Rim countries. The investment opportunities available to the company involve rates of return and initial investment amounts that differ because of differences in operating costs and consumer demand in the countries involved. The total investment (K) that Hard Rock can undertake is constrained by the cost of capital (i), which is defined by the following function:

$$i = 6 + 0.8 \, K$$

The initial investment and rate of return for each country are listed below in order of decreasing rate of return.

Country	Initial Investment ($ millions)	Rate of Return
Bangkok	$3.8	16.0%
Belgium	1.3	15.0
France	2.4	13.0
Germany	3.1	11.0
Japan	1.9	9.0

Plot the investment supply function and the investment demand schedule on the graph below. Determine the optimal level of investment and the corresponding cost of capital for the firm.

Chapter 14: Problem 1

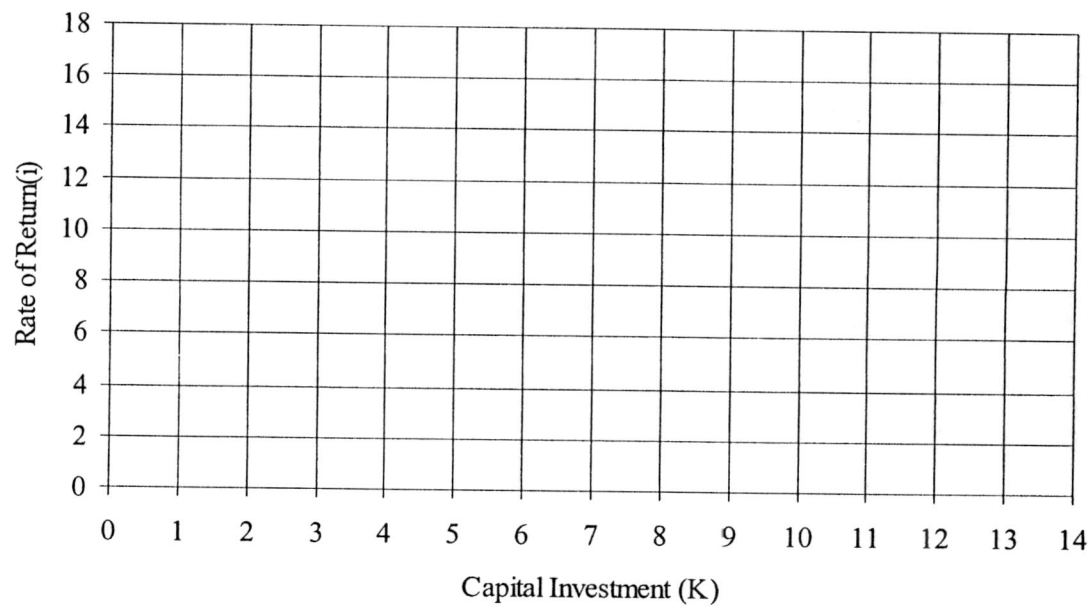

Capital Investment (K)

Adam Snaff is the owner and operator of Hot Diggity's Doggies. He sells hot dogs with all the appropriate condiments from a cart on the streets of Metro City. He is considering three alternative replacements for his existing vending cart. Each has a productive life of four years. They differ in capacity and, hence, in the amount of revenue per day that each can generate. The initial cost, annual net cash flow at the end of each year, and salvage value that will be realized at the end of the fourth year for each of the replacement carts (in $1,000s) are listed below. Use this information to solve Problems 2 through 5.

Type of Cart	Initial Cost	Annual Net Revenue	Salvage Value
Minicart	$ 6	$ 2	$ 1
Midicart	8	3	1
Megacart	12	4	3

2. Calculate the net present value of each of the carts using a discount rate of 10%. Which cart is preferred?

3.   Snaff has decided that the riskiness of profits from the three carts depends directly on the initial cost and predicted annual net revenue from each. He believes that the appropriate risk-adjusted discount rates are 9%, 12%, and 15% for the Minicart, Midicart, and Megacart, respectively. Calculate the net present value of each cart using the appropriate risk-adjusted rate of return for each. Which cart is preferred?

4.   If you have a computer available, use it to calculate the internal rate of return of each of the three carts. Which is preferred?

5.   Why is the preferred cart determined in Problem 2 different from that determined in Problem 4? Which is the better approach (NPV or IRR) to use in this case? Why?

Profligate Sons, Incorporated (PSI), wants to raise funds to expand its executive recreational facilities. The senior financial officer at PSI has gathered the following information in an effort to determine the firm's cost of capital. PSI typically obtains 75% of its capital by issuing debt. The interest rate on U.S. Treasury bills is 3.7%. The marginal tax rate is 45%. Projected profit for next year is $10,700,000. Profit is expected to grow at an annual rate of 5%. PSI long-term bonds yield 10.2%. The firm typically pays out 60% of its annual profit in dividends. It currently has 1,250,000 shares of stock outstanding and shares are trading at a price of $50. PSI's beta coefficient is 1.2 and the industry of which PSI is a part offers an average rate of return of 9%. Use this information to solve Problems 6 through 10.

6. Calculate the firm's after-tax cost of debt.

7. Calculate the firm's cost of equity capital using the "risk-free rate plus premium" model. What is the weighted cost of capital based on this model?

8. Calculate the firm's cost of equity capital using the "dividend valuation" model. What is the weighted cost of capital based on this model?

9. Calculate the firm's cost of equity capital using the "capital asset pricing model" model. What is the weighted cost of capital based on this model?

True-False Answers

1	T	7	T	13	F	19	F	25	F
2	T	8	T	14	F	20	T	26	T
3	F	9	F	15	T	21	F	27	F
4	F	10	F	16	T	22	T	28	T
5	T	11	T	17	F	23	F	29	F
6	F	12	F	18	T	24	T	30	T

Multiple Choice Answers

1	B	5	D	9	C	13	C	17	C
2	D	6	A	10	C	14	D	18	D
3	C	7	D	11	A	15	A	19	B
4	A	8	C	12	B	16	C	20	B

Solutions to Problems

1. The optimal total initial investment for the firm is $7.5 million at a cost of capital of 12%. Investments should be undertaken in Bangkok, Belgium, and France, but not in Germany or Japan.

Chapter 14: Problem 1

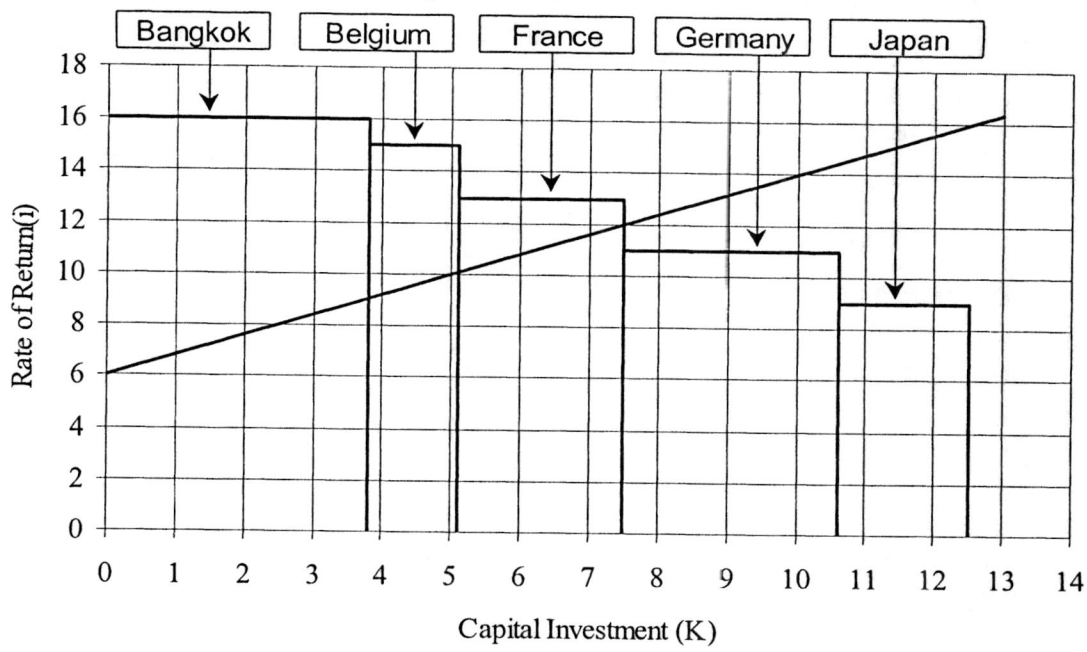

2.   The net present value of each cart is calculated as follows:

Minicart: NPV = -6 + (2)(PVIFA$_{10\%,4}$) + (1)(PVIF$_{10\%,4}$) = -6 + (2)(3.1699) + (1)(0.6830) = \$1,022,800

Midicart: NPV = -8 + (3)(PVIFA$_{10\%,4}$) + (1)(PVIF$_{10\%,4}$) = -8 + (3)(3.1699) + (1)(0.6830) = \$2,192,700

Megacart: NPV = -12 + (4)(PVIFA$_{10\%,4}$) + (3)(PVIF$_{10\%,4}$) = -12 + (4)(3.1699) + (3)(0.6830) = \$2,728,600

The Megacart has the highest net present value and is therefore preferred.

3.   The net present value of each cart is calculated using risk-adjusted rates of return as follows:

Minicart: NPV = -6 + (2)(PVIFA$_{9\%,4}$) + (1)(PVIF$_{9\%,4}$) = -6 + (2)(3.2397) + (1)(0.7084) = \$1,187,800

Midicart: NPV = -8 + (3)(PVIFA$_{12\%,4}$) + (1)(PVIF$_{12\%,4}$) = -8 + (3)(3.0373) + (1)(0.6355) = \$1,747,400

Megacart: NPV = -12 + (4)(PVIFA$_{15\%,4}$) + (3)(PVIF$_{15\%,4}$) = -12 + (4)(2.8550) + (3)(0.5718) = \$1,135,400

The Midicart has the highest risk-adjusted net present value and is therefore preferred.

4.   The internal rates of return (IRR) are 17.16%, 21.56%, and 19.20% for the Minicart, Midicart, and Megacart, respectively. The Midicart has the highest IRR and is therefore preferred.

5.   The NPV calculations implicitly assume that any funds left over after expenses are paid can be invested to yield a rate of return equal to the discount rate. The IRR calculations implicitly assume that any funds left over after expenses are paid can be invested to yield a rate of return equal to the internal rate of return. The former assumption is more conservative and more reasonable. Consequently, the NPV is the better approach in this case and, ignoring adjustments for risk, the Megacart would be the better choice.

6.   The after-tax cost of debt is equal to the before-tax cost of debt times one minus the marginal tax rate. In this case that is

$$k_d = (10.2\%)(1 - 0.45) = 5.6\%$$

7.   Using the rule of thumb value of 4% as the risk premium of stocks over the firm's corporate bonds, the cost of equity capital is

$$k_e = 10.2 + 4 = 14.2\%$$

Note that this result implies that the risk premium associated with the firm's bonds is the difference between the yield on the firm's bonds (10.2%) and the risk-free rate (3.7%), i.e., $10.2 - 3.7 = 6.5\%$.

The firm's weighted cost of capital is:

$$k_c = (.75)(5.6) + (.25)(14.2) = 7.8\%$$

8.   The projected dividend per share for the coming year is equal to total profit ($10,700,000) times the percentage of profit paid out in dividends (60%) divided by the number of shares outstanding (1,250,000). This yields D = $5.136. The cost of equity capital calculated using the dividend valuation model is

$$k_e = (5.136/50) + 0.05 = 15.3\%$$

The firm's weighted cost of capital is

$$k_c = (.75)(5.6) + (.25)(15.3) = 8.0\%$$

9.   The cost of capital according to the capital asset pricing model is

$$k_e = 3.7 + (1.20)(9 - 3.7) = 10.1\%$$

The firm's weighted cost of capital is

$$k_c = (.75)(5.6) + (.25)(10.1) = 6.7\%$$